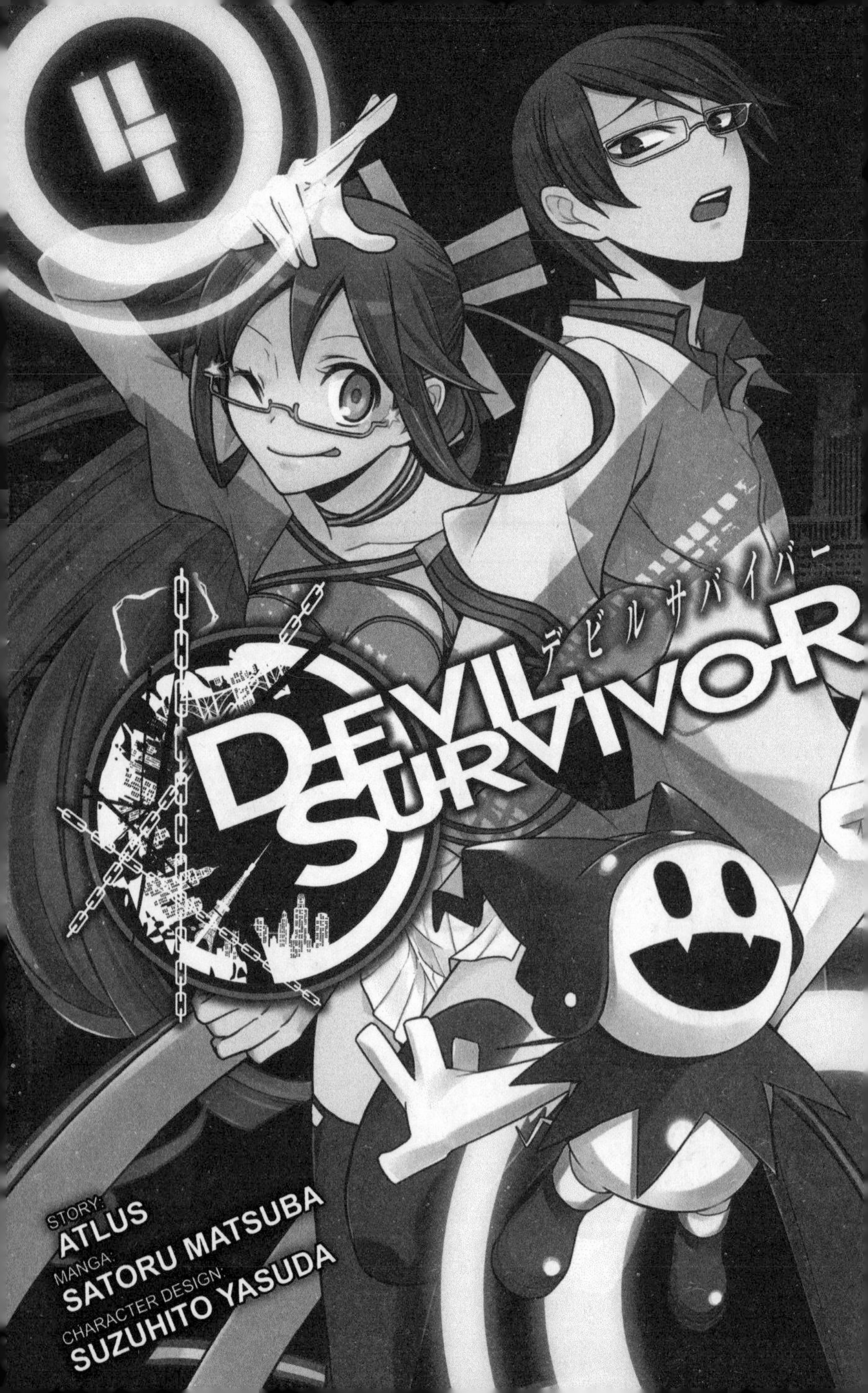
4
デビルサバイバー
DEVIL SURVIVOR
STORY:
ATLUS
MANGA:
SATORU MATSUBA
CHARACTER DESIGN:
SUZUHITO YASUDA

MAIN CHARACTER

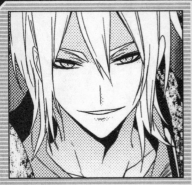

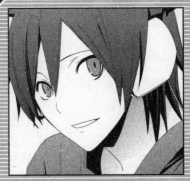

KAZUYA MINEGISHI
(KAZUYA)

Uses a portable gaming device known as a COMP to make contracts with demons after gaining the power to command them.

NAOYA
(NAOYA)

Kazuya's cousin. He lost his parents at a young age and lived with Kazuya's family until last year. He's known as a genius programmer with staggering insight.

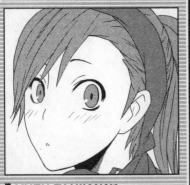

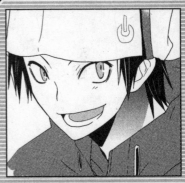

ATSURO KIHARA
(AT-LOW)

Kazuya's classmate and best friend. He's an aspiring programmer, and has been hanging with the big boys on the Internet since he was in grade school.

YUZU TANIKAWA
(YUZ)

A friend of Kazuya's since childhood. They currently attend the same high school.

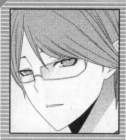

KEISUKE TAKAGI (K-T)

A middle school classmate of Atsuro's. He has a righteous streak, which led him to save Atsuro from bullying, and hates all kinds of wrongdoing.

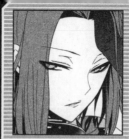

YOSHINO HARUSAWA (HARU)

Current lead vocalist of the indie band D-Va. She worries about the band's former vocalist, Aya, who was a strong influence in her career. Her singing voice seems to have the power to summon demons, but...

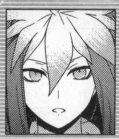

AMANE KUZURYU (AMANE)

A priestess of the Shomonkai religious organization. She can create barriers to prevent demons from approaching.

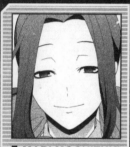

MARI MOCHIZUKI (MARI)

A nurse at an elementary school. She once worked as Atsuro's tutor. A friend of Kaido and his brother since childhood, she has an ongoing hatred for the killer who took Kaido's brother from them in the Bloodless Murders.

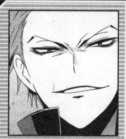

TADASHI "KAIDO" NIKAIDO (NIKAIDO)

Leader of the Daemons, a gang based in the Shibuya area. He's searching for his brother's killer so he can settle the score. He harbors a secret fondness for his childhood friend Mari.

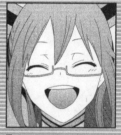

MIDORI KOMAKI (DOLLY)

An internet idol who enjoys tremendous popularity as the cosplayer Dolly. The influence of her late father, combined with her own desire to transform herself, gives her a strong yearning to be a defender of justice.

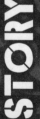

3RD DAY (BELDR)

Having been defeated once, our heroes face the immortal Beldr again. With help from friends, the party pulls off a narrow victory, but suddenly something happens to Kazuya—he absorbs Beldr's power. At that moment, he became an unwitting participant in a battle for supremacy fought between the most powerful demons in the lockdown!!

Our story begins on the **4TH DAY** (CRUMBLING REASON)

CONTENTS

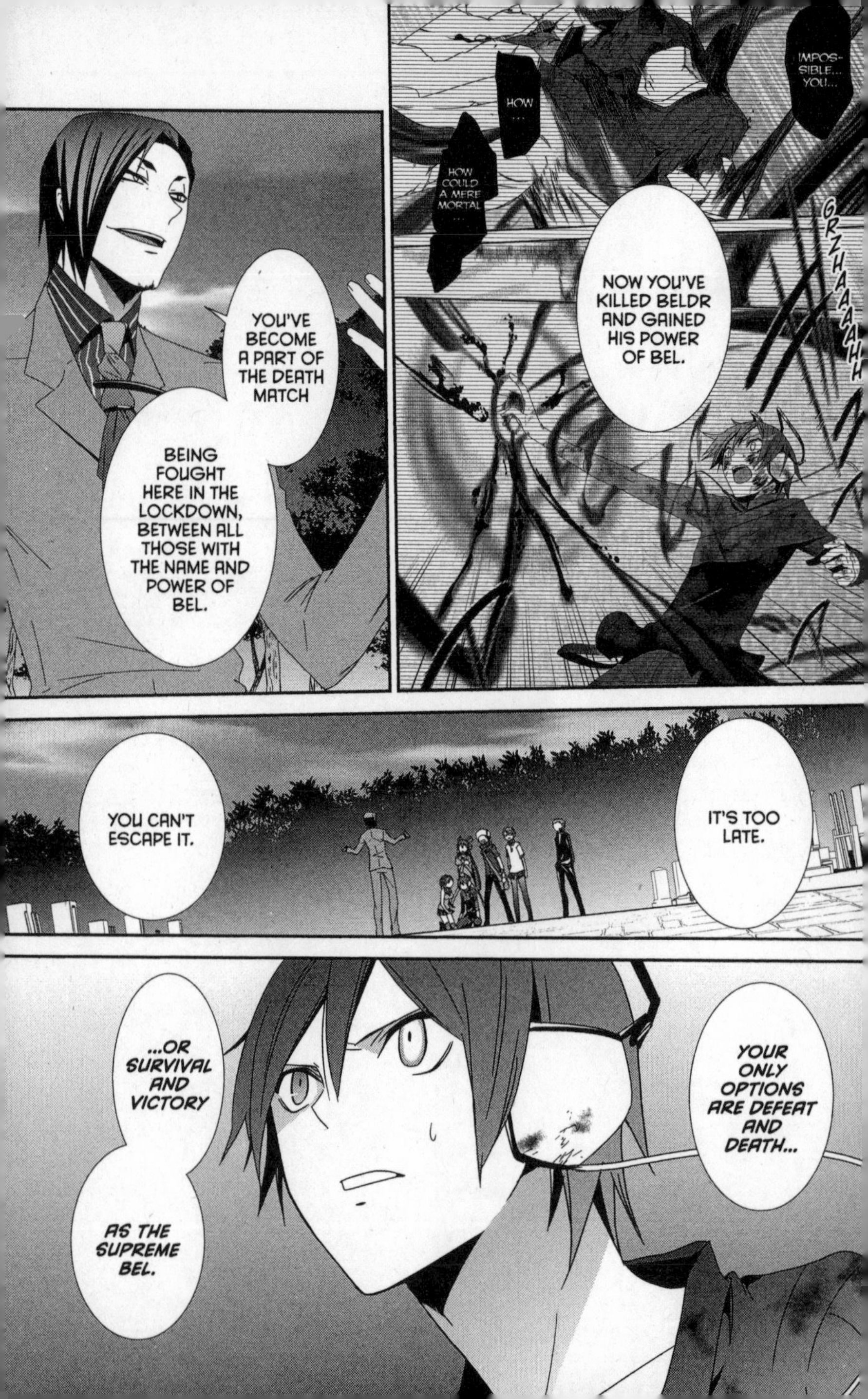
IMPOS-SIBLE... YOU...
HOW ...
HOW COULD A MERE MORTAL ...
GRZHAAAAAHH
NOW YOU'VE KILLED BELDR AND GAINED HIS POWER OF BEL.
YOU'VE BECOME A PART OF THE DEATH MATCH
BEING FOUGHT HERE IN THE LOCKDOWN, BETWEEN ALL THOSE WITH THE NAME AND POWER OF BEL.
IT'S TOO LATE.
YOU CAN'T ESCAPE IT.
YOUR ONLY OPTIONS ARE DEFEAT AND DEATH...
...OR SURVIVAL AND VICTORY
AS THE SUPREME BEL.

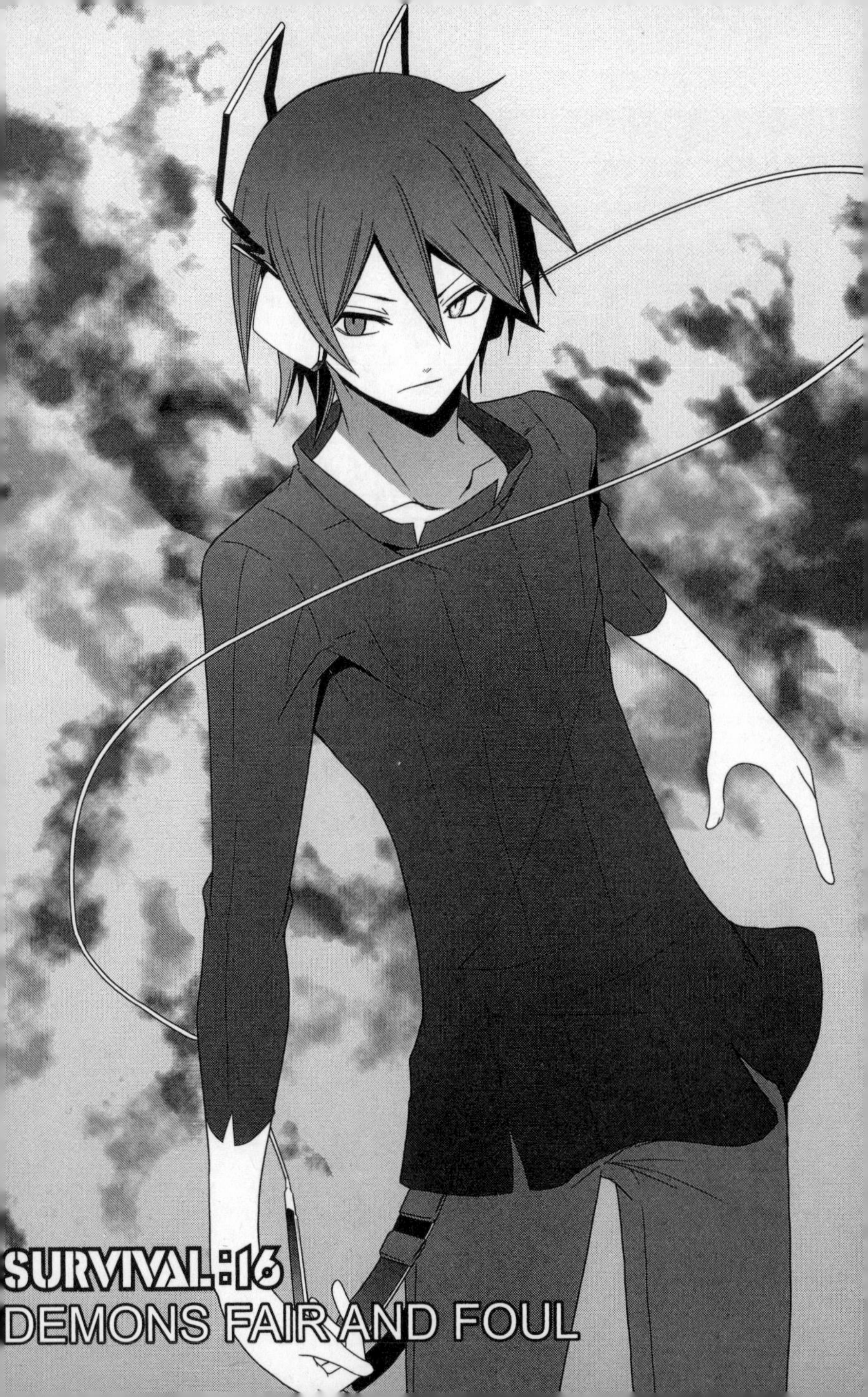

SURVIVAL:16
DEMONS FAIR AND FOUL

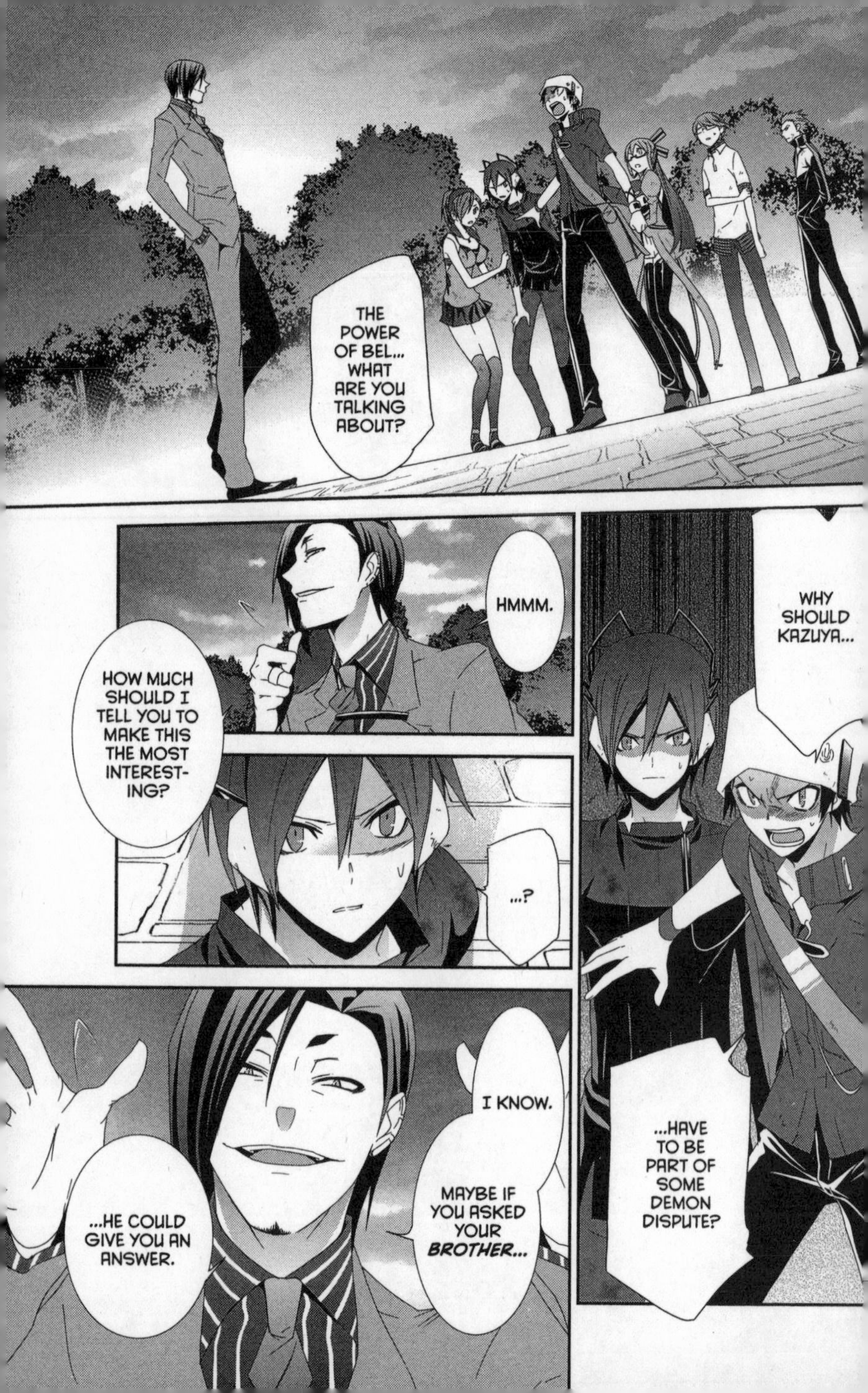
THE POWER OF BEL... WHAT ARE YOU TALKING ABOUT?
WHY SHOULD KAZUYA...
...HAVE TO BE PART OF SOME DEMON DISPUTE?
HMMM.
HOW MUCH SHOULD I TELL YOU TO MAKE THIS THE MOST INTEREST-ING?
...?
I KNOW.
MAYBE IF YOU ASKED YOUR *BROTHER*...
...HE COULD GIVE YOU AN ANSWER.

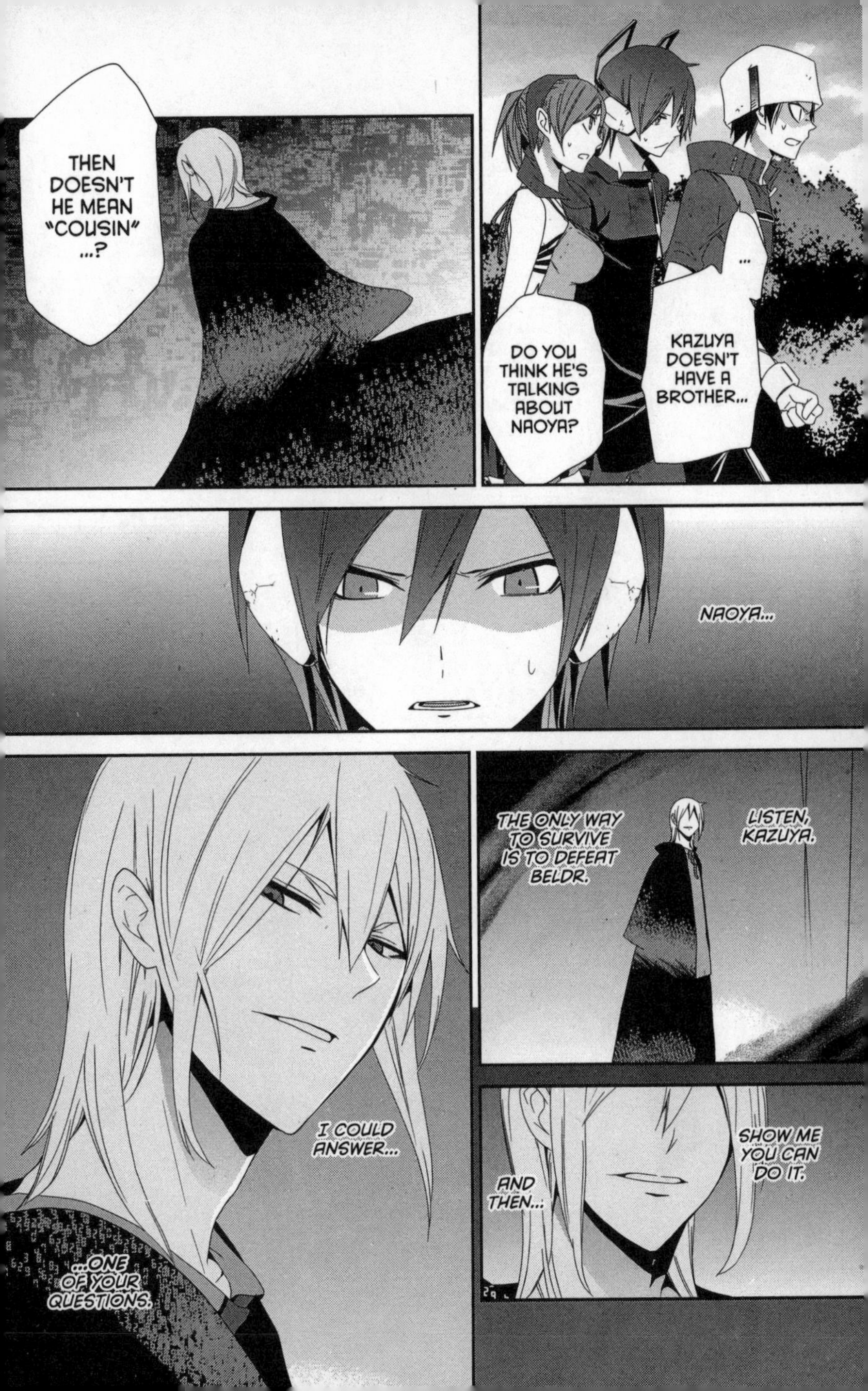
...
KAZUYA DOESN'T HAVE A BROTHER...
DO YOU THINK HE'S TALKING ABOUT NAOYA?
THEN DOESN'T HE MEAN "COUSIN" ...?
NAOYA...
LISTEN, KAZUYA.
THE ONLY WAY TO SURVIVE IS TO DEFEAT BELDR.
SHOW ME YOU CAN DO IT.
AND THEN...
I COULD ANSWER...
...ONE OF YOUR QUESTIONS.

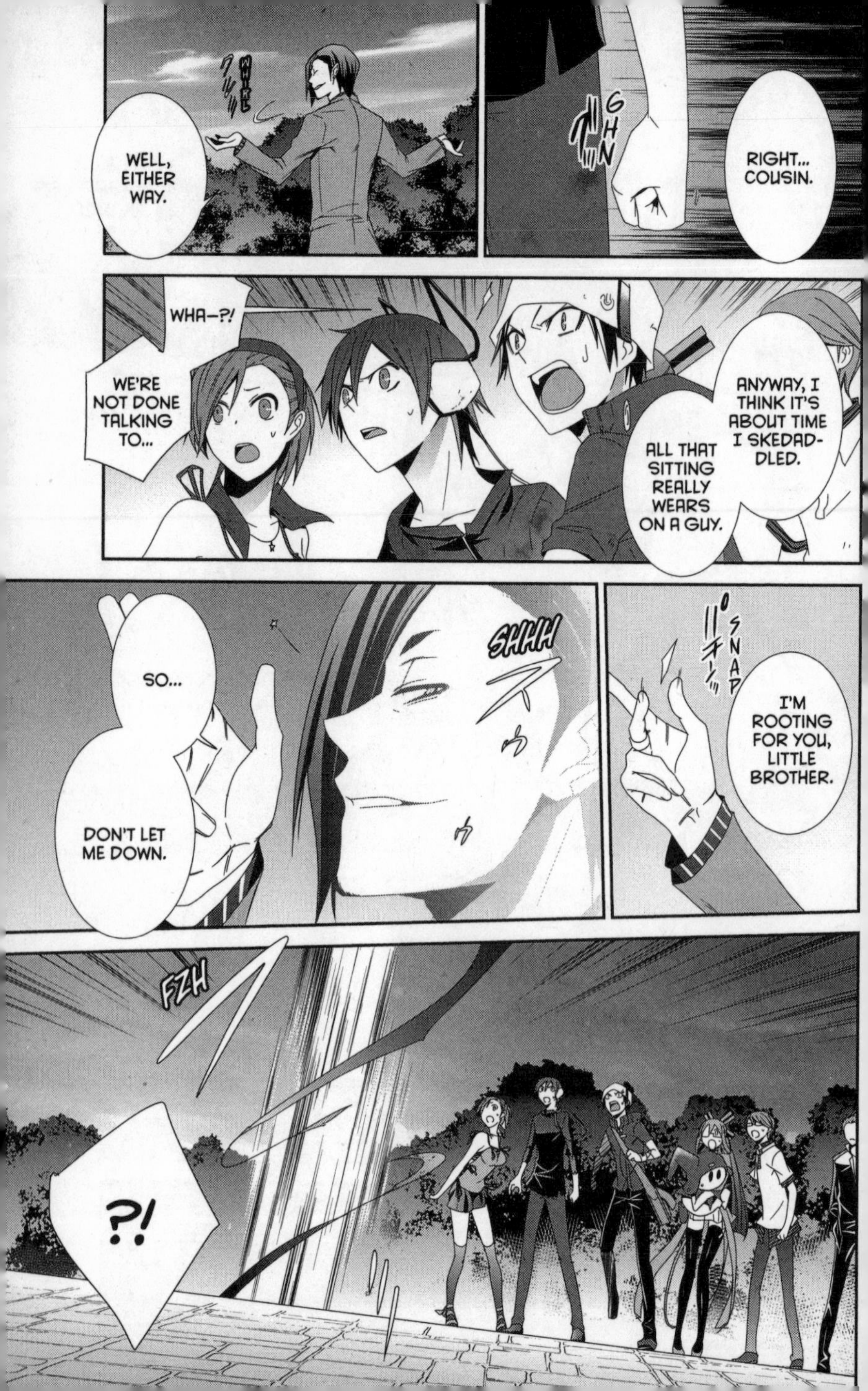
GHN
RIGHT... COUSIN.
WHIRL
WELL, EITHER WAY.
ANYWAY, I THINK IT'S ABOUT TIME I SKEDADDLED.
ALL THAT SITTING REALLY WEARS ON A GUY.
WHA-?!
WE'RE NOT DONE TALKING TO...
SNAP
I'M ROOTING FOR YOU, LITTLE BROTHER.
SHHH
SO...
DON'T LET ME DOWN.
FZH
?!

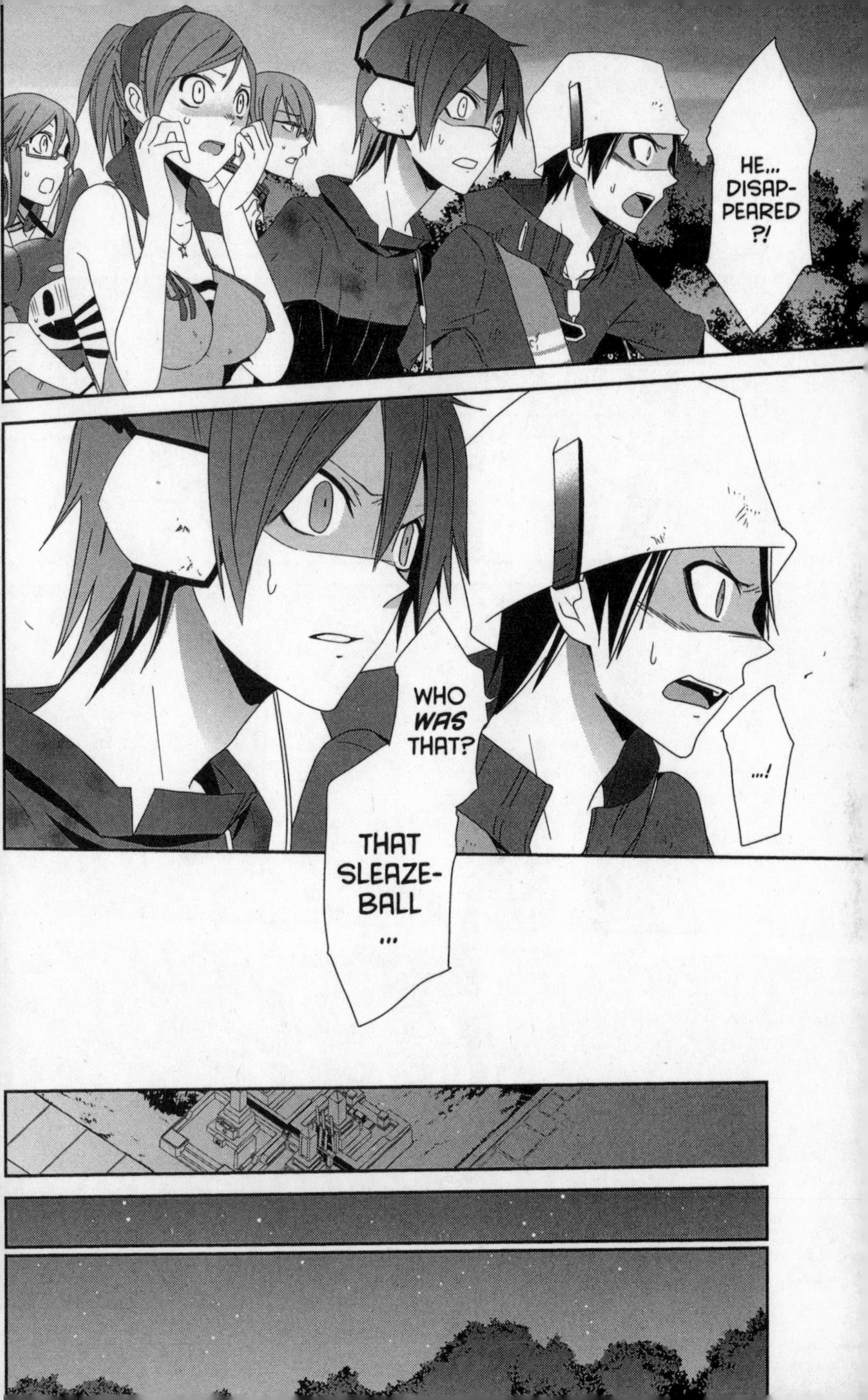
HE... DISAPPEARED ?!
...!
WHO *WAS* THAT?
THAT SLEAZE-BALL ...

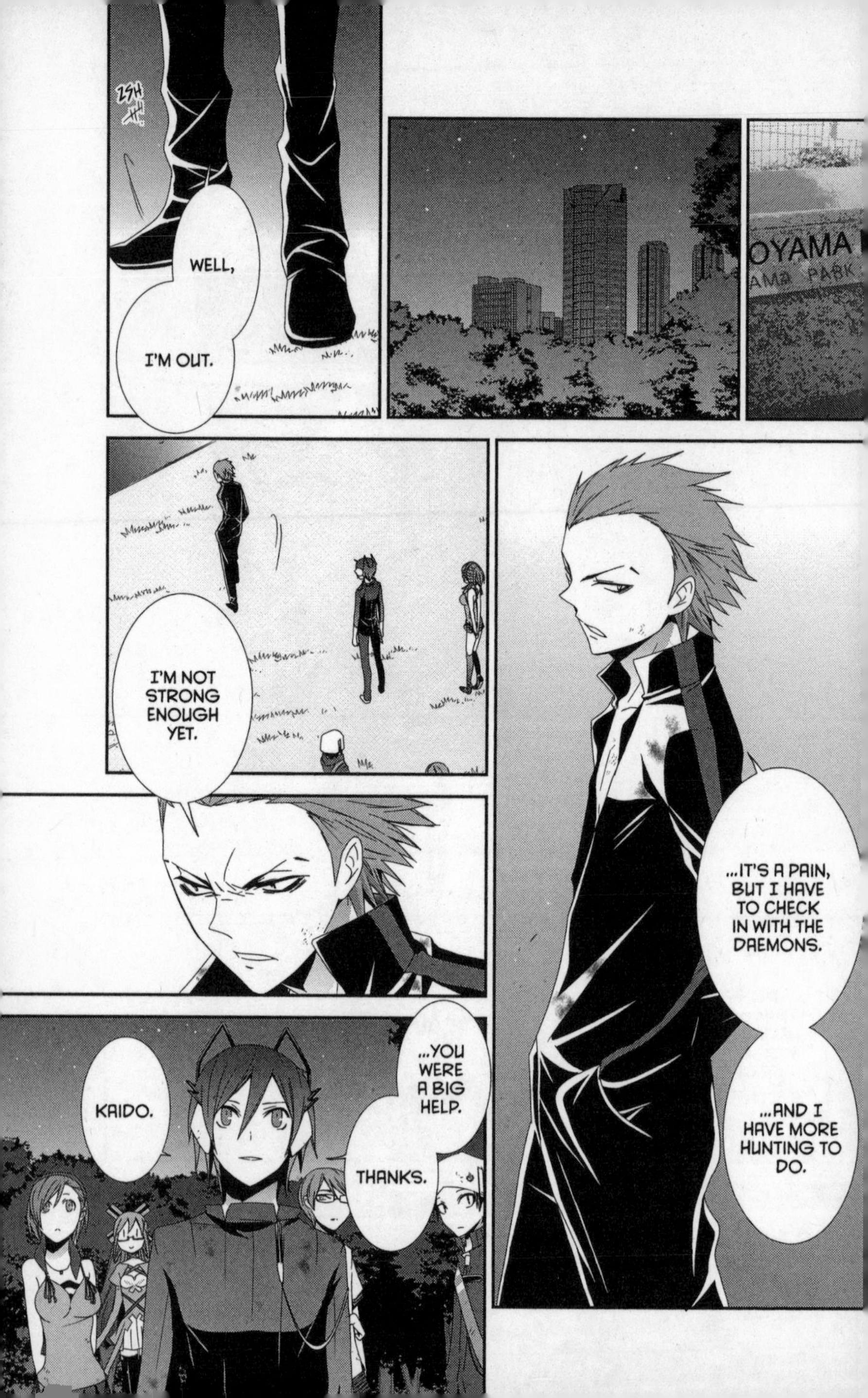
OYAMA
ZSH
WELL,
I'M OUT.
...IT'S A PAIN, BUT I HAVE TO CHECK IN WITH THE DAEMONS.
...AND I HAVE MORE HUNTING TO DO.
I'M NOT STRONG ENOUGH YET.
...YOU WERE A BIG HELP.
THANKS.
KAIDO.

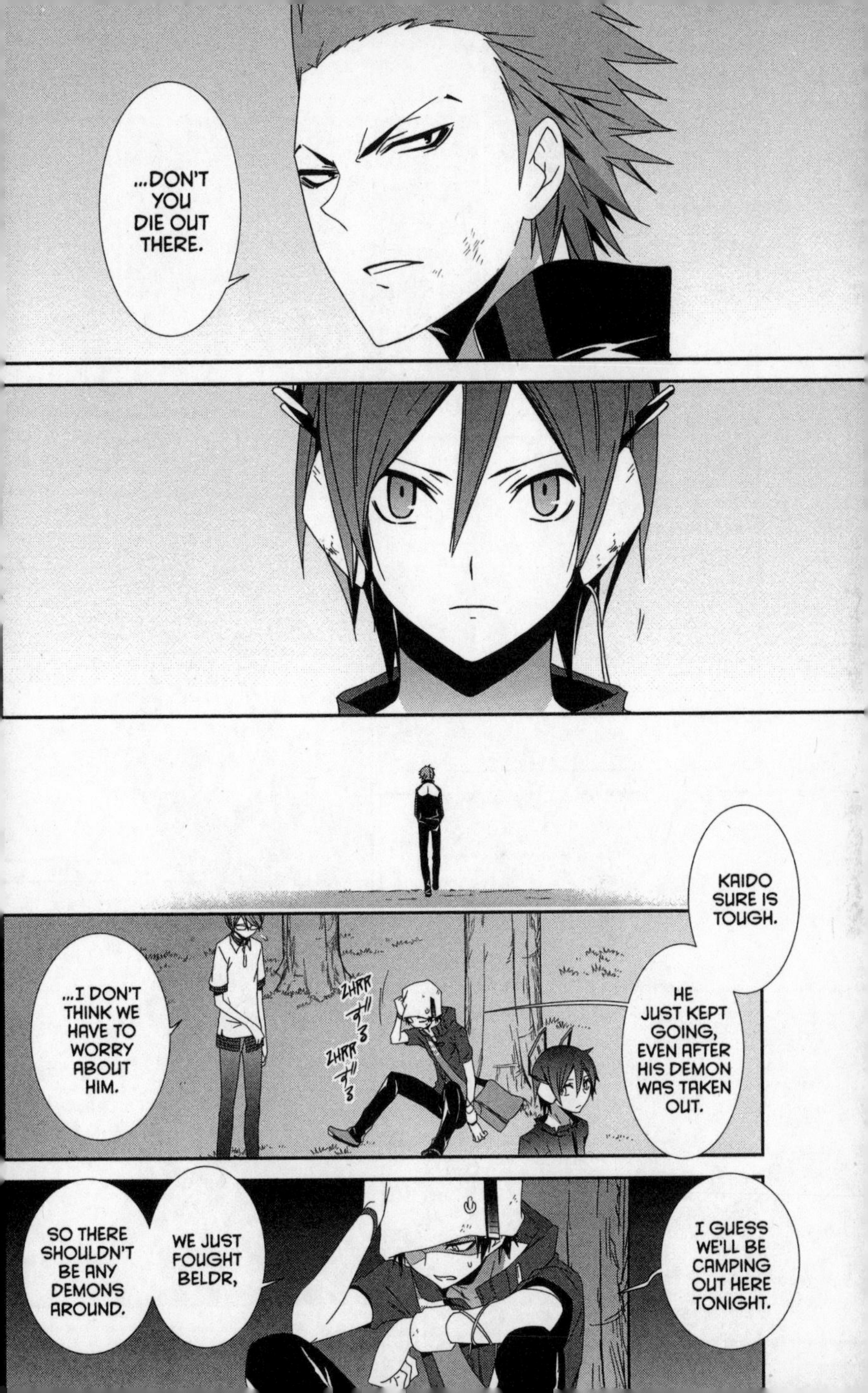
...DON'T YOU DIE OUT THERE.
KAIDO SURE IS TOUGH.
HE JUST KEPT GOING, EVEN AFTER HIS DEMON WAS TAKEN OUT.
ZHRR
ずる
ZHRR
ずる
...I DON'T THINK WE HAVE TO WORRY ABOUT HIM.
I GUESS WE'LL BE CAMPING OUT HERE TONIGHT.
WE JUST FOUGHT BELDR,
SO THERE SHOULDN'T BE ANY DEMONS AROUND.

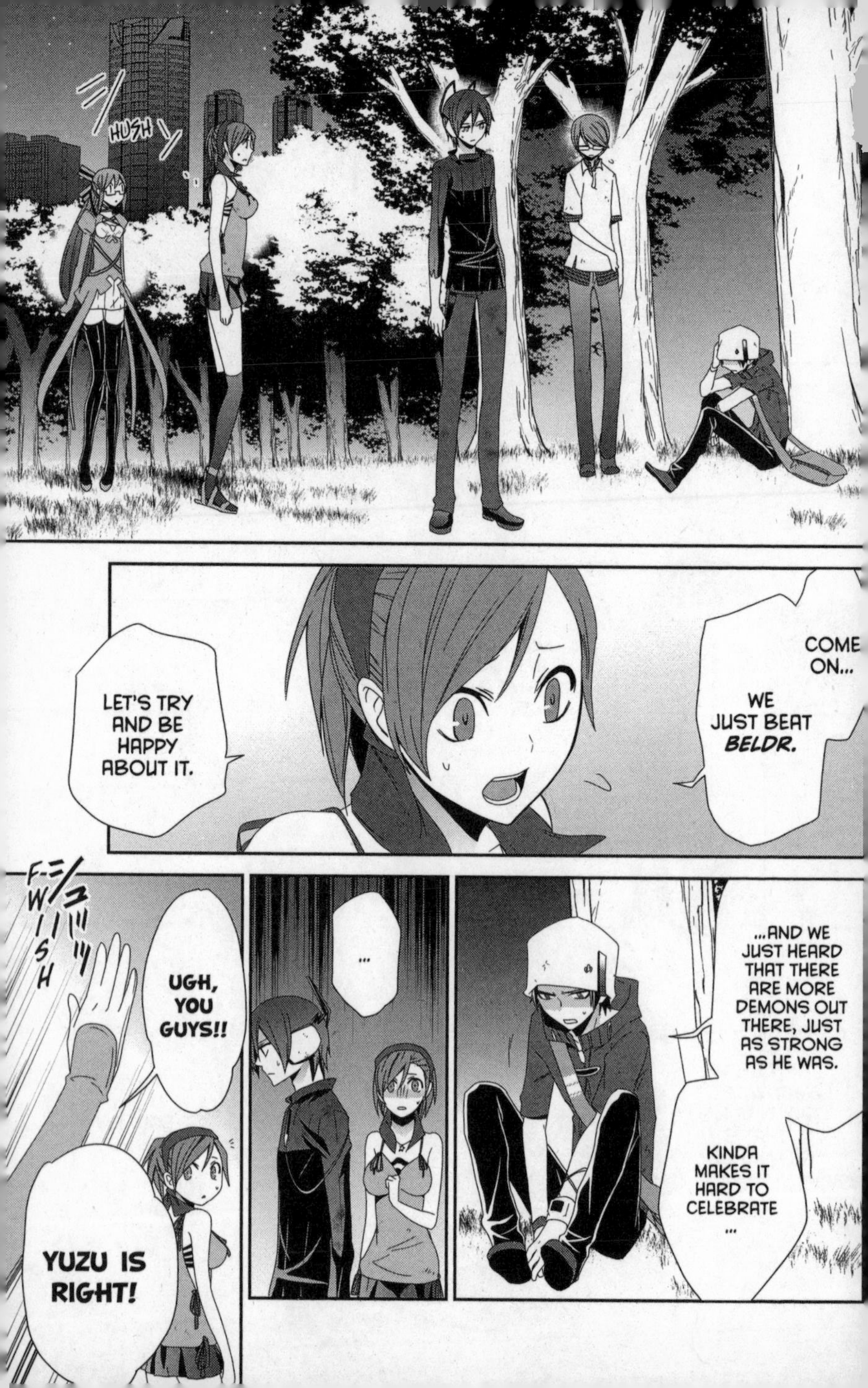
HUSH
COME ON... WE JUST BEAT BELDR.
LET'S TRY AND BE HAPPY ABOUT IT.
...AND WE JUST HEARD THAT THERE ARE MORE DEMONS OUT THERE, JUST AS STRONG AS HE WAS.
KINDA MAKES IT HARD TO CELEBRATE ...
...
F-WISH
UGH, YOU GUYS!!
YUZU IS RIGHT!

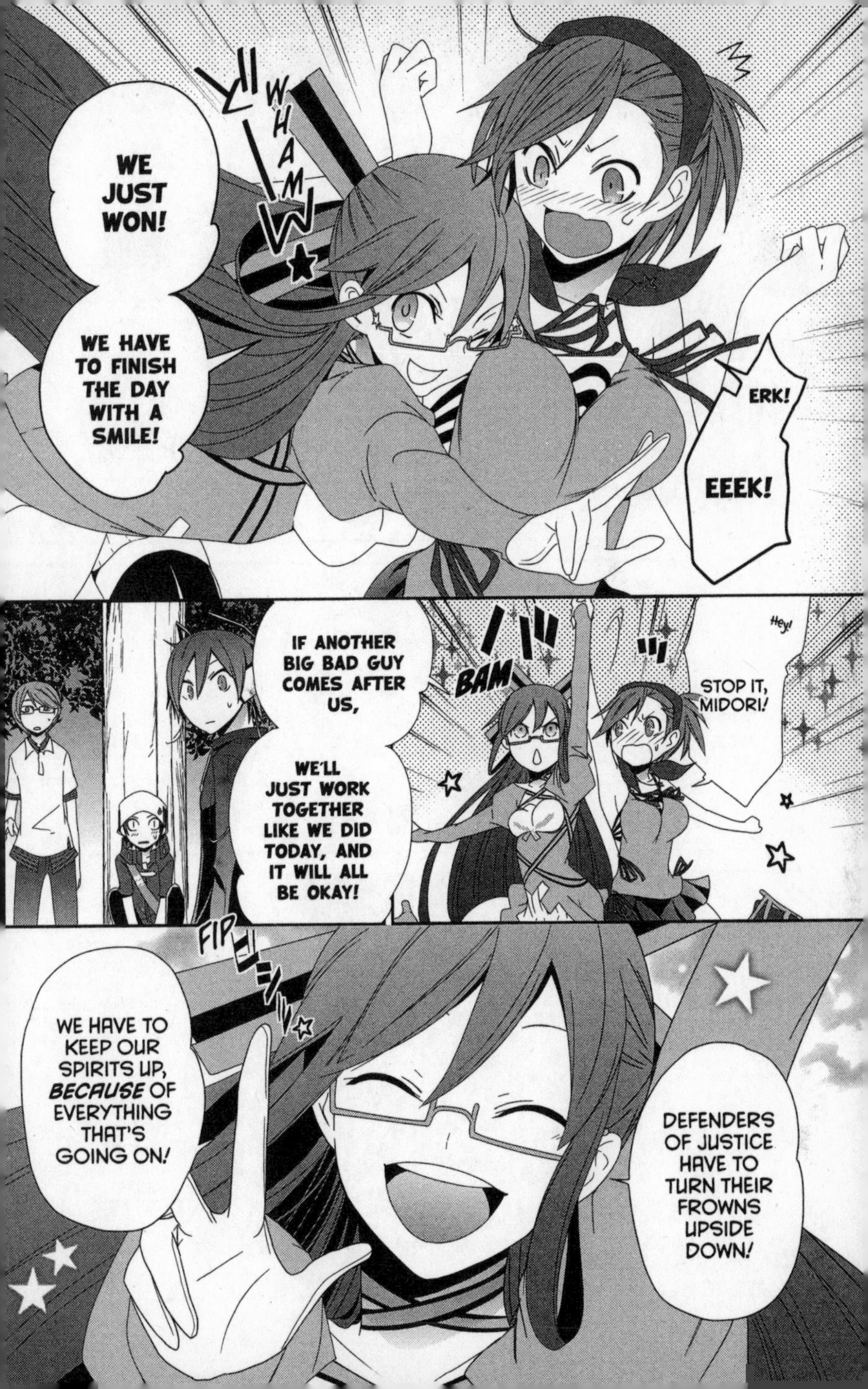
ERK!
EEEK!
WHAM
WE JUST WON!
WE HAVE TO FINISH THE DAY WITH A SMILE!
Hey!
STOP IT, MIDORI!
BAM
IF ANOTHER BIG BAD GUY COMES AFTER US,
WE'LL JUST WORK TOGETHER LIKE WE DID TODAY, AND IT WILL ALL BE OKAY!
DEFENDERS OF JUSTICE HAVE TO TURN THEIR FROWNS UPSIDE DOWN!
FIP
WE HAVE TO KEEP OUR SPIRITS UP, *BECAUSE* OF EVERYTHING THAT'S GOING ON!

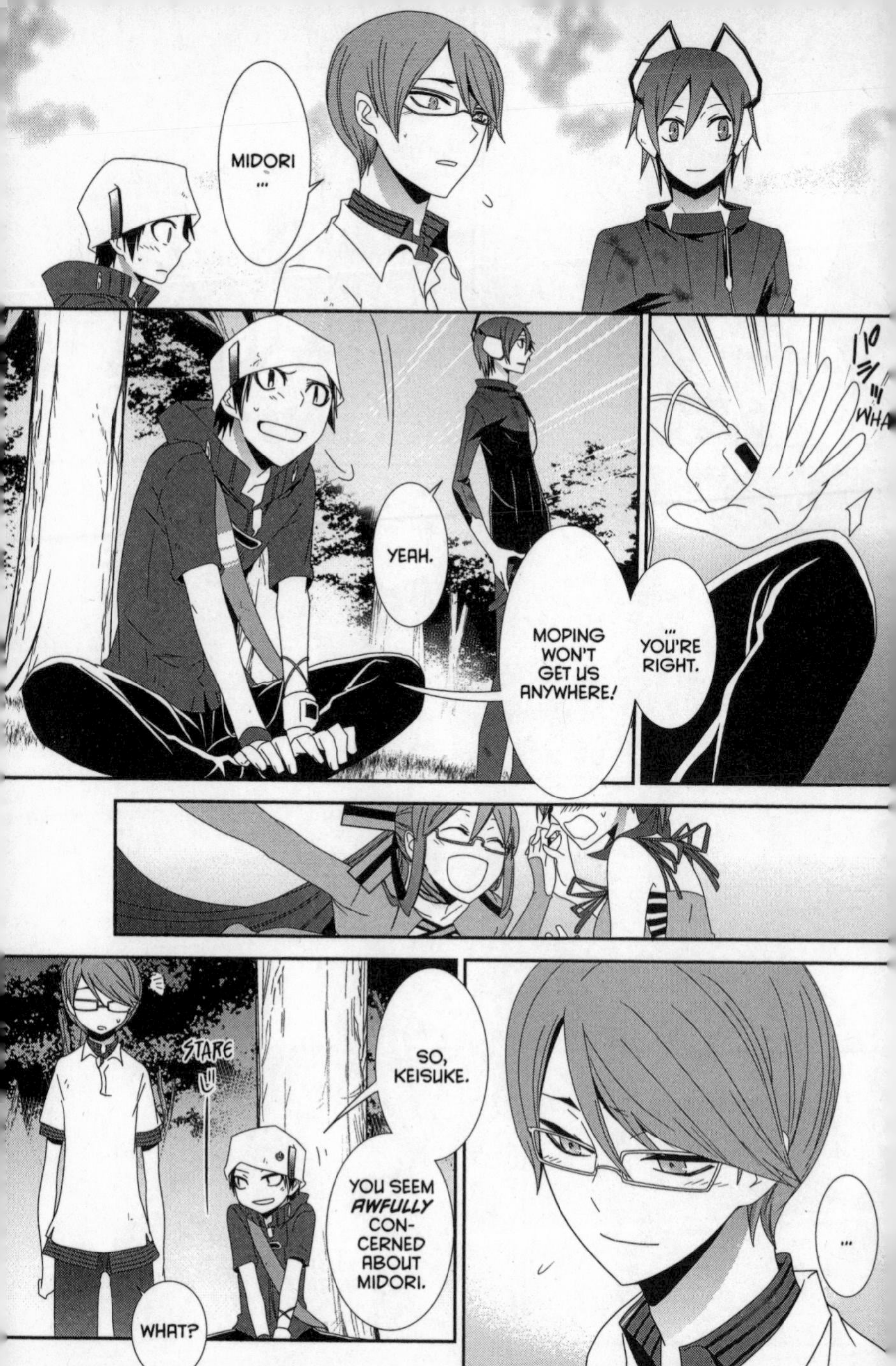
MIDORI ...
WHA
YEAH.
MOPING WON'T GET US ANYWHERE!
... YOU'RE RIGHT.
...
SO, KEISUKE.
YOU SEEM **AWFULLY** CON-CERNED ABOUT MIDORI.
STARE
WHAT?

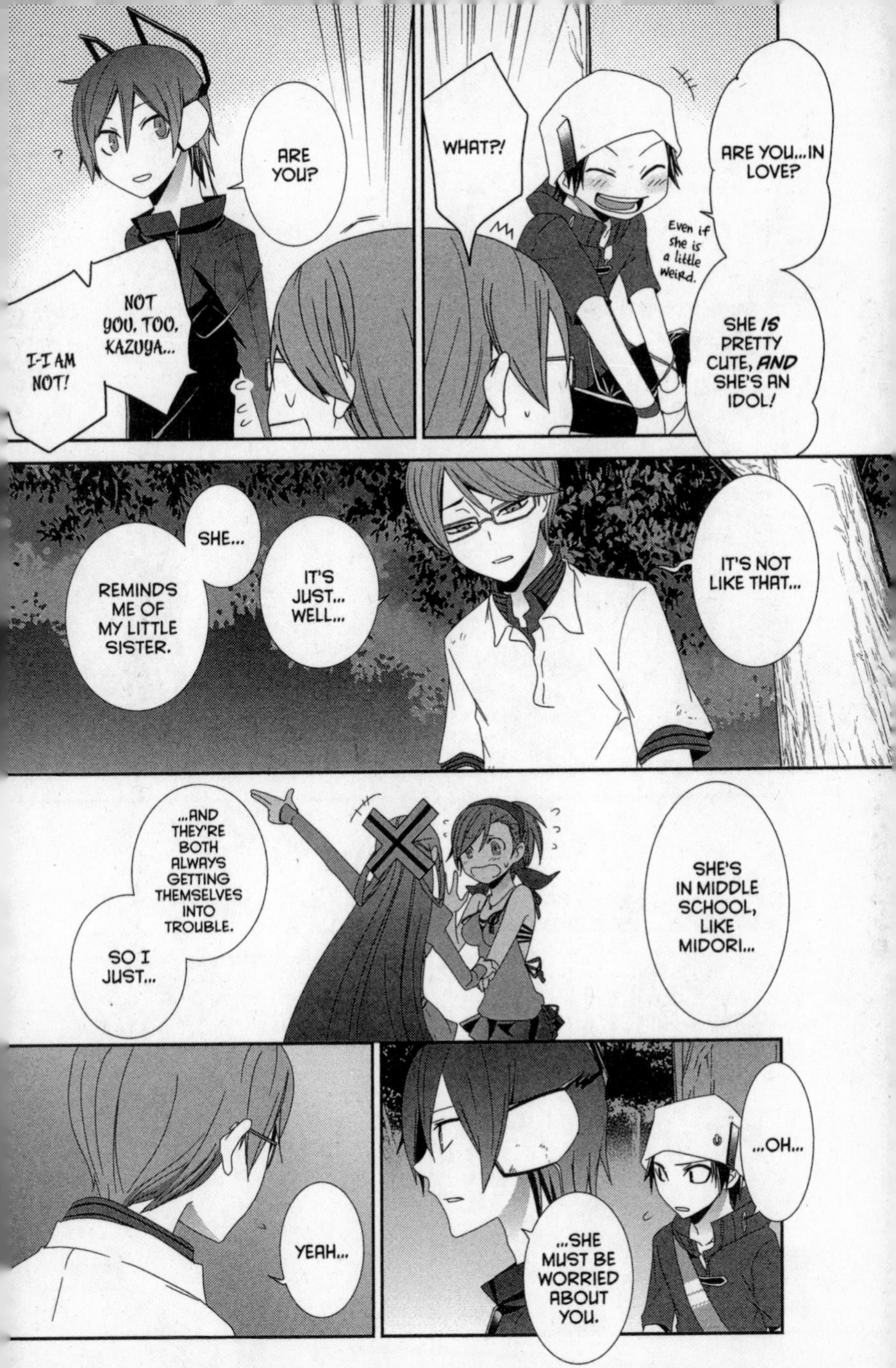
ARE YOU...IN LOVE?
SHE IS PRETTY CUTE, AND SHE'S AN IDOL!
Even if she is a little weird.
WHAT?!
ARE YOU?
NOT YOU, TOO, KAZUYA...
I-I AM NOT!
IT'S NOT LIKE THAT...
IT'S JUST... WELL...
SHE...
REMINDS ME OF MY LITTLE SISTER.
SHE'S IN MIDDLE SCHOOL, LIKE MIDORI...
...AND THEY'RE BOTH ALWAYS GETTING THEMSELVES INTO TROUBLE.
SO I JUST...
...OH...
...SHE MUST BE WORRIED ABOUT YOU.
YEAH...

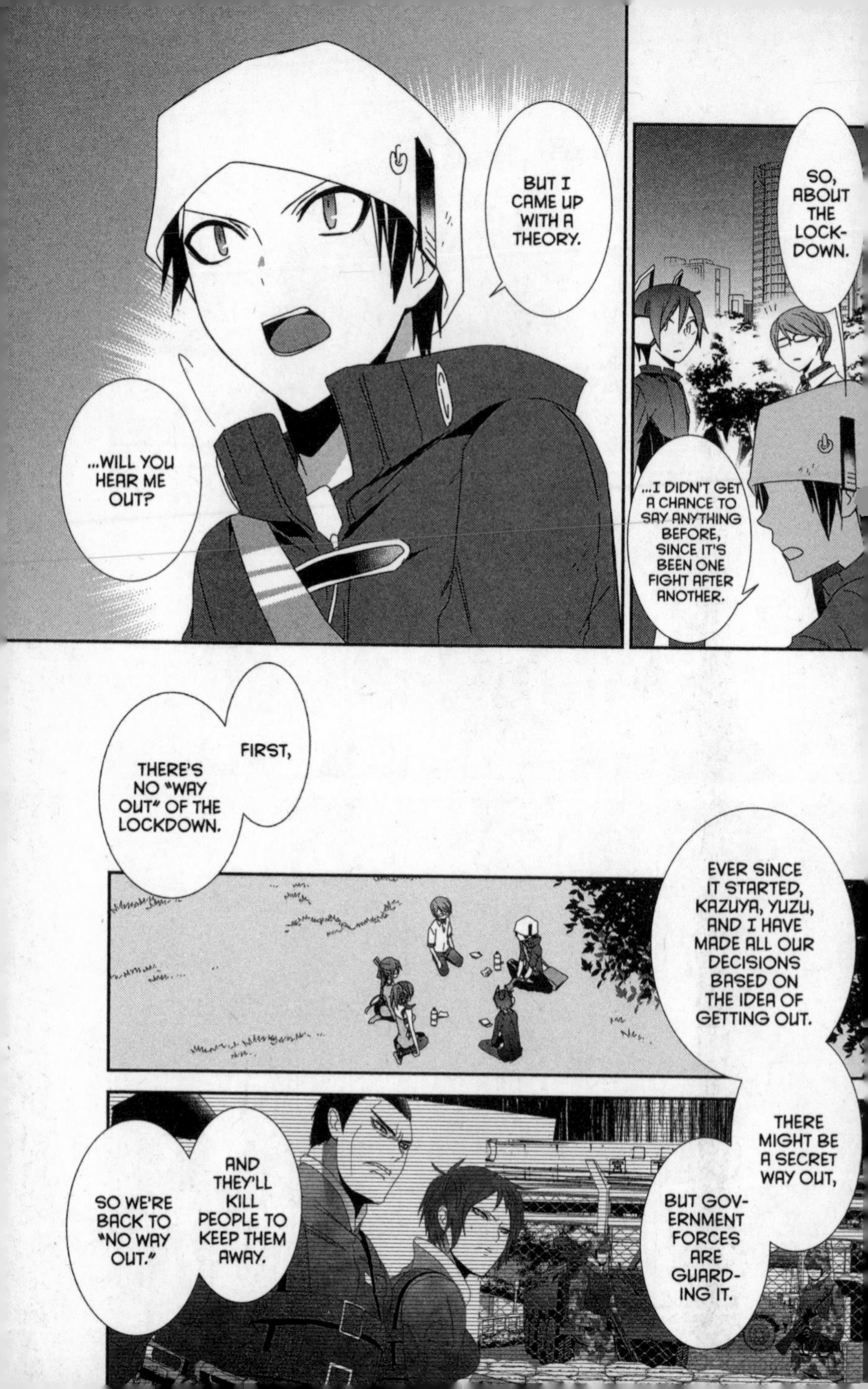
SO, ABOUT THE LOCK-DOWN.
...I DIDN'T GET A CHANCE TO SAY ANYTHING BEFORE, SINCE IT'S BEEN ONE FIGHT AFTER ANOTHER.
BUT I CAME UP WITH A THEORY.
...WILL YOU HEAR ME OUT?
FIRST,
THERE'S NO "WAY OUT" OF THE LOCKDOWN.
EVER SINCE IT STARTED, KAZUYA, YUZU, AND I HAVE MADE ALL OUR DECISIONS BASED ON THE IDEA OF GETTING OUT.
THERE MIGHT BE A SECRET WAY OUT,
BUT GOVERNMENT FORCES ARE GUARDING IT.
AND THEY'LL KILL PEOPLE TO KEEP THEM AWAY.
SO WE'RE BACK TO "NO WAY OUT."

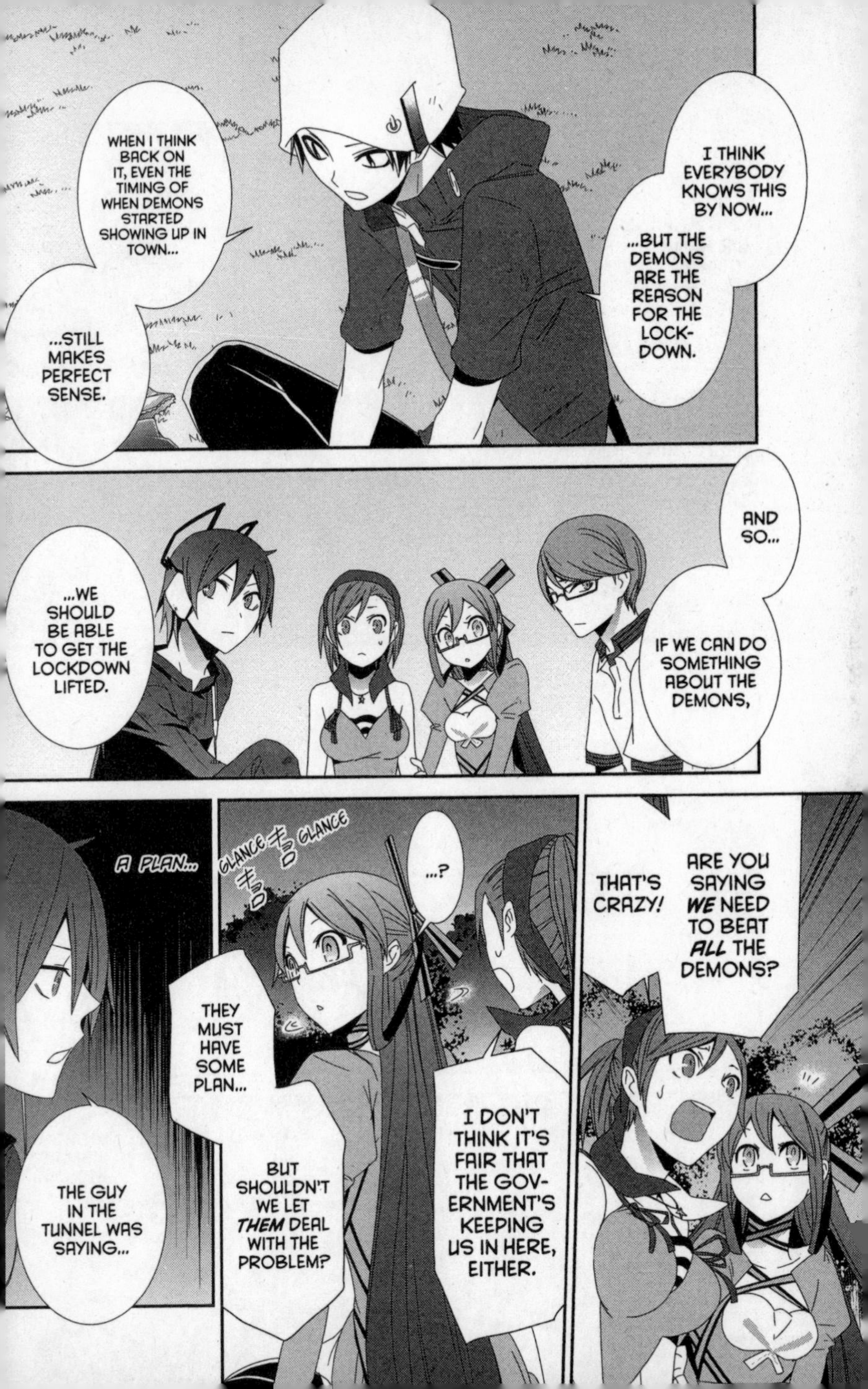
I THINK EVERYBODY KNOWS THIS BY NOW...
...BUT THE DEMONS ARE THE REASON FOR THE LOCK-DOWN.
WHEN I THINK BACK ON IT, EVEN THE TIMING OF WHEN DEMONS STARTED SHOWING UP IN TOWN...
...STILL MAKES PERFECT SENSE.
AND SO...
IF WE CAN DO SOMETHING ABOUT THE DEMONS,
...WE SHOULD BE ABLE TO GET THE LOCKDOWN LIFTED.
ARE YOU SAYING *WE* NEED TO BEAT *ALL* THE DEMONS?
THAT'S CRAZY!
GLANCE GLANCE
...?
THEY MUST HAVE SOME PLAN...
BUT SHOULDN'T WE LET *THEM* DEAL WITH THE PROBLEM?
I DON'T THINK IT'S FAIR THAT THE GOV-ERNMENT'S KEEPING US IN HERE, EITHER.
A PLAN...
THE GUY IN THE TUNNEL WAS SAYING...

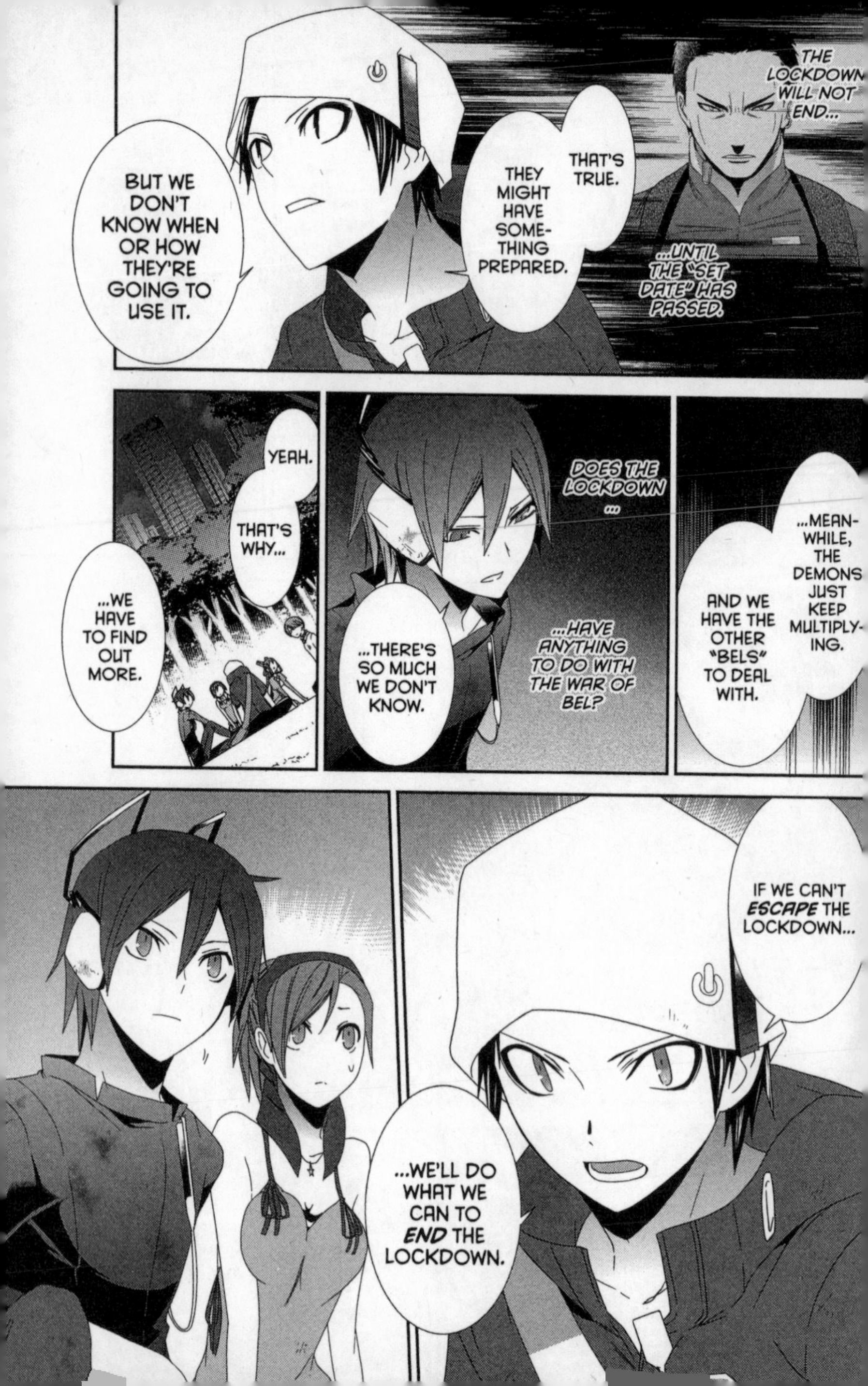
THE LOCKDOWN WILL NOT END...
...UNTIL THE "SET DATE" HAS PASSED.
THAT'S TRUE.
THEY MIGHT HAVE SOME-THING PREPARED.
BUT WE DON'T KNOW WHEN OR HOW THEY'RE GOING TO USE IT.
...MEAN-WHILE, THE DEMONS JUST KEEP MULTIPLY-ING.
AND WE HAVE THE OTHER "BELS" TO DEAL WITH.
DOES THE LOCKDOWN...
...HAVE ANYTHING TO DO WITH THE WAR OF BEL?
...THERE'S SO MUCH WE DON'T KNOW.
YEAH.
THAT'S WHY...
...WE HAVE TO FIND OUT MORE.
IF WE CAN'T *ESCAPE* THE LOCKDOWN...
...WE'LL DO WHAT WE CAN TO *END* THE LOCKDOWN.

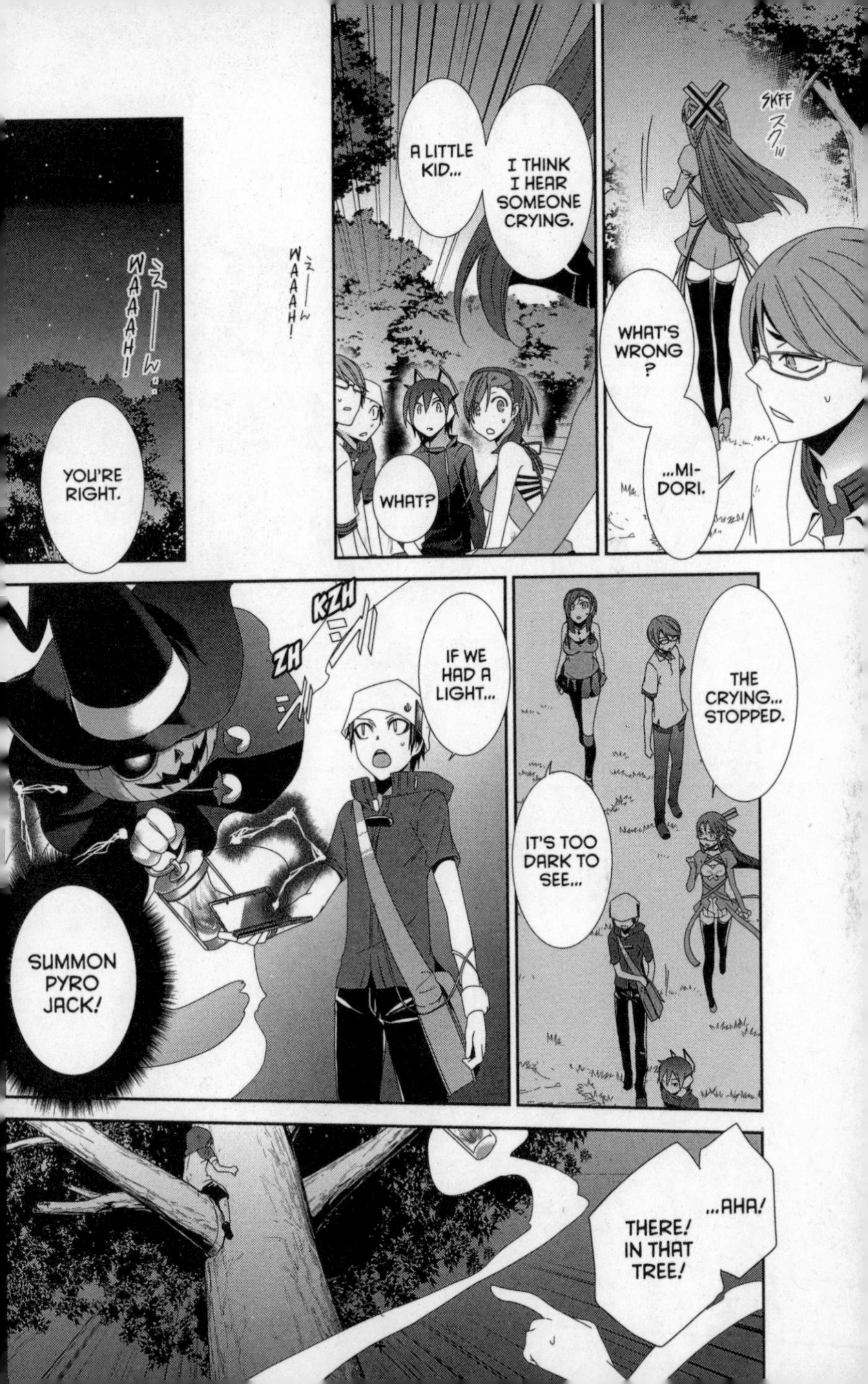
SKFF
WHAT'S WRONG?
...MI-DORI.
I THINK I HEAR SOMEONE CRYING.
A LITTLE KID...
WHAT?
WAAAAH!
WAAAAH!
YOU'RE RIGHT.
THE CRYING... STOPPED.
IT'S TOO DARK TO SEE...
IF WE HAD A LIGHT...
KZH
ZH
SUMMON PYRO JACK!
...AHA!
THERE! IN THAT TREE!

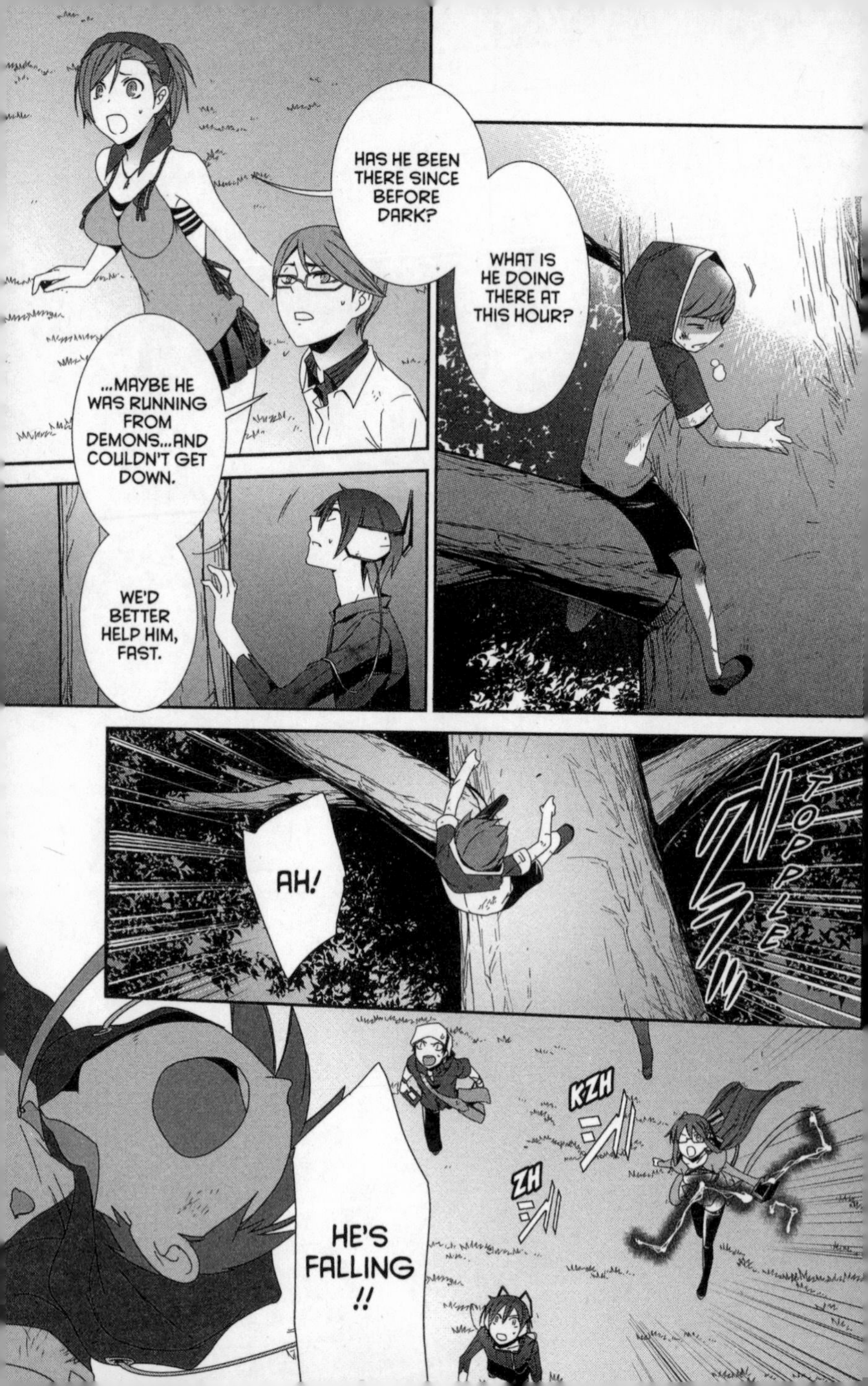
HAS HE BEEN THERE SINCE BEFORE DARK?
WHAT IS HE DOING THERE AT THIS HOUR?
...MAYBE HE WAS RUNNING FROM DEMONS...AND COULDN'T GET DOWN.
WE'D BETTER HELP HIM, FAST.
TOPPLE
AH!
KZH
ZH
HE'S FALLING!!

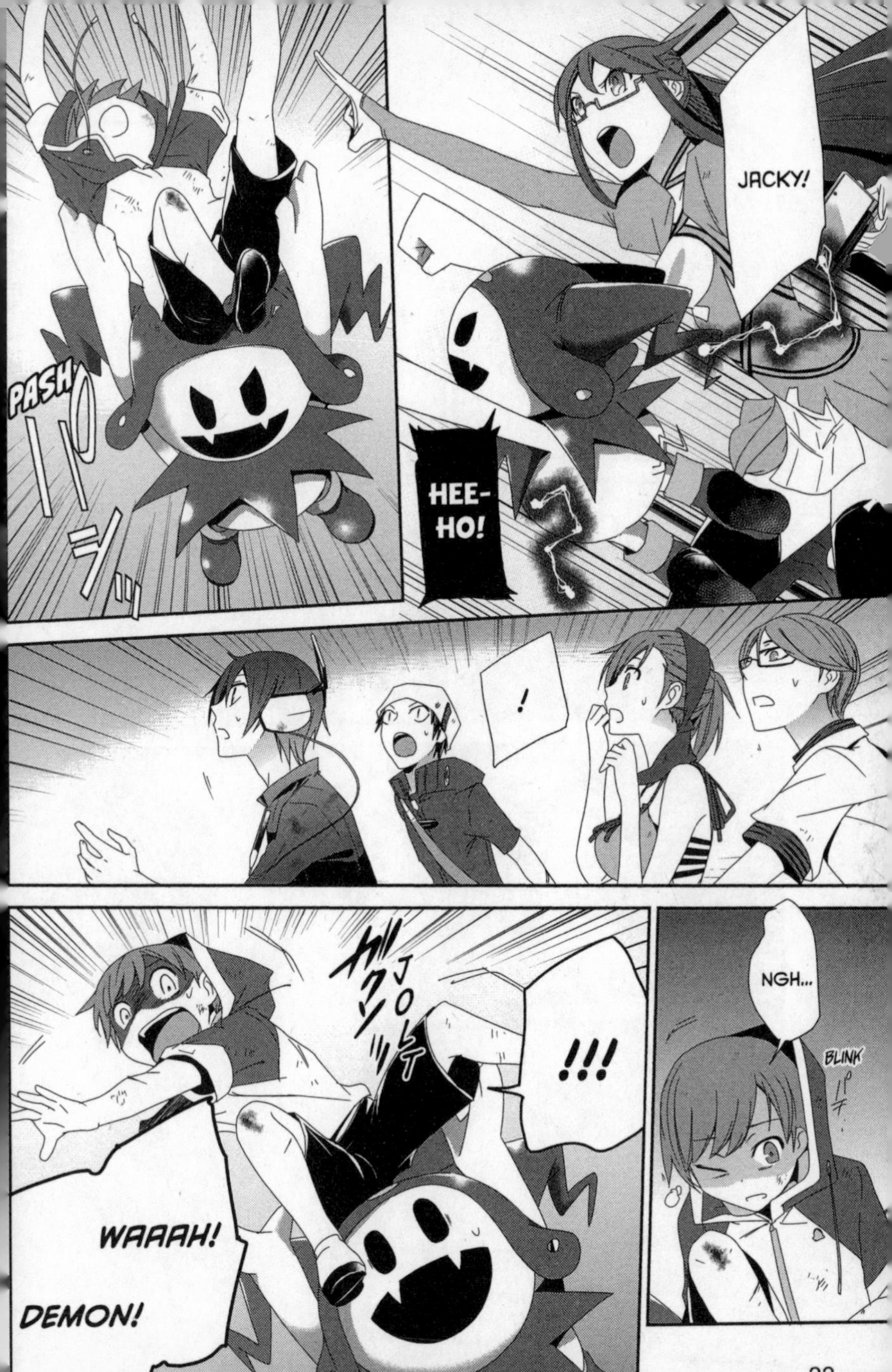
JACKY!
HEE-
HO!
PASH
!
NGH...
BLINK
JOLT
!!!
WAAAH!
DEMON!

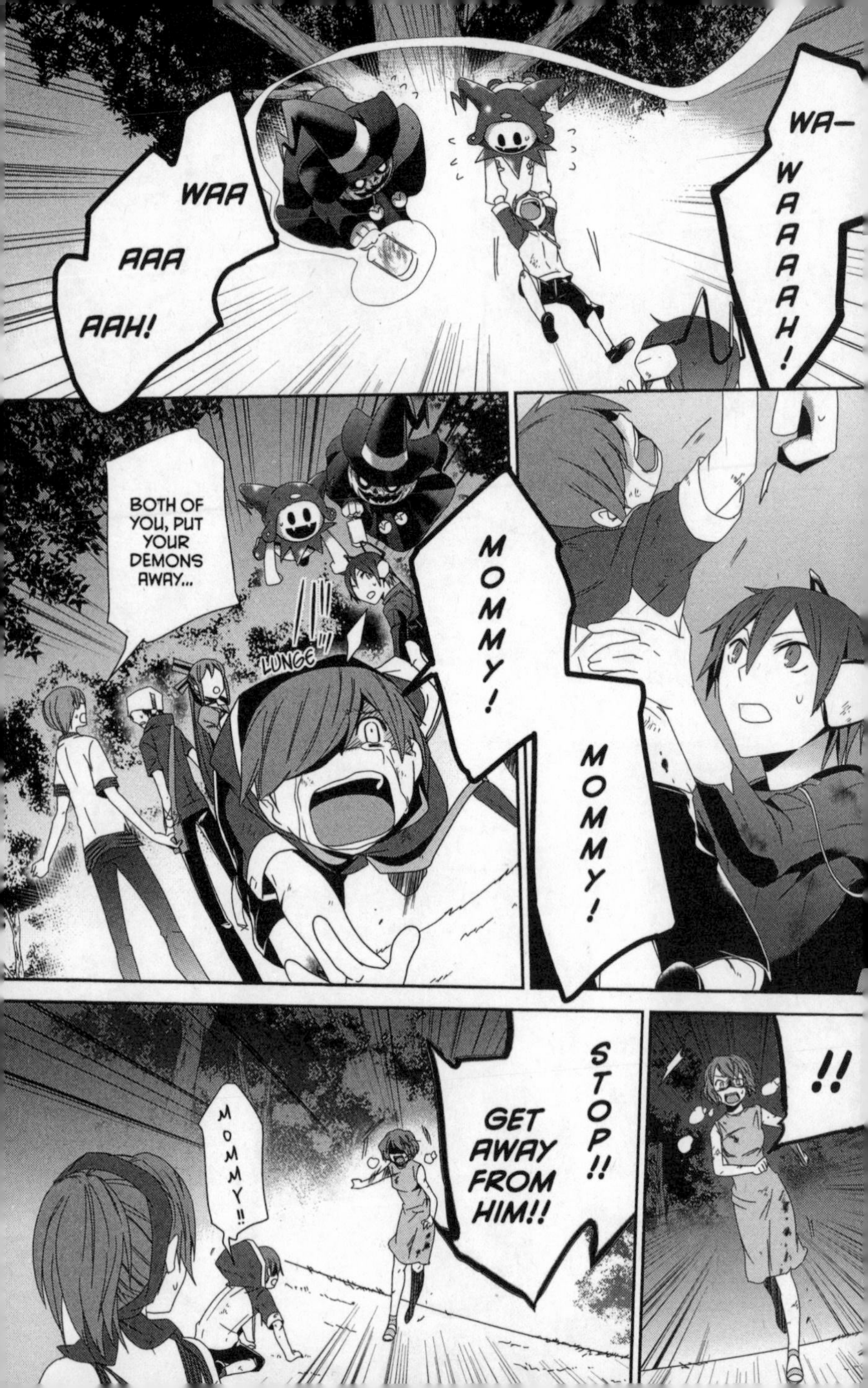

WA— WAAAAAH!
WAAAAAAAH!
MOMMY!
MOMMY!
BOTH OF YOU, PUT YOUR DEMONS AWAY...
LUNGE
!!
STOP!!
GET AWAY FROM HIM!!
MOMMY!!

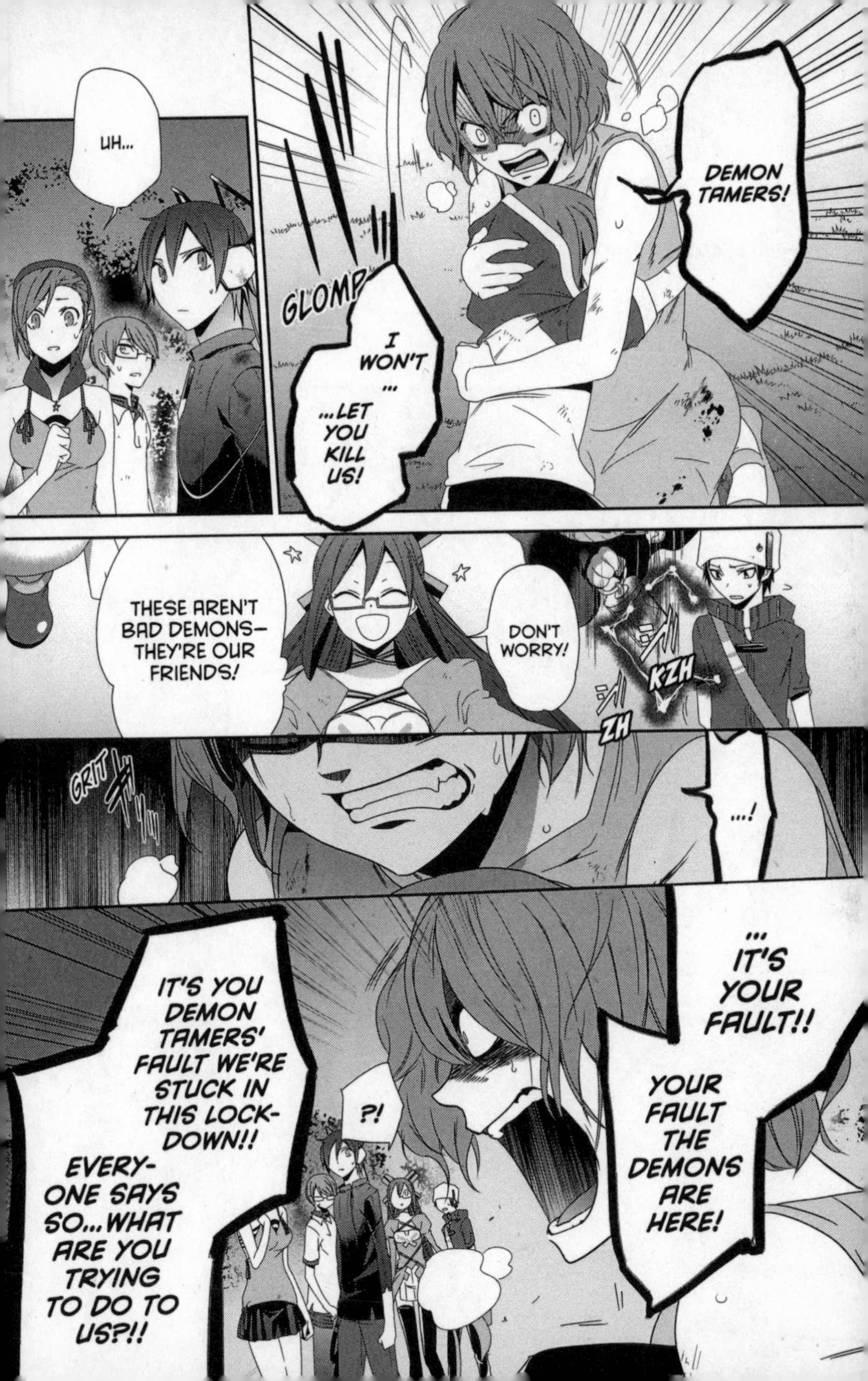
DEMON TAMERS!
GLOMP
I WON'T ...
...LET YOU KILL US!
UH...
KZH
ZH
DON'T WORRY!
THESE AREN'T BAD DEMONS—THEY'RE OUR FRIENDS!
...!
GRIT
...IT'S YOUR FAULT!!
YOUR FAULT THE DEMONS ARE HERE!
?!
IT'S YOU DEMON TAMERS' FAULT WE'RE STUCK IN THIS LOCK-DOWN!!
EVERY-ONE SAYS SO...WHAT ARE YOU TRYING TO DO TO US?!!

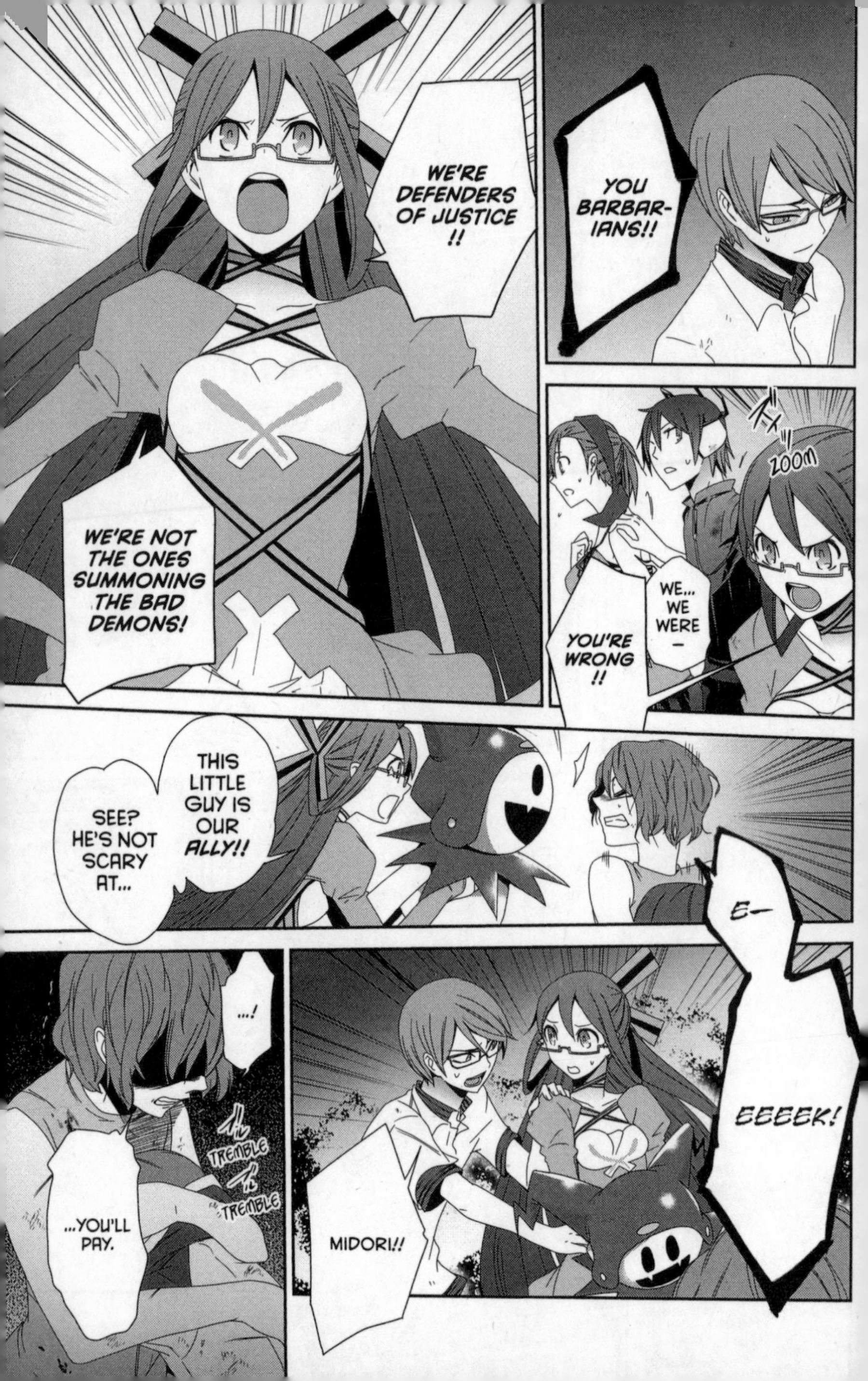
YOU BARBAR-IANS!!
ZOOM
WE... WE WERE —
YOU'RE WRONG !!
WE'RE DEFENDERS OF JUSTICE !!
WE'RE NOT THE ONES SUMMONING THE BAD DEMONS!
THIS LITTLE GUY IS OUR ALLY!!
SEE? HE'S NOT SCARY AT...
E—
EEEEK!
MIDORI!!
...!
TREMBLE TREMBLE
...YOU'LL PAY.

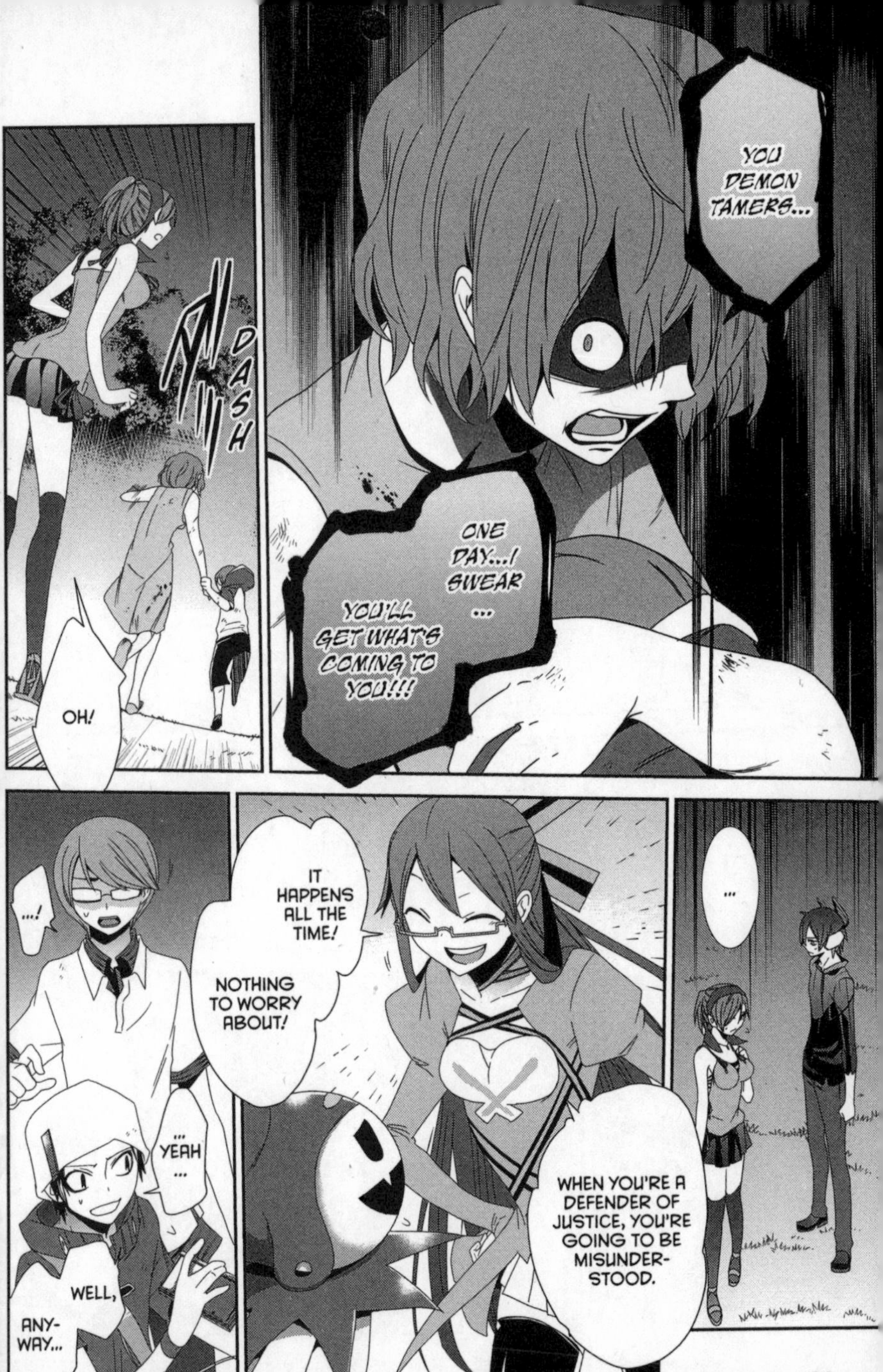
YOU DEMON TAMERS...
ONE DAY...I SWEAR...
YOU'LL GET WHAT'S COMING TO YOU!!!
DASH
OH!
...
IT HAPPENS ALL THE TIME!
NOTHING TO WORRY ABOUT!
WHEN YOU'RE A DEFENDER OF JUSTICE, YOU'RE GOING TO BE MISUNDER-STOOD.
...!
...YEAH...
WELL, ANYWAY...

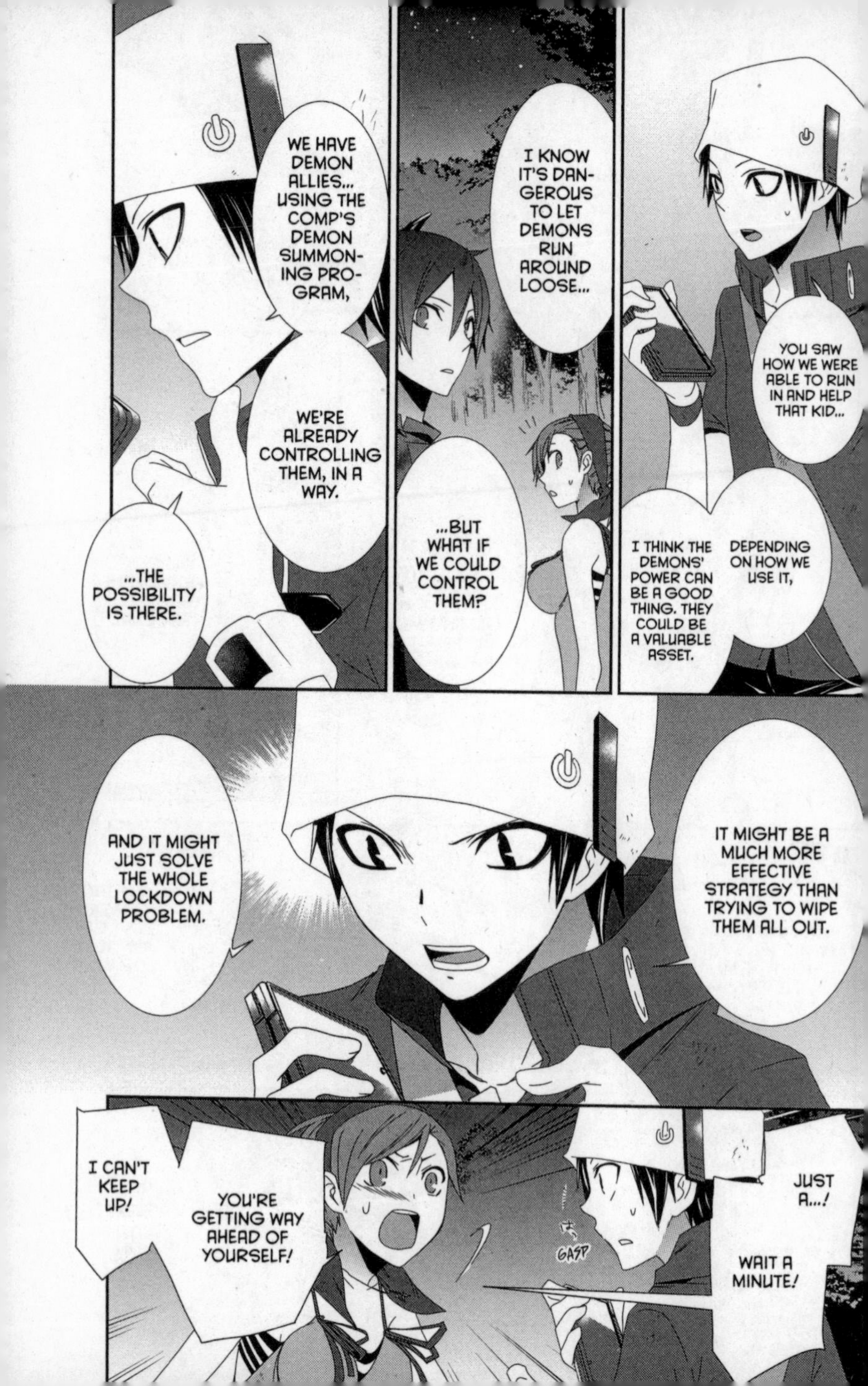
YOU SAW HOW WE WERE ABLE TO RUN IN AND HELP THAT KID...
DEPENDING ON HOW WE USE IT,
I THINK THE DEMONS' POWER CAN BE A GOOD THING. THEY COULD BE A VALUABLE ASSET.
I KNOW IT'S DANGEROUS TO LET DEMONS RUN AROUND LOOSE...
...BUT WHAT IF WE COULD CONTROL THEM?
WE HAVE DEMON ALLIES... USING THE COMP'S DEMON SUMMONING PROGRAM,
WE'RE ALREADY CONTROLLING THEM, IN A WAY.
...THE POSSIBILITY IS THERE.
IT MIGHT BE A MUCH MORE EFFECTIVE STRATEGY THAN TRYING TO WIPE THEM ALL OUT.
AND IT MIGHT JUST SOLVE THE WHOLE LOCKDOWN PROBLEM.
JUST A...!
WAIT A MINUTE!
GASP
YOU'RE GETTING WAY AHEAD OF YOURSELF!
I CAN'T KEEP UP!

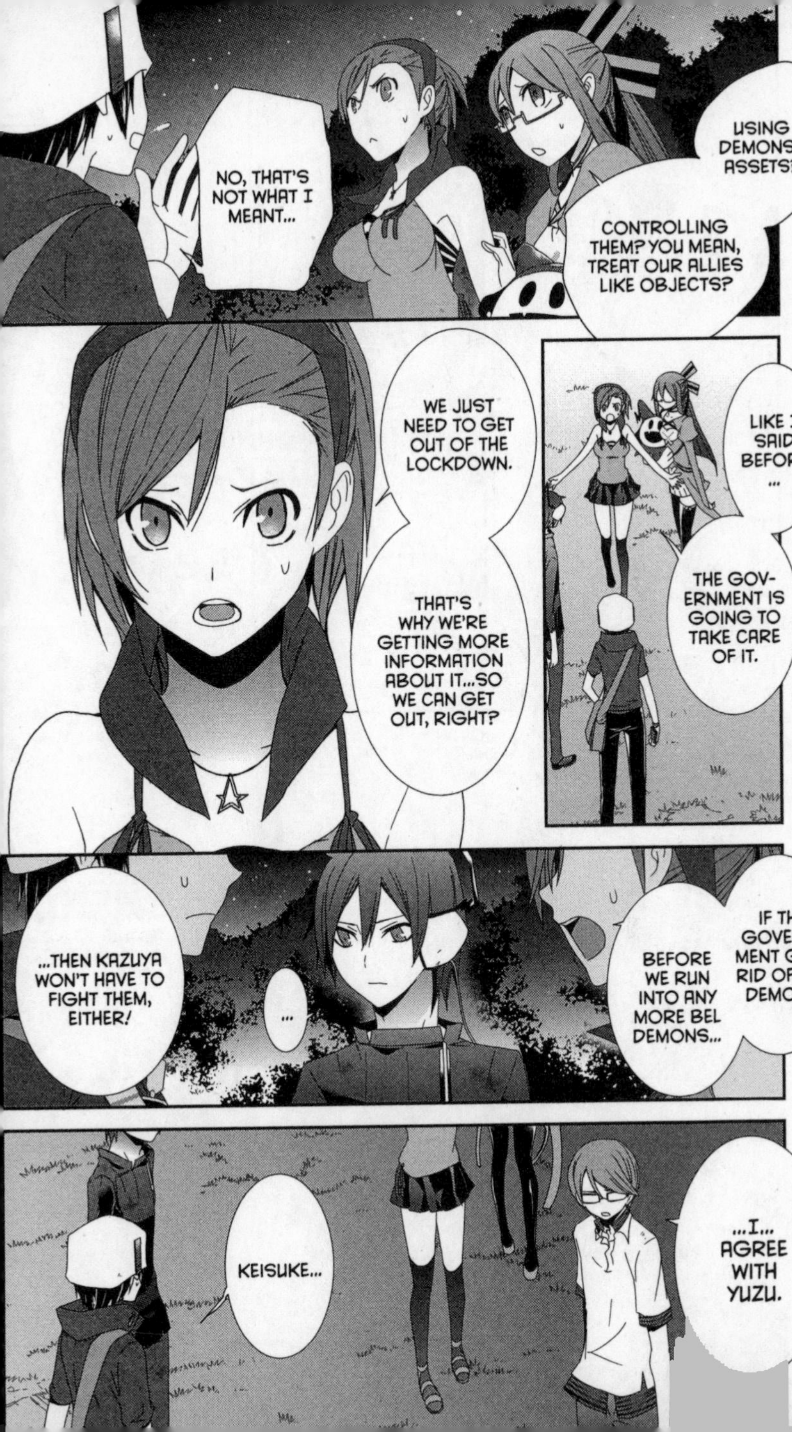
USING DEMONS? ASSETS?
CONTROLLING THEM? YOU MEAN, TREAT OUR ALLIES LIKE OBJECTS?
NO, THAT'S NOT WHAT I MEANT...
LIKE I SAID BEFORE ...
THE GOV-ERNMENT IS GOING TO TAKE CARE OF IT.
WE JUST NEED TO GET OUT OF THE LOCKDOWN.
THAT'S WHY WE'RE GETTING MORE INFORMATION ABOUT IT...SO WE CAN GET OUT, RIGHT?
IF THE GOVERN-MENT GETS RID OF THE DEMONS
BEFORE WE RUN INTO ANY MORE BEL DEMONS...
...
...THEN KAZUYA WON'T HAVE TO FIGHT THEM, EITHER!
...I... AGREE WITH YUZU.
KEISUKE...

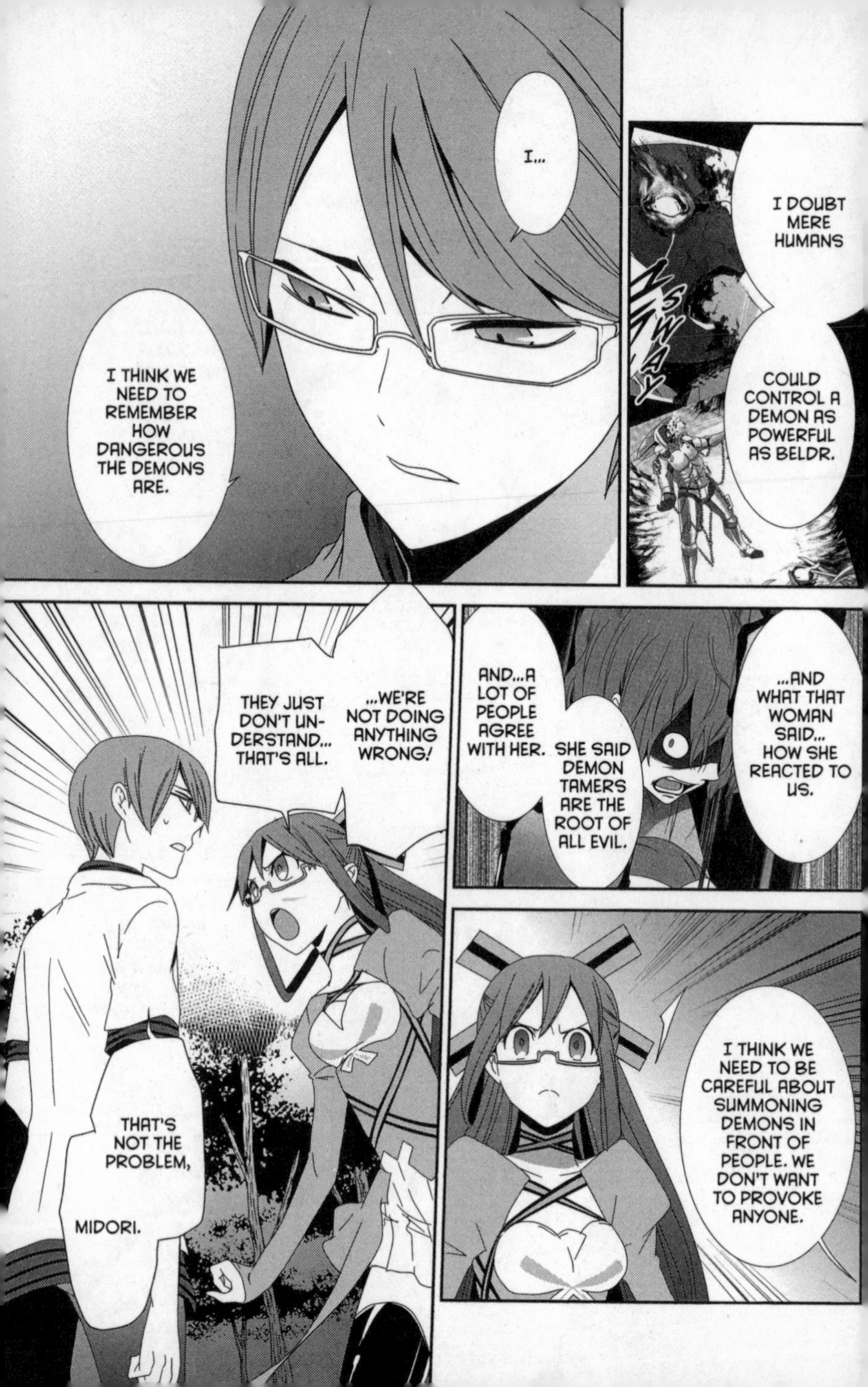
I DOUBT MERE HUMANS
SWAY
COULD CONTROL A DEMON AS POWERFUL AS BELDR.
I...
I THINK WE NEED TO REMEMBER HOW DANGEROUS THE DEMONS ARE.
...AND WHAT THAT WOMAN SAID... HOW SHE REACTED TO US.
SHE SAID DEMON TAMERS ARE THE ROOT OF ALL EVIL.
AND...A LOT OF PEOPLE AGREE WITH HER.
I THINK WE NEED TO BE CAREFUL ABOUT SUMMONING DEMONS IN FRONT OF PEOPLE. WE DON'T WANT TO PROVOKE ANYONE.
...WE'RE NOT DOING ANYTHING WRONG!
THEY JUST DON'T UN-DERSTAND... THAT'S ALL.
THAT'S NOT THE PROBLEM,
MIDORI.

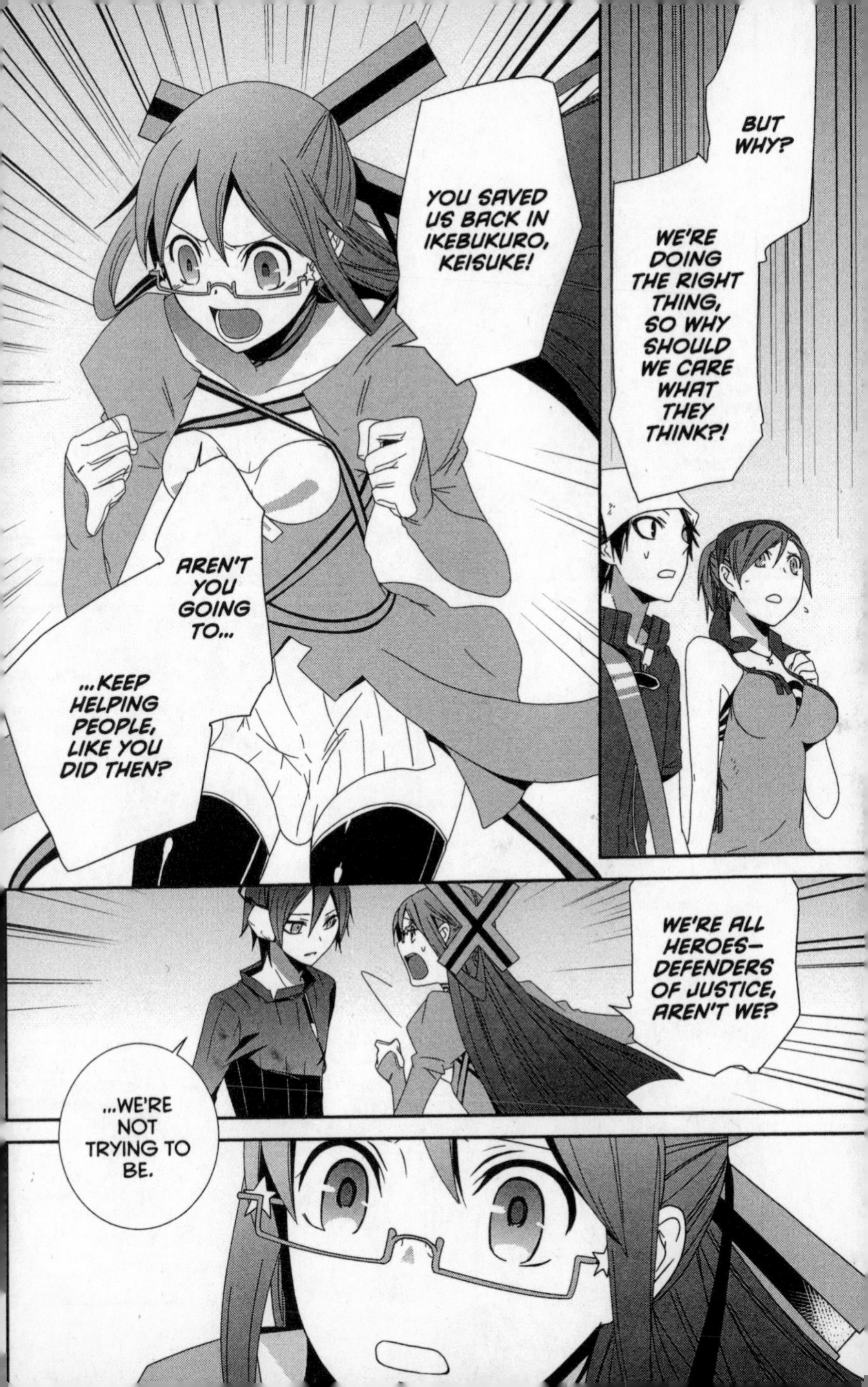
BUT WHY?
WE'RE DOING THE RIGHT THING, SO WHY SHOULD WE CARE WHAT THEY THINK?!
YOU SAVED US BACK IN IKEBUKURO, KEISUKE!
AREN'T YOU GOING TO...
...KEEP HELPING PEOPLE, LIKE YOU DID THEN?
WE'RE ALL HEROES—DEFENDERS OF JUSTICE, AREN'T WE?
...WE'RE NOT TRYING TO BE.

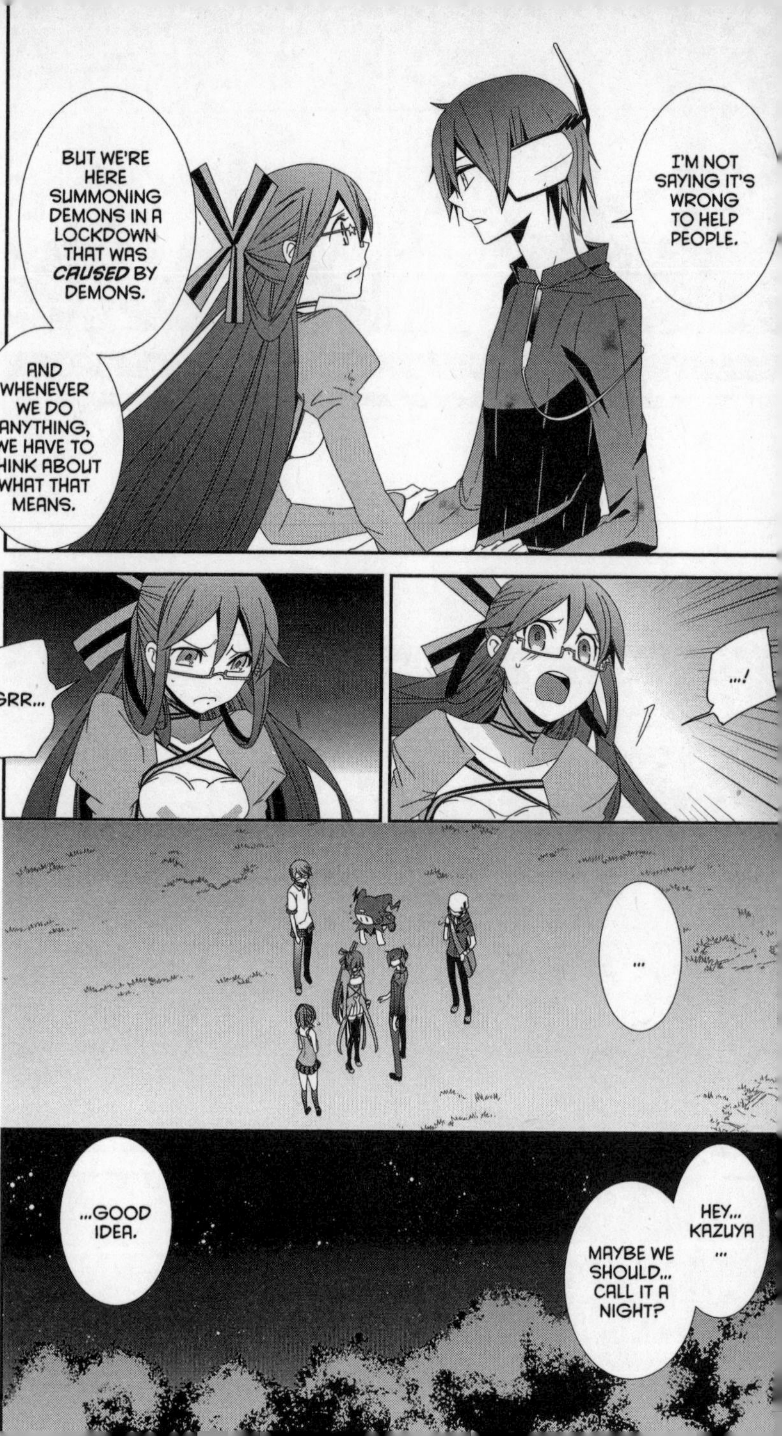
I'M NOT SAYING IT'S WRONG TO HELP PEOPLE.
BUT WE'RE HERE SUMMONING DEMONS IN A LOCKDOWN THAT WAS *CAUSED* BY DEMONS.
AND WHENEVER WE DO ANYTHING, WE HAVE TO THINK ABOUT WHAT THAT MEANS.
...!
GRR...
...
HEY... KAZUYA ...
MAYBE WE SHOULD... CALL IT A NIGHT?
...GOOD IDEA.

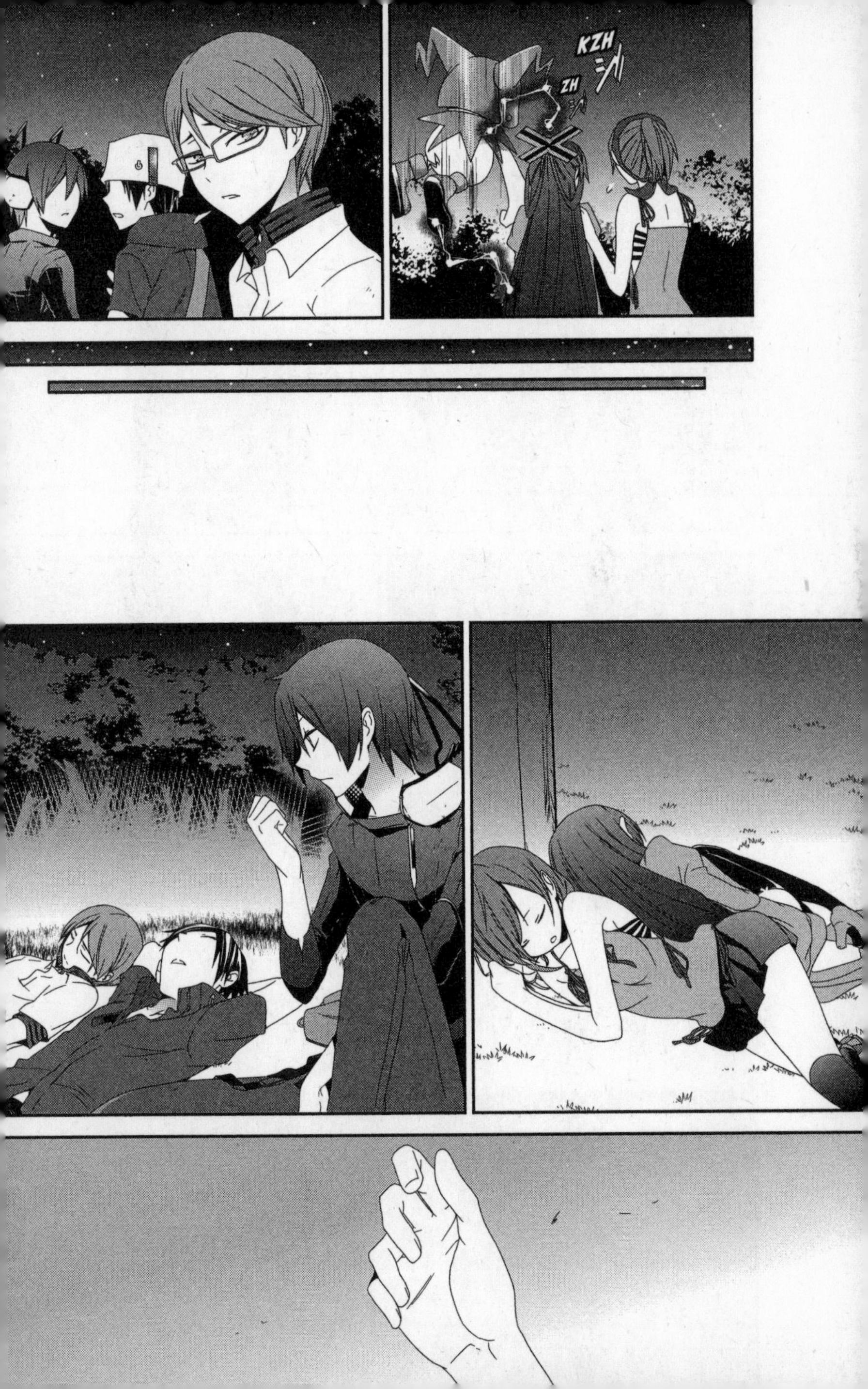
KZH
ZH

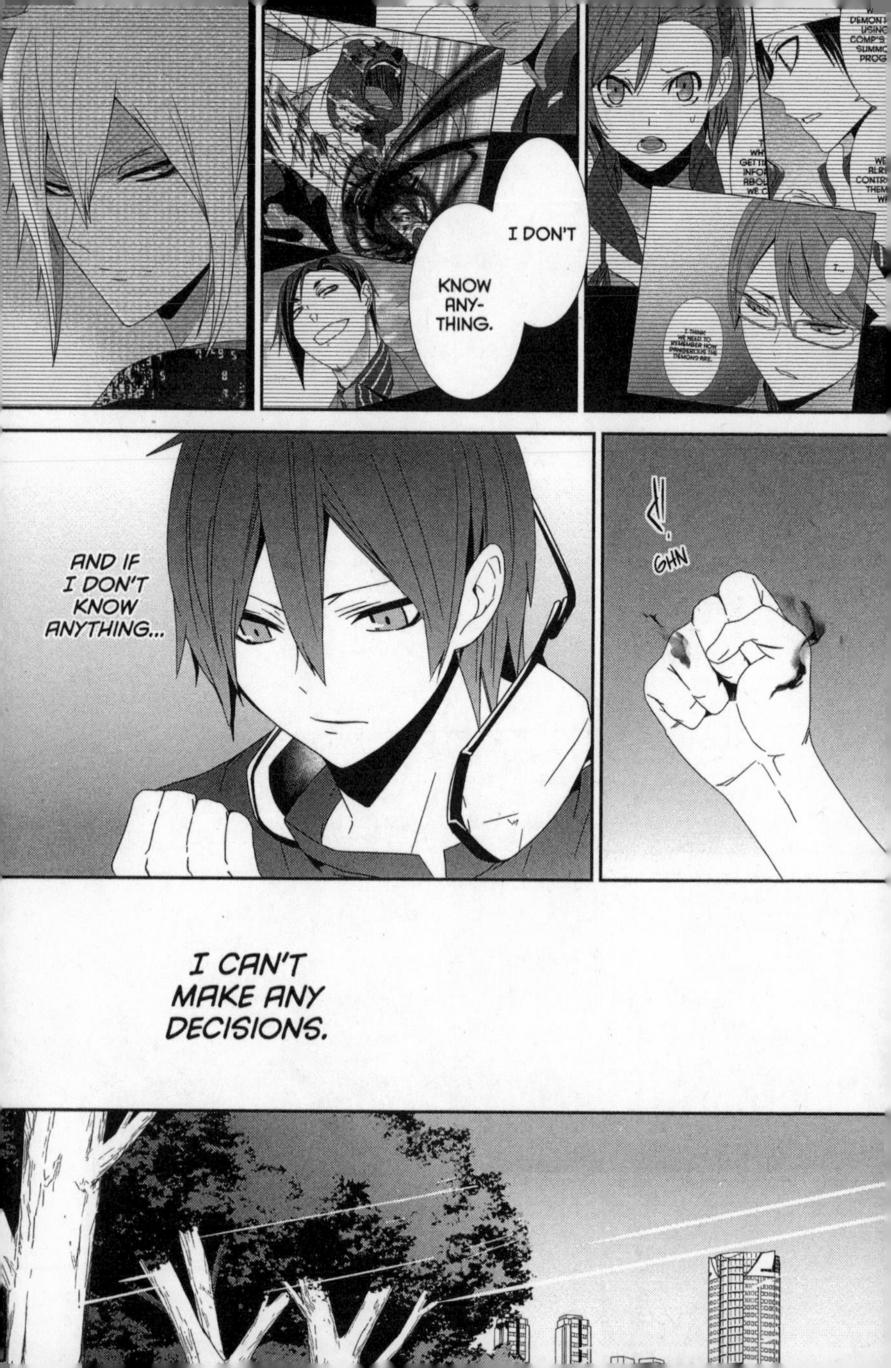
I...
I THINK WE NEED TO REMEMBER HOW DANGEROUS THE DEMONS ARE.
I DON'T
KNOW ANY-THING.
GHN
AND IF I DON'T KNOW ANYTHING...
I CAN'T MAKE ANY DECISIONS.

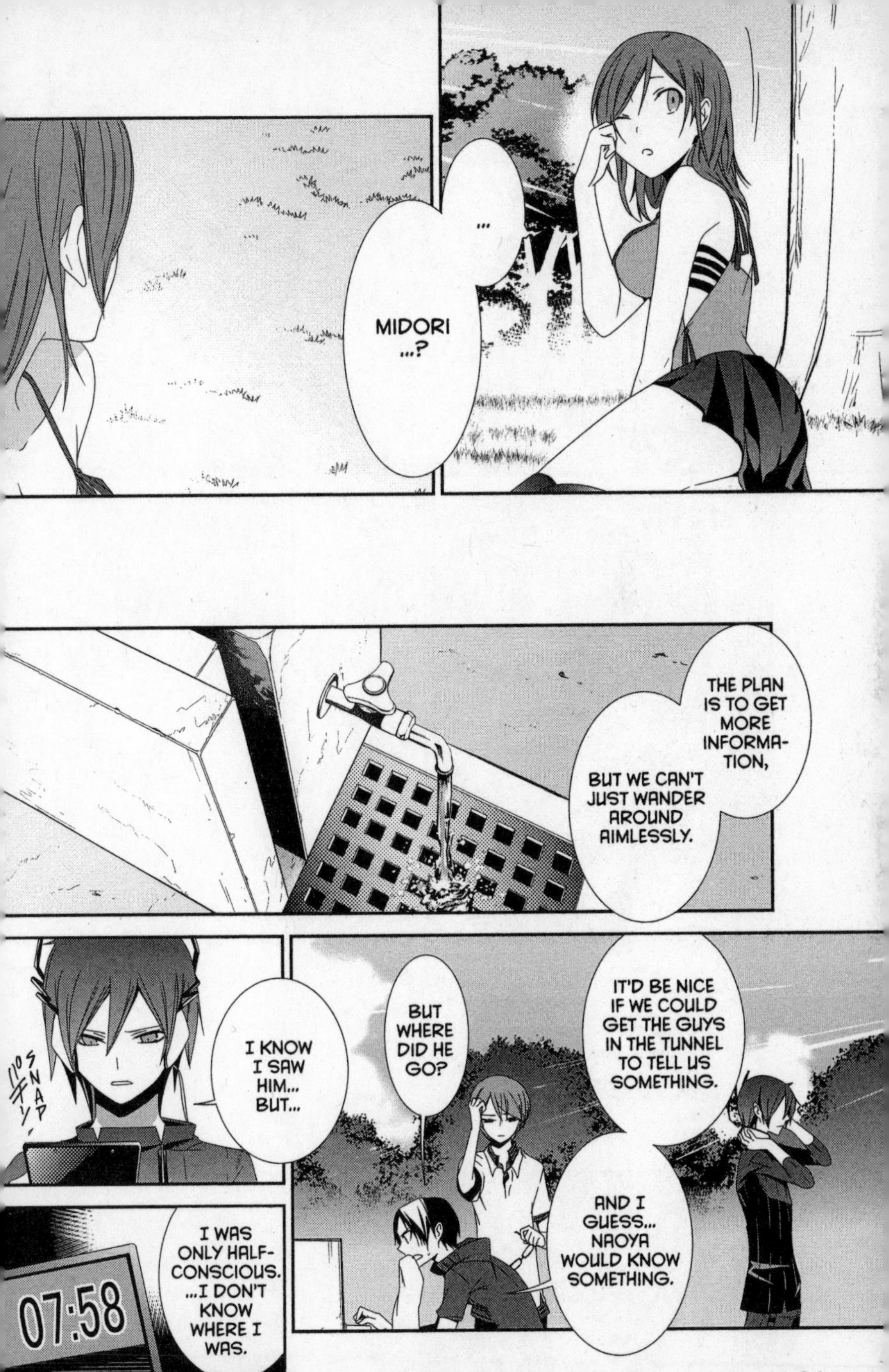
...
MIDORI ...?
THE PLAN IS TO GET MORE INFORMATION,
BUT WE CAN'T JUST WANDER AROUND AIMLESSLY.
IT'D BE NICE IF WE COULD GET THE GUYS IN THE TUNNEL TO TELL US SOMETHING.
AND I GUESS... NAOYA WOULD KNOW SOMETHING.
BUT WHERE DID HE GO?
I KNOW I SAW HIM... BUT...
SNAP
07:58
I WAS ONLY HALF-CONSCIOUS. ...I DON'T KNOW WHERE I WAS.

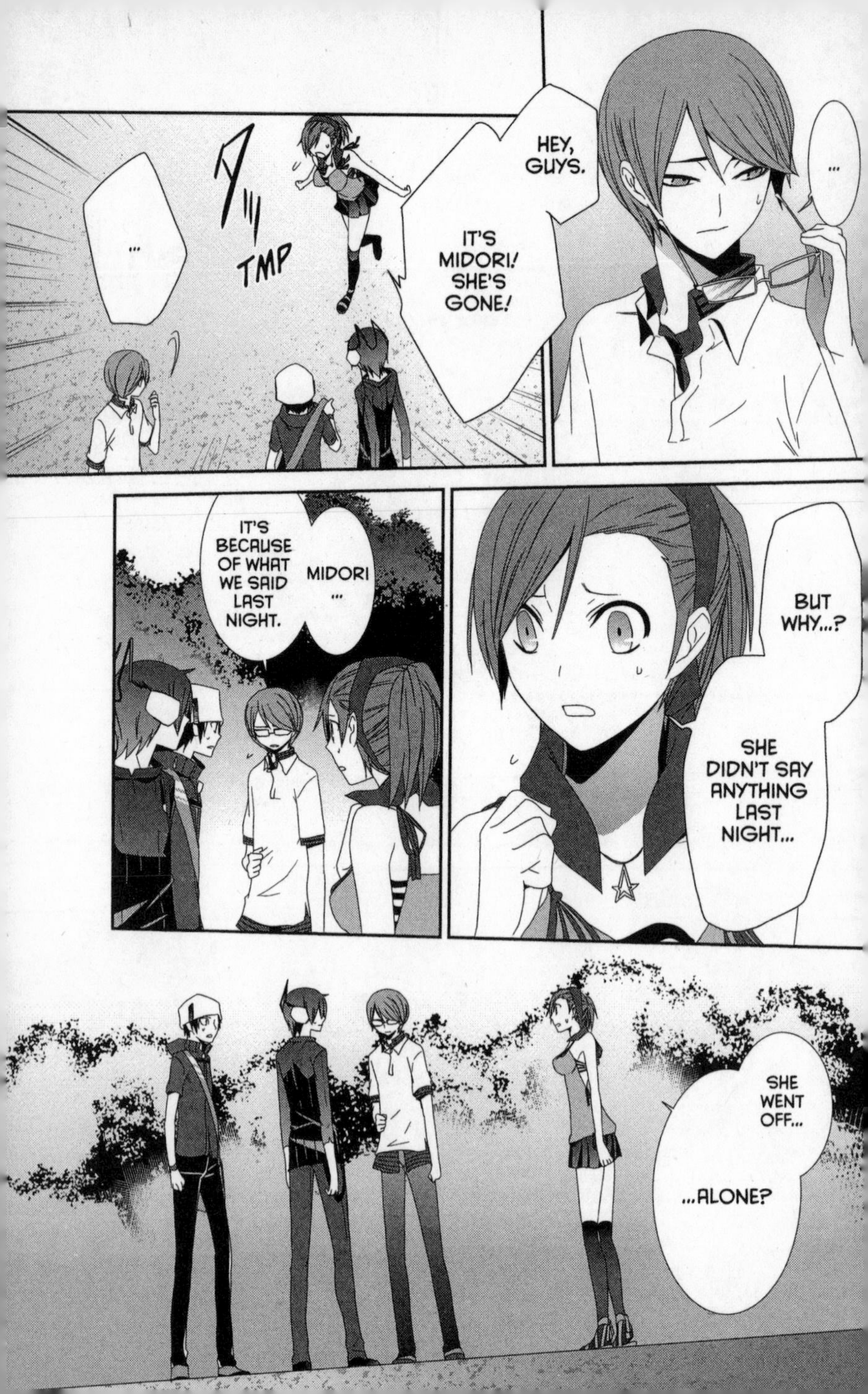
...
HEY, GUYS.
IT'S MIDORI! SHE'S GONE!
TMP
...
BUT WHY...?
SHE DIDN'T SAY ANYTHING LAST NIGHT...
MIDORI...
IT'S BECAUSE OF WHAT WE SAID LAST NIGHT.
SHE WENT OFF...
...ALONE?

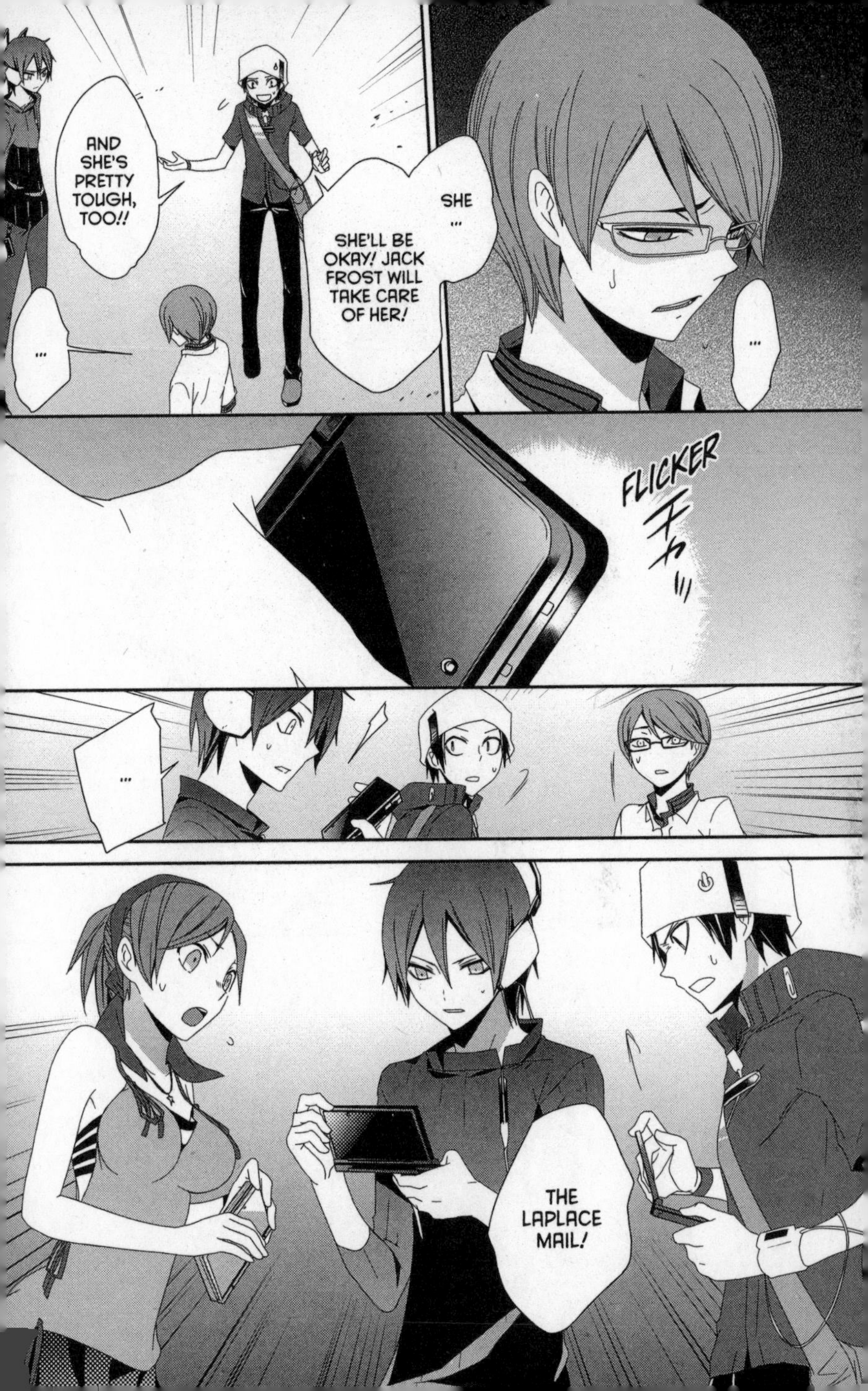
SHE ...
...
SHE'LL BE OKAY! JACK FROST WILL TAKE CARE OF HER!
AND SHE'S PRETTY TOUGH, TOO!!
...
FLICKER
...
THE LAPLACE MAIL!

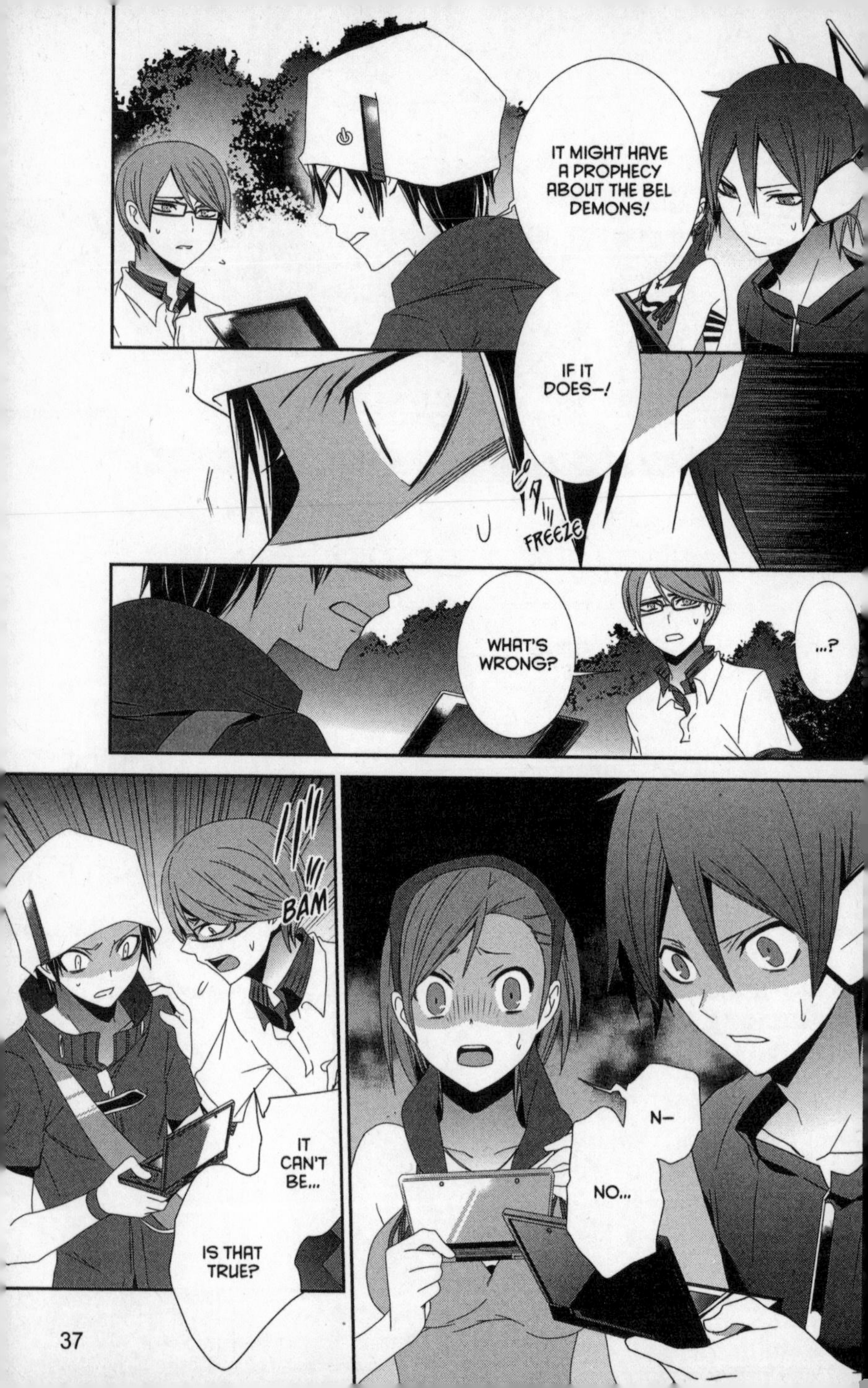
IT MIGHT HAVE A PROPHECY ABOUT THE BEL DEMONS!
IF IT DOES—!
FREEZE
...?
WHAT'S WRONG?
N—
NO...
BAM
IT CAN'T BE...
IS THAT TRUE?

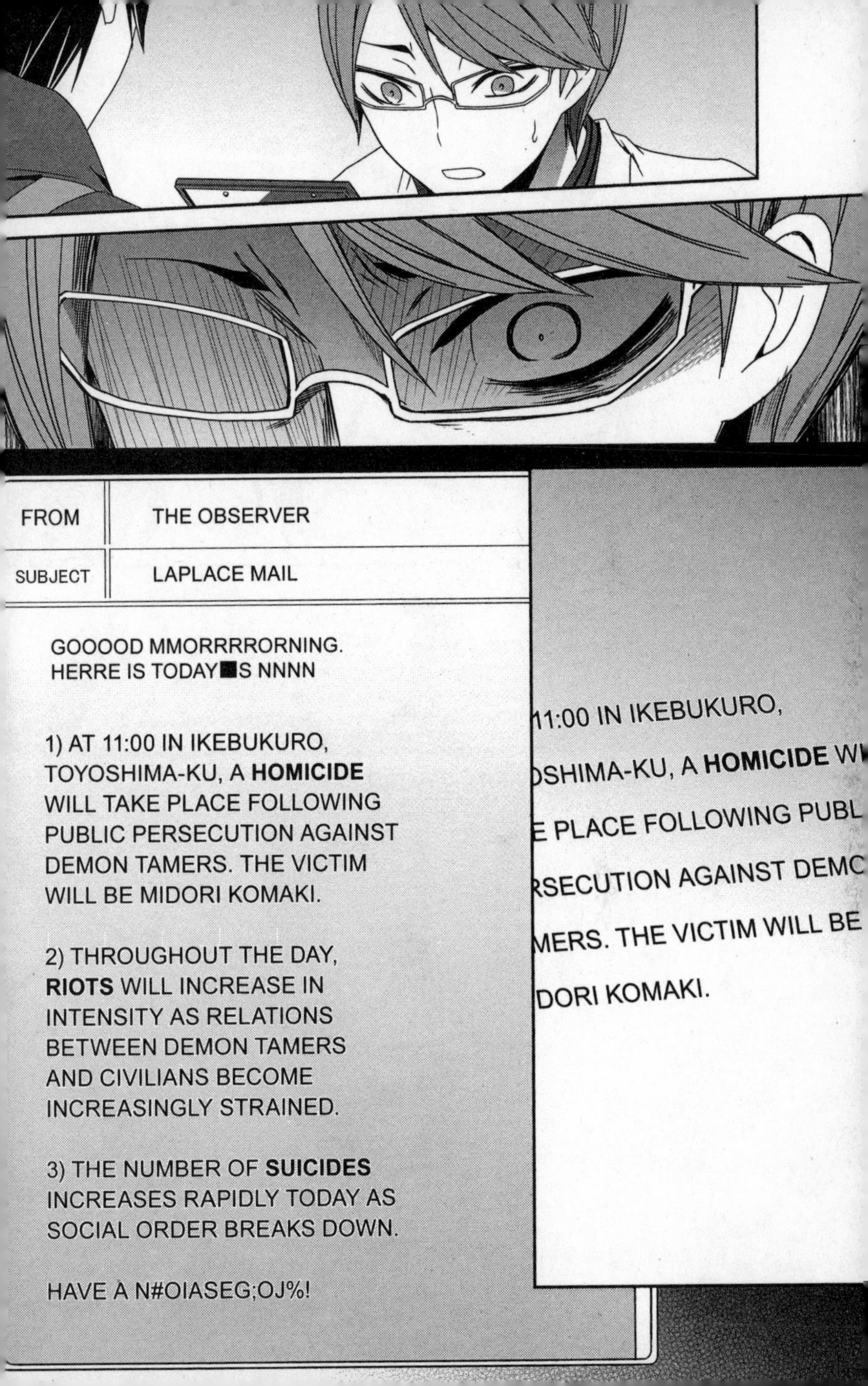

11:00 IN IKEBUKURO,
SHIMA-KU, A HOMICIDE
PLACE FOLLOWING
RSECUTION AGAINST
MERS. THE VICTIM WILL BE
DORI KOMAKI.
FROM THE OBSERVER
SUBJECT LAPLACE MAIL
GOOOOD MMORRRRORNING.
HERRE IS TODAY■S NNNN
1) AT 11:00 IN IKEBUKURO, TOYOSHIMA-KU, A HOMICIDE WILL TAKE PLACE FOLLOWING PUBLIC PERSECUTION AGAINST DEMON TAMERS. THE VICTIM WILL BE MIDORI KOMAKI.
2) THROUGHOUT THE DAY, RIOTS WILL INCREASE IN INTENSITY AS RELATIONS BETWEEN DEMON TAMERS AND CIVILIANS BECOME INCREASINGLY STRAINED.
3) THE NUMBER OF SUICIDES INCREASES RAPIDLY TODAY AS SOCIAL ORDER BREAKS DOWN.
HAVE A N#OIASEG;OJ%!

DEVIL SURVIVOR
デビルサバイバー

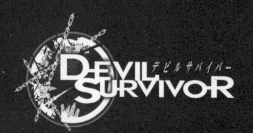

DEVIL SURVIVOR
デビルサバイバー

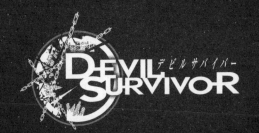

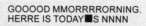

SUBJECT	LAPLACE MAIL

GOOOOD MMORRRRORNING.
HERRE IS TODAY■S NNNN

1) AT 11:00 IN IKEBUKURO, TOYOSHIMA-KU, A **HOMICIDE** WILL TAKE PLACE FOLLOWING PUBLIC PERSECUTION AGAINST DEMON TAMERS. THE VICTIM WILL BE MIDORI KOMAKI.

2) THROUGHOUT THE DAY, **RIOTS** WILL INCREASE IN INTENSITY AS RELATIONS BETWEEN DEMON TAMERS AND CIVILIANS BECOME INCREASINGLY STRAINED.

3) THE NUMBER OF **SUICIDES** INCREASES RAPIDLY TODAY AS SOCIAL ORDER BREAKS DOWN.

NO...

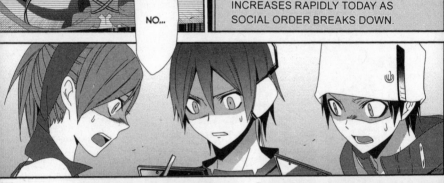

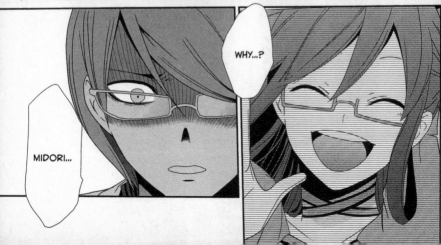

WHY...?

MIDORI...

SURVIVAL:17
THE COLLAPSE OF ORDER

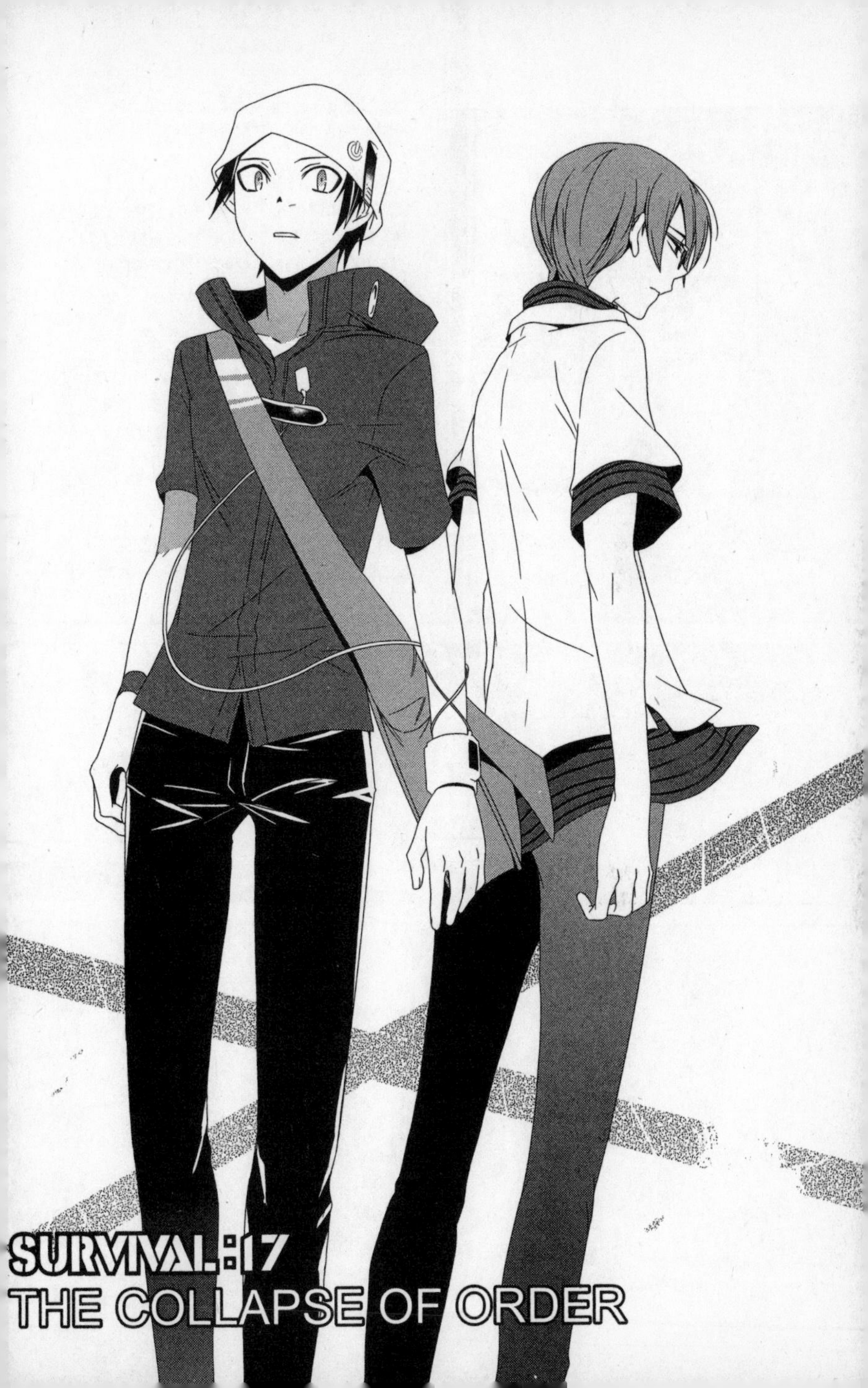

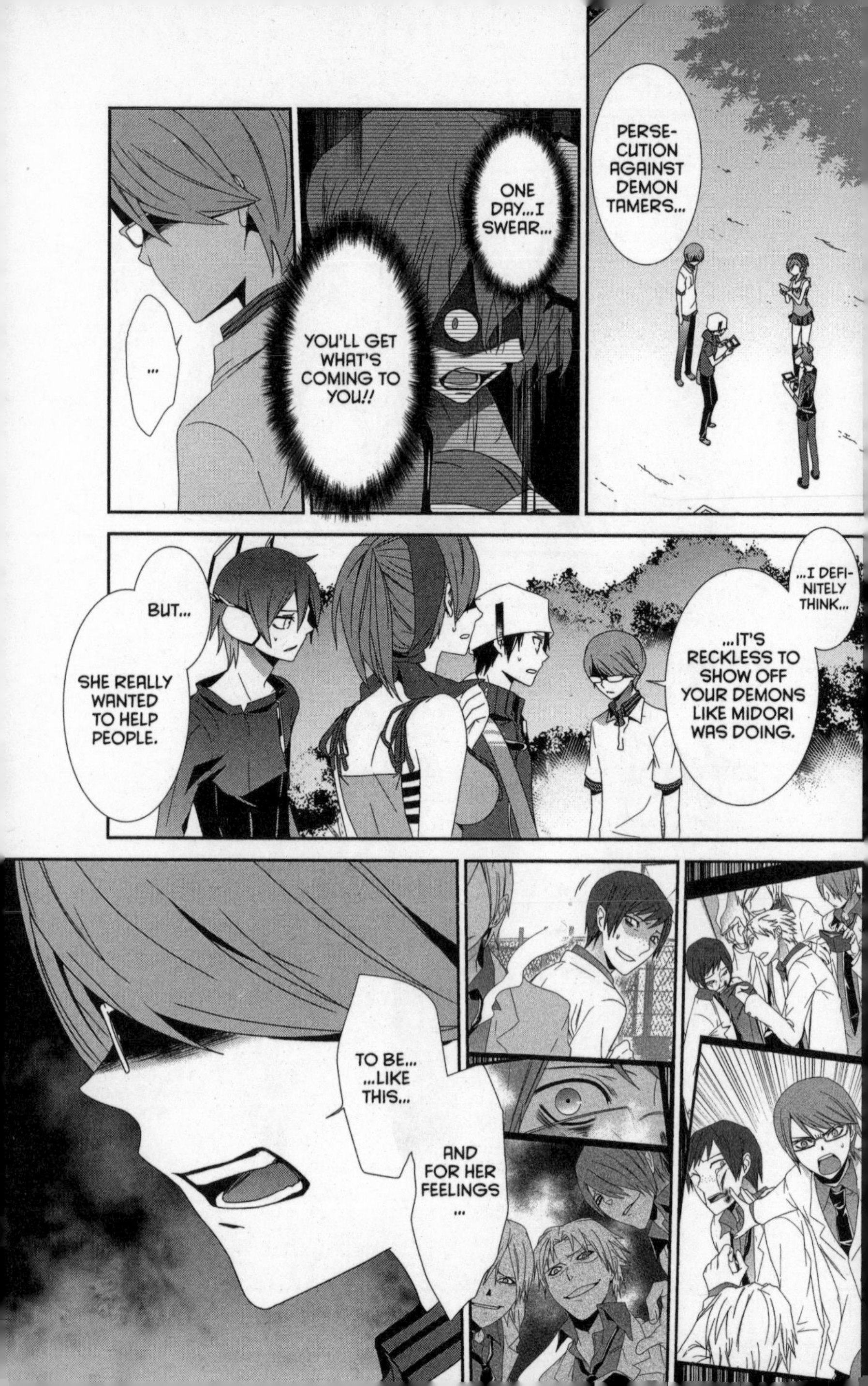
PERSE-
CUTION
AGAINST
DEMON
TAMERS...
ONE
DAY...I
SWEAR...
YOU'LL GET
WHAT'S
COMING TO
YOU!!
...
...I DEFI-
NITELY
THINK...
...IT'S
RECKLESS TO
SHOW OFF
YOUR DEMONS
LIKE MIDORI
WAS DOING.
BUT...
SHE REALLY
WANTED
TO HELP
PEOPLE.
TO BE...
...LIKE
THIS...
AND
FOR HER
FEELINGS
...

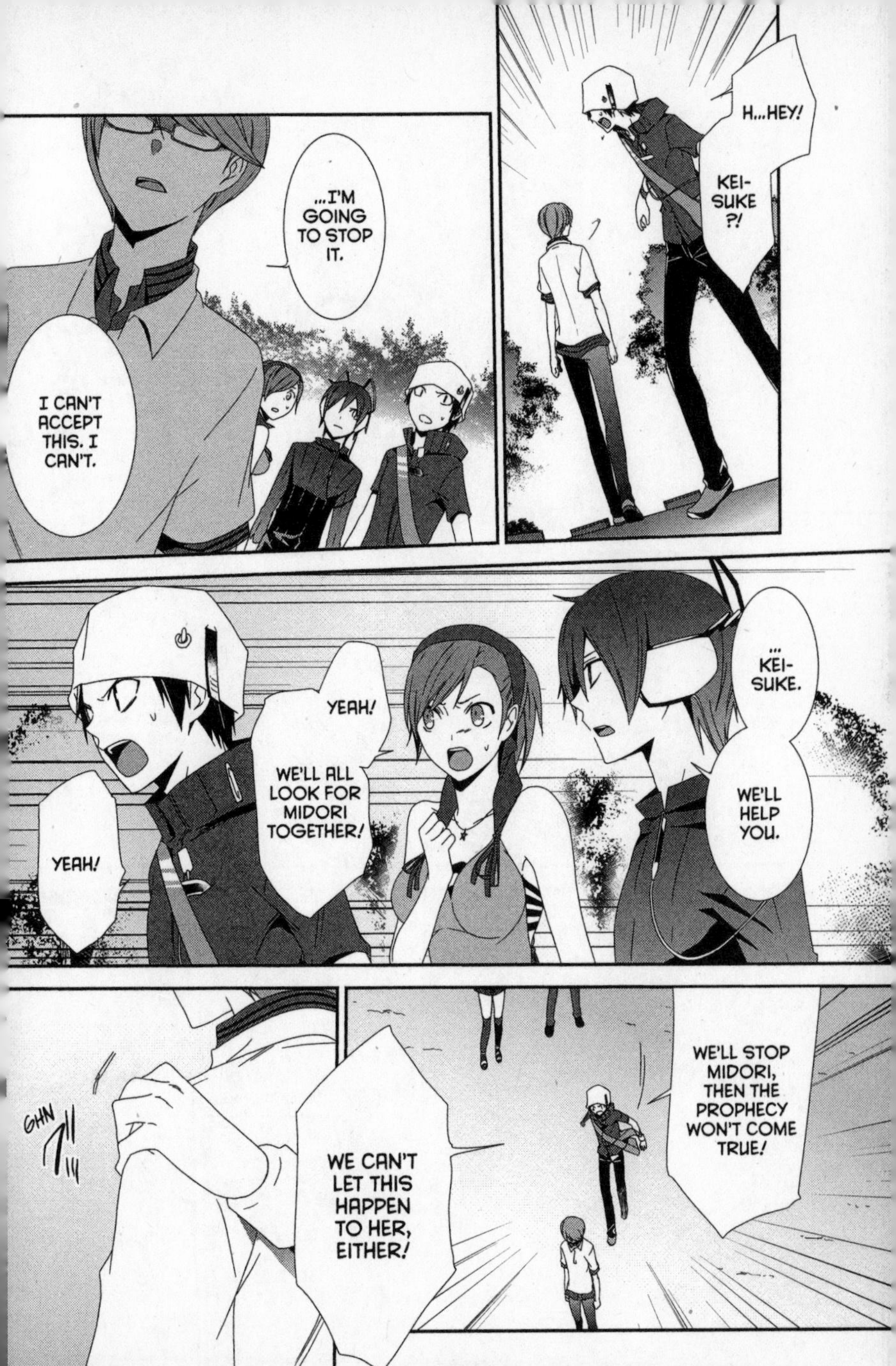
H...HEY!
KEI-SUKE?!
...I'M GOING TO STOP IT.
I CAN'T ACCEPT THIS. I CAN'T.
... KEI-SUKE.
WE'LL HELP YOU.
YEAH!
WE'LL ALL LOOK FOR MIDORI TOGETHER!
YEAH!
WE'LL STOP MIDORI, THEN THE PROPHECY WON'T COME TRUE!
WE CAN'T LET THIS HAPPEN TO HER, EITHER!
GHN

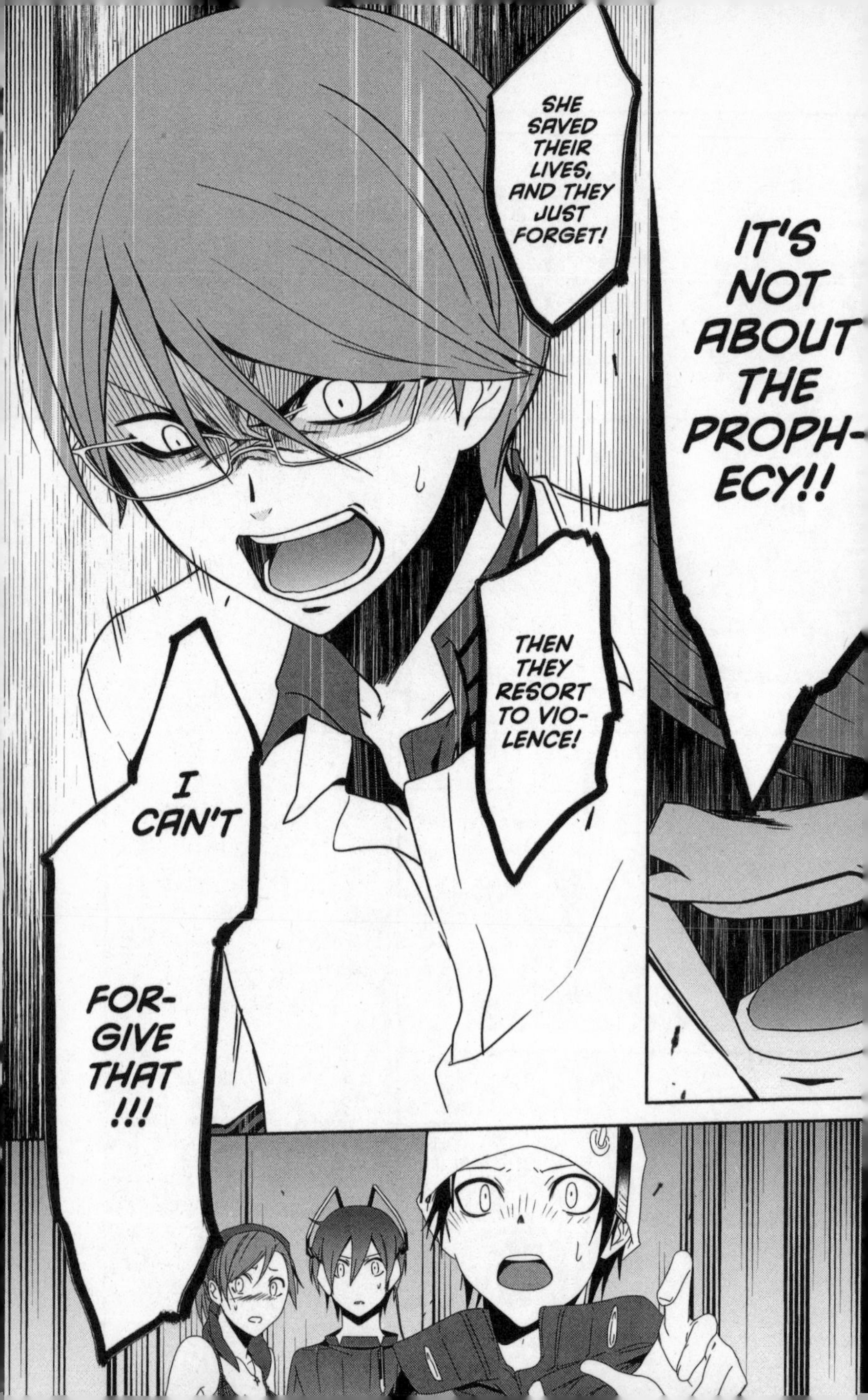
IT'S NOT ABOUT THE PROPH-ECY!!
SHE SAVED THEIR LIVES, AND THEY JUST FORGET!
THEN THEY RESORT TO VIO-LENCE!
I CAN'T
FOR-GIVE THAT !!!

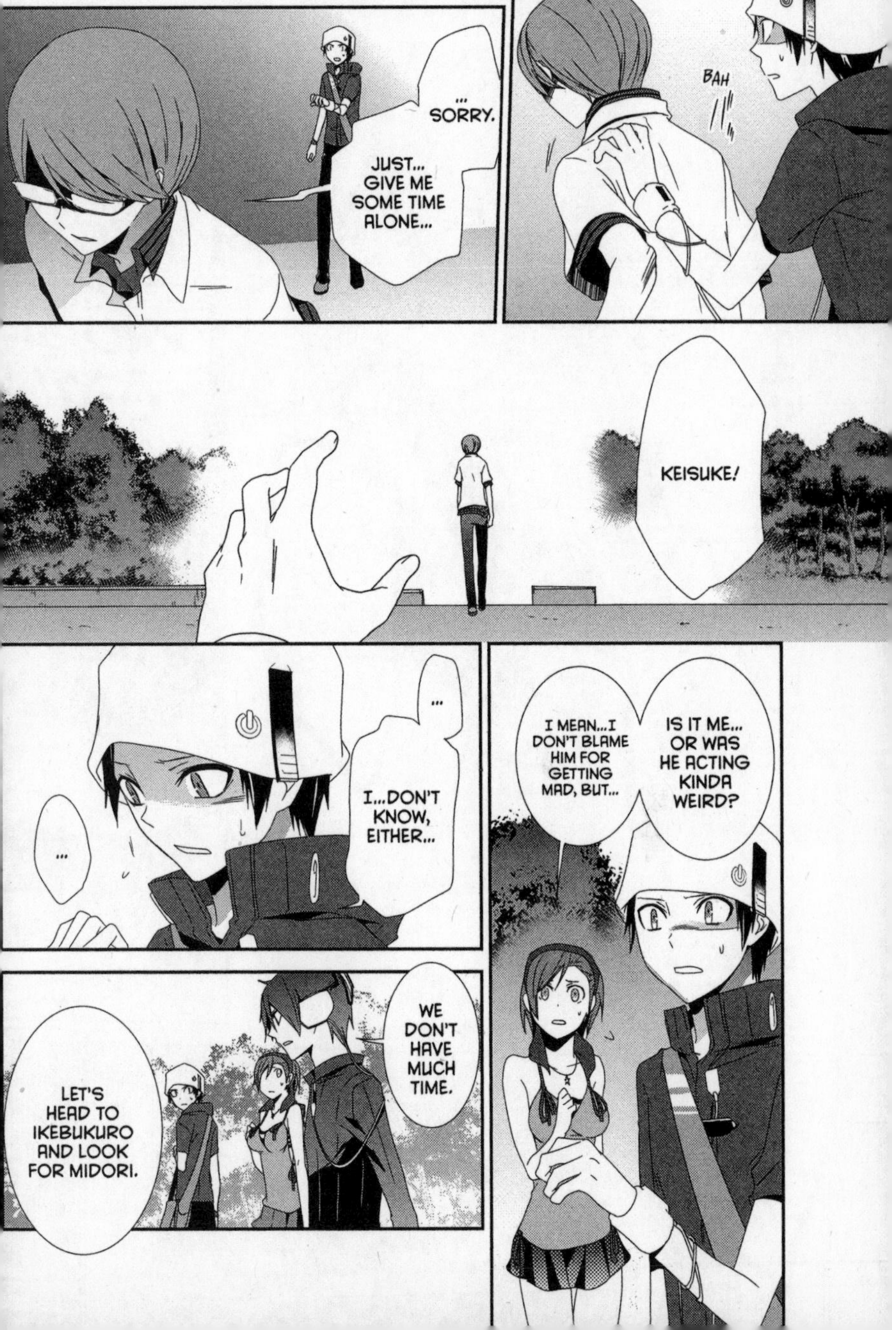
BAH
... SORRY.
JUST... GIVE ME SOME TIME ALONE...
KEISUKE!
IS IT ME... OR WAS HE ACTING KINDA WEIRD?
I MEAN...I DON'T BLAME HIM FOR GETTING MAD, BUT...
...
I...DON'T KNOW, EITHER...
...
WE DON'T HAVE MUCH TIME.
LET'S HEAD TO IKEBUKURO AND LOOK FOR MIDORI.

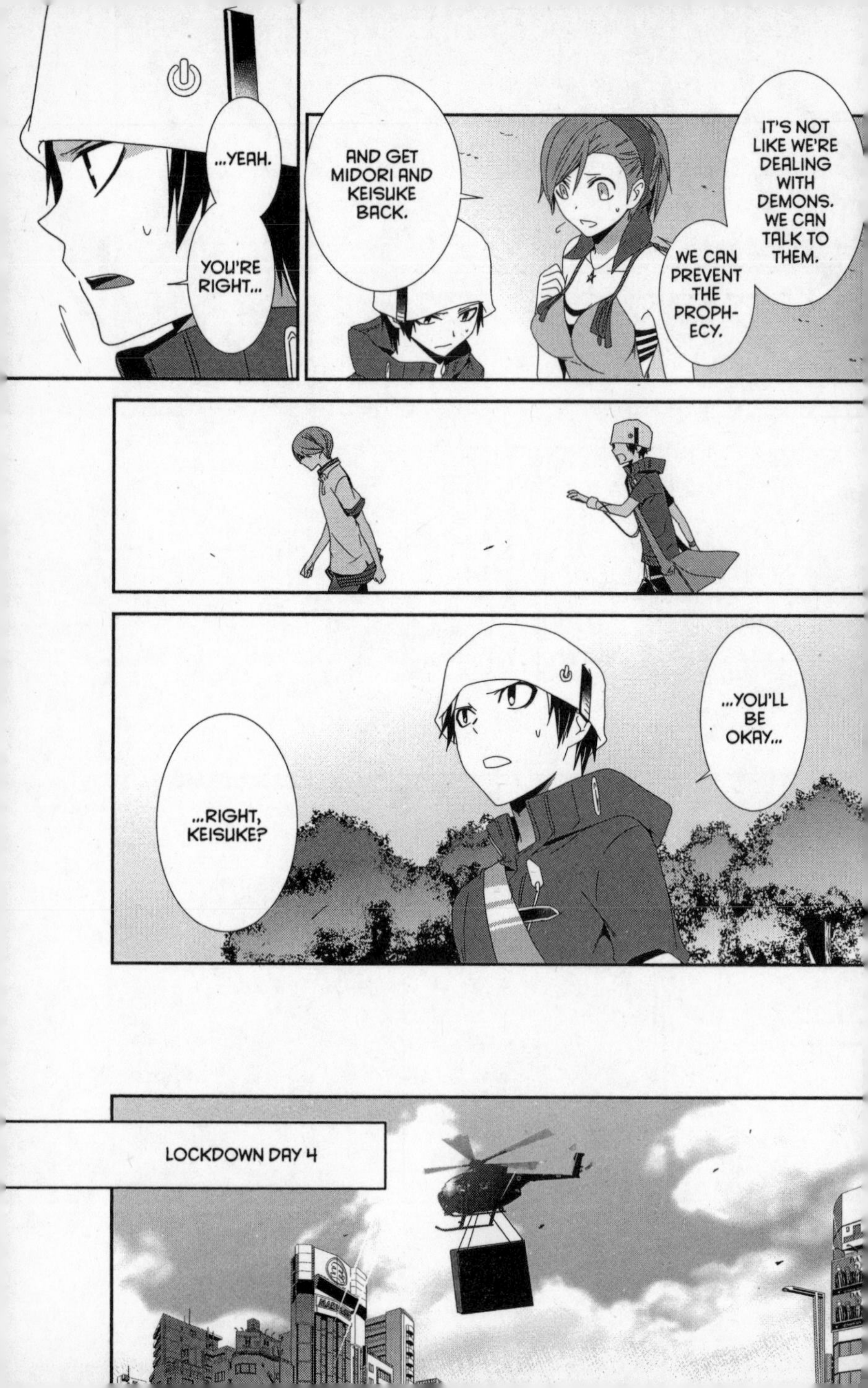
IT'S NOT LIKE WE'RE DEALING WITH DEMONS. WE CAN TALK TO THEM.
WE CAN PREVENT THE PROPHECY.
AND GET MIDORI AND KEISUKE BACK.
...YEAH.
YOU'RE RIGHT...
...YOU'LL BE OKAY...
...RIGHT, KEISUKE?
LOCKDOWN DAY 4

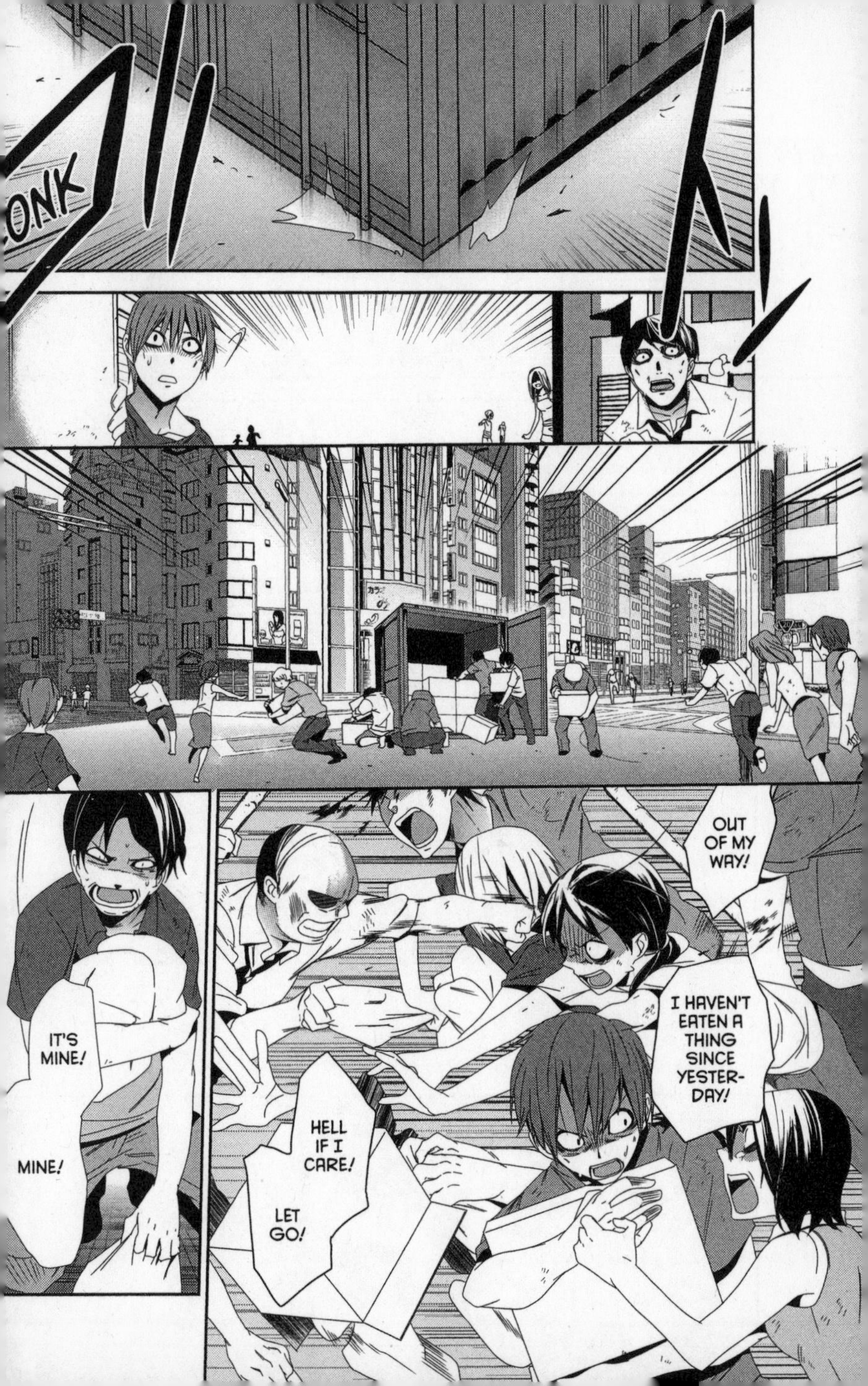
ONK
OUT OF MY WAY!
I HAVEN'T EATEN A THING SINCE YESTER-DAY!
HELL IF I CARE!
LET GO!
IT'S MINE!
MINE!

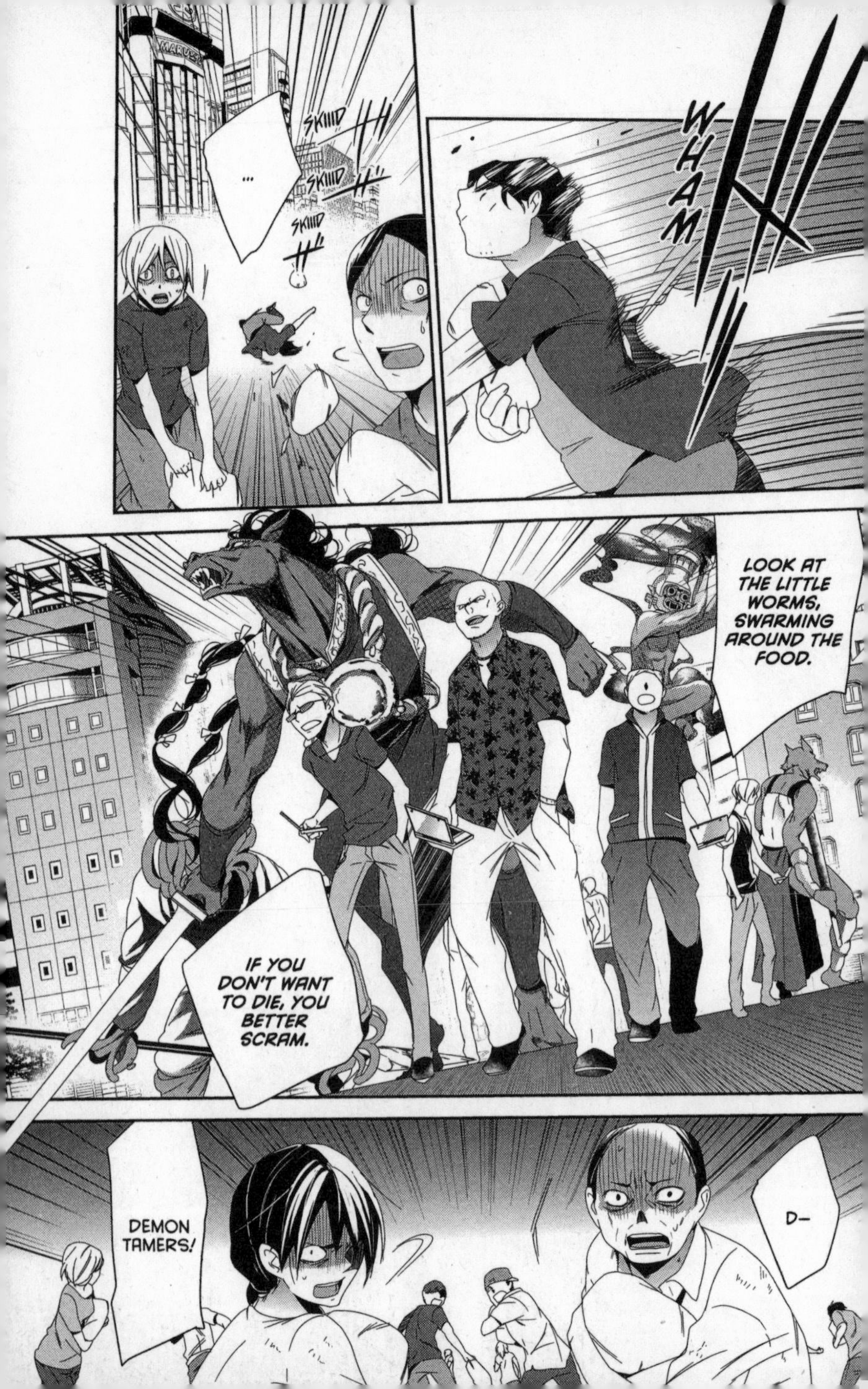

WHAM
...
SKIIID
SKIIID
SKIIID
...
LOOK AT THE LITTLE WORMS, SWARMING AROUND THE FOOD.
IF YOU DON'T WANT TO DIE, YOU BETTER SCRAM.
D—
DEMON TAMERS!

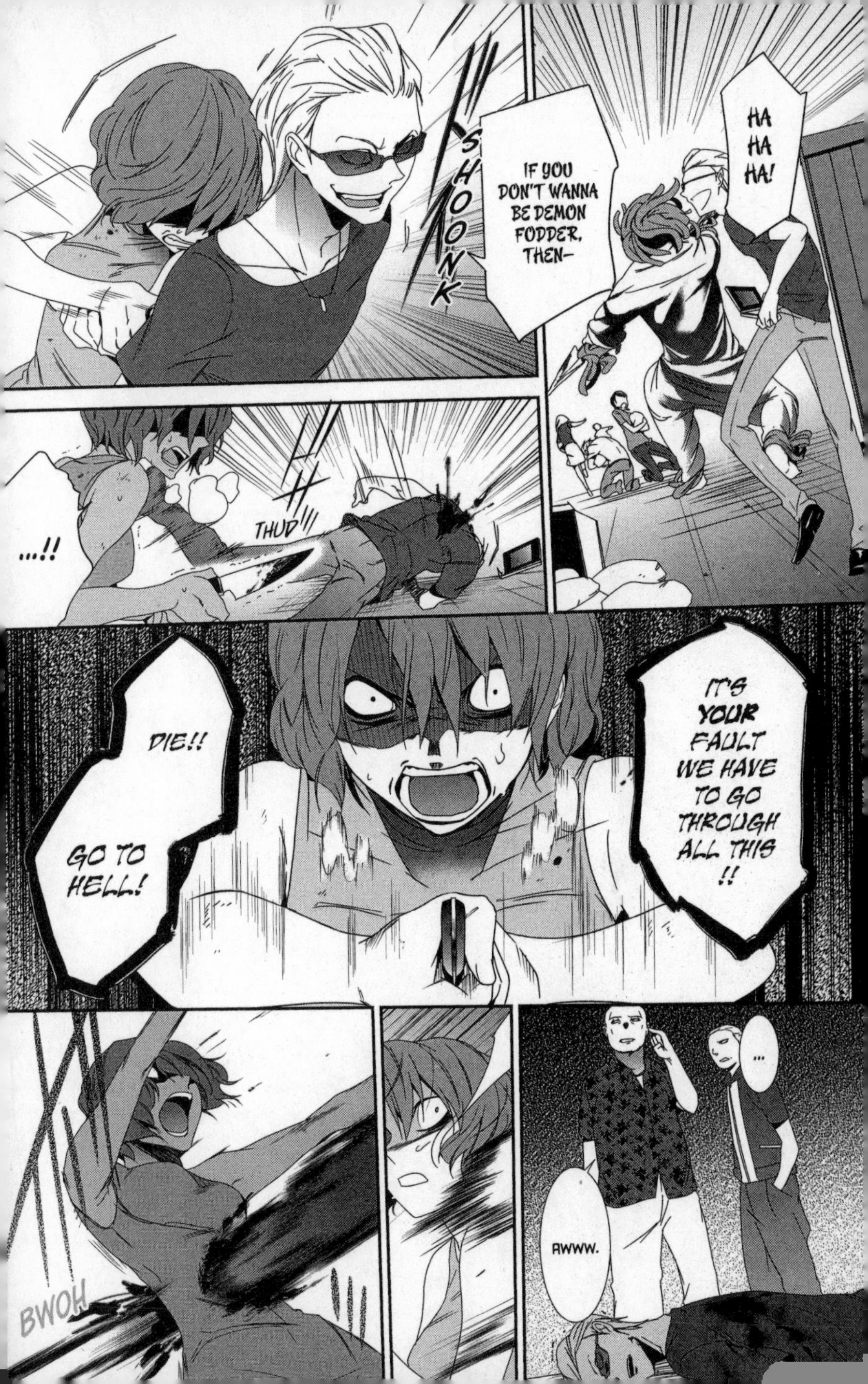
HA HA HA!
IF YOU DON'T WANNA BE DEMON FODDER, THEN-
SHOOONK
THUD
...!!
IT'S YOUR FAULT WE HAVE TO GO THROUGH ALL THIS !!
DIE!!
GO TO HELL!
...
AWWW.
BWOH

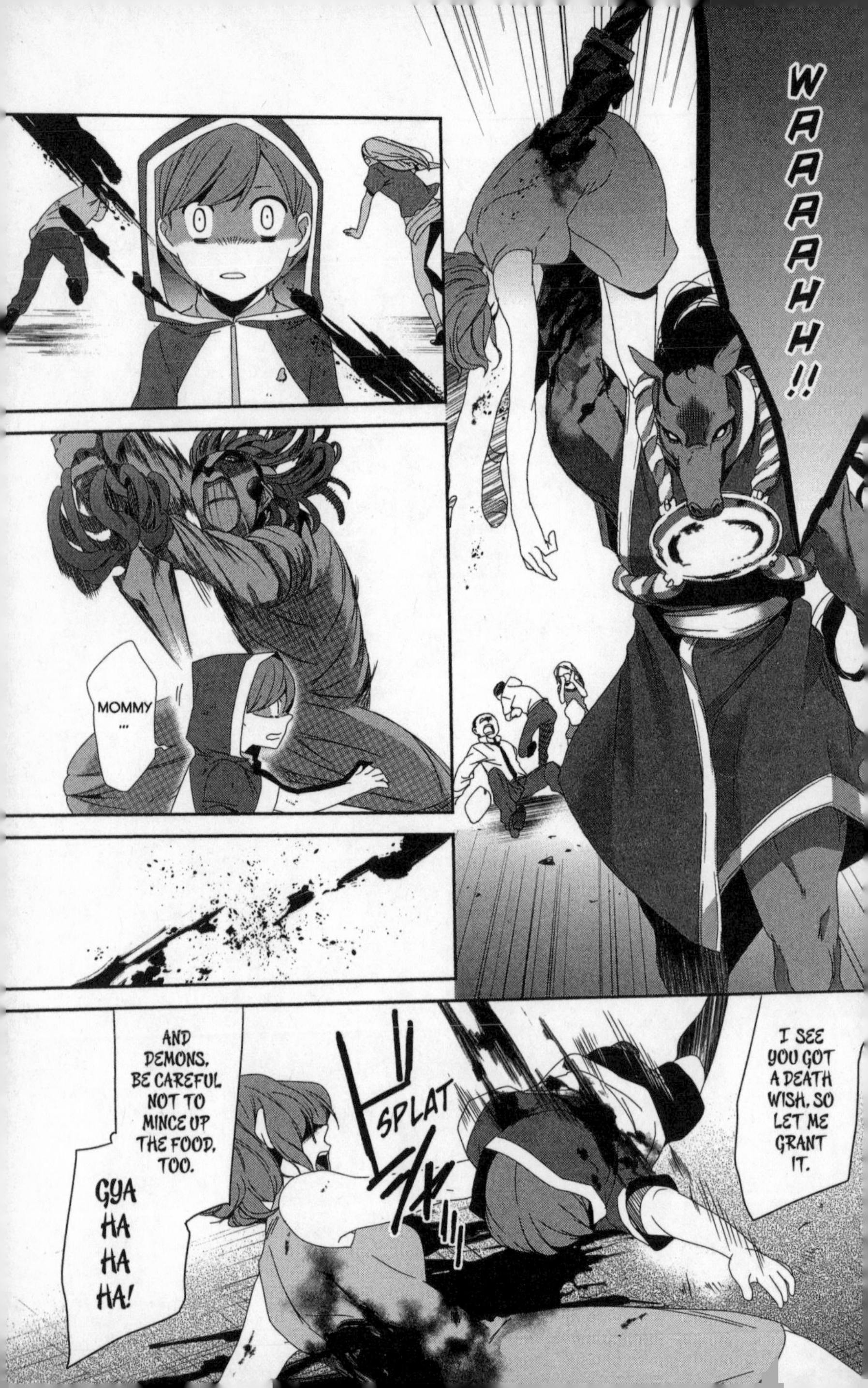
WAAAAAHH!!
MOMMY ...
I SEE YOU GOT A DEATH WISH, SO LET ME GRANT IT.
SPLAT
AND DEMONS, BE CAREFUL NOT TO MINCE UP THE FOOD, TOO.
GYA HA HA HA!

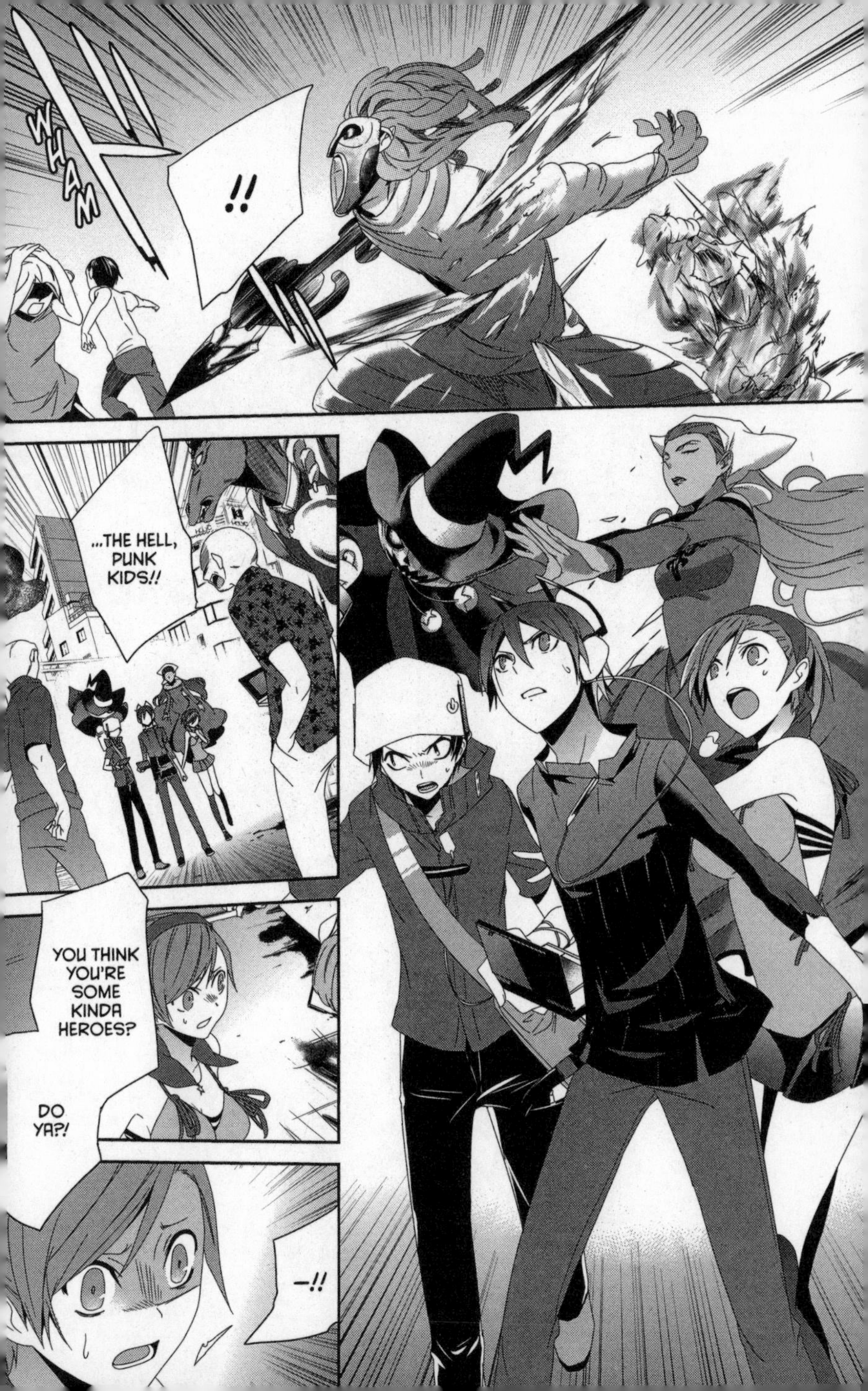
!!
WHAM
...THE HELL, PUNK KIDS!!
YOU THINK YOU'RE SOME KINDA HEROES?
DO YA?!
—!!

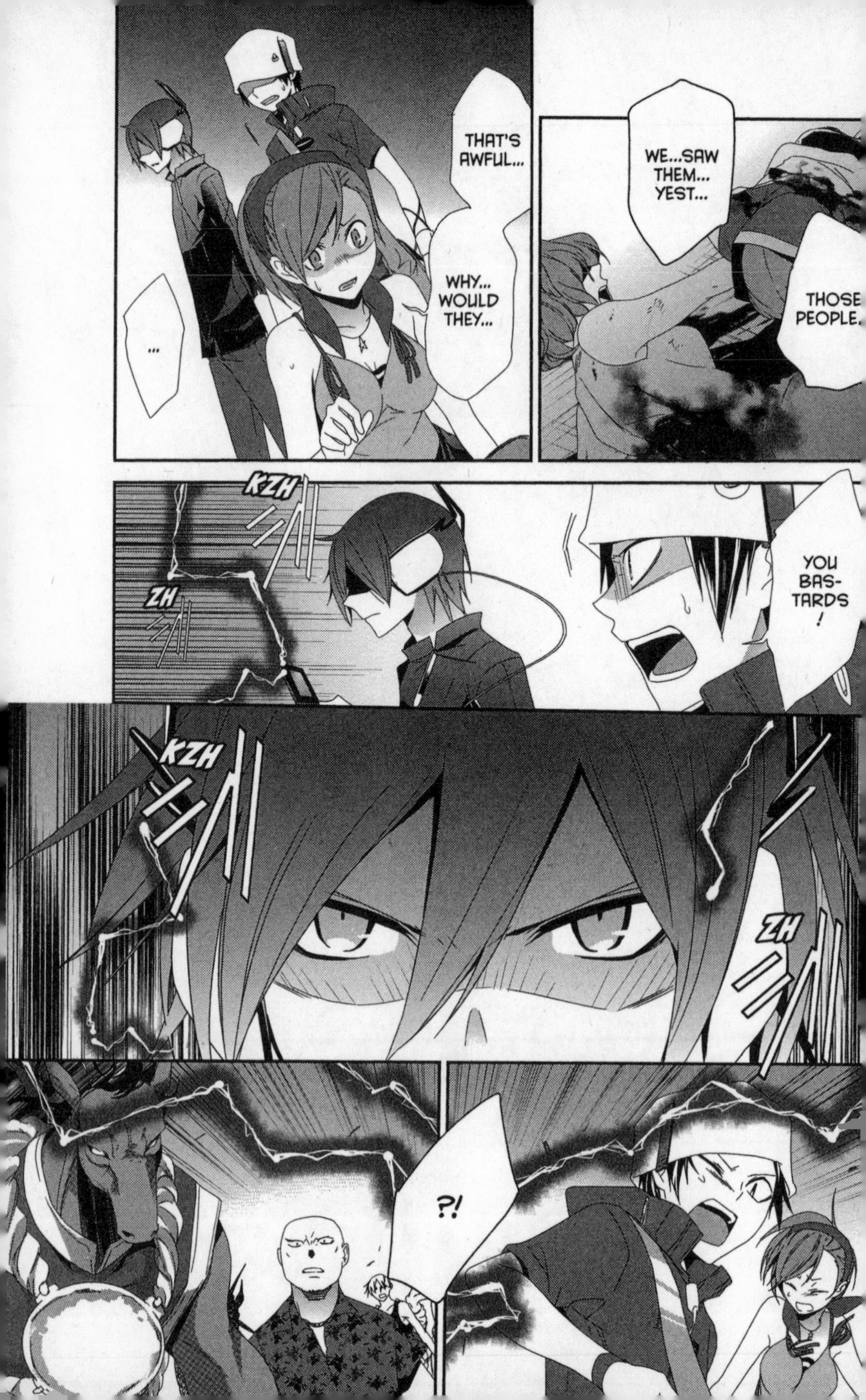
WE...SAW THEM... YEST...
THOSE PEOPLE.
THAT'S AWFUL...
WHY... WOULD THEY...
...
YOU BAS-TARDS!
KZH
ZH
KZH
ZH
?!

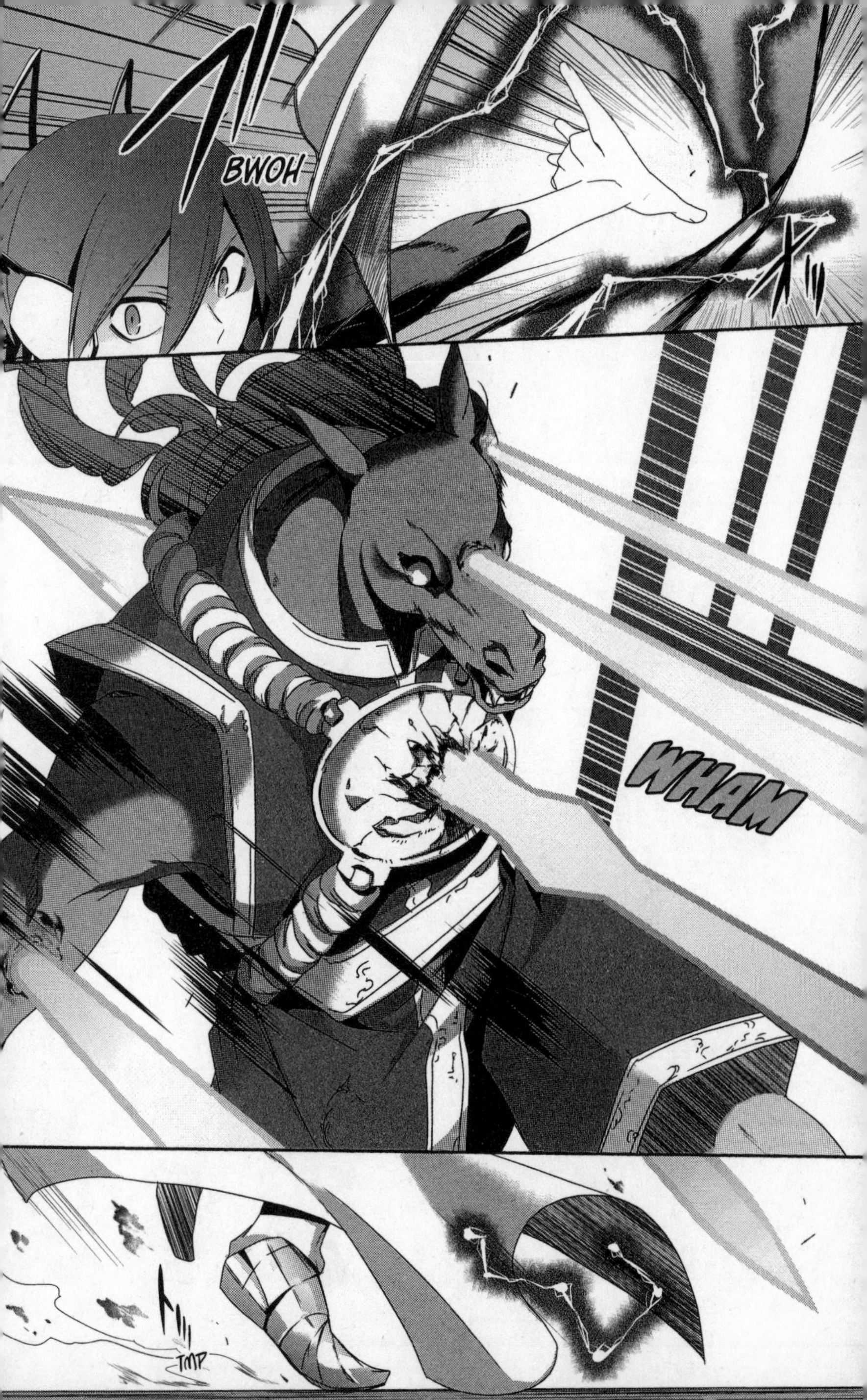
BWOH
WHAM
TMP

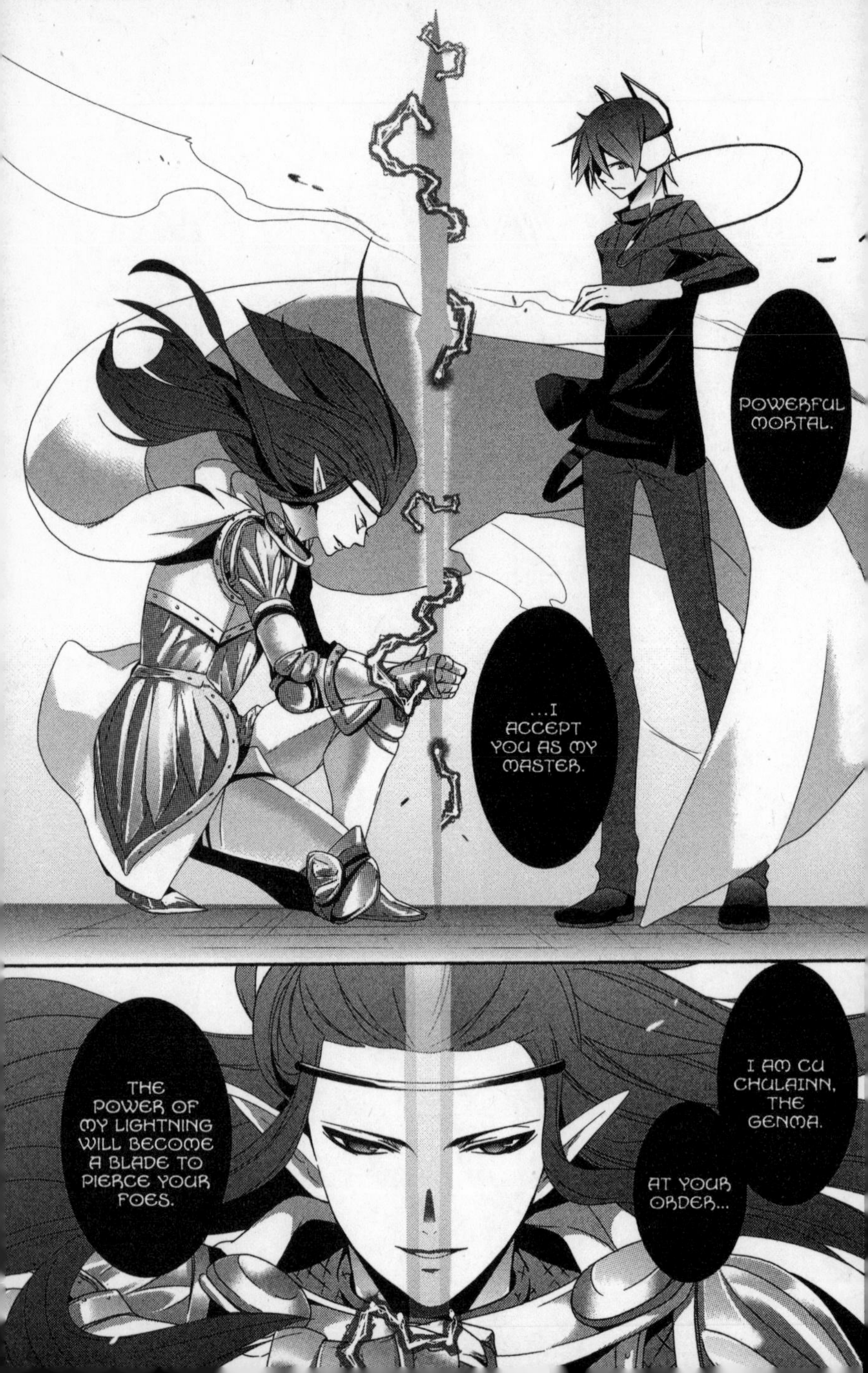
POWERFUL MORTAL.
...I ACCEPT YOU AS MY MASTER.
I AM CU CHULAINN, THE GENMA.
AT YOUR ORDER...
THE POWER OF MY LIGHTNING WILL BECOME A BLADE TO PIERCE YOUR FOES.

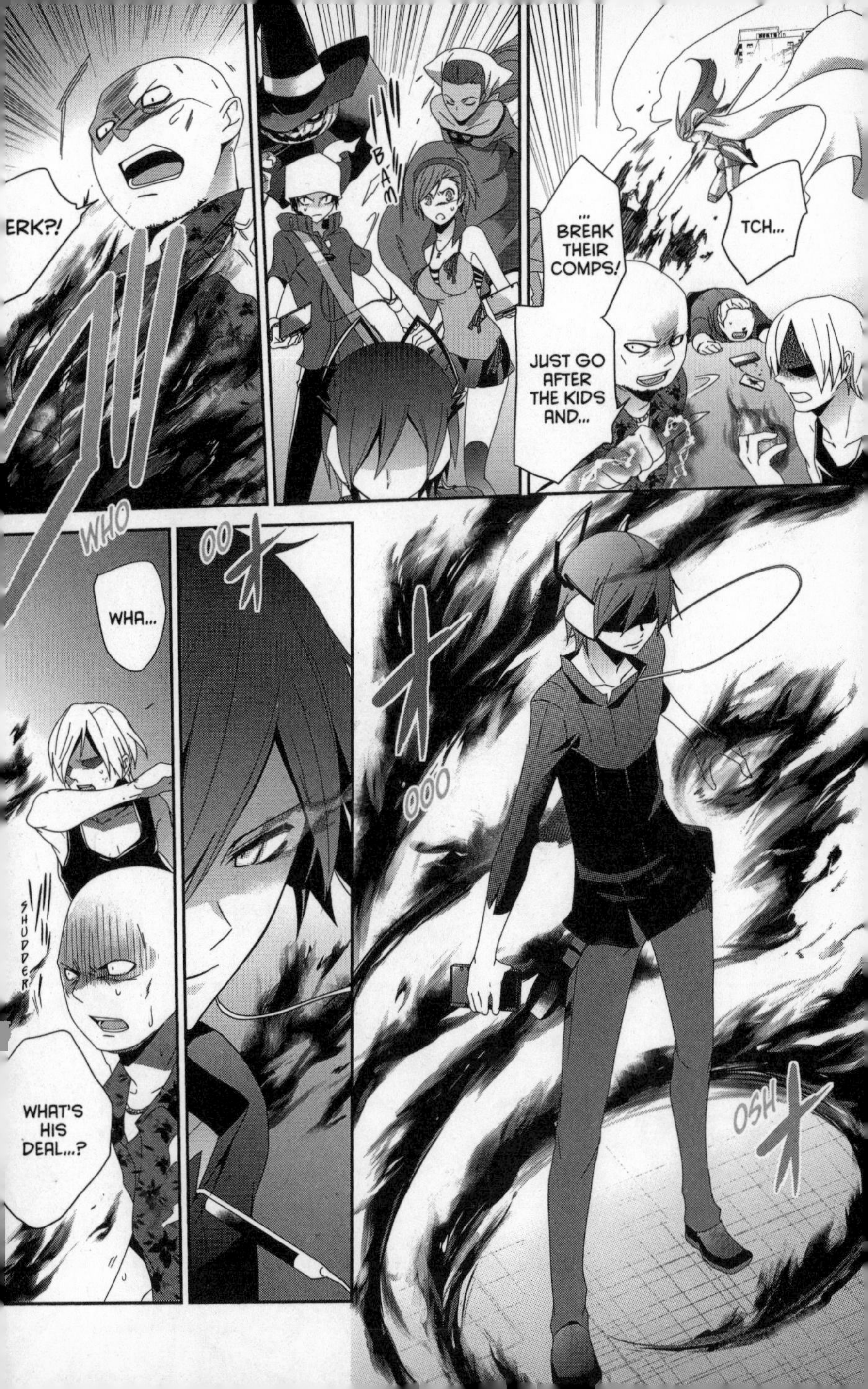
TCH...
JUST GO AFTER THE KIDS AND...
...BREAK THEIR COMPS!
BAM
ERK?!
WHO
OO
OOO
OSH
WHA...
SHUDDER
WHAT'S HIS DEAL...?

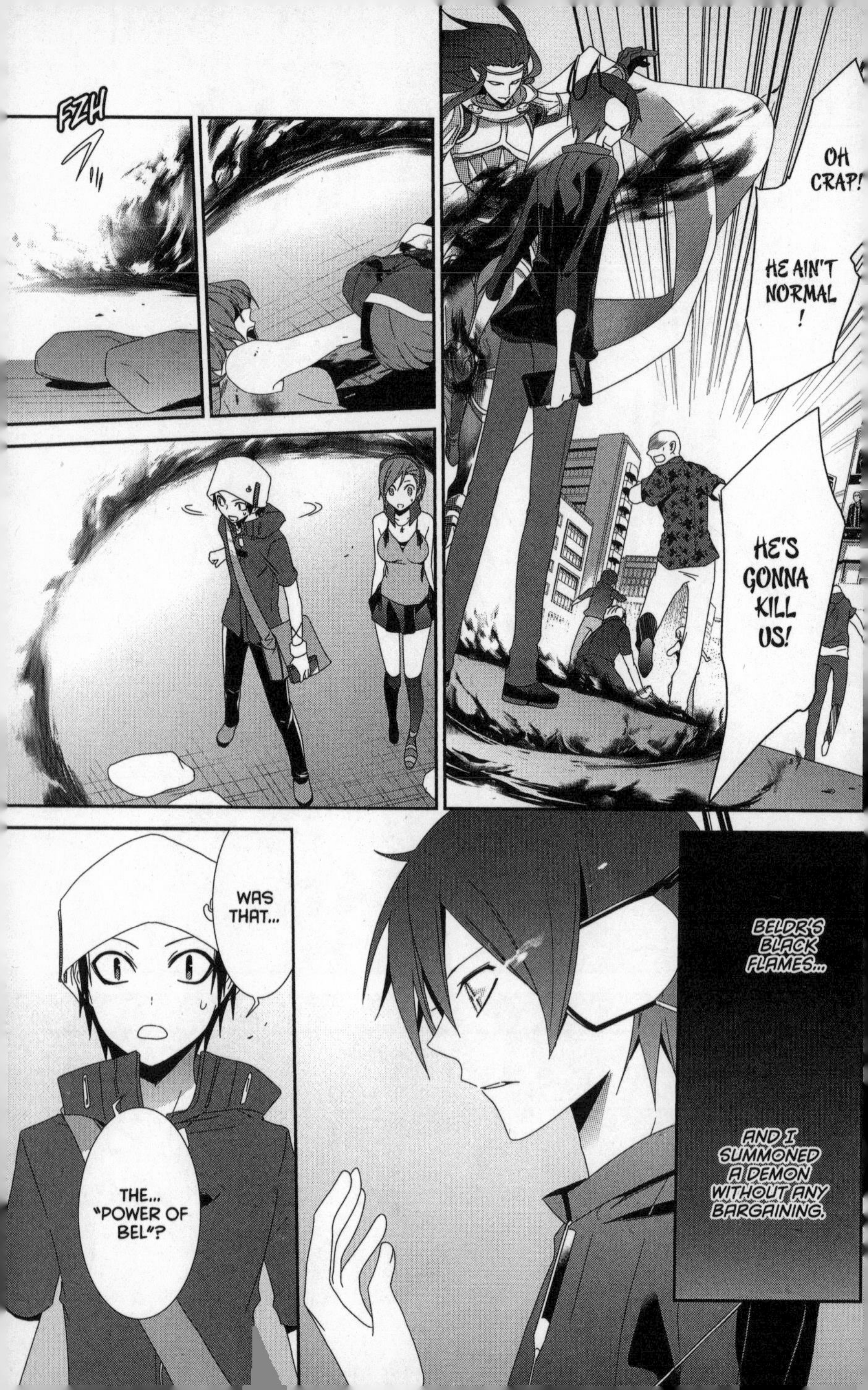
OH CRAP!
HE AIN'T NORMAL!
HE'S GONNA KILL US!
FZH
BELDR'S BLACK FLAMES...
AND I SUMMONED A DEMON WITHOUT ANY BARGAINING.
WAS THAT...
THE... "POWER OF BEL"?

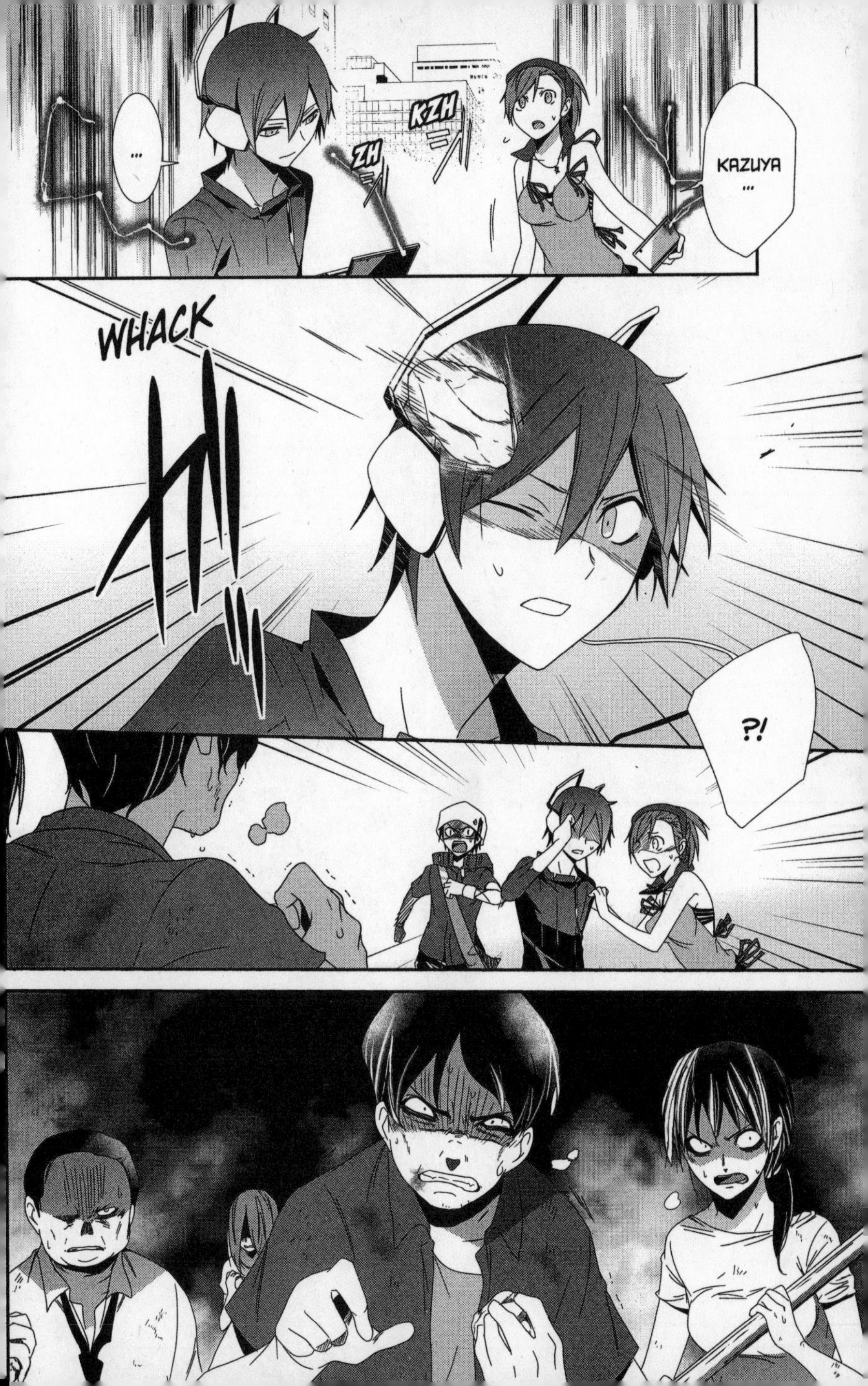
KAZUYA ...
KZH
ZH
...
WHACK
?!

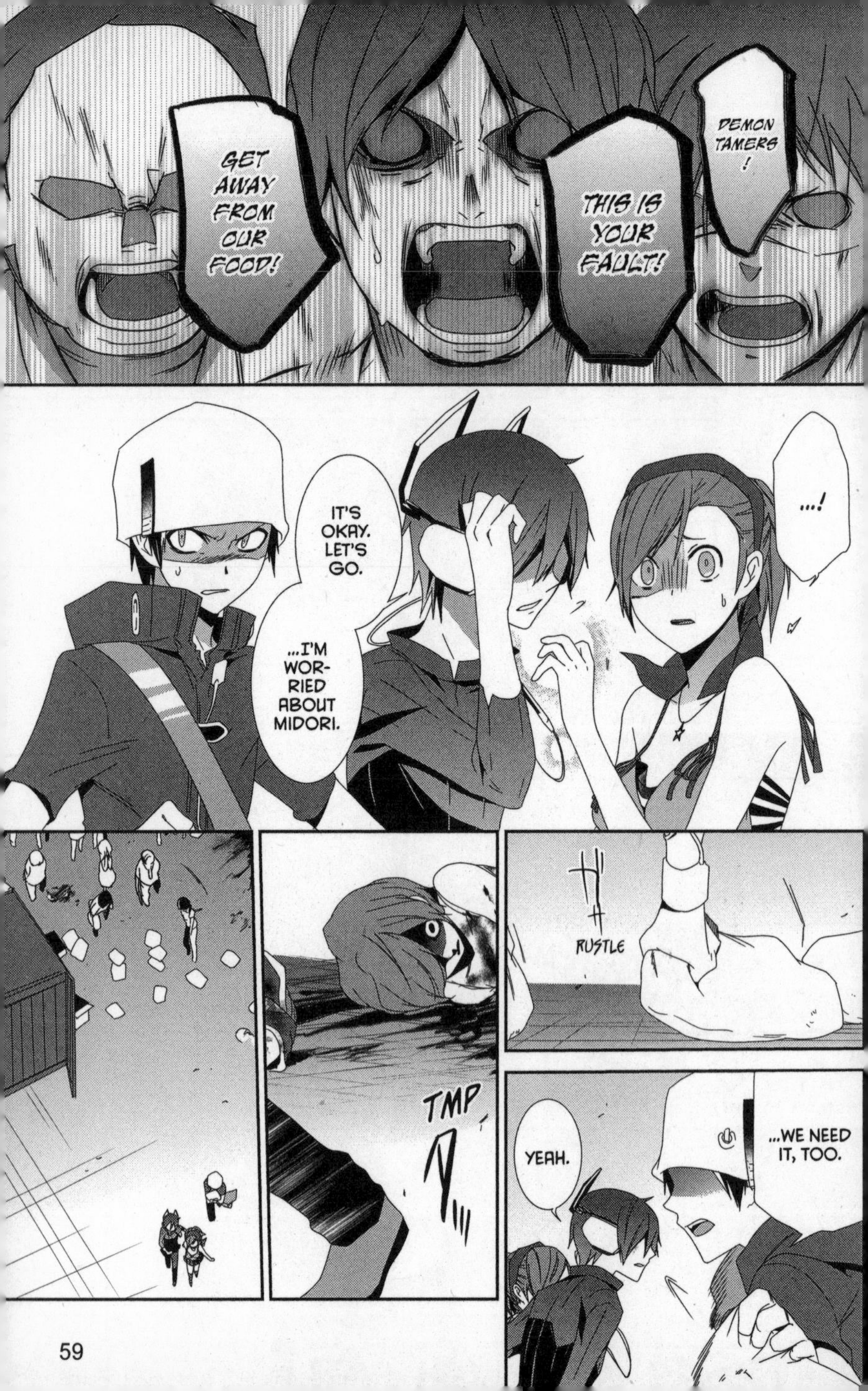
DEMON TAMERS!
THIS IS YOUR FAULT!
GET AWAY FROM OUR FOOD!
...!
IT'S OKAY. LET'S GO.
...I'M WORRIED ABOUT MIDORI.
RUSTLE
...WE NEED IT, TOO.
YEAH.
TMP

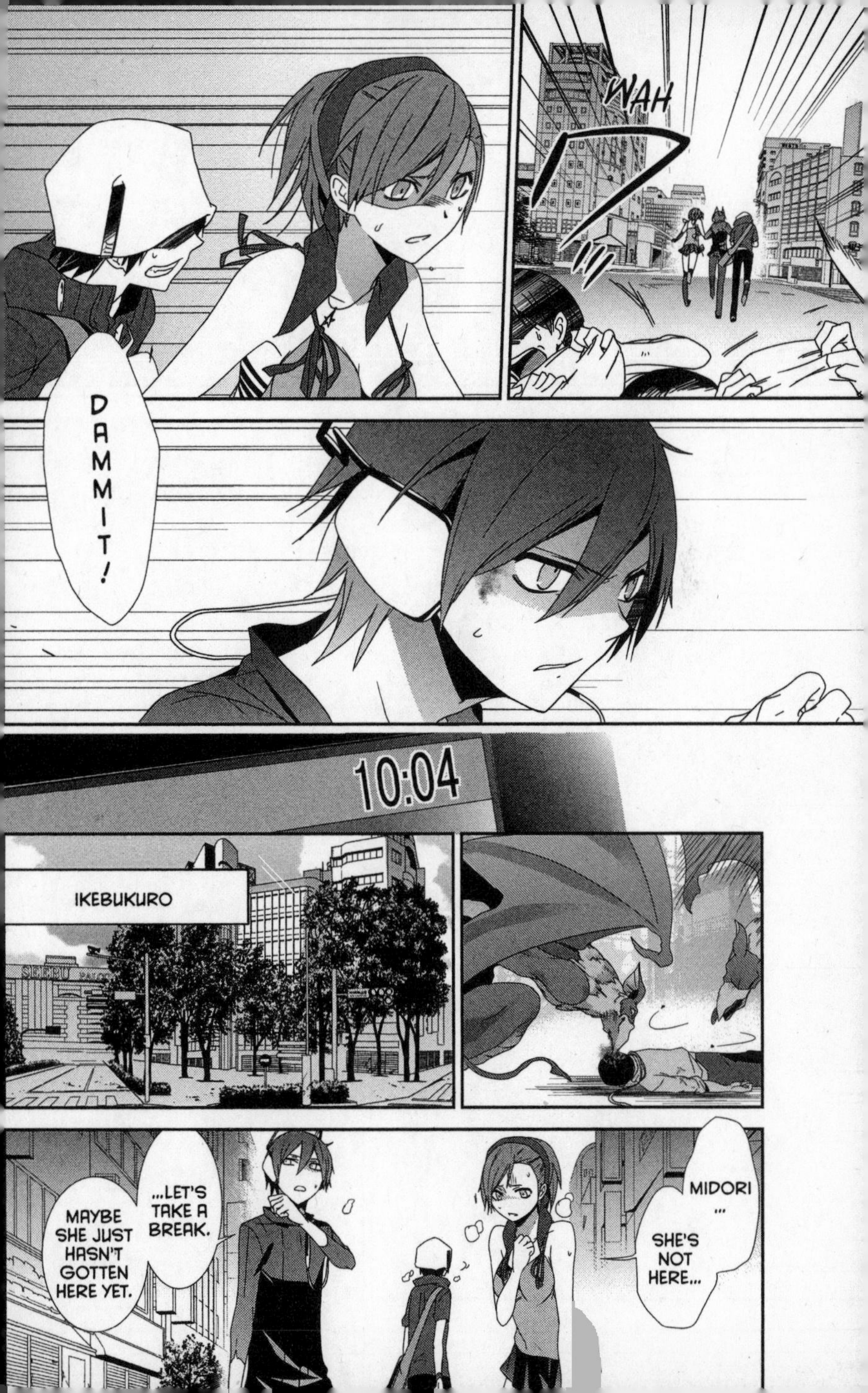
WAH
DAMMIT!
10:04
IKEBUKURO
MIDORI ... SHE'S NOT HERE...
...LET'S TAKE A BREAK.
MAYBE SHE JUST HASN'T GOTTEN HERE YET.

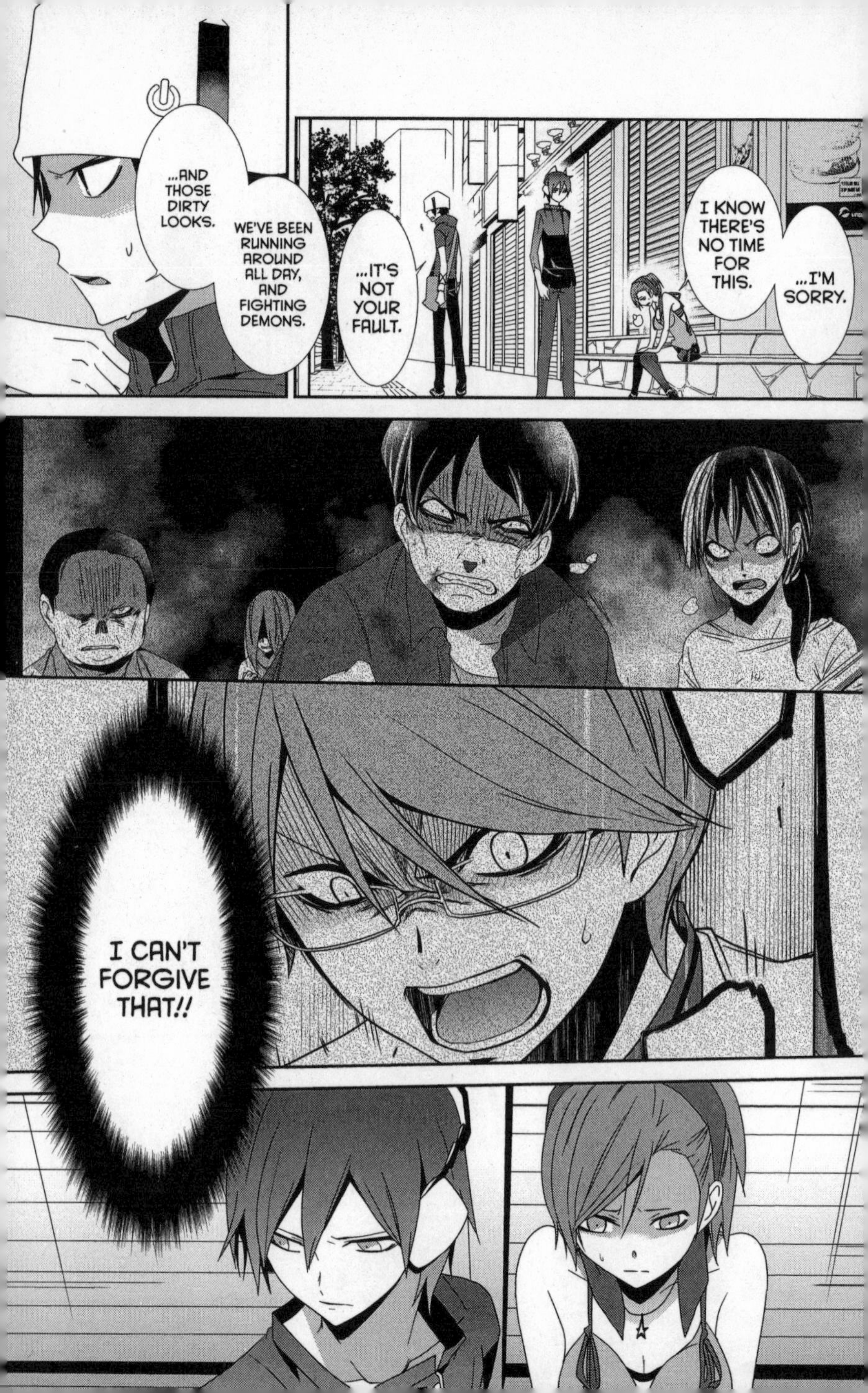
...I'M SORRY.
I KNOW THERE'S NO TIME FOR THIS.
...IT'S NOT YOUR FAULT.
WE'VE BEEN RUNNING AROUND ALL DAY, AND FIGHTING DEMONS.
...AND THOSE DIRTY LOOKS.
I CAN'T FORGIVE THAT!!

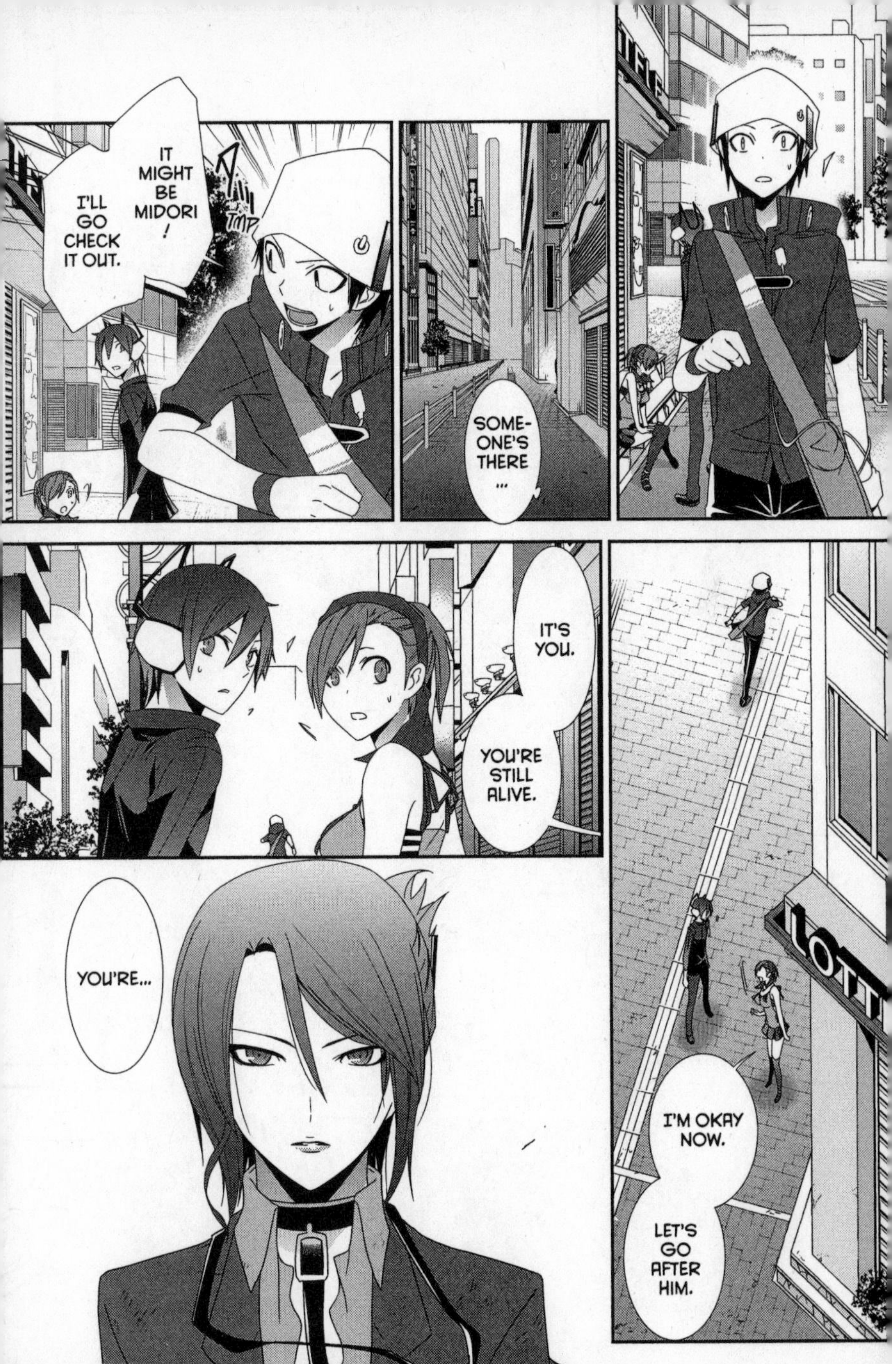
SOME-ONE'S THERE ...
IT MIGHT BE MIDORI!
TMP
I'LL GO CHECK IT OUT.
I'M OKAY NOW.
LET'S GO AFTER HIM.
IT'S YOU.
YOU'RE STILL ALIVE.
YOU'RE...

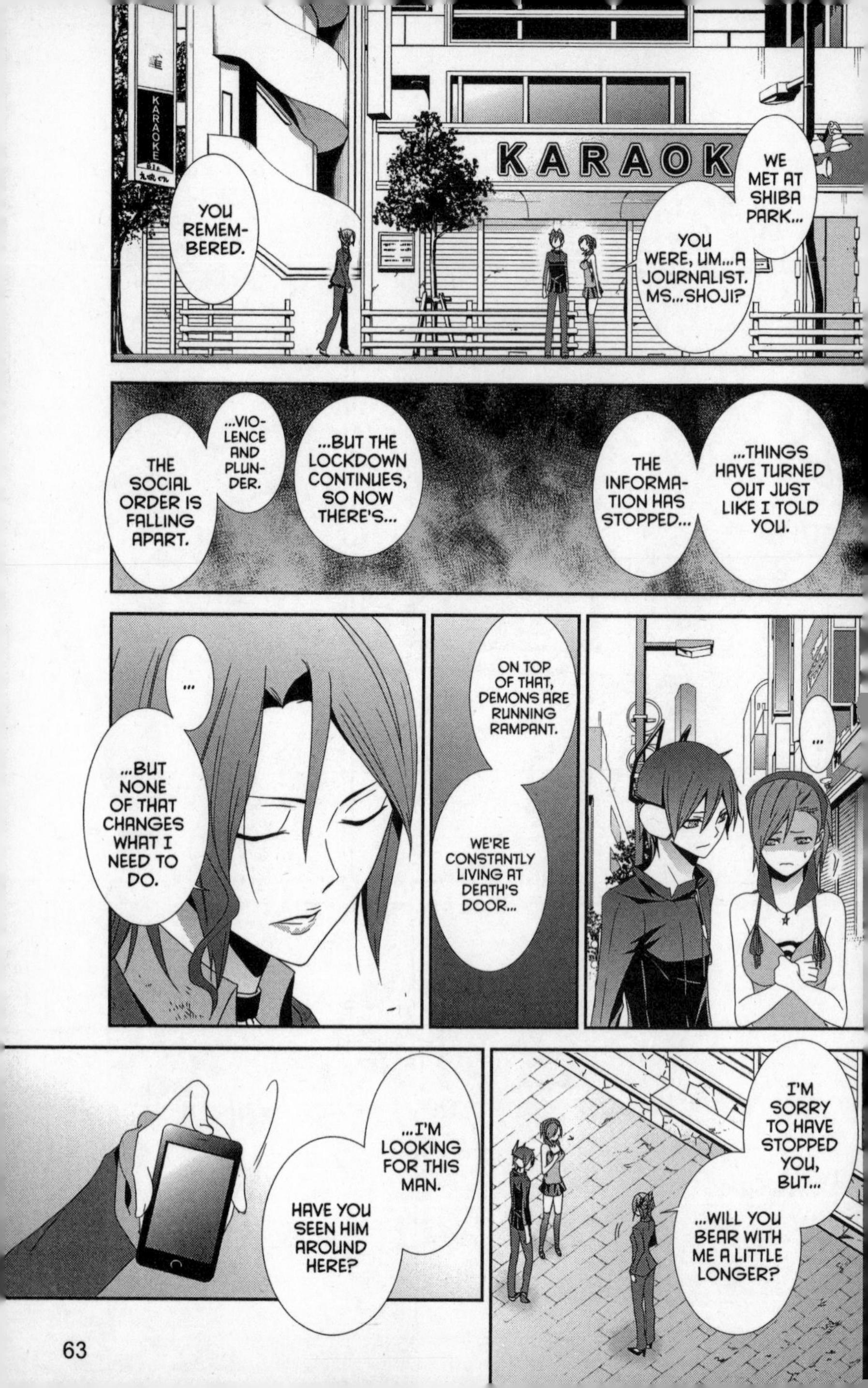
KARAOKE
KARAOK
WE MET AT SHIBA PARK...
YOU WERE, UM...A JOURNALIST. MS...SHOJI?
YOU REMEMBERED.
...THINGS HAVE TURNED OUT JUST LIKE I TOLD YOU.
THE INFORMATION HAS STOPPED...
...BUT THE LOCKDOWN CONTINUES, SO NOW THERE'S...
...VIOLENCE AND PLUNDER.
THE SOCIAL ORDER IS FALLING APART.
...
ON TOP OF THAT, DEMONS ARE RUNNING RAMPANT.
WE'RE CONSTANTLY LIVING AT DEATH'S DOOR...
...
...BUT NONE OF THAT CHANGES WHAT I NEED TO DO.
I'M SORRY TO HAVE STOPPED YOU, BUT...
...WILL YOU BEAR WITH ME A LITTLE LONGER?
...I'M LOOKING FOR THIS MAN.
HAVE YOU SEEN HIM AROUND HERE?

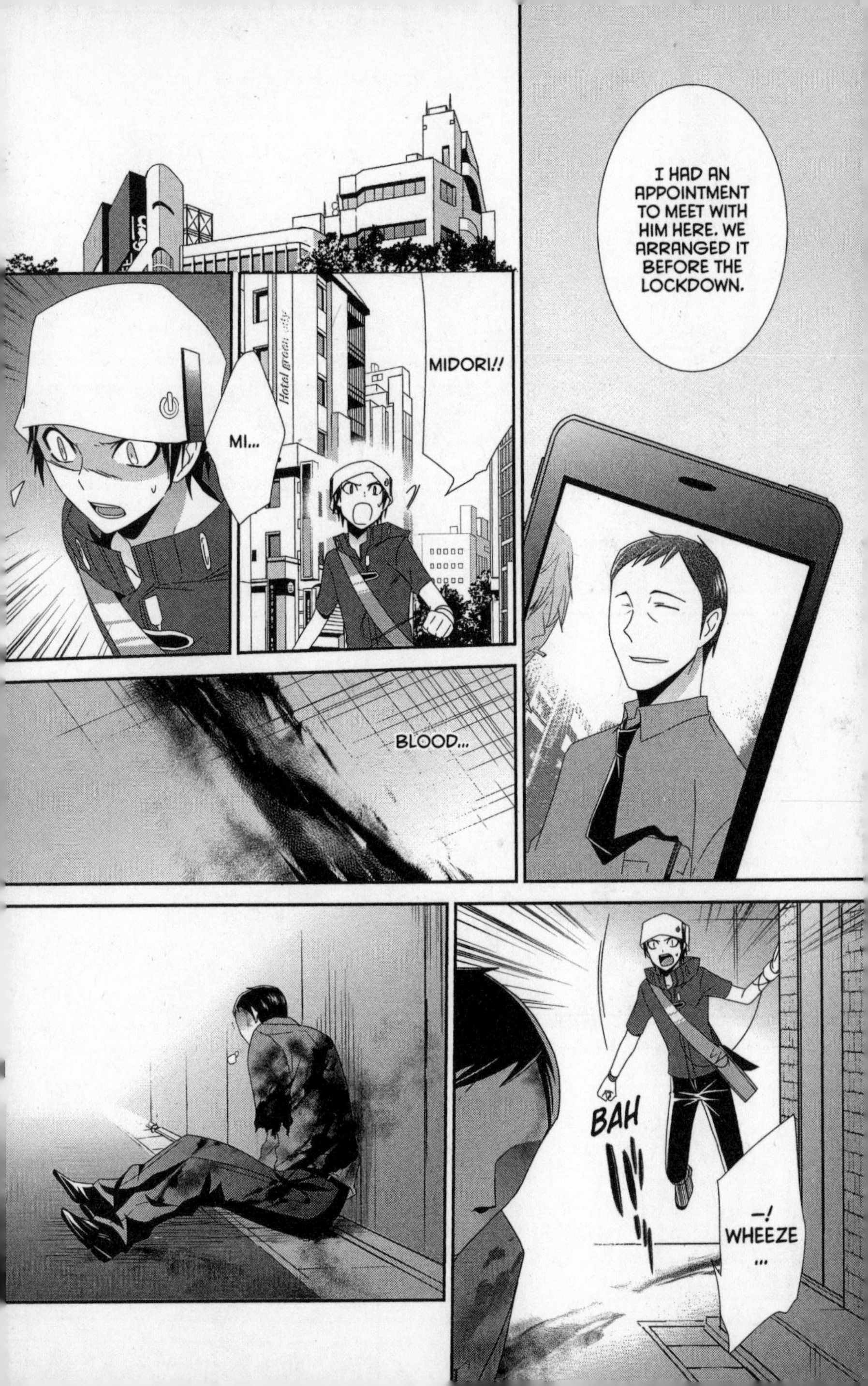
I HAD AN APPOINTMENT TO MEET WITH HIM HERE. WE ARRANGED IT BEFORE THE LOCKDOWN.
Hotel green city
MIDORI!!
MI...
BLOOD...
BAH
—! WHEEZE ...

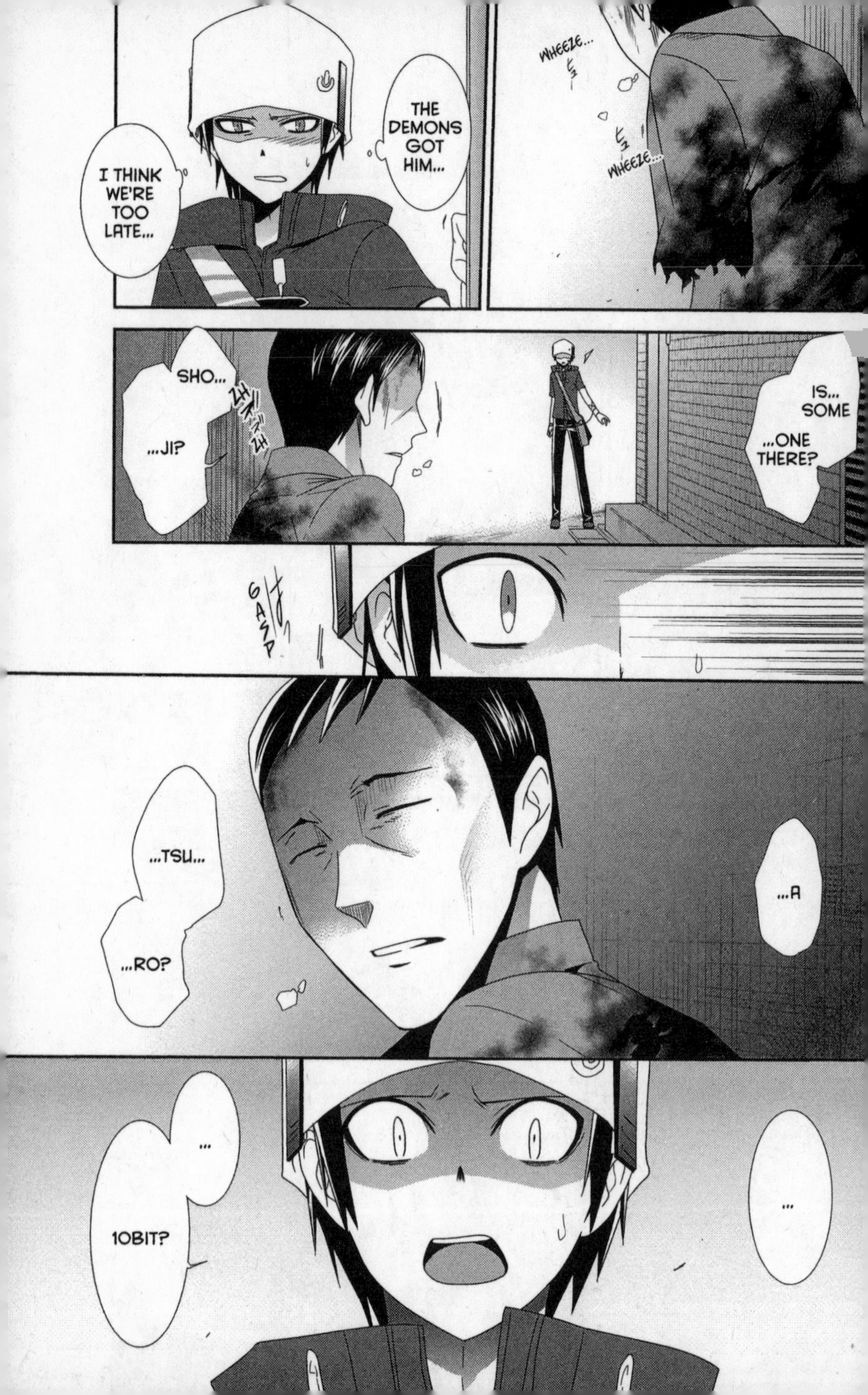
WHEEZE...
WHEEZE...
THE DEMONS GOT HIM...
I THINK WE'RE TOO LATE...
IS... SOME ...ONE THERE?
ZH
ZH
SHO... ...JI?
GASP
...A
...TSU... ...RO?
...
... 10BIT?

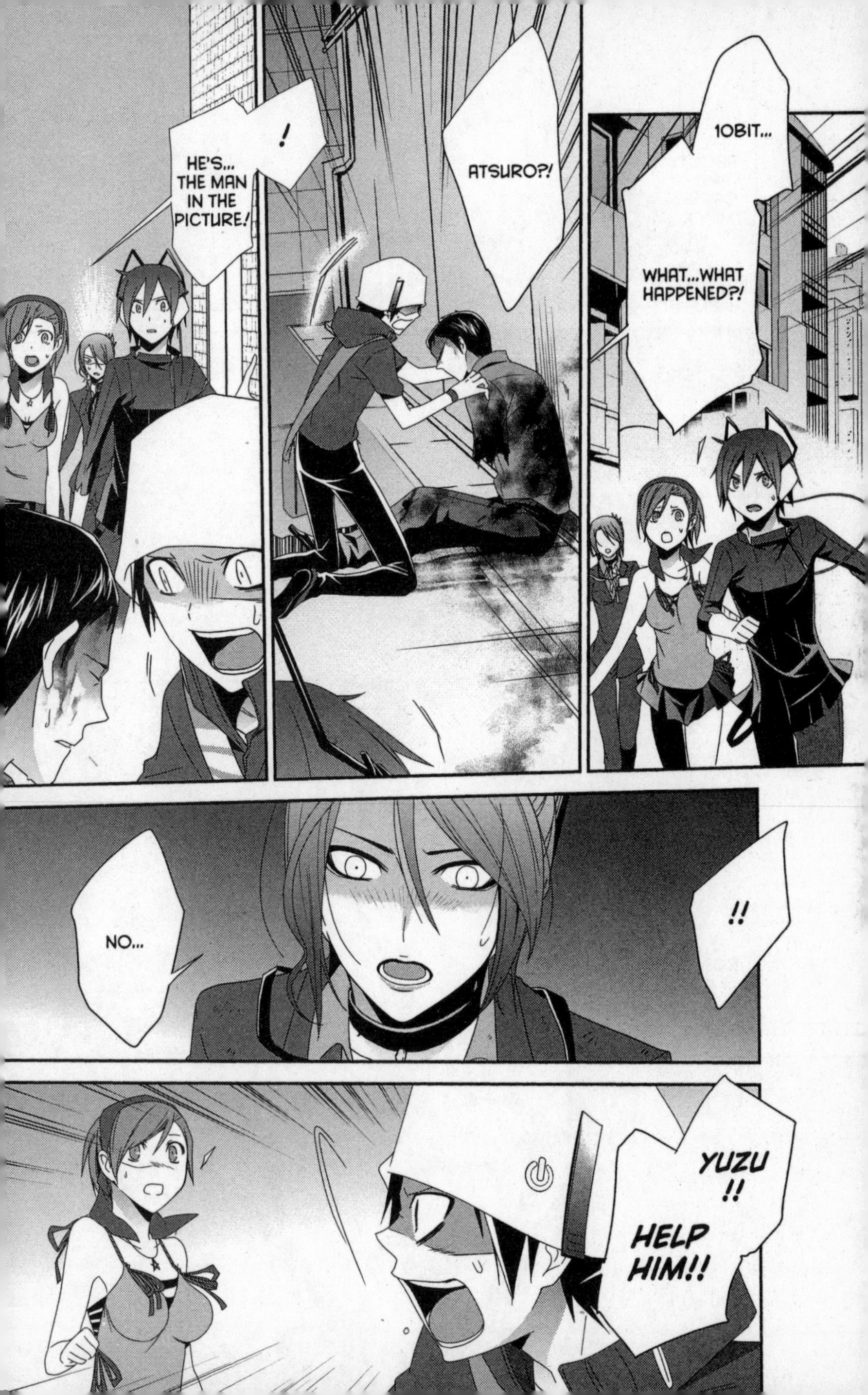
10BIT...
WHAT...WHAT HAPPENED?!
ATSURO?!
!
HE'S... THE MAN IN THE PICTURE!
!!
NO...
YUZU!!
HELP HIM!!

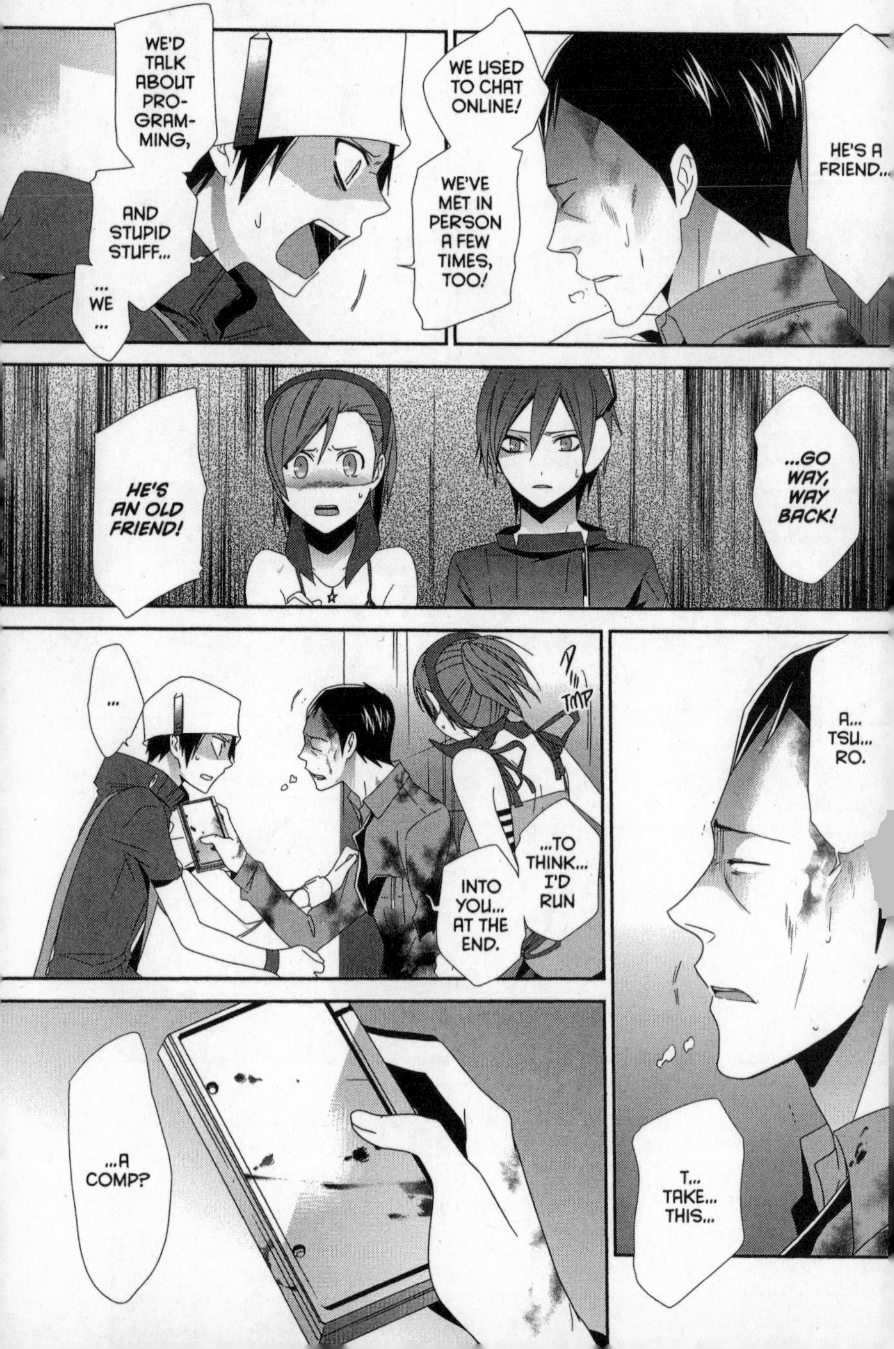
HE'S A FRIEND...
WE USED TO CHAT ONLINE!
WE'VE MET IN PERSON A FEW TIMES, TOO!
WE'D TALK ABOUT PRO-GRAM-MING,
AND STUPID STUFF...
...WE...
...GO WAY, WAY BACK!
HE'S AN OLD FRIEND!
A... TSU... RO.
T... TAKE... THIS...
TMP
...TO THINK... I'D RUN
INTO YOU... AT THE END.
...
...A COMP?

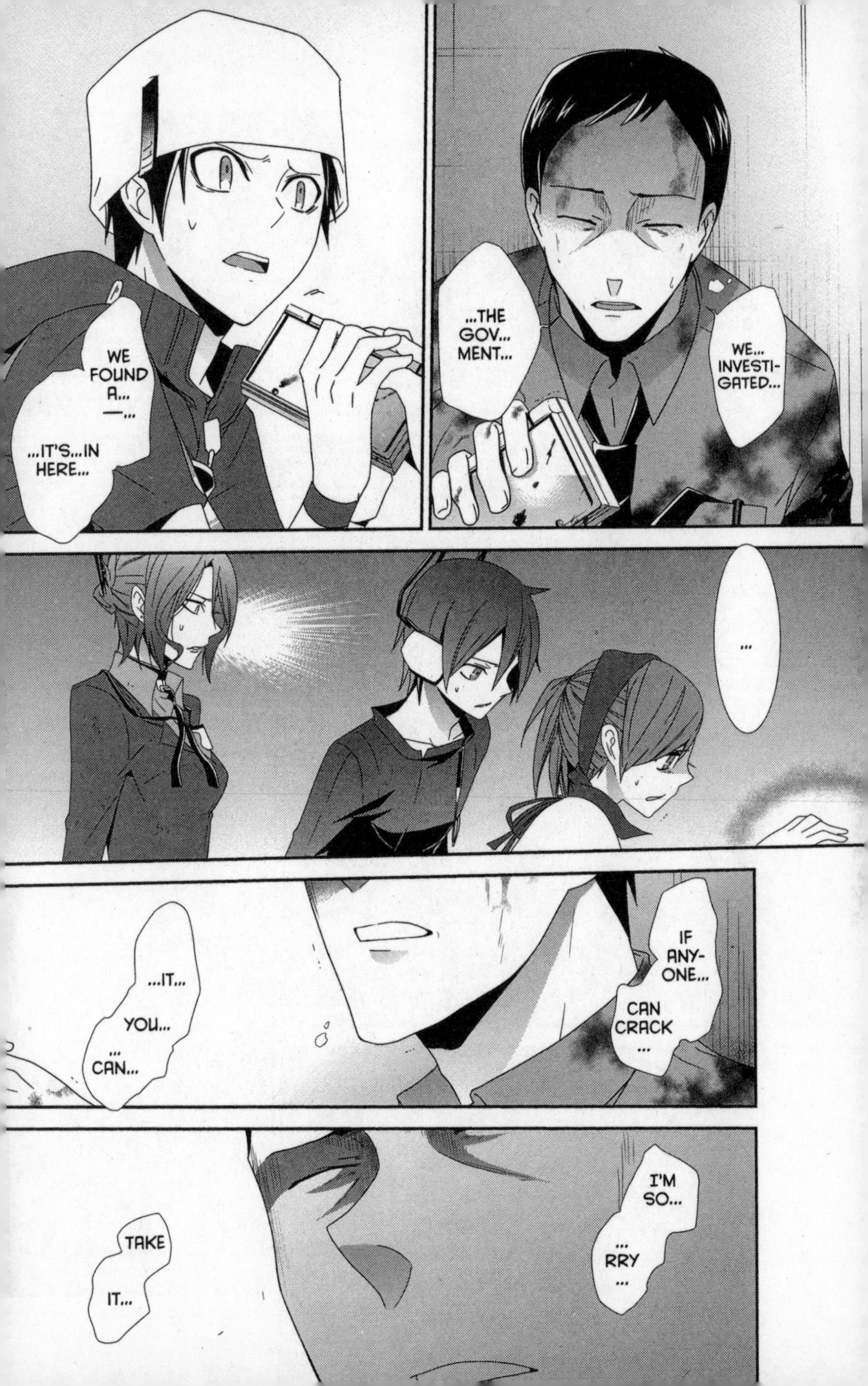
WE... INVESTI-GATED...
...THE GOV... MENT...
WE FOUND A... —...
...IT'S...IN HERE...
...
IF ANY-ONE...
CAN CRACK ...
...IT...
YOU...
... CAN...
I'M SO...
... RRY ...
TAKE IT...

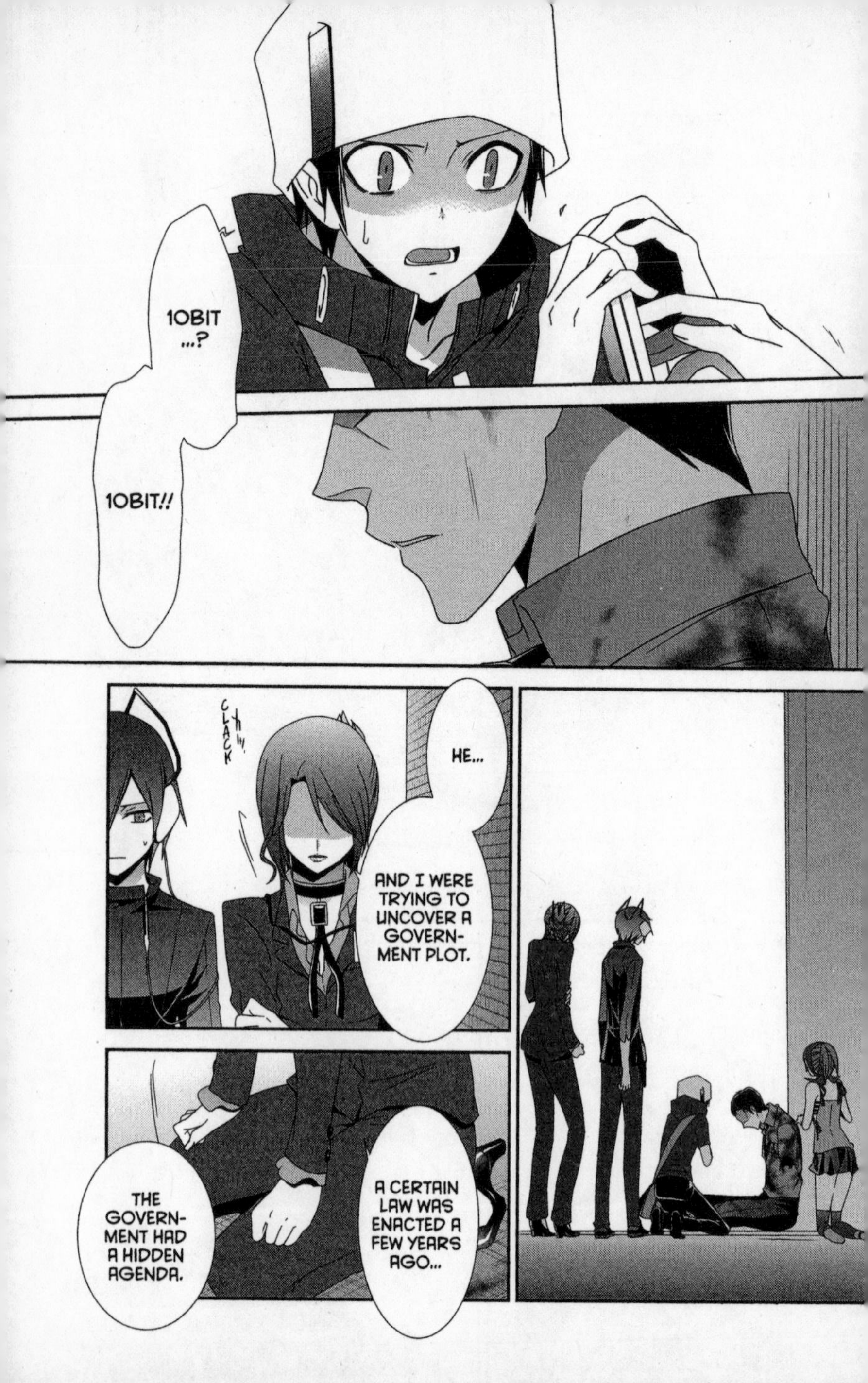
10BIT ...?
10BIT!!
HE...
CLACK
AND I WERE TRYING TO UNCOVER A GOVERNMENT PLOT.
A CERTAIN LAW WAS ENACTED A FEW YEARS AGO...
THE GOVERNMENT HAD A HIDDEN AGENDA.

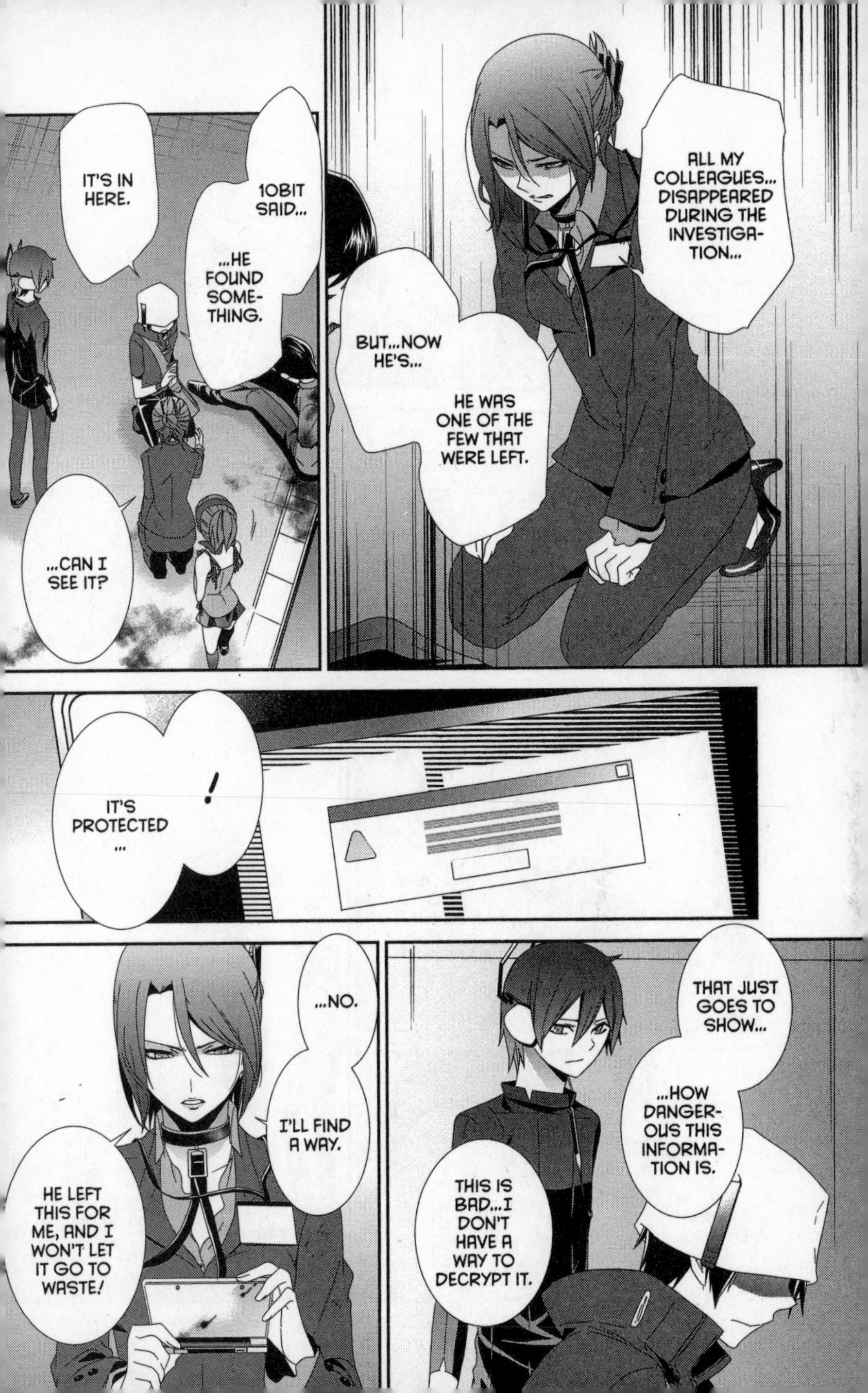
ALL MY COLLEAGUES... DISAPPEARED DURING THE INVESTIGATION...
BUT...NOW HE'S...
HE WAS ONE OF THE FEW THAT WERE LEFT.
10BIT SAID...
...HE FOUND SOMETHING.
IT'S IN HERE.
...CAN I SEE IT?
!
IT'S PROTECTED ...
THAT JUST GOES TO SHOW...
...HOW DANGEROUS THIS INFORMATION IS.
THIS IS BAD...I DON'T HAVE A WAY TO DECRYPT IT.
...NO.
I'LL FIND A WAY.
HE LEFT THIS FOR ME, AND I WON'T LET IT GO TO WASTE!

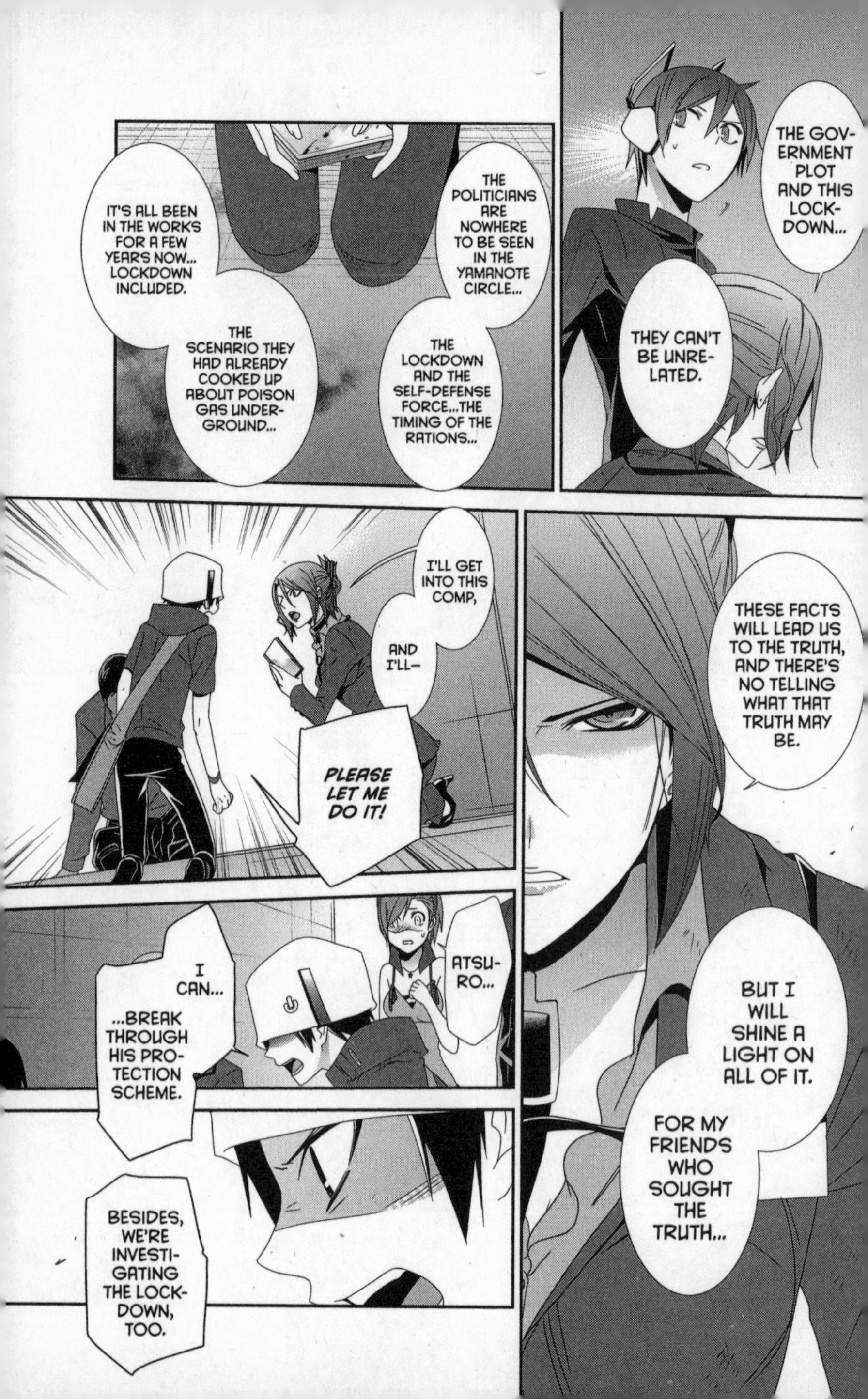
THE GOVERNMENT PLOT AND THIS LOCKDOWN...
THEY CAN'T BE UNRELATED.
THE POLITICIANS ARE NOWHERE TO BE SEEN IN THE YAMANOTE CIRCLE...
IT'S ALL BEEN IN THE WORKS FOR A FEW YEARS NOW... LOCKDOWN INCLUDED.
THE LOCKDOWN AND THE SELF-DEFENSE FORCE...THE TIMING OF THE RATIONS...
THE SCENARIO THEY HAD ALREADY COOKED UP ABOUT POISON GAS UNDERGROUND...
THESE FACTS WILL LEAD US TO THE TRUTH, AND THERE'S NO TELLING WHAT THAT TRUTH MAY BE.
BUT I WILL SHINE A LIGHT ON ALL OF IT.
FOR MY FRIENDS WHO SOUGHT THE TRUTH...
I'LL GET INTO THIS COMP,
AND I'LL—
PLEASE LET ME DO IT!
ATSURO...
I CAN... ...BREAK THROUGH HIS PROTECTION SCHEME.
BESIDES, WE'RE INVESTIGATING THE LOCKDOWN, TOO.

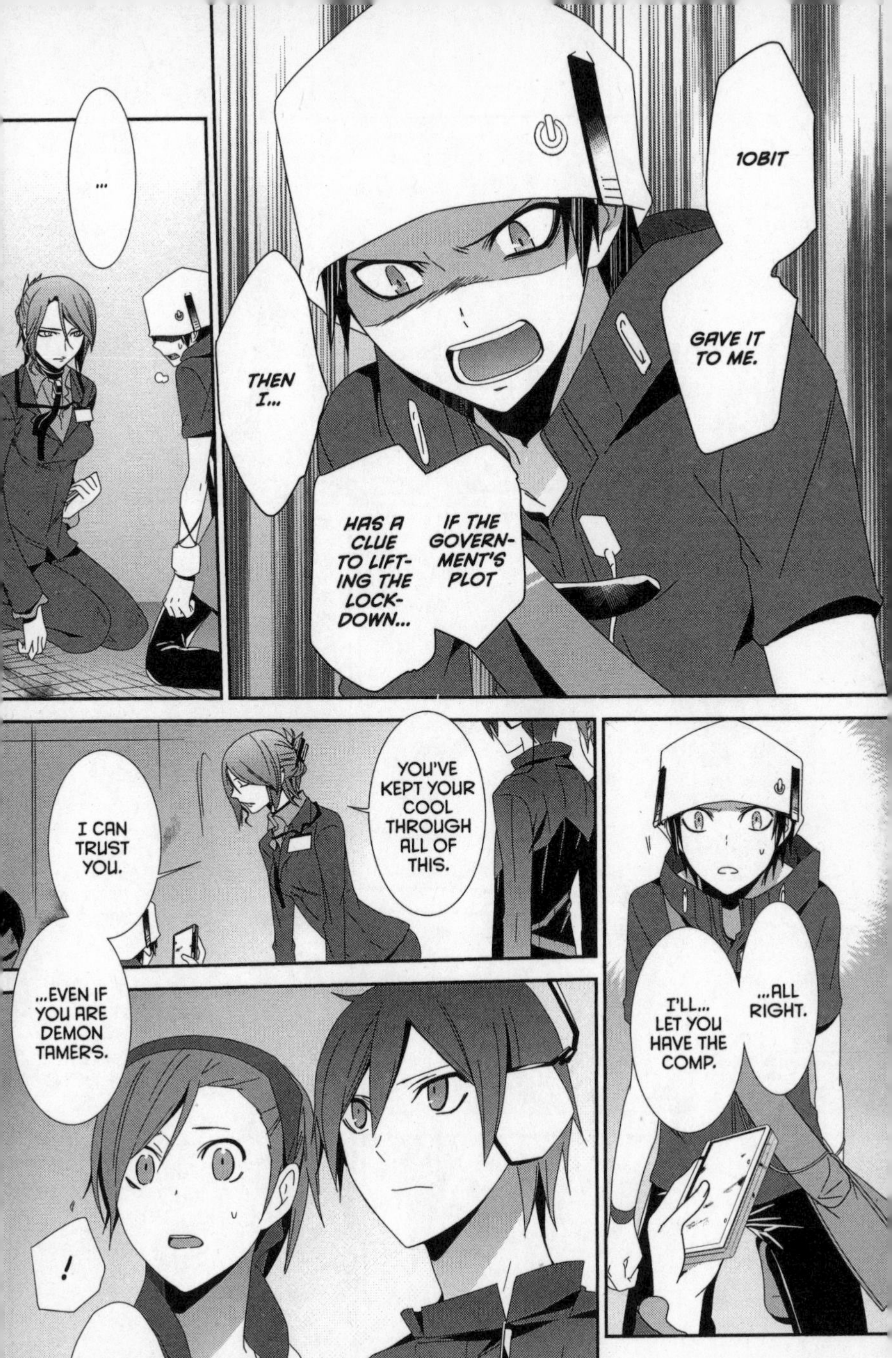
10BIT
GAVE IT TO ME.
THEN I...
IF THE GOVERNMENT'S PLOT
HAS A CLUE TO LIFTING THE LOCKDOWN...
...
...ALL RIGHT.
I'LL... LET YOU HAVE THE COMP.
YOU'VE KEPT YOUR COOL THROUGH ALL OF THIS.
I CAN TRUST YOU.
...EVEN IF YOU ARE DEMON TAMERS.
!

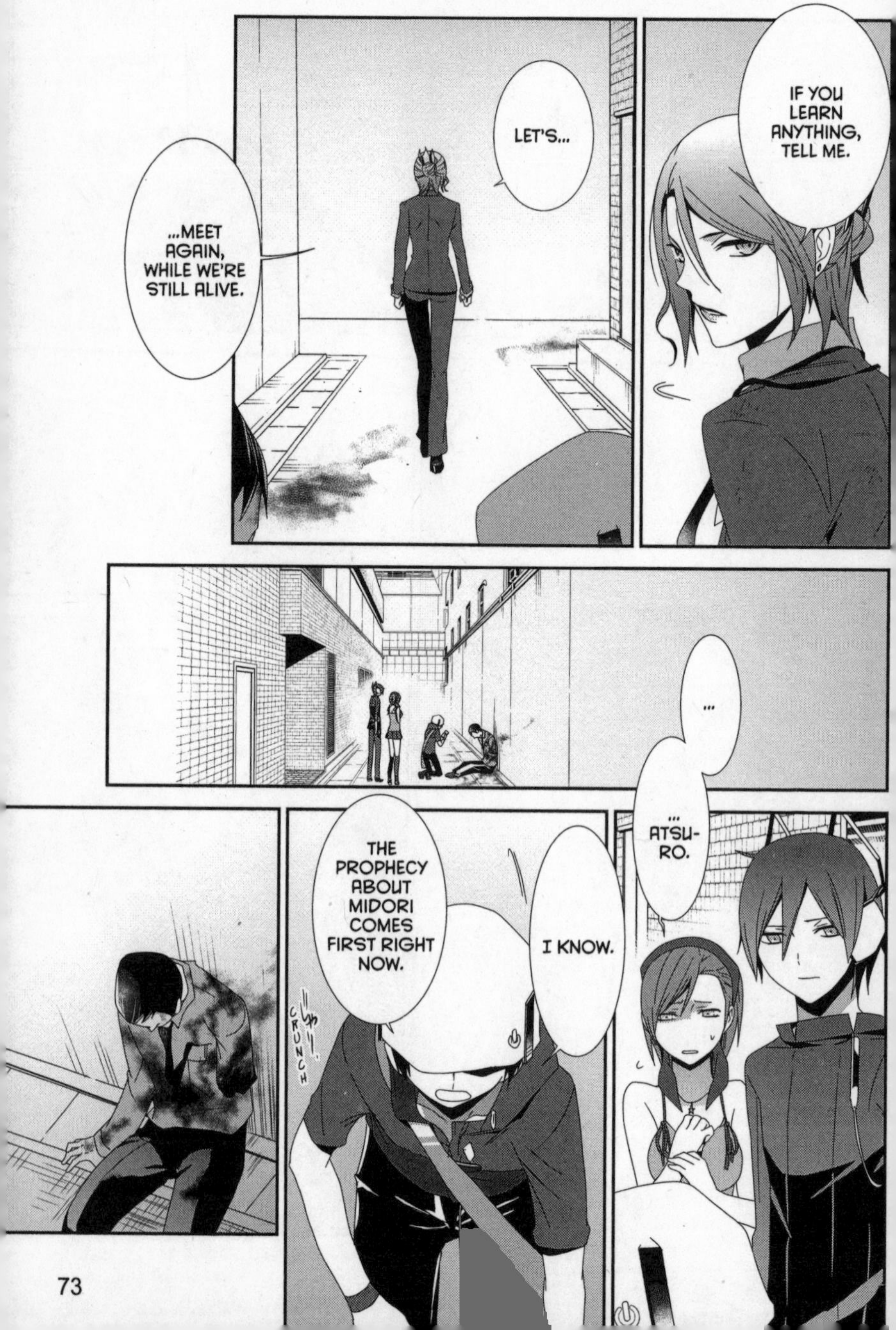
IF YOU LEARN ANYTHING, TELL ME.
LET'S...
...MEET AGAIN, WHILE WE'RE STILL ALIVE.
...
...ATSU-RO.
THE PROPHECY ABOUT MIDORI COMES FIRST RIGHT NOW.
I KNOW.
CRUNCH

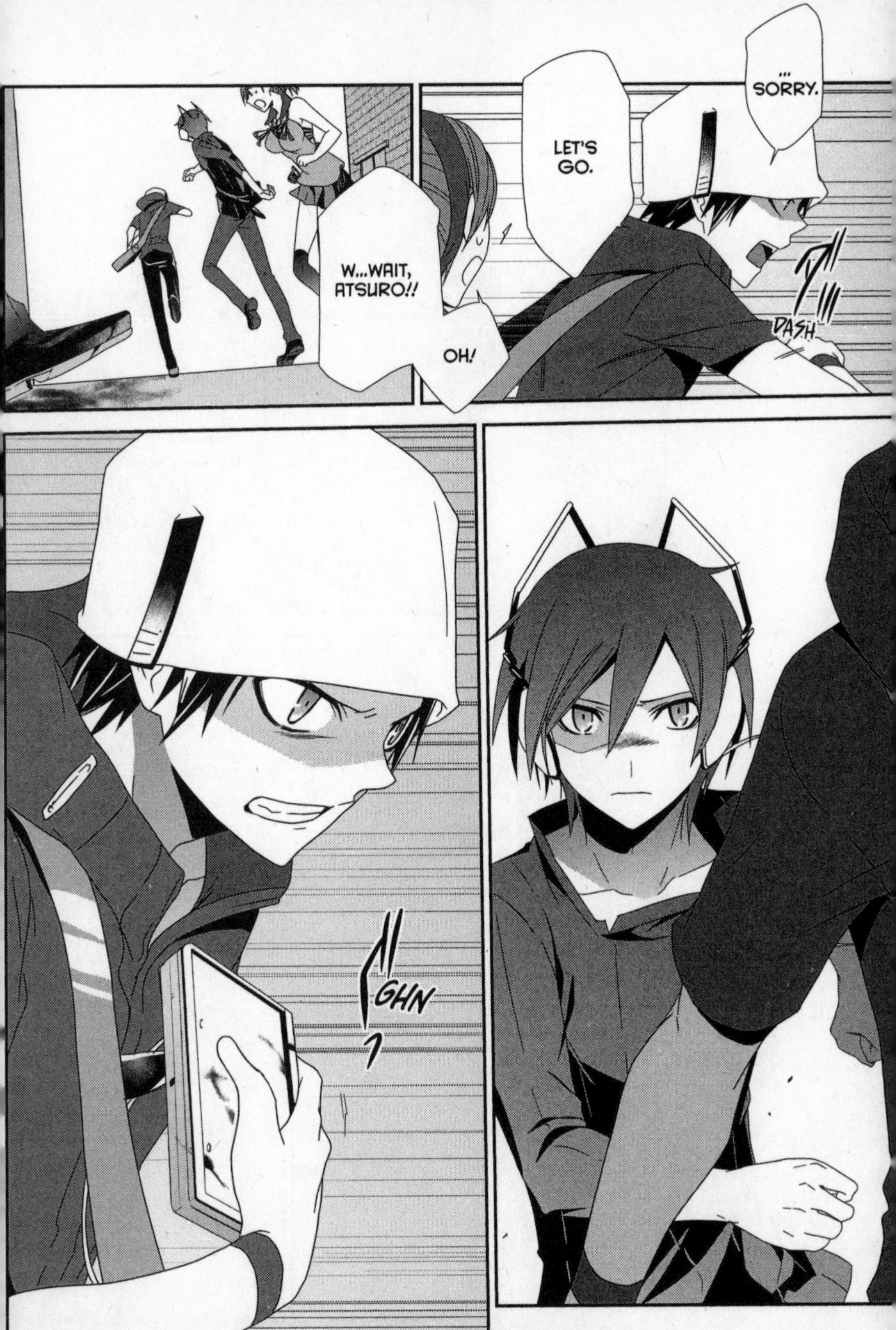

...SORRY.
LET'S GO.
DASH
OH!
W...WAIT, ATSURO!!
GHN

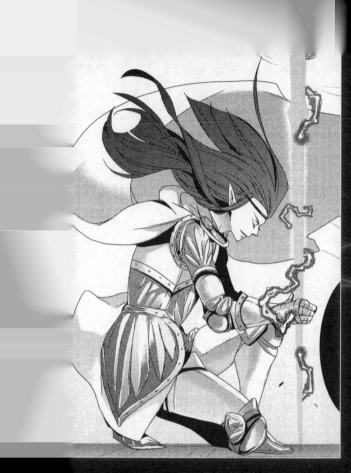

CU CHULAINN

GALLANT HERO FROM CELTIC MYTHOLOGY WHO
DS THE MAGIC SPEAR, GAE BOLG. THE SON OF THE
GOD LUGH AND DEICHTINE, HE HAD BEEN BLESSED
MIGHTY STRENGTH SINCE CHILDHOOD. IN BATTLE,
NORMALLY BEAUTIFUL COUNTENANCE TURNED
SOME, AND IT IS SAID HE HAD THE SKILL AND VALOR
OVERTURN ENTIRE ARMIES SINGLE-HANDEDLY. HE
CURSED TO DIE FOR SPURNING THE WAR GODDESS
GAN'S LOVE, AND WAS IMPALED BY HIS OWN SPEAR.
T INSTANT, HE TIED HIMSELF TO A STONE PILLAR SO
THAT HE NEVER FELL, EVEN IN DEATH.

DEVIL SURVIVOR
デビルサバイバー

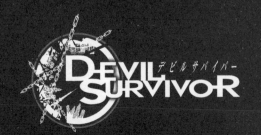

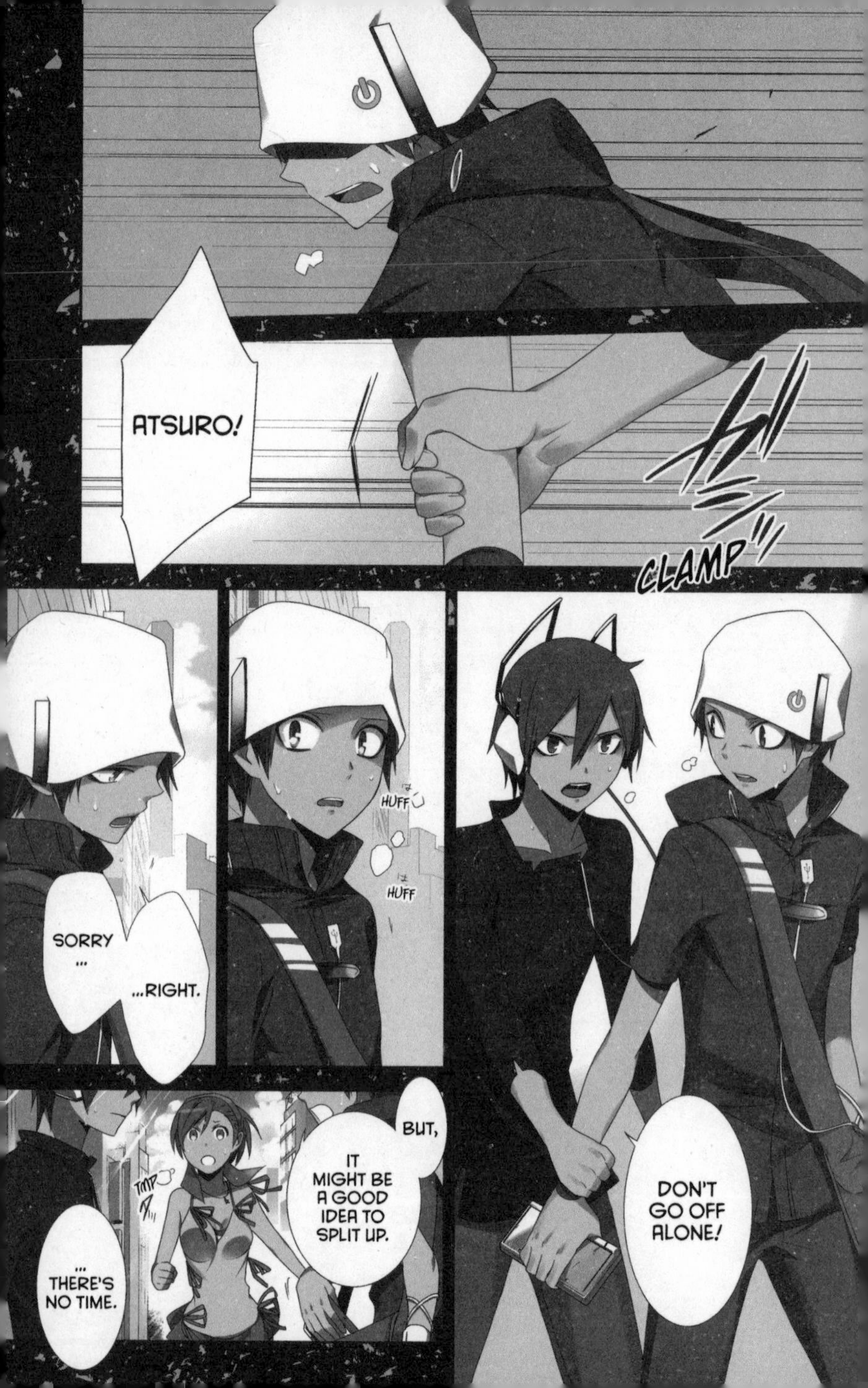
ATSURO!
CLAMP
DON'T GO OFF ALONE!
HUFF
HUFF
SORRY ... ...RIGHT.
BUT,
IT MIGHT BE A GOOD IDEA TO SPLIT UP.
TMP
... THERE'S NO TIME.

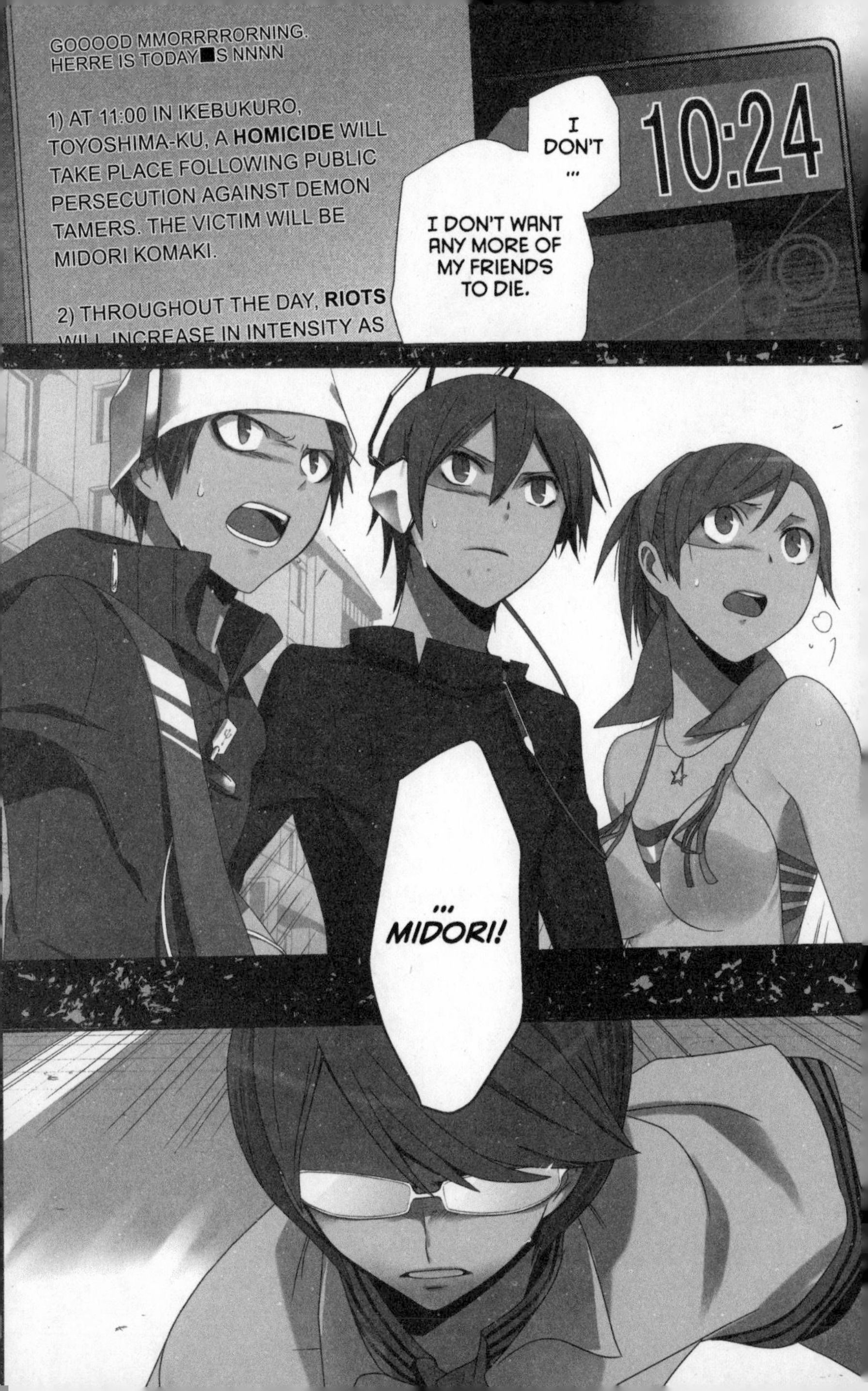
10:24
I DON'T ...
I DON'T WANT ANY MORE OF MY FRIENDS TO DIE.
GOOOOD MMORRRRORNING.
HERRE IS TODAY■S NNNN
1) AT 11:00 IN IKEBUKURO, TOYOSHIMA-KU, A HOMICIDE WILL TAKE PLACE FOLLOWING PUBLIC PERSECUTION AGAINST DEMON TAMERS. THE VICTIM WILL BE MIDORI KOMAKI.
2) THROUGHOUT THE DAY, RIOTS WILL INCREASE IN INTENSITY AS
... MIDORI!

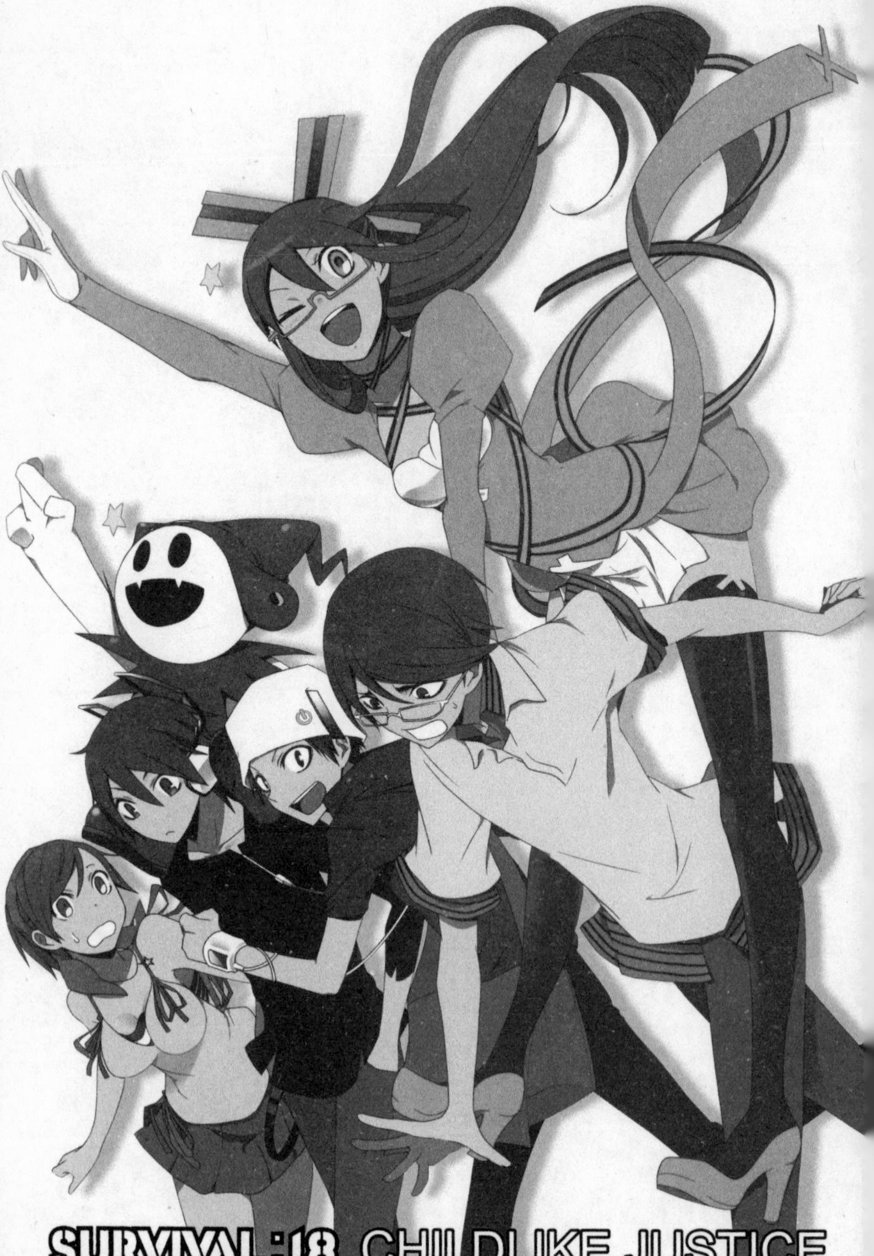

SURVIVAL:18 CHILDLIKE JUSTICE

DEVIL SURVIVOR
デビルサバイバー

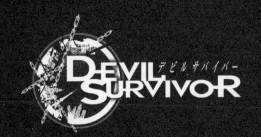

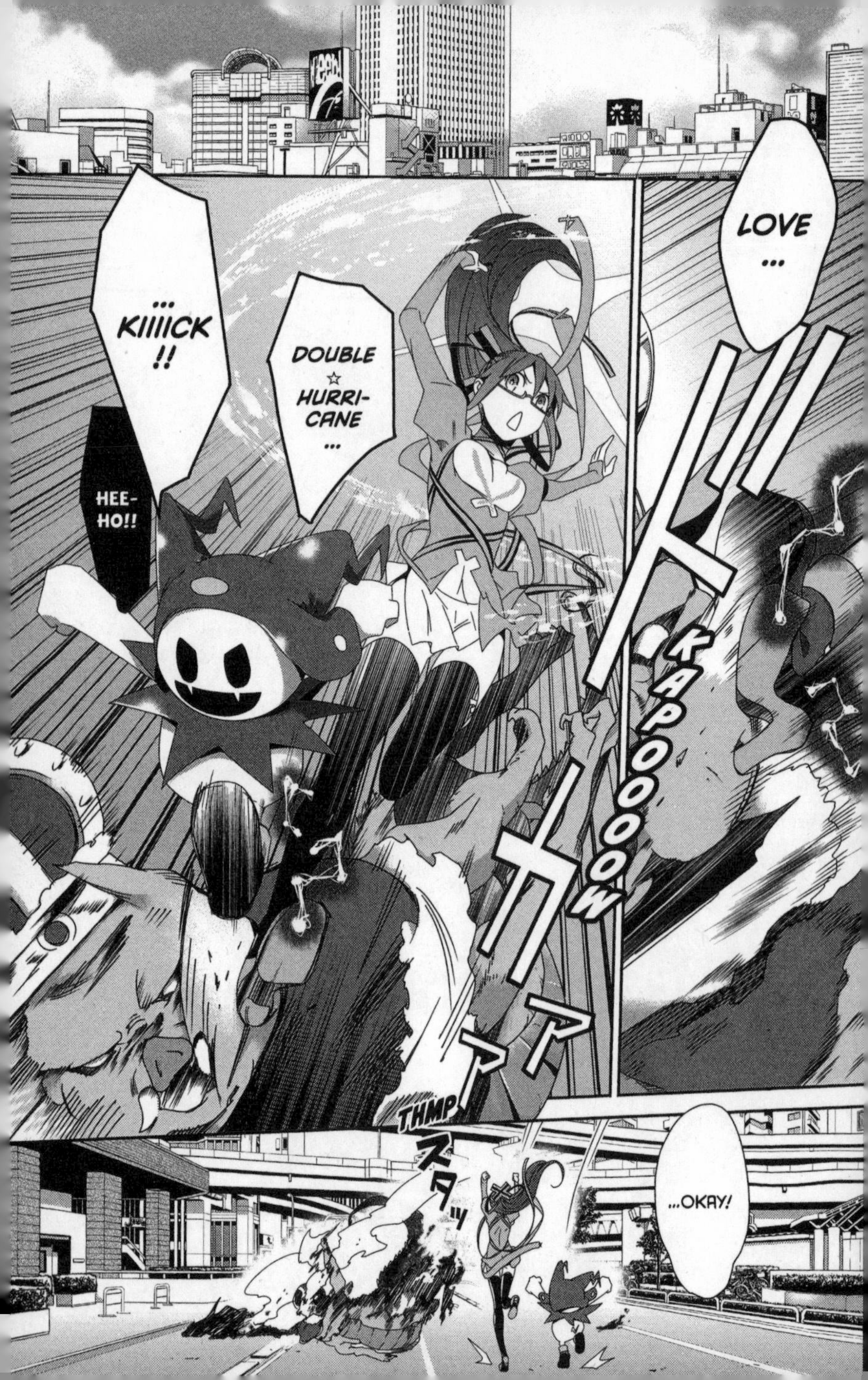
LOVE ...
DOUBLE ☆ HURRI-CANE ...
... KIIICK !!
HEE-HO!!
KAPOOOOOOW
THMP
...OKAY!

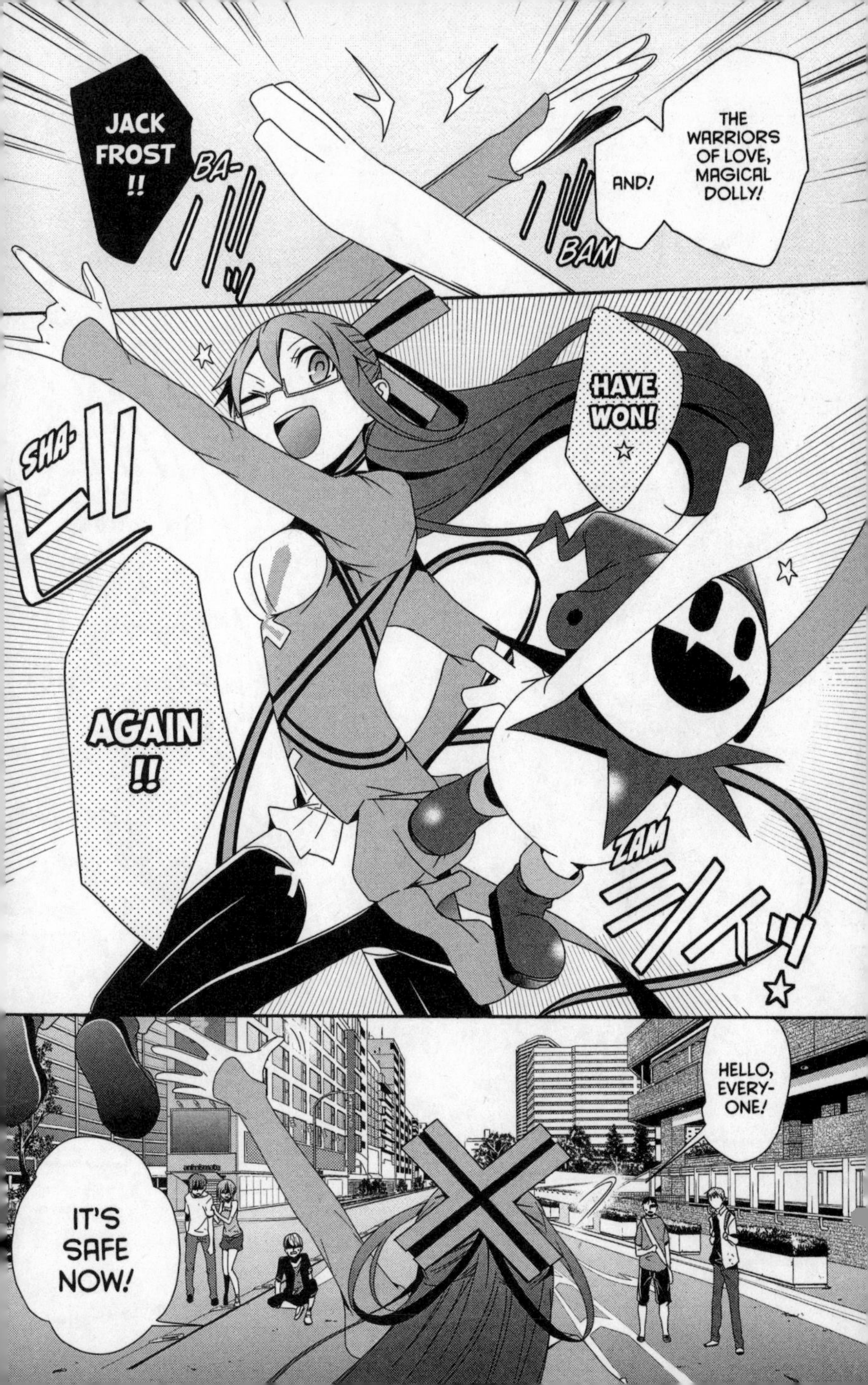
THE WARRIORS OF LOVE, MAGICAL DOLLY!
AND!
BAM
BA-
JACK FROST !!
HAVE WON!
ZAM
SHA-
AGAIN !!
HELLO, EVERY-ONE!
IT'S SAFE NOW!

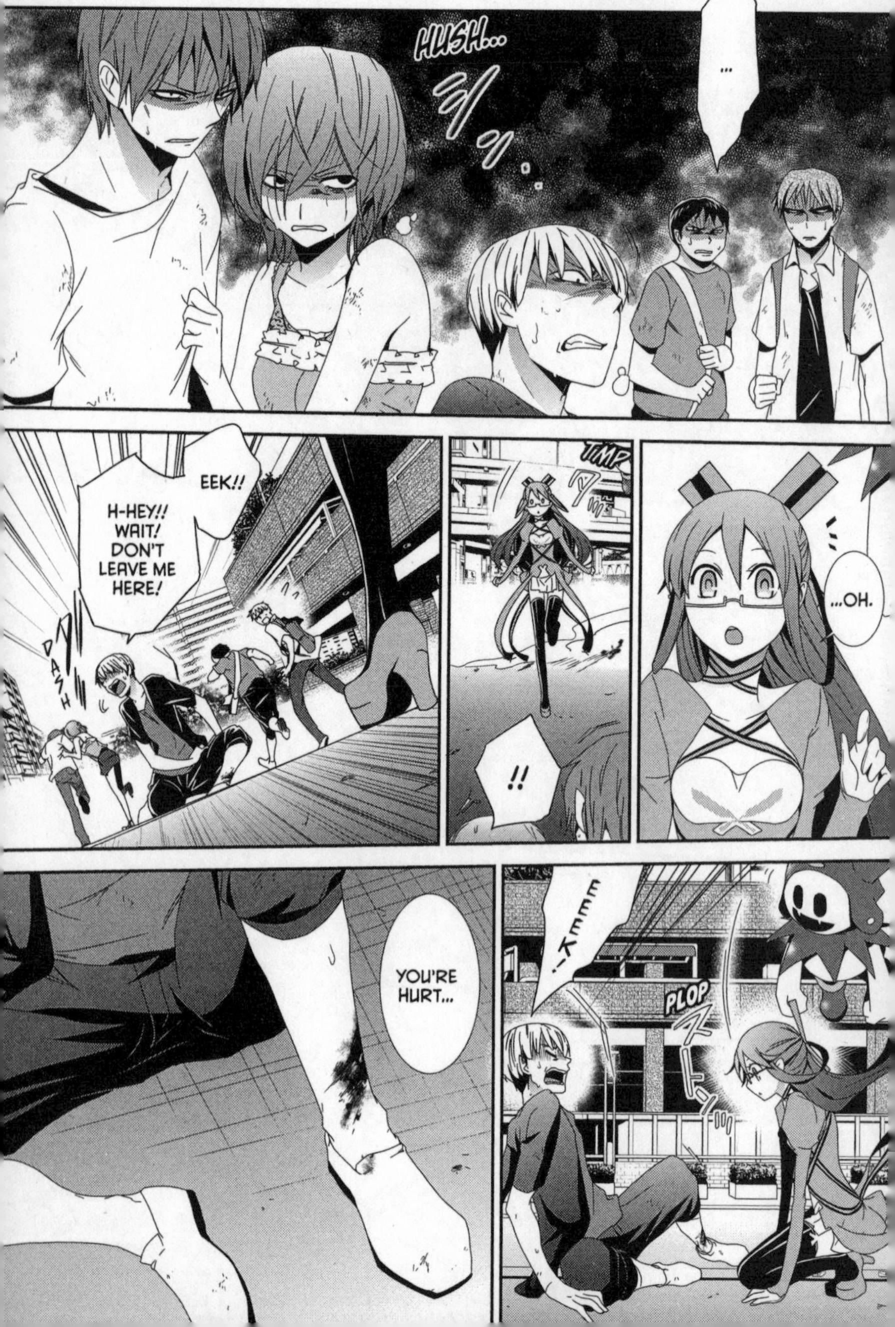
...
HUSH...
...OH.
TMP
!!
EEK!!
H-HEY!! WAIT! DON'T LEAVE ME HERE!
DASH
EEEEK!
PLOP
YOU'RE HURT...

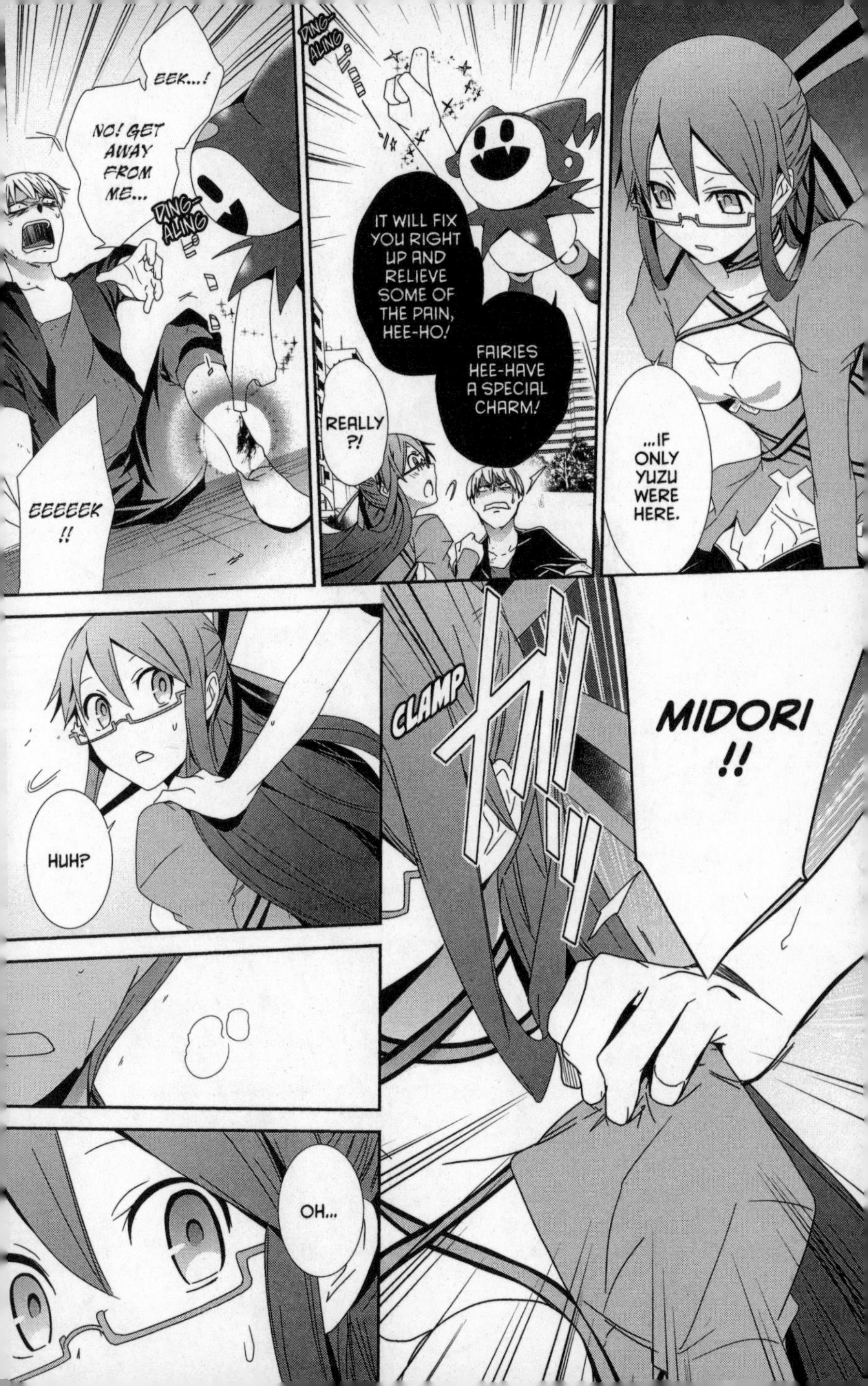
...IF ONLY YUZU WERE HERE.
DING-ALING
FAIRIES HEE-HAVE A SPECIAL CHARM!
IT WILL FIX YOU RIGHT UP AND RELIEVE SOME OF THE PAIN, HEE-HO!
REALLY ?!
EEK...!
NO! GET AWAY FROM ME...
DING-ALING
EEEEEK !!
MIDORI !!
CLAMP
HUH?
OH...

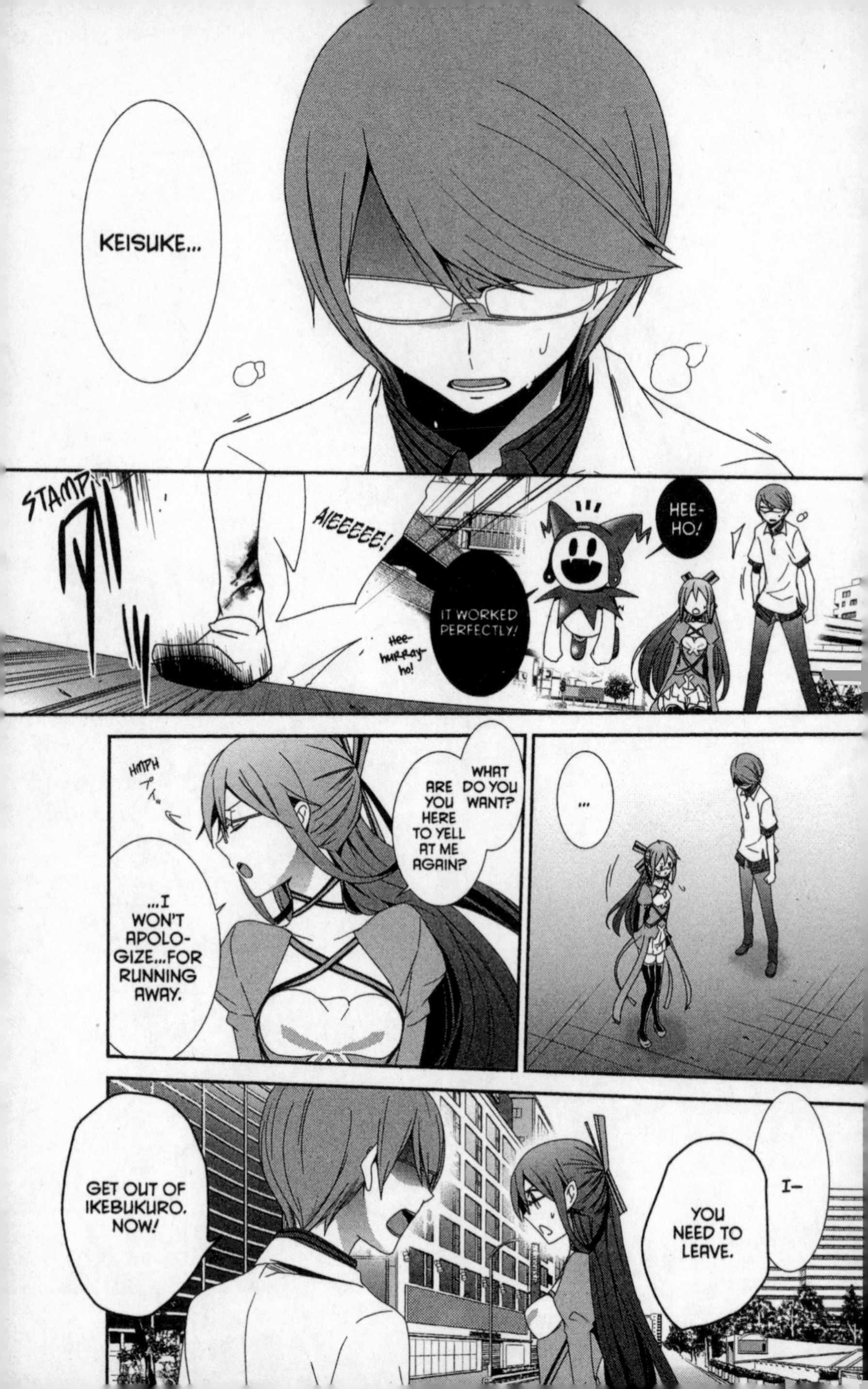
KEISUKE...
HEE-HO!
IT WORKED PERFECTLY!
Hee-hurray-ho!
AIEEEEE!
STAMP
...
WHAT DO YOU WANT? ARE YOU HERE TO YELL AT ME AGAIN?
HMPH
...I WON'T APOLOGIZE...FOR RUNNING AWAY.
I—
YOU NEED TO LEAVE.
GET OUT OF IKEBUKURO. NOW!

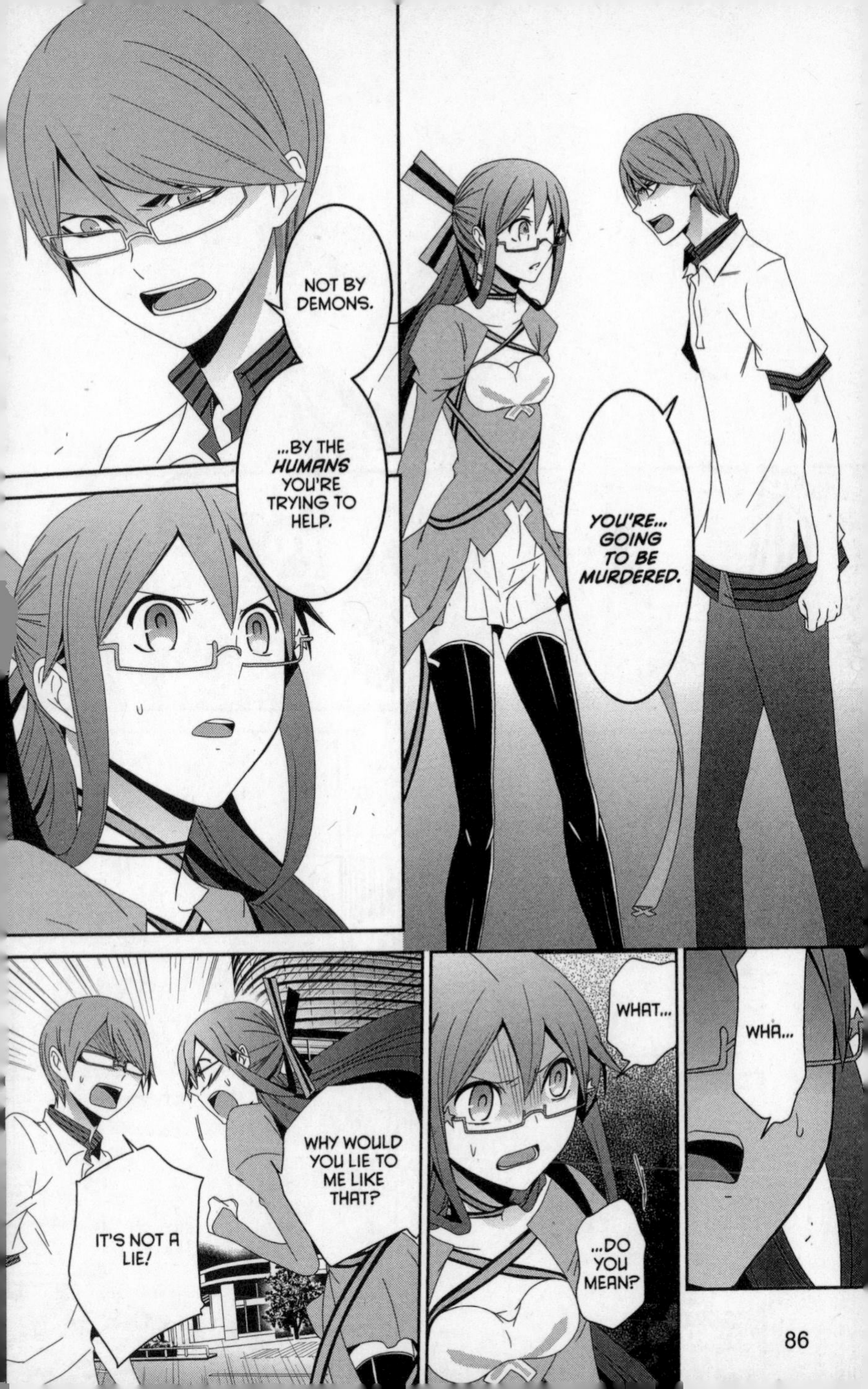
YOU'RE... GOING TO BE MURDERED.
NOT BY DEMONS.
...BY THE *HUMANS* YOU'RE TRYING TO HELP.
WHA...
WHAT...
...DO YOU MEAN?
WHY WOULD YOU LIE TO ME LIKE THAT?
IT'S NOT A LIE!

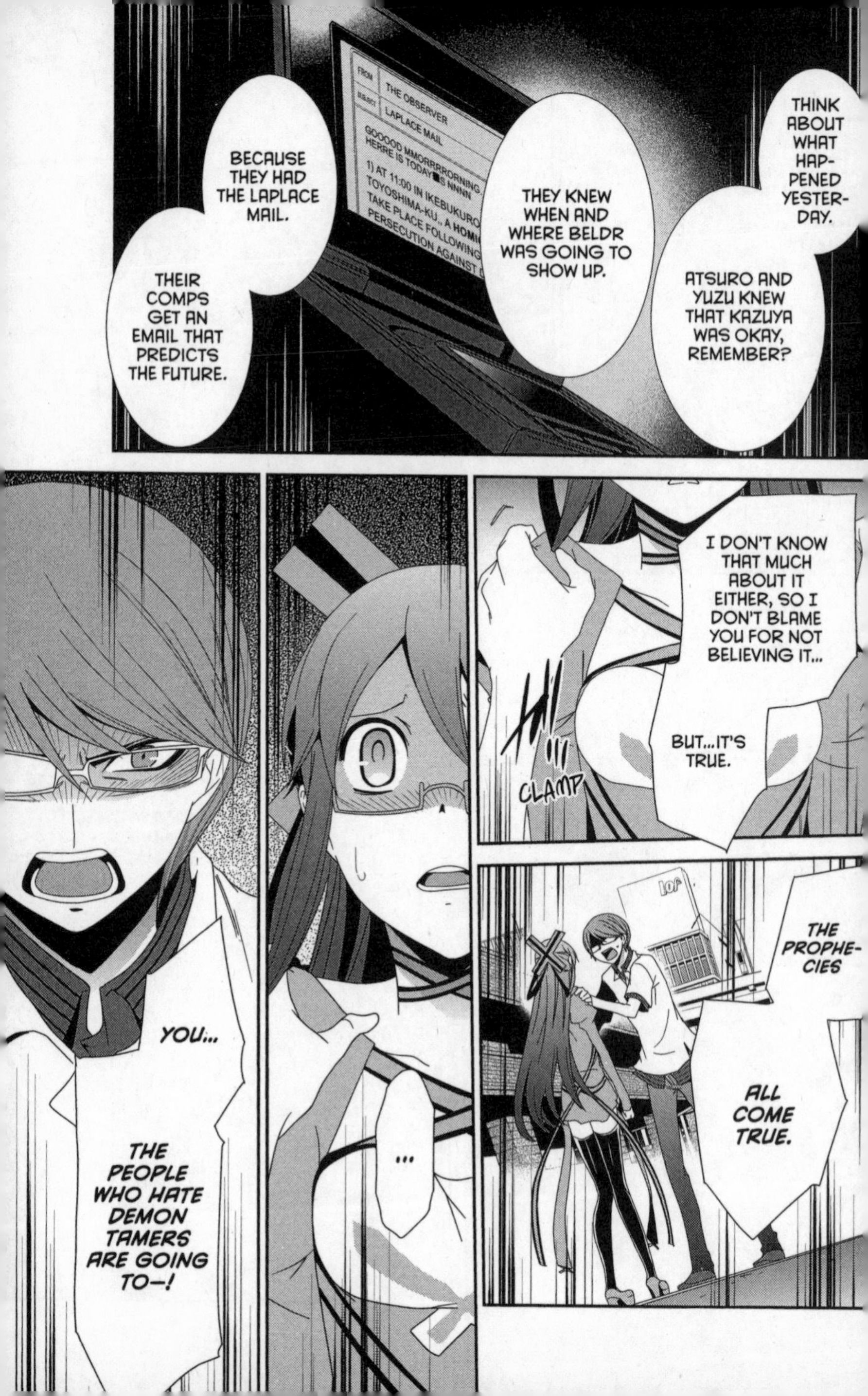
THINK ABOUT WHAT HAP-PENED YESTER-DAY.
ATSURO AND YUZU KNEW THAT KAZUYA WAS OKAY, REMEMBER?
THEY KNEW WHEN AND WHERE BELDR WAS GOING TO SHOW UP.
FROM
THE OBSERVER
LAPLACE MAIL
GOOOOD MMORRRRORNING.
BECAUSE THEY HAD THE LAPLACE MAIL.
THEIR COMPS GET AN EMAIL THAT PREDICTS THE FUTURE.
I DON'T KNOW THAT MUCH ABOUT IT EITHER, SO I DON'T BLAME YOU FOR NOT BELIEVING IT...
BUT...IT'S TRUE.
CLAMP
THE PROPHE-CIES
ALL COME TRUE.
...
YOU...
THE PEOPLE WHO HATE DEMON TAMERS ARE GOING TO—!

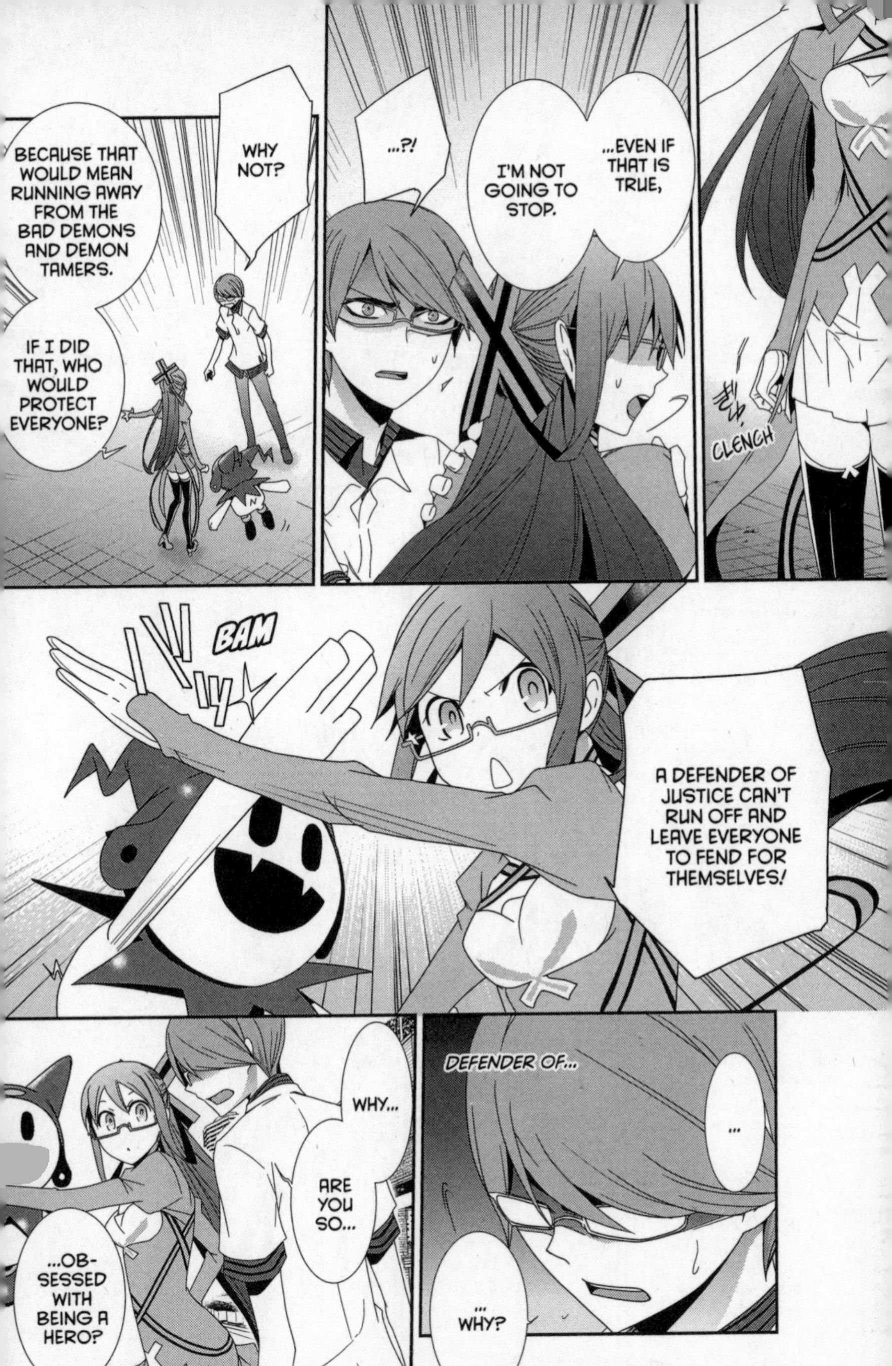
CLENCH
...EVEN IF THAT IS TRUE,
I'M NOT GOING TO STOP.
...?!
WHY NOT?
BECAUSE THAT WOULD MEAN RUNNING AWAY FROM THE BAD DEMONS AND DEMON TAMERS.
IF I DID THAT, WHO WOULD PROTECT EVERYONE?
BAM
A DEFENDER OF JUSTICE CAN'T RUN OFF AND LEAVE EVERYONE TO FEND FOR THEMSELVES!
DEFENDER OF...
...
... WHY?
WHY...
ARE YOU SO...
...OB-SESSED WITH BEING A HERO?

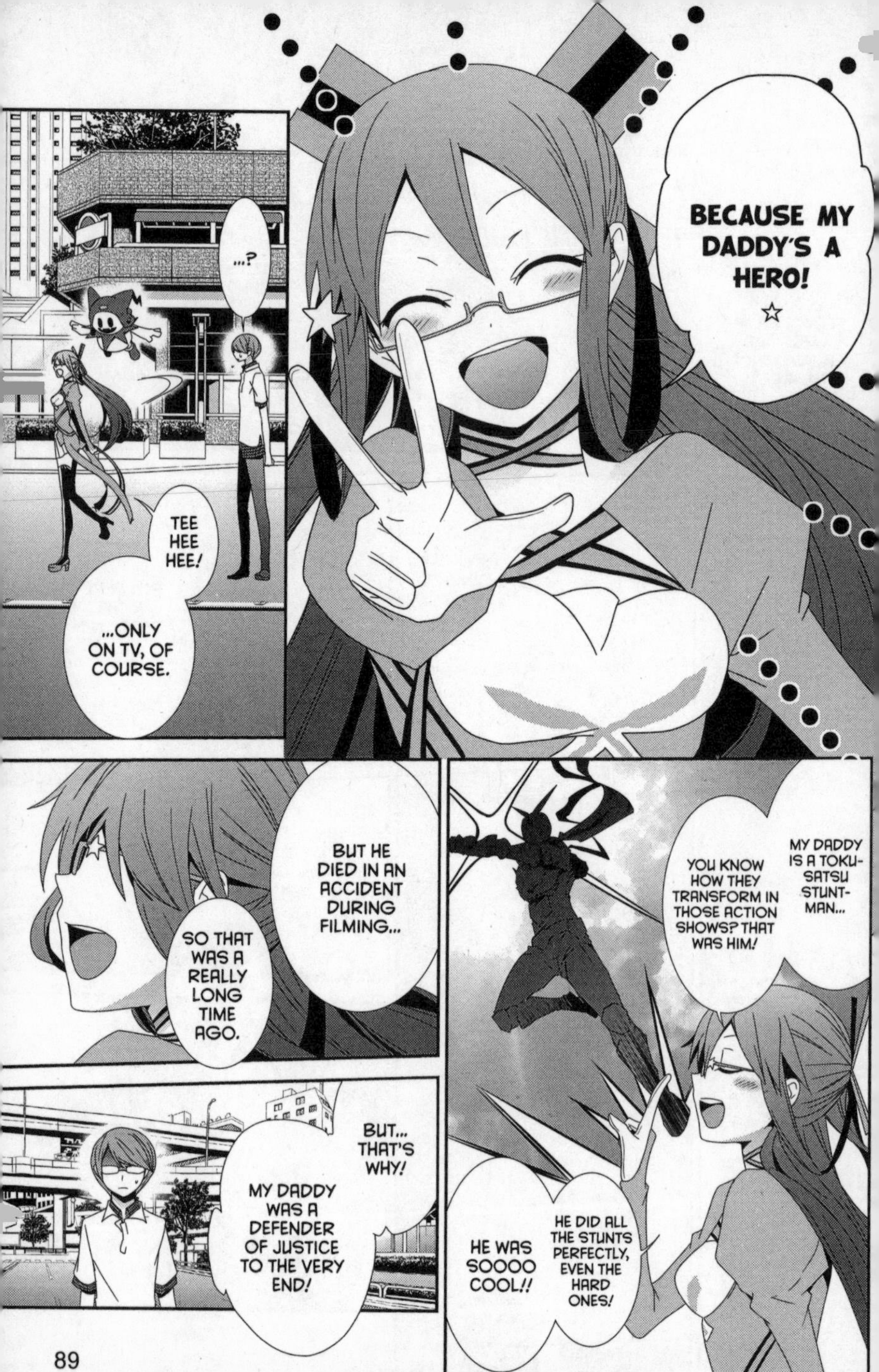
BECAUSE MY DADDY'S A HERO! ☆
...?
TEE HEE HEE!
...ONLY ON TV, OF COURSE.
MY DADDY IS A TOKU-SATSU STUNT-MAN...
YOU KNOW HOW THEY TRANSFORM IN THOSE ACTION SHOWS? THAT WAS HIM!
HE DID ALL THE STUNTS PERFECTLY, EVEN THE HARD ONES!
HE WAS SOOOO COOL!!
BUT HE DIED IN AN ACCIDENT DURING FILMING...
SO THAT WAS A REALLY LONG TIME AGO.
BUT... THAT'S WHY!
MY DADDY WAS A DEFENDER OF JUSTICE TO THE VERY END!

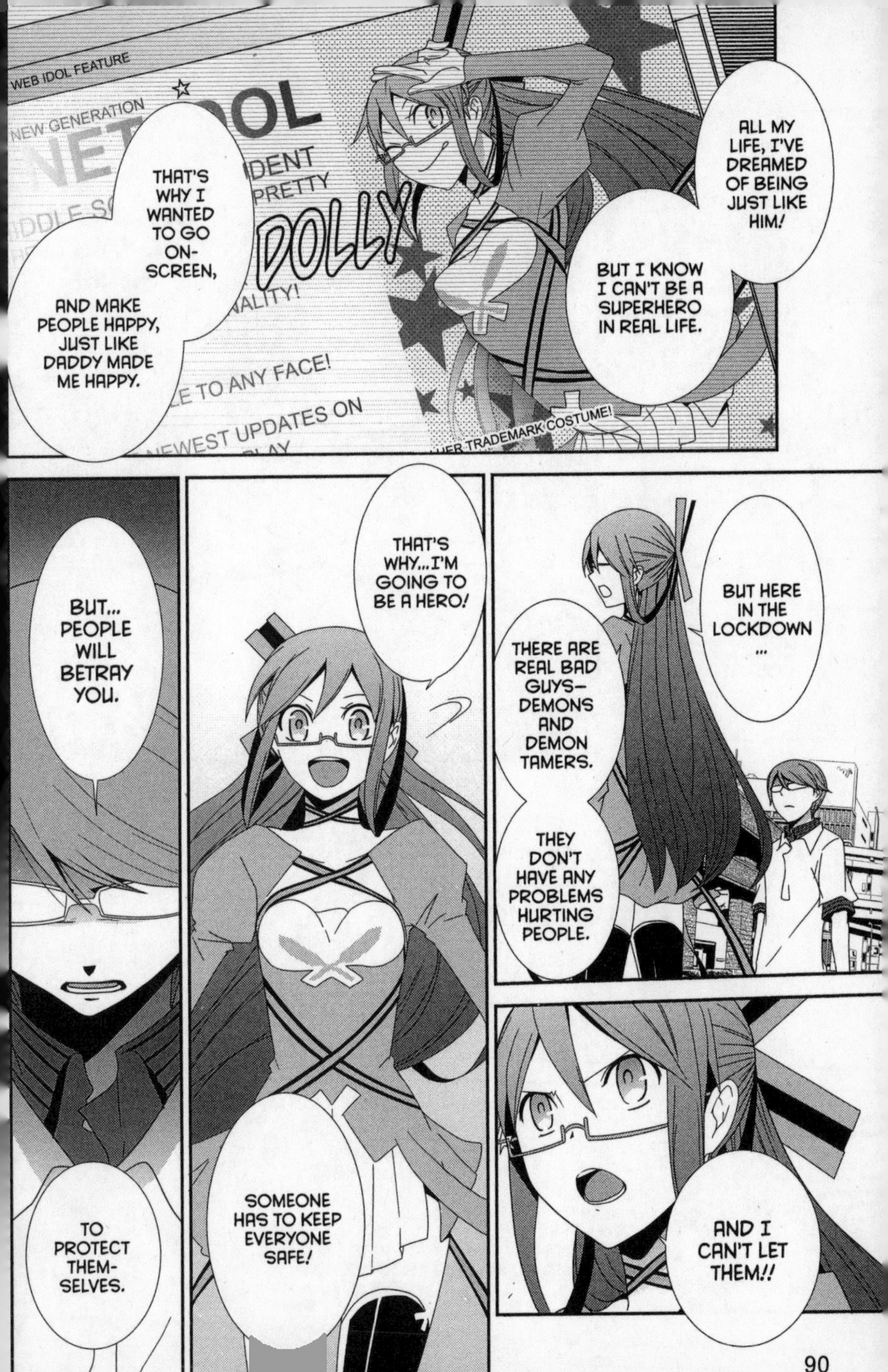
WEB IDOL FEATURE
NEW GENERATION
DOLLY
ALL MY LIFE, I'VE DREAMED OF BEING JUST LIKE HIM!
BUT I KNOW I CAN'T BE A SUPERHERO IN REAL LIFE.
HER TRADEMARK COSTUME!
THAT'S WHY I WANTED TO GO ON-SCREEN,
AND MAKE PEOPLE HAPPY, JUST LIKE DADDY MADE ME HAPPY.
BUT HERE IN THE LOCKDOWN ...
THERE ARE REAL BAD GUYS—DEMONS AND DEMON TAMERS.
THEY DON'T HAVE ANY PROBLEMS HURTING PEOPLE.
AND I CAN'T LET THEM!!
THAT'S WHY...I'M GOING TO BE A HERO!
SOMEONE HAS TO KEEP EVERYONE SAFE!
BUT... PEOPLE WILL BETRAY YOU.
TO PROTECT THEM-SELVES.

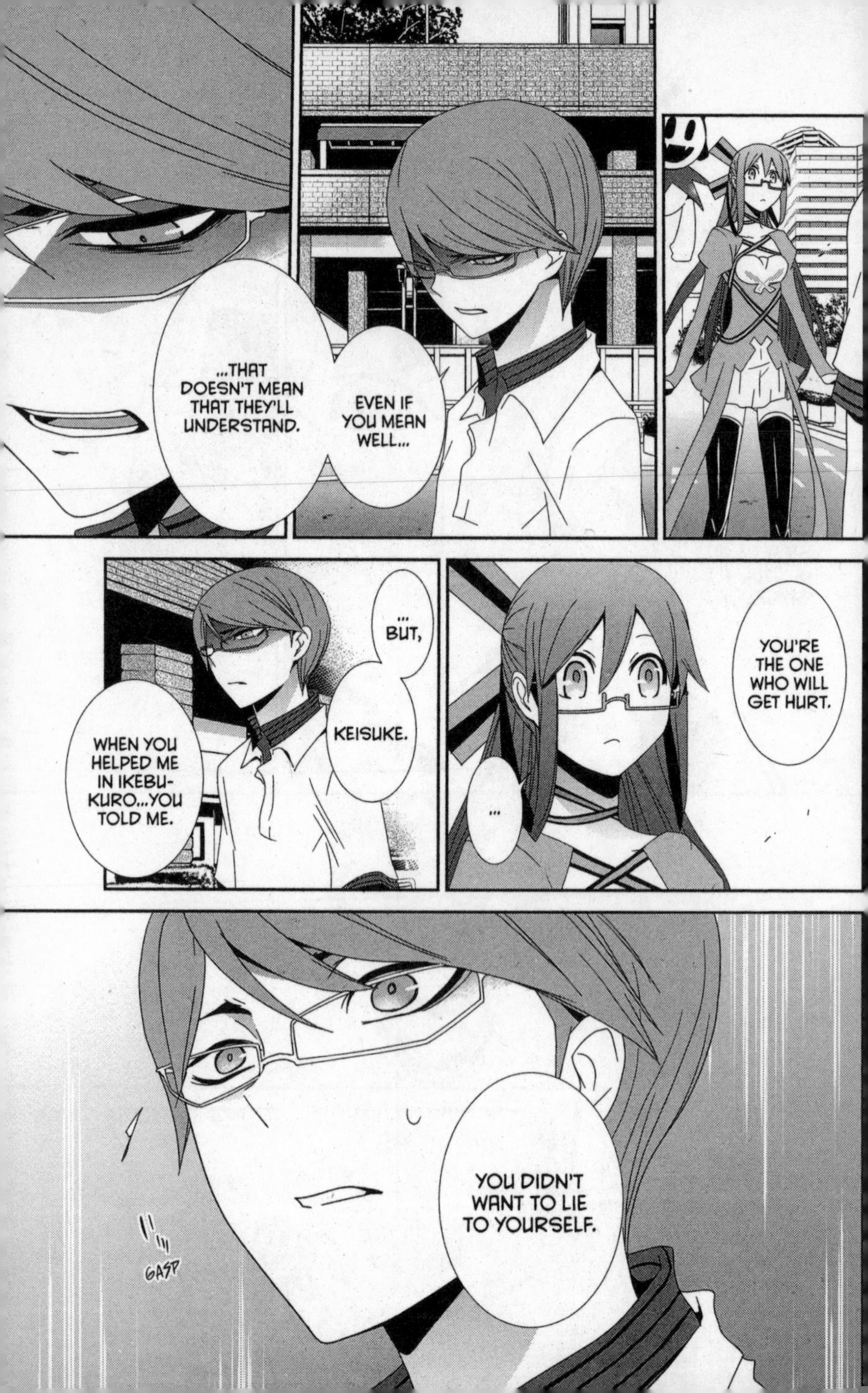
EVEN IF YOU MEAN WELL...
...THAT DOESN'T MEAN THAT THEY'LL UNDERSTAND.
YOU'RE THE ONE WHO WILL GET HURT.
...
... BUT,
KEISUKE.
WHEN YOU HELPED ME IN IKEBU-KURO...YOU TOLD ME.
YOU DIDN'T WANT TO LIE TO YOURSELF.
GASP

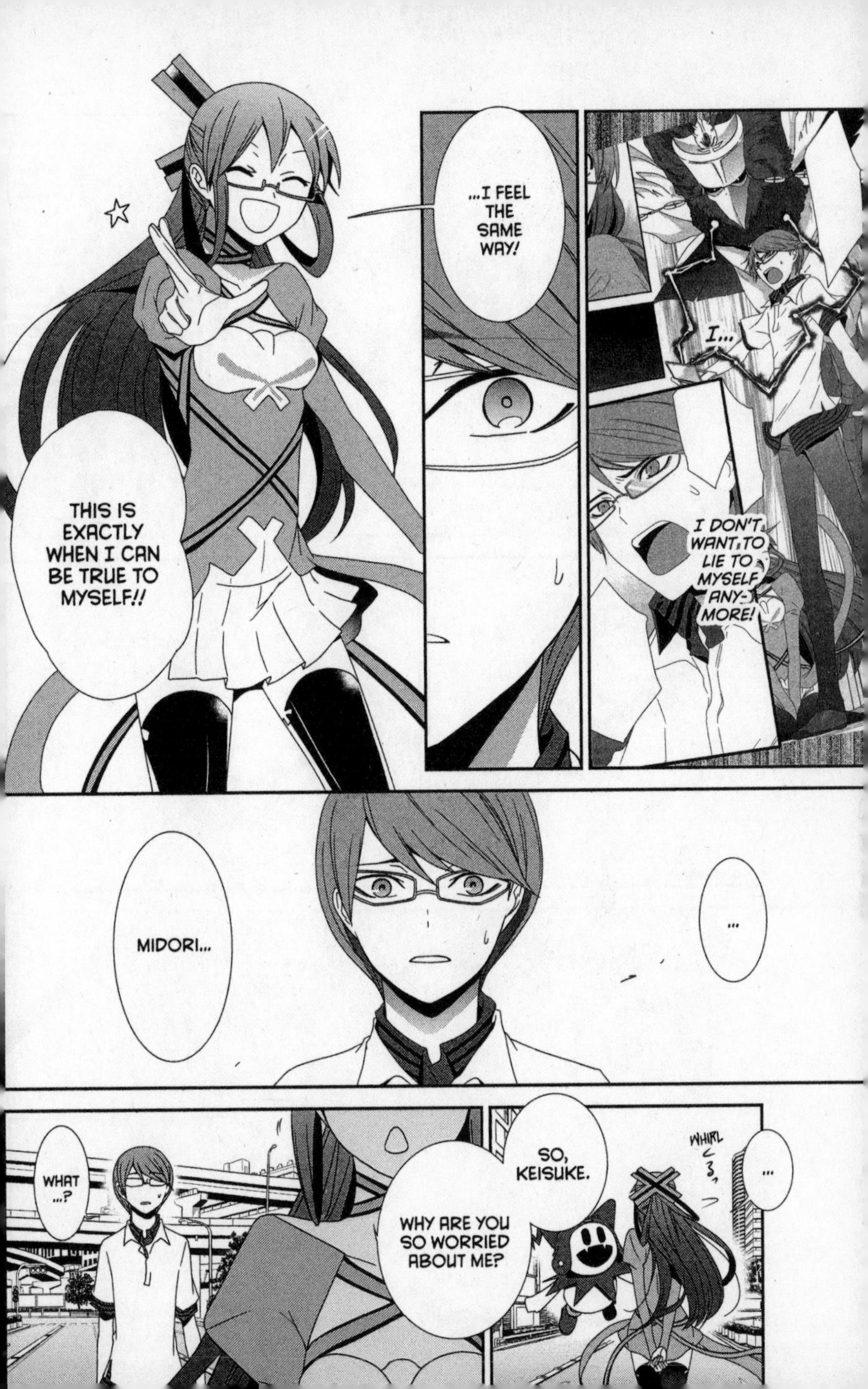
I...
I DON'T WANT TO LIE TO MYSELF ANYMORE!
...I FEEL THE SAME WAY!
THIS IS EXACTLY WHEN I CAN BE TRUE TO MYSELF!!
...
MIDORI...
WHIRL
...
SO, KEISUKE.
WHY ARE YOU SO WORRIED ABOUT ME?
WHAT...?

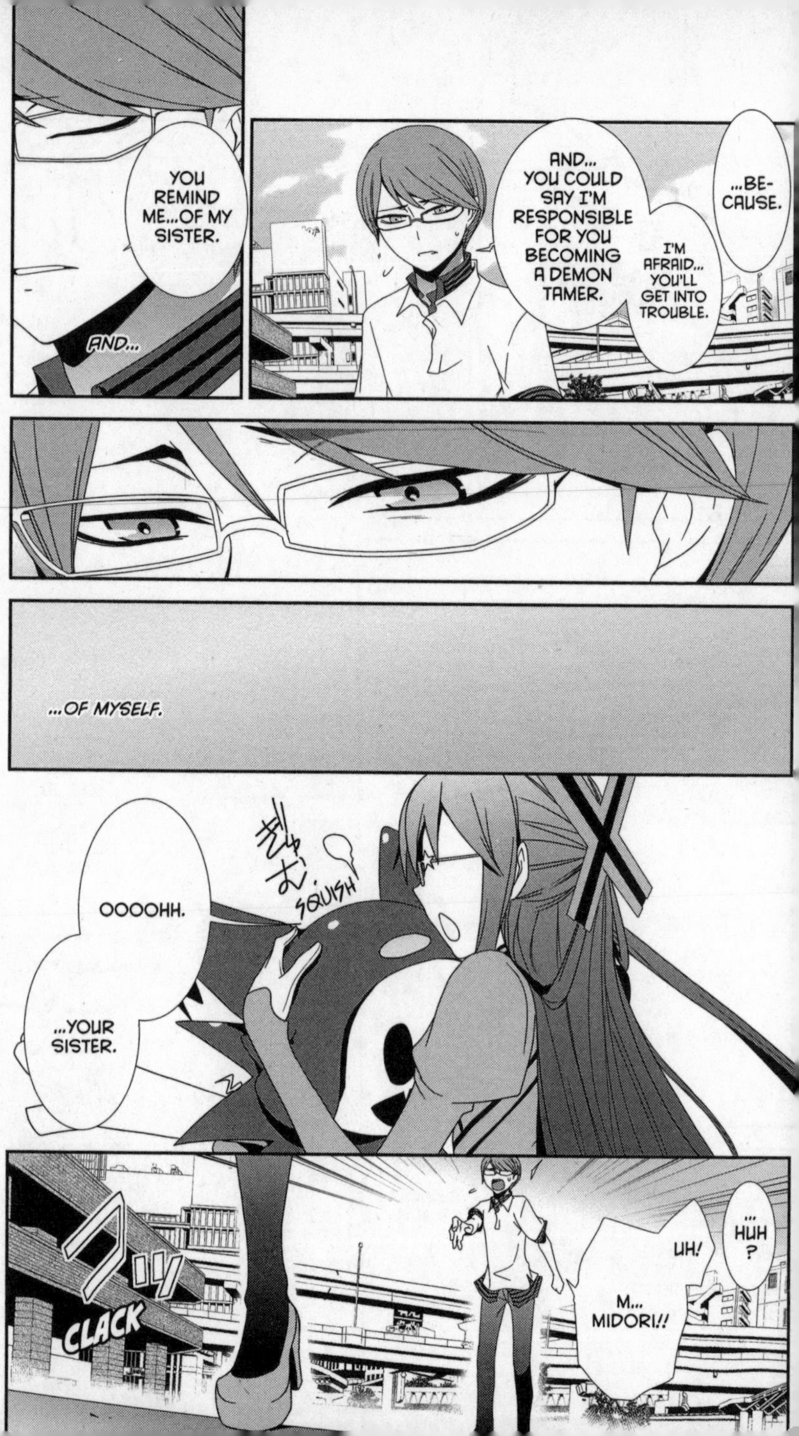
...BE-CAUSE.
I'M AFRAID... YOU'LL GET INTO TROUBLE.
AND... YOU COULD SAY I'M RESPONSIBLE FOR YOU BECOMING A DEMON TAMER.
YOU REMIND ME...OF MY SISTER.
AND...
...OF MYSELF.
SQUISH
OOOOHH.
...YOUR SISTER.
... HUH?
UH!
M... MIDORI!!
CLACK

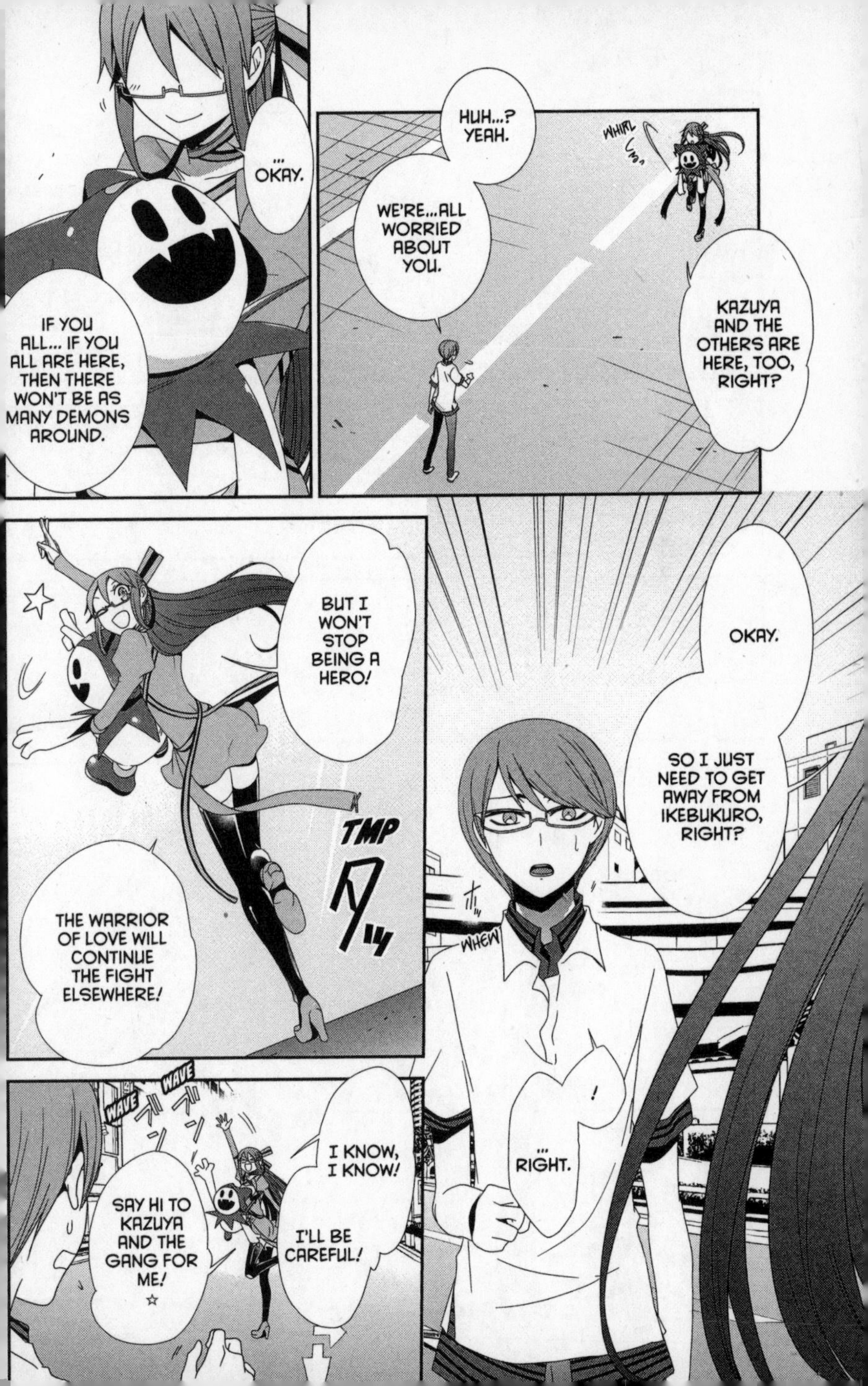
WHIRL
KAZUYA AND THE OTHERS ARE HERE, TOO, RIGHT?
HUH...? YEAH.
WE'RE...ALL WORRIED ABOUT YOU.
... OKAY.
IF YOU ALL... IF YOU ALL ARE HERE, THEN THERE WON'T BE AS MANY DEMONS AROUND.
OKAY.
SO I JUST NEED TO GET AWAY FROM IKEBUKURO, RIGHT?
WHEW
... RIGHT.
BUT I WON'T STOP BEING A HERO!
TMP
THE WARRIOR OF LOVE WILL CONTINUE THE FIGHT ELSEWHERE!
I KNOW, I KNOW!
I'LL BE CAREFUL!
WAVE
WAVE
SAY HI TO KAZUYA AND THE GANG FOR ME! ☆

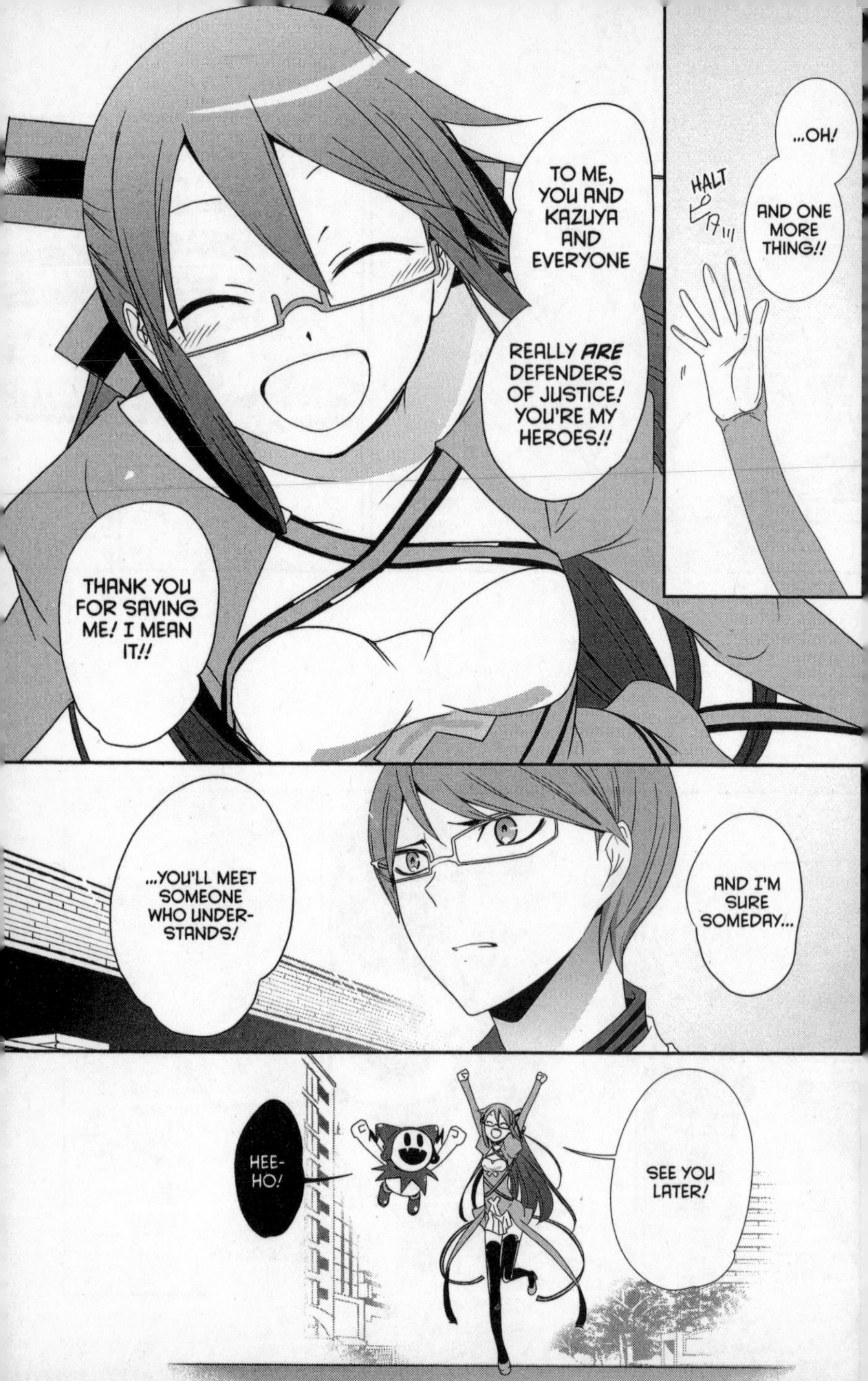

...OH!
HALT
AND ONE MORE THING!!
TO ME, YOU AND KAZUYA AND EVERYONE
REALLY *ARE* DEFENDERS OF JUSTICE! YOU'RE MY HEROES!!
THANK YOU FOR SAVING ME! I MEAN IT!!
AND I'M SURE SOMEDAY...
...YOU'LL MEET SOMEONE WHO UNDER-STANDS!
SEE YOU LATER!
HEE-HO!

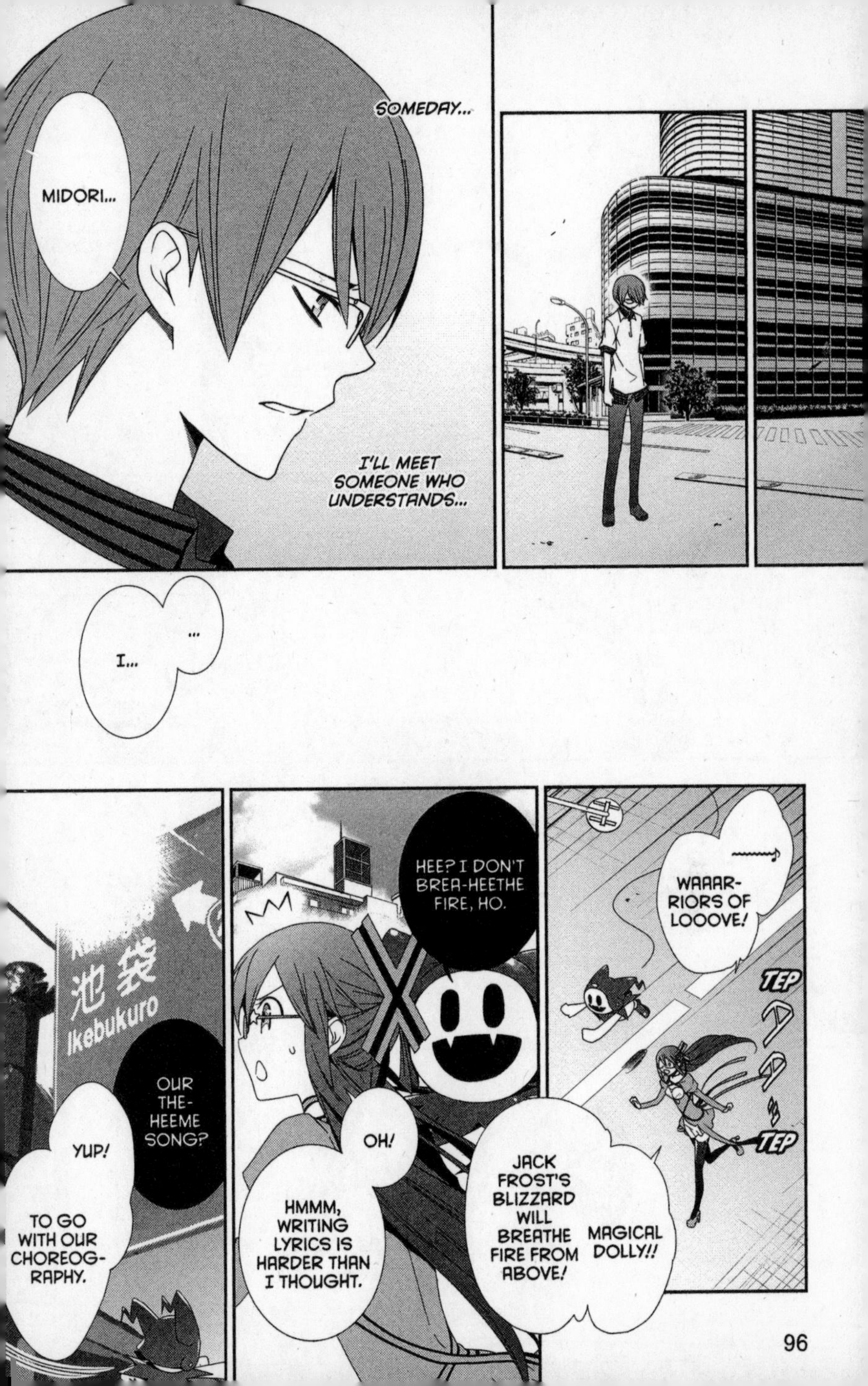
SOMEDAY...
MIDORI...
I'LL MEET SOMEONE WHO UNDERSTANDS...
...
I...
WAAAR-RIORS OF LOOOVE!
TEP
TEP
MAGICAL DOLLY!!
JACK FROST'S BLIZZARD WILL BREATHE FIRE FROM ABOVE!
HEE? I DON'T BREA-HEETHE FIRE, HO.
OH!
HMMM, WRITING LYRICS IS HARDER THAN I THOUGHT.
OUR THE-HEEME SONG?
YUP!
TO GO WITH OUR CHOREOG-RAPHY.
池袋
Ikebukuro

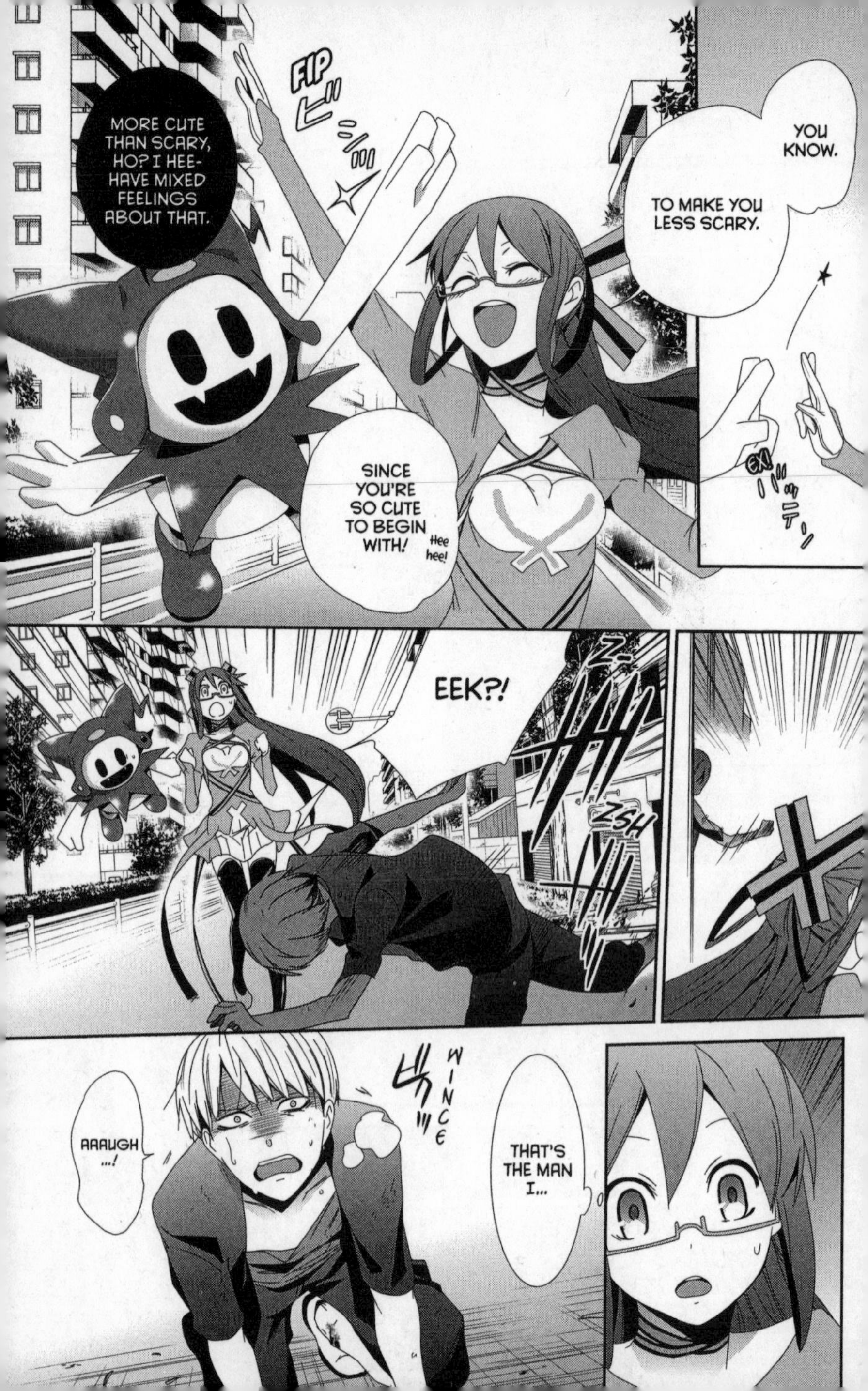
YOU KNOW.
TO MAKE YOU LESS SCARY.
EX!
FIP
SINCE YOU'RE SO CUTE TO BEGIN WITH!
Hee hee!
MORE CUTE THAN SCARY, HO? I HEE-HAVE MIXED FEELINGS ABOUT THAT.
EEK?!
ZSH
THAT'S THE MAN I...
WINCE
AAAUGH ...!

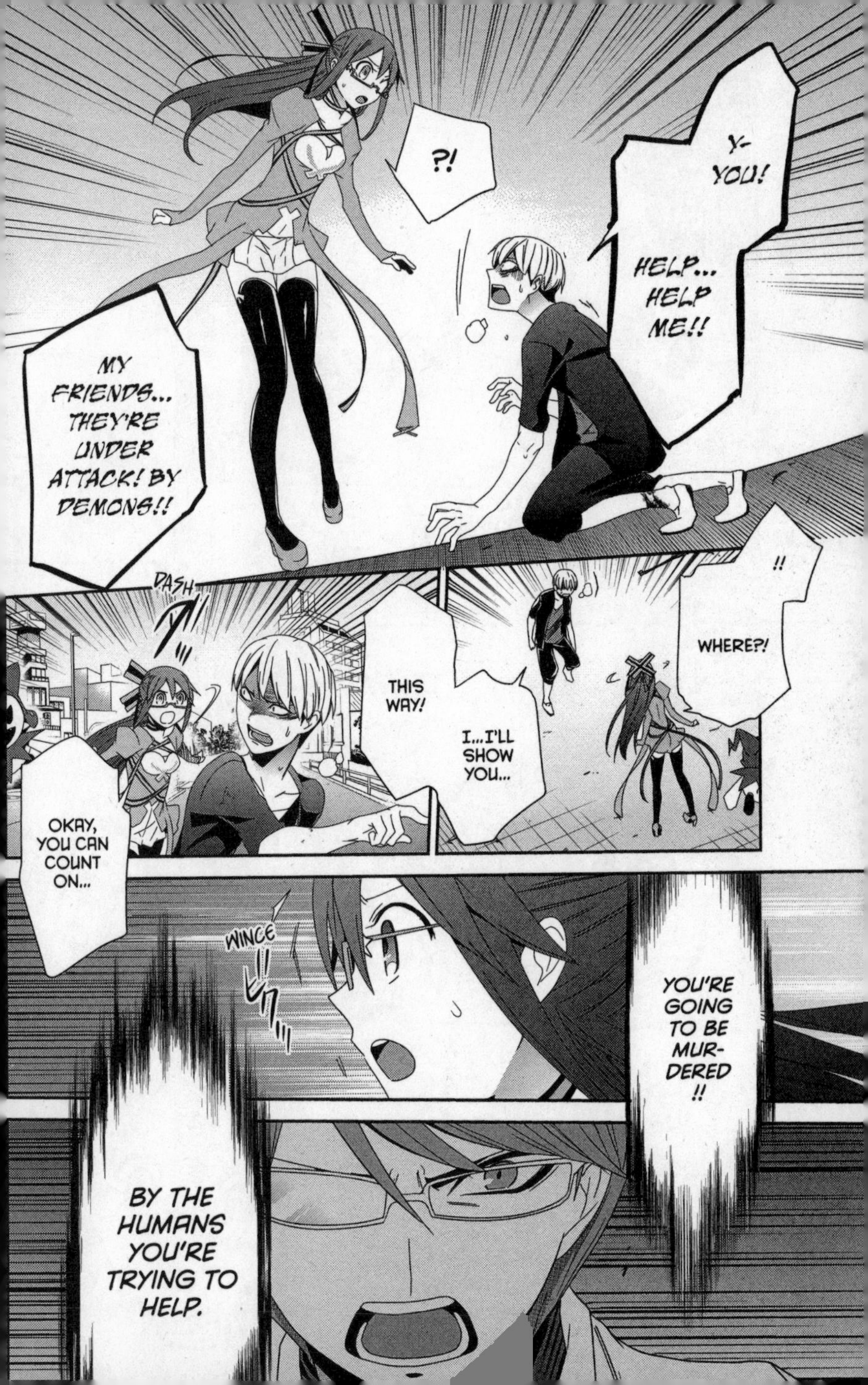
Y- YOU!
HELP... HELP ME!!
?!
MY FRIENDS... THEY'RE UNDER ATTACK! BY DEMONS!!
!!
WHERE?!
THIS WAY!
I...I'LL SHOW YOU...
DASH
OKAY, YOU CAN COUNT ON...
WINCE
YOU'RE GOING TO BE MUR-DERED!!
BY THE HUMANS YOU'RE TRYING TO HELP.

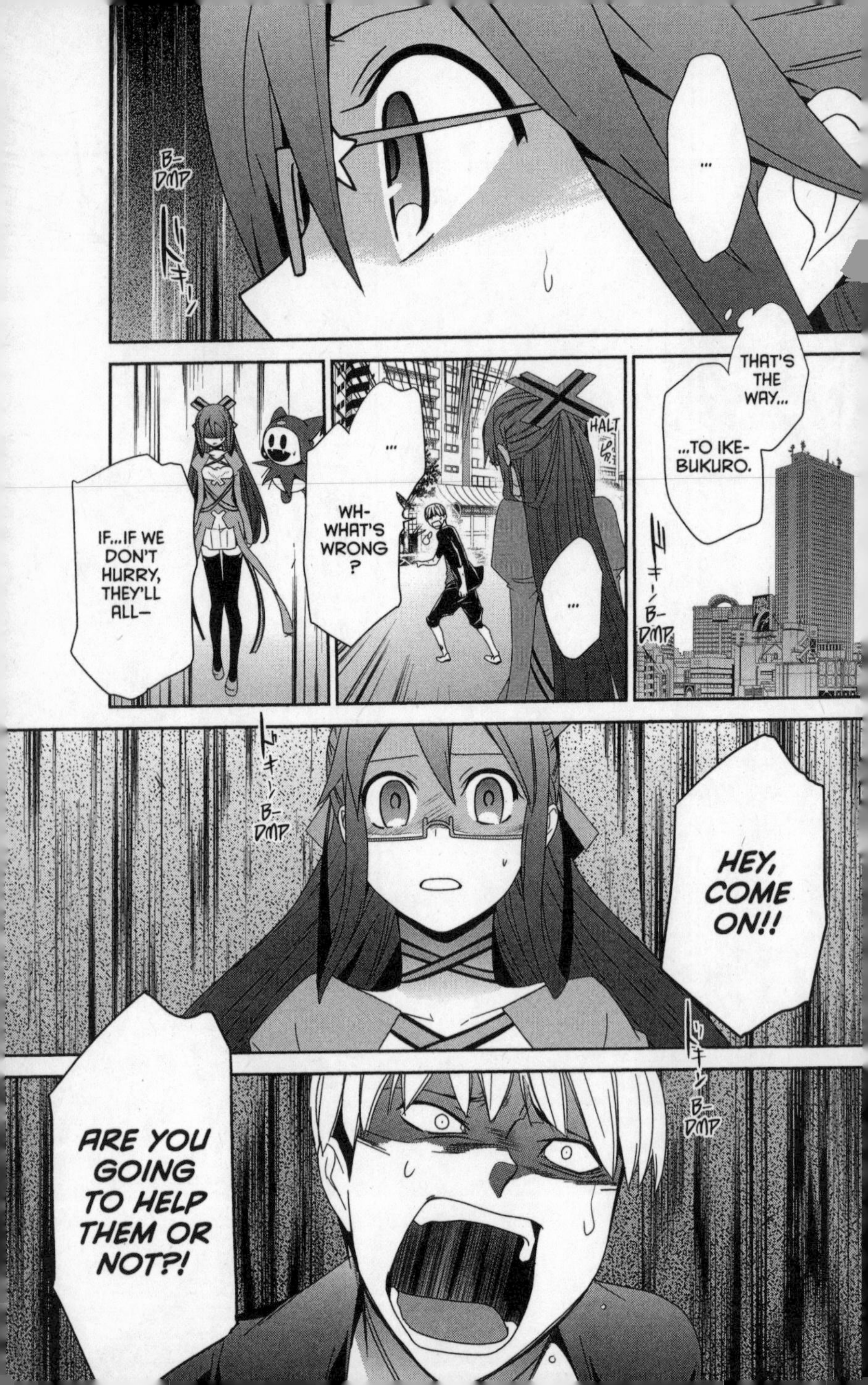
...
B-DMP
THAT'S THE WAY...
...TO IKE-BUKURO.
B-DMP
HALT
...
...
WH-WHAT'S WRONG?
IF...IF WE DON'T HURRY, THEY'LL ALL—
B-DMP
HEY, COME ON!!
B-DMP
ARE YOU GOING TO HELP THEM OR NOT?!

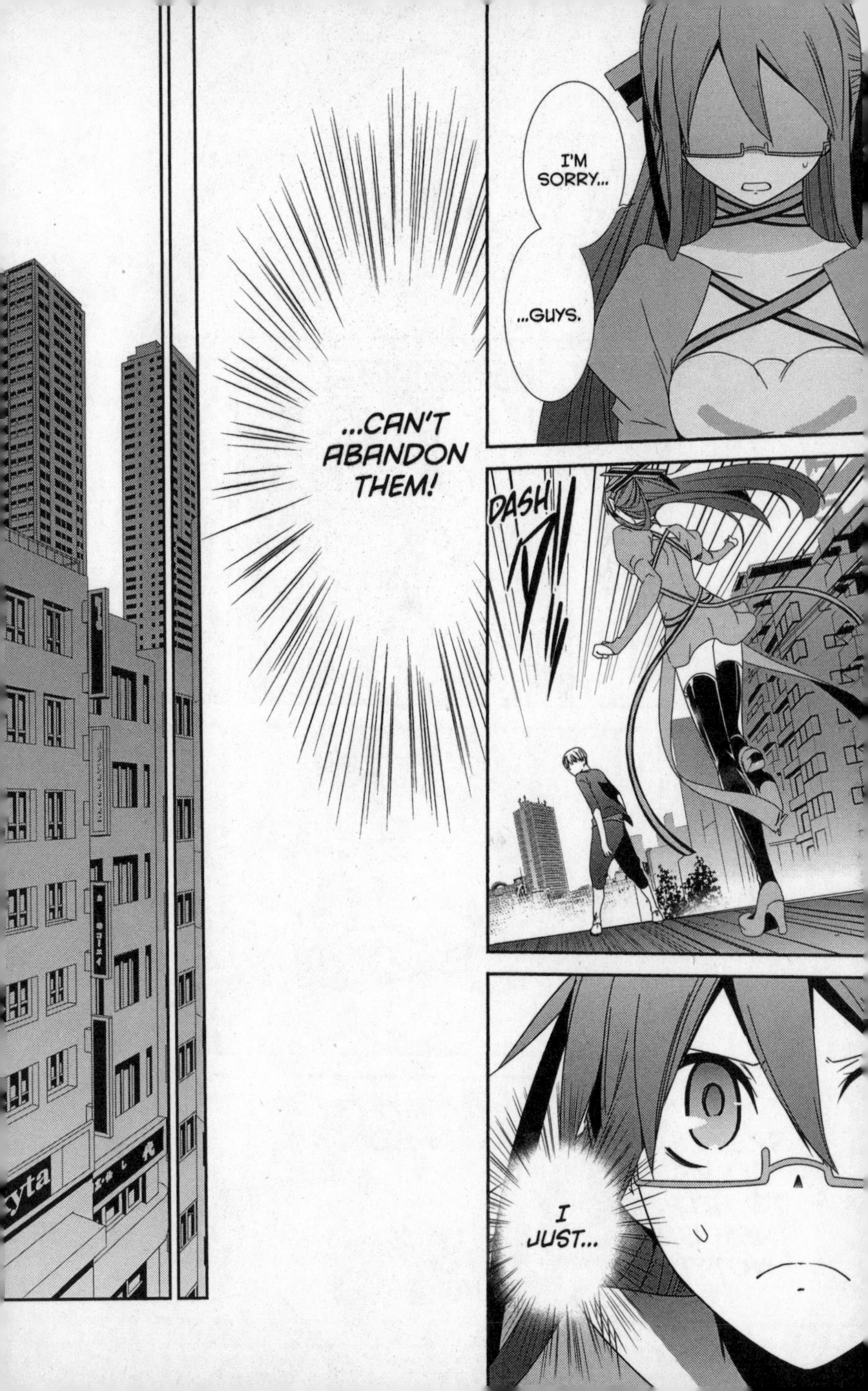
I'M SORRY...
...GUYS.
DASH
I JUST...
...CAN'T ABANDON THEM!

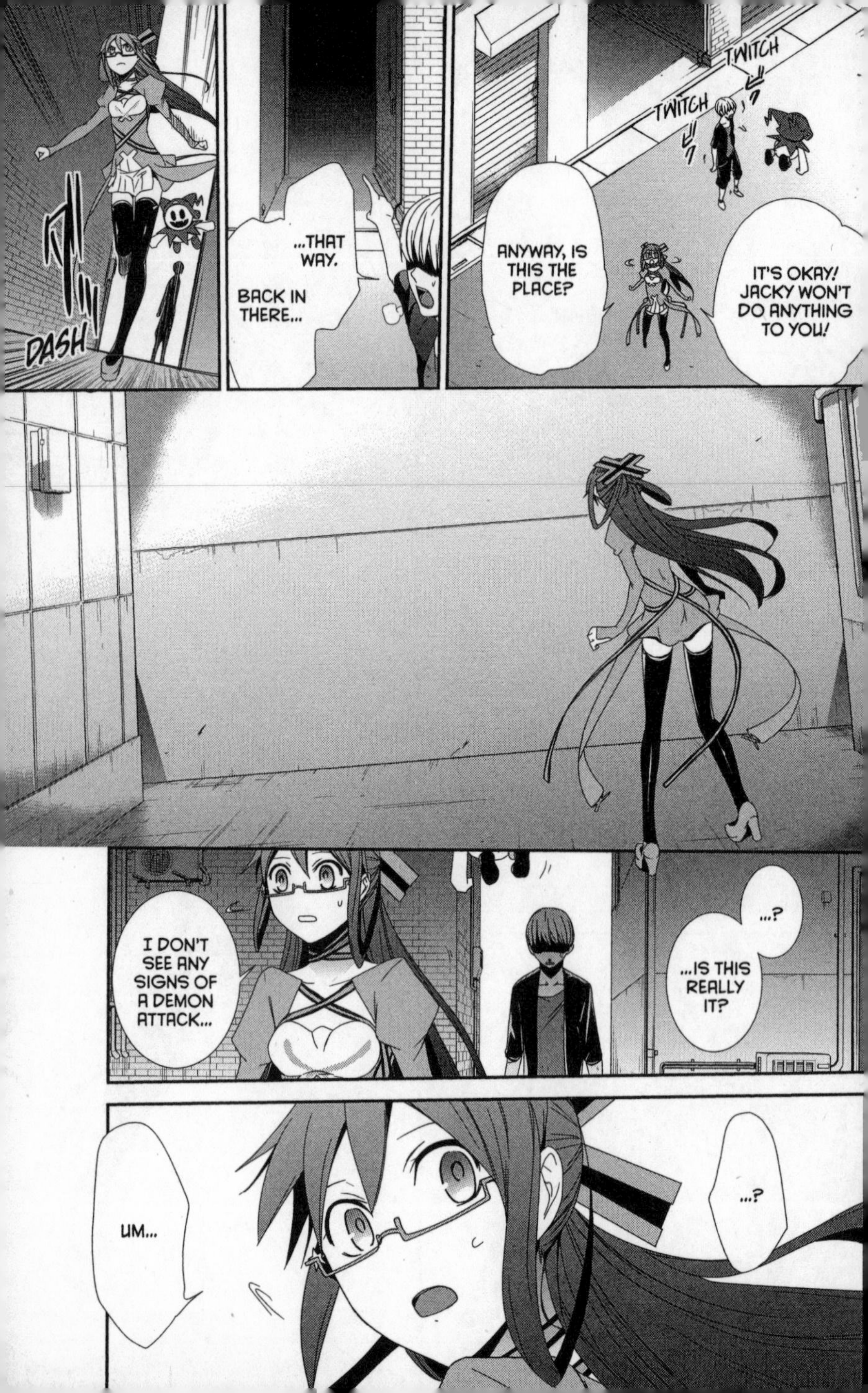
TWITCH
TWITCH
IT'S OKAY! JACKY WON'T DO ANYTHING TO YOU!
ANYWAY, IS THIS THE PLACE?
...THAT WAY.
BACK IN THERE...
DASH
...?
...IS THIS REALLY IT?
I DON'T SEE ANY SIGNS OF A DEMON ATTACK...
...?
UM...

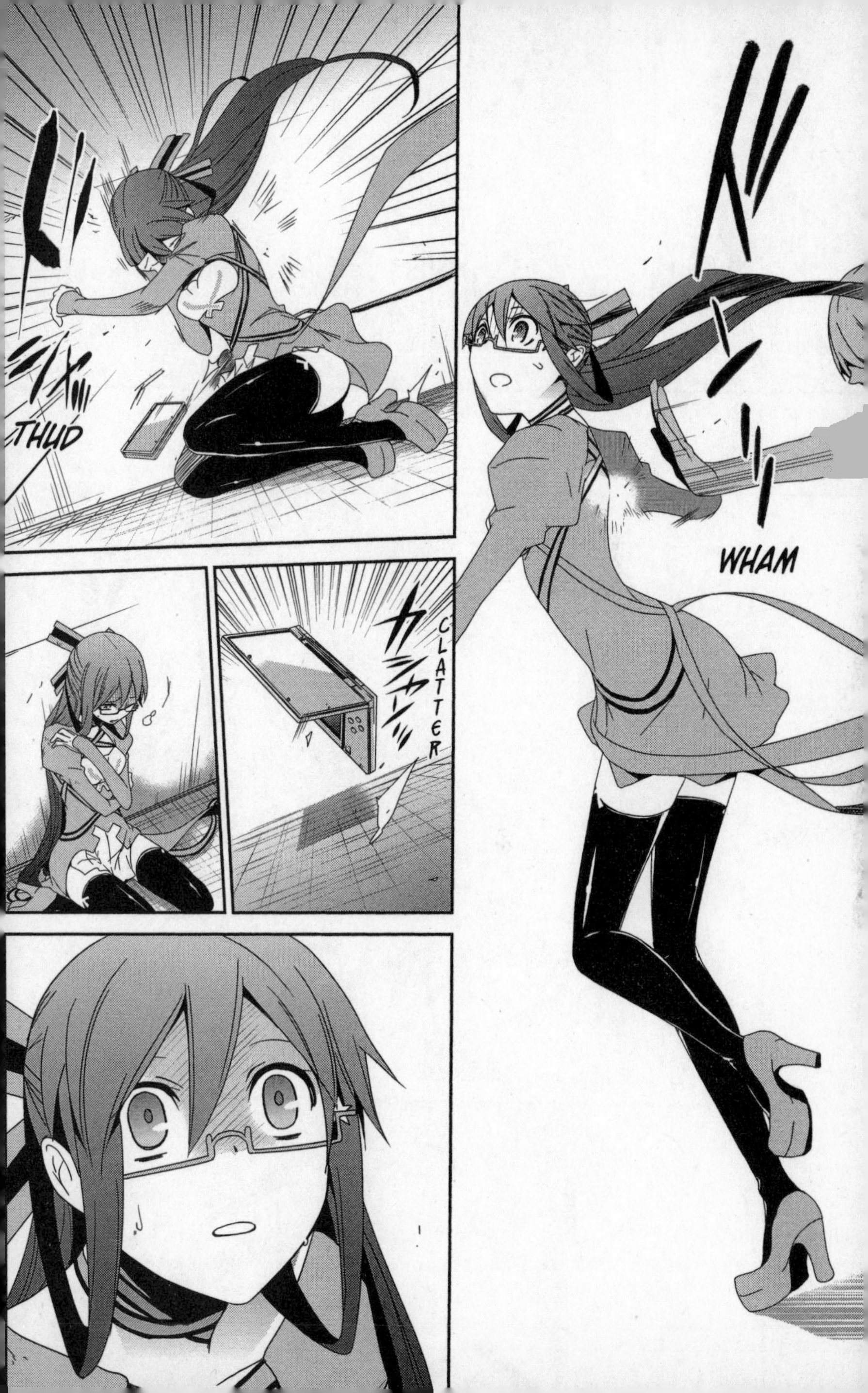
WHAM
THUD
CLATTER

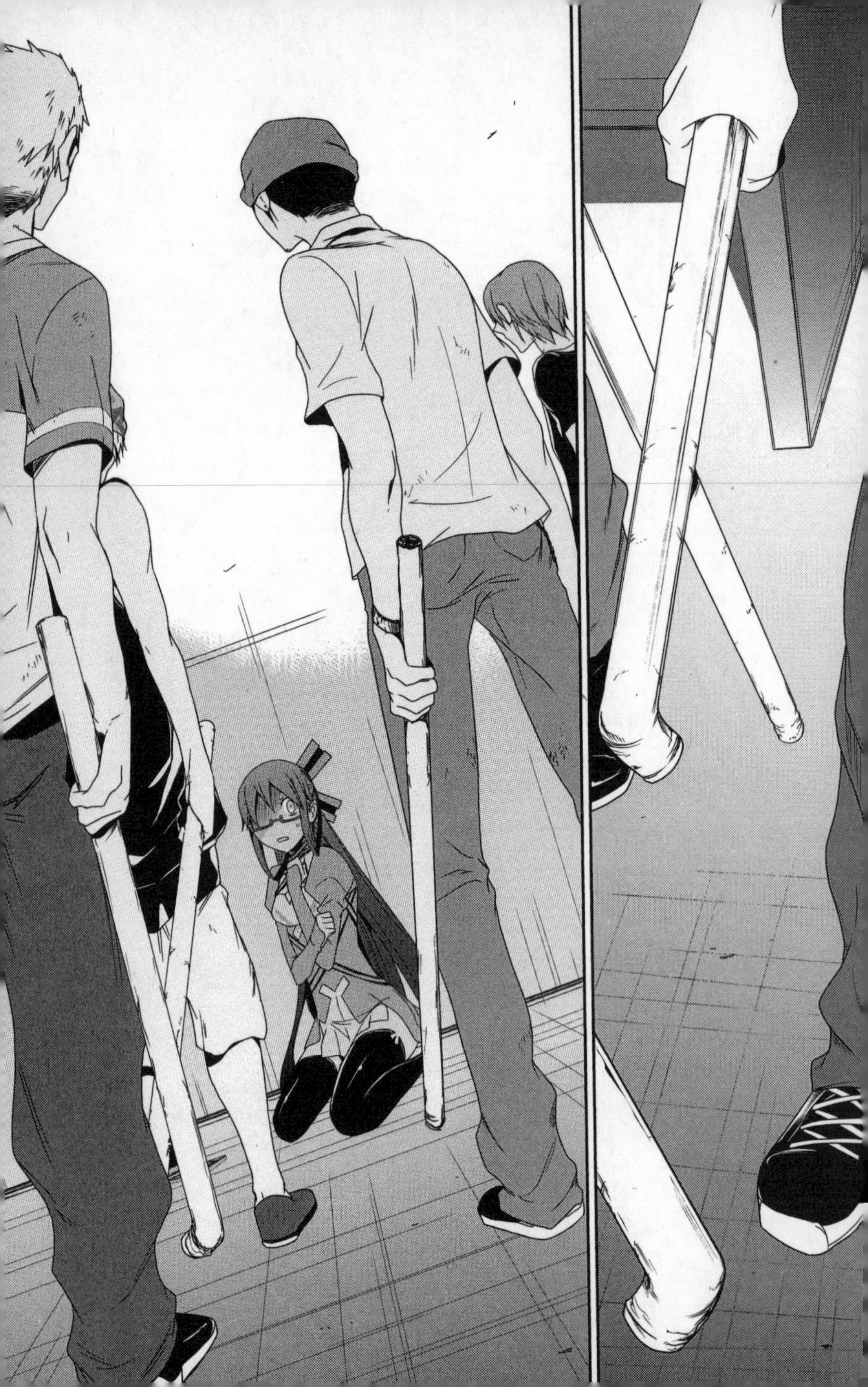

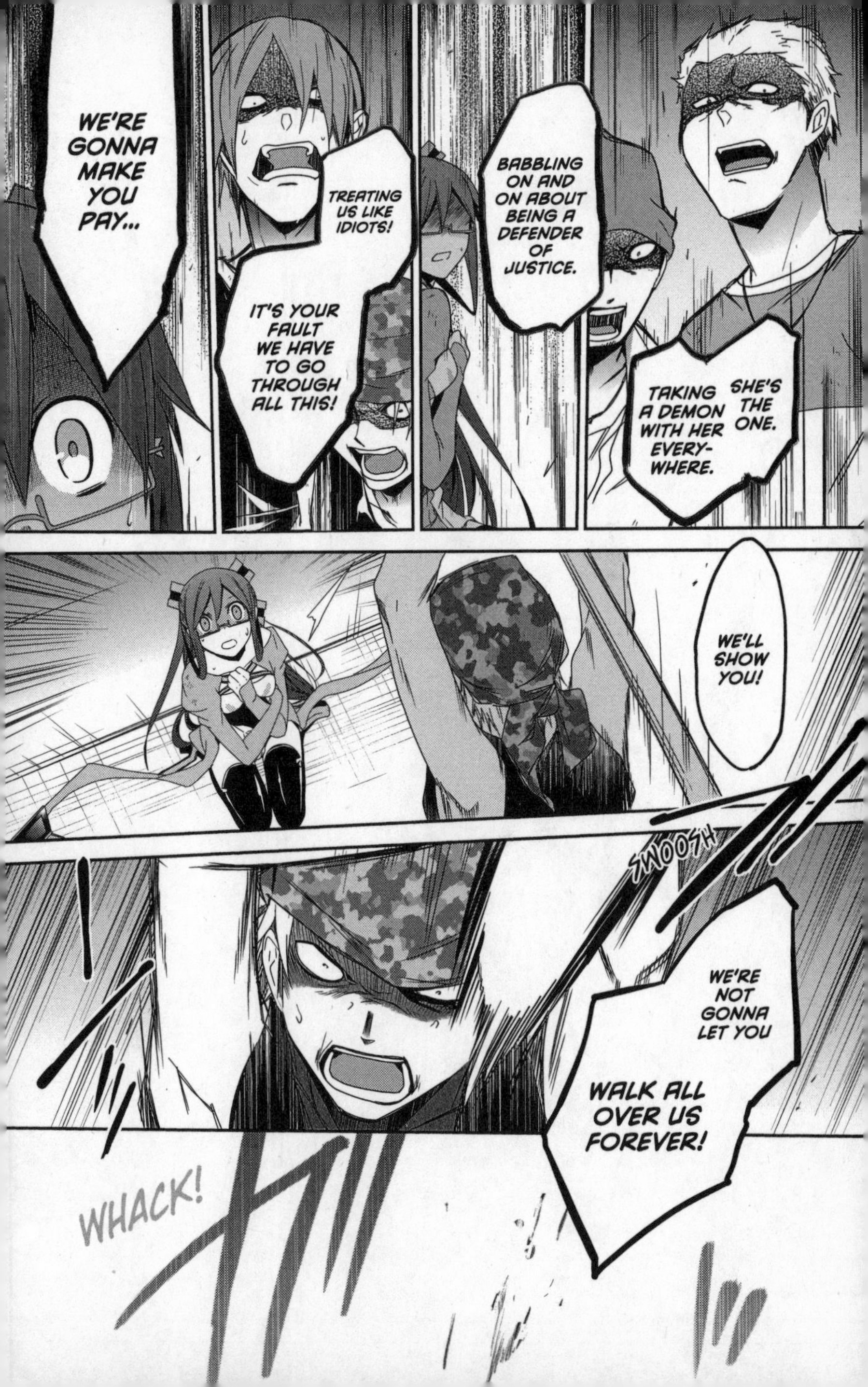
SHE'S THE ONE.
TAKING A DEMON WITH HER EVERY-WHERE.
BABBLING ON AND ON ABOUT BEING A DEFENDER OF JUSTICE.
TREATING US LIKE IDIOTS!
IT'S YOUR FAULT WE HAVE TO GO THROUGH ALL THIS!
WE'RE GONNA MAKE YOU PAY...
WE'LL SHOW YOU!
SWOOSH
WE'RE NOT GONNA LET YOU
WALK ALL OVER US FOREVER!
WHACK!

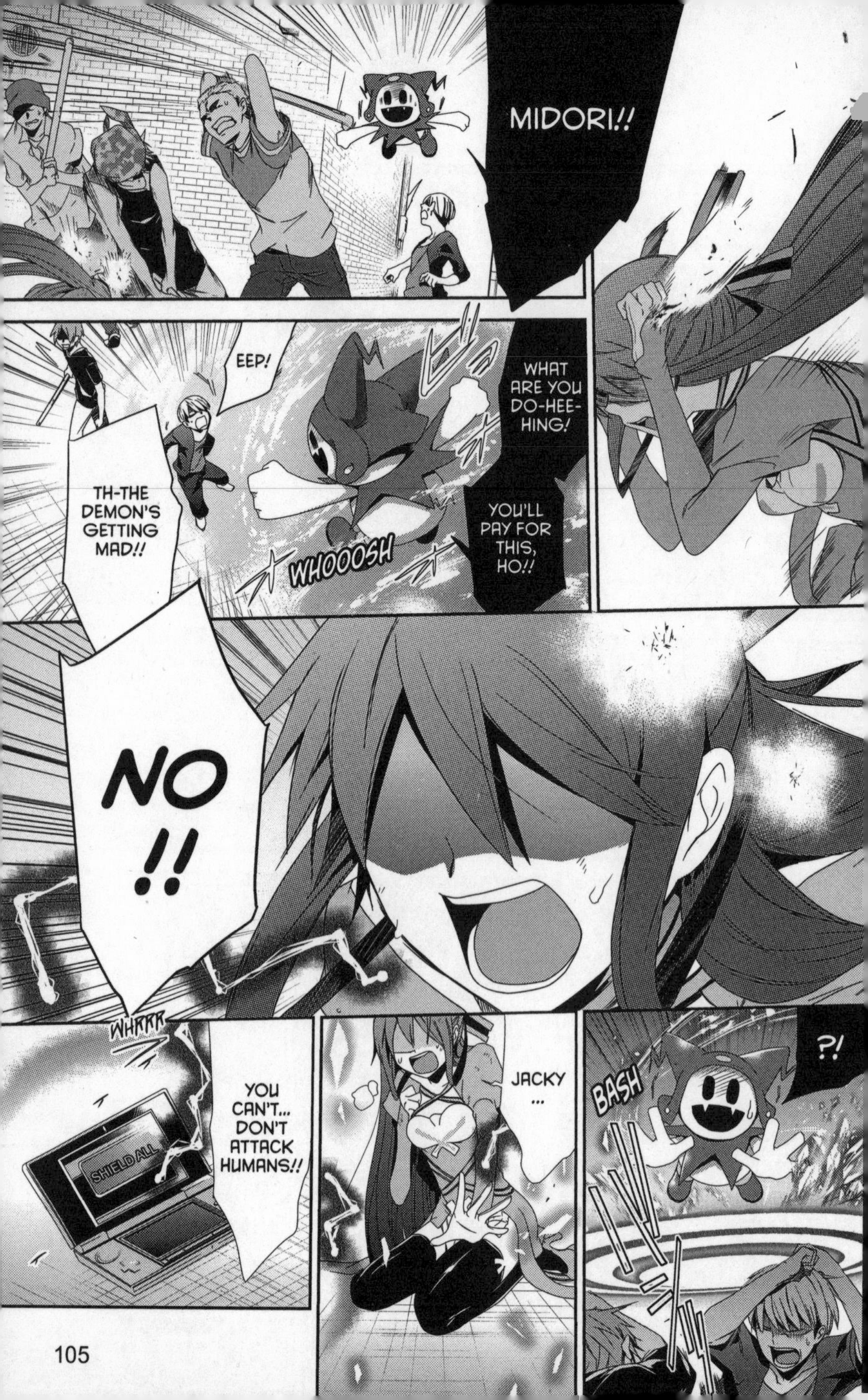
MIDORI!!
WHAT ARE YOU DO-HEE-HING!
EEP!
YOU'LL PAY FOR THIS, HO!!
WHOOOSH
TH-THE DEMON'S GETTING MAD!!
NO!!
?!
BASH
JACKY...
YOU CAN'T... DON'T ATTACK HUMANS!!
WHRRR
SHIELD ALL

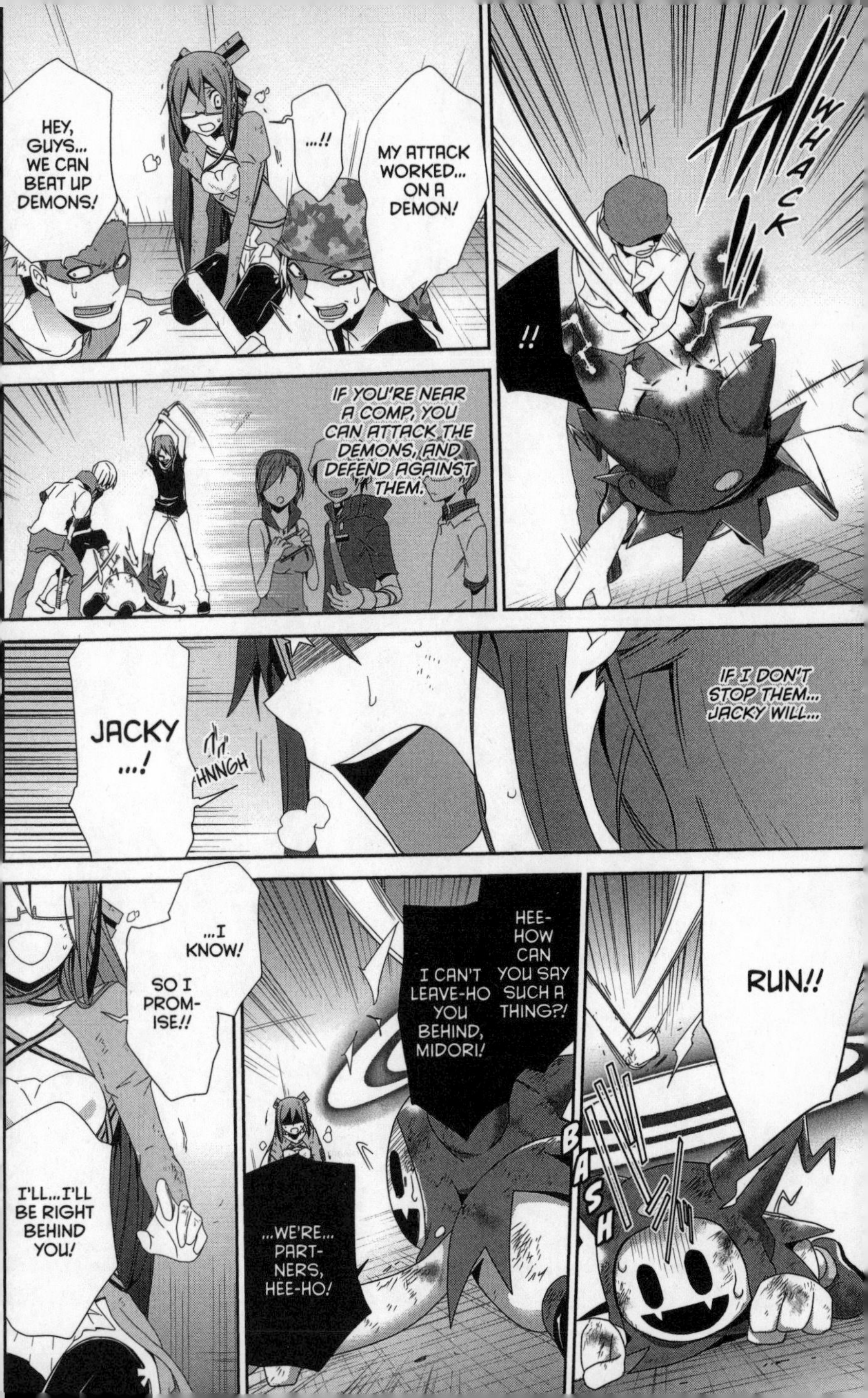
WHACK
!!
MY ATTACK WORKED... ON A DEMON!
...!!
HEY, GUYS... WE CAN BEAT UP DEMONS!
IF YOU'RE NEAR A COMP, YOU CAN ATTACK THE DEMONS, AND DEFEND AGAINST THEM.
IF I DON'T STOP THEM... JACKY WILL...
HNNGH
JACKY ...!
RUN!!
BASH
HEE-HOW CAN YOU SAY SUCH A THING?!
I CAN'T LEAVE-HO YOU BEHIND, MIDORI!
...WE'RE... PART-NERS, HEE-HO!
...I KNOW!
SO I PROM-ISE!!
I'LL...I'LL BE RIGHT BEHIND YOU!

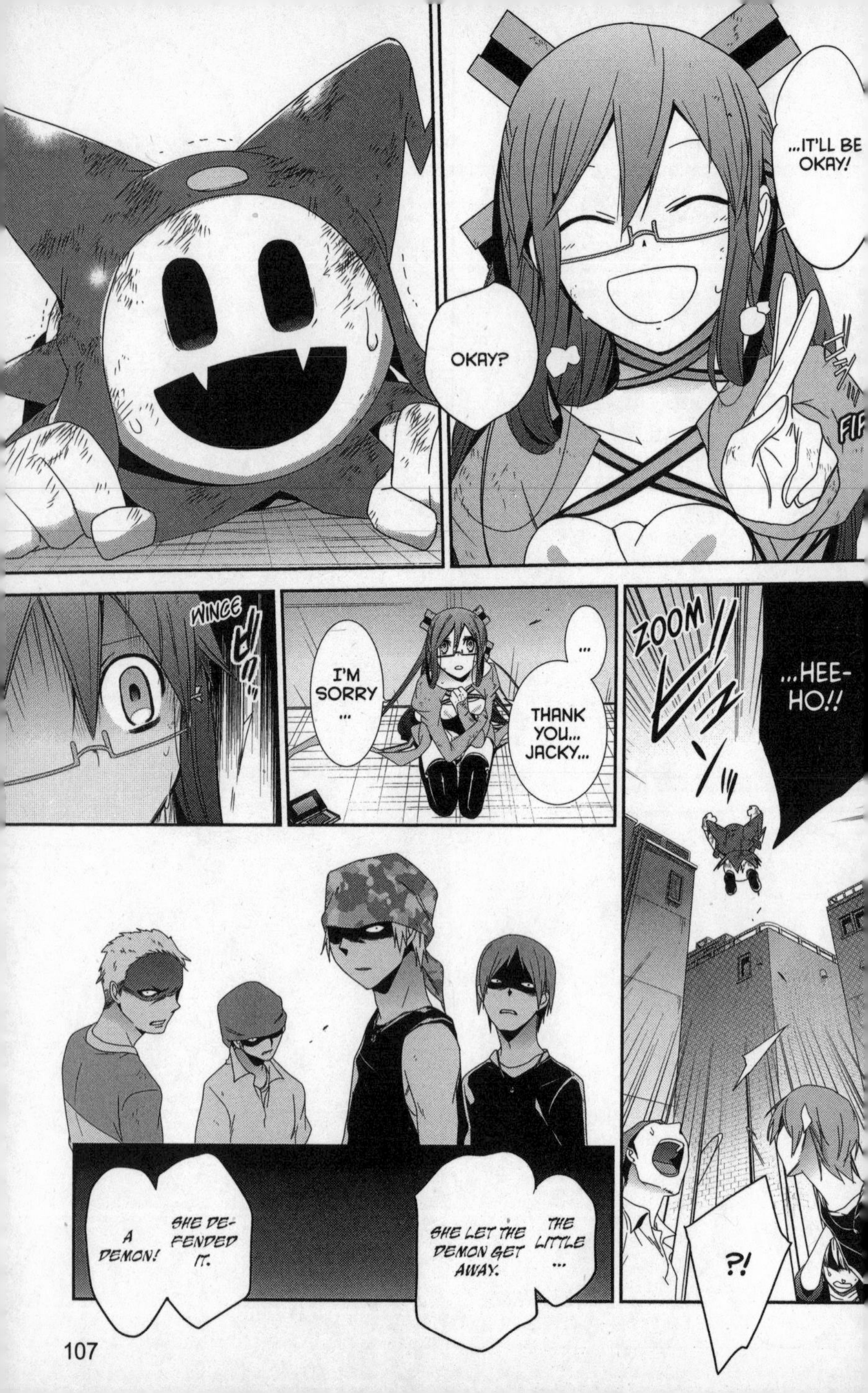
...IT'LL BE OKAY!
OKAY?
ZOOM
...HEE-HO!!
...
THANK YOU... JACKY...
I'M SORRY ...
WINCE
?!
THE LITTLE ...
SHE LET THE DEMON GET AWAY.
SHE DE-FENDED IT.
A DEMON!

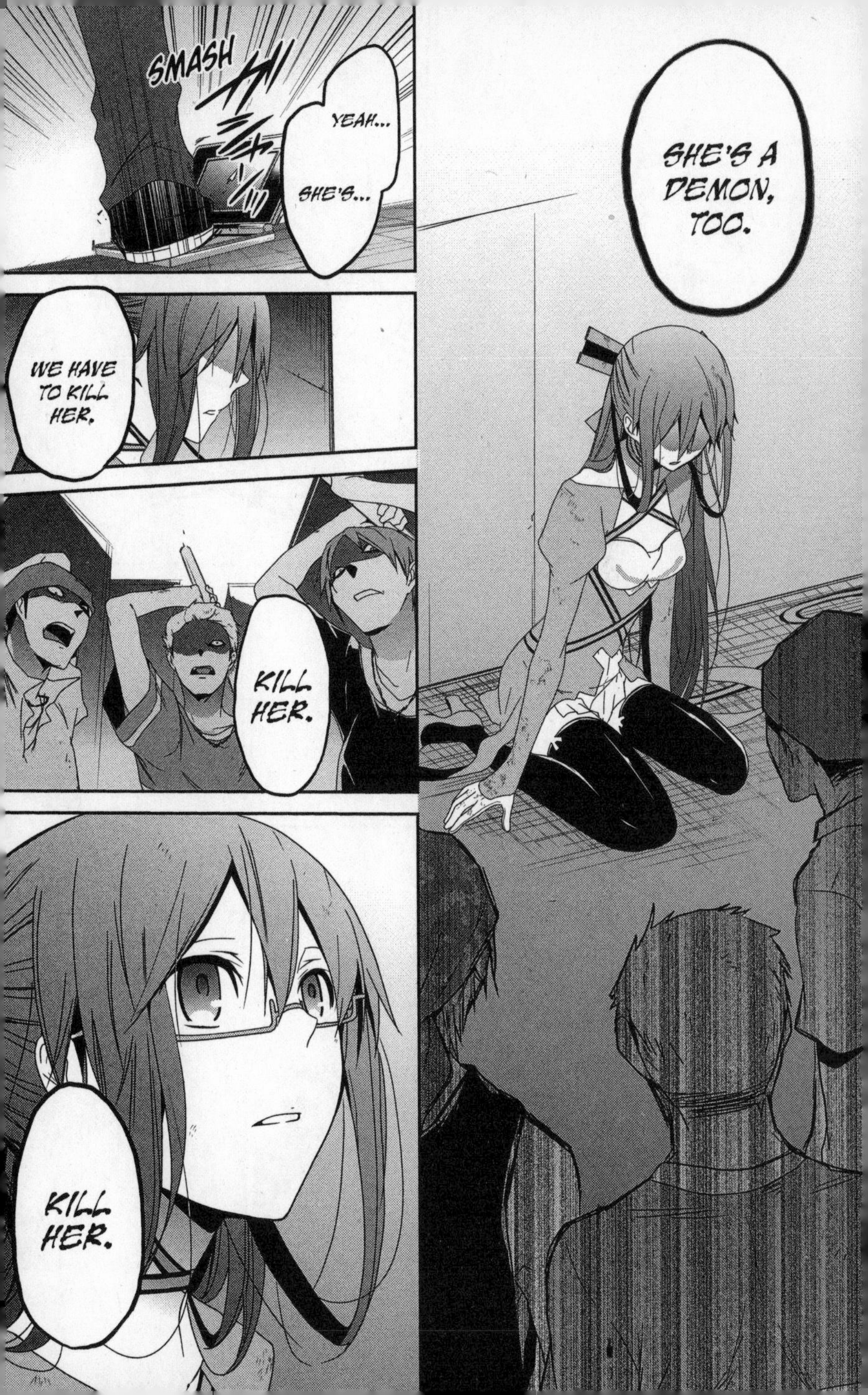
SHE'S A DEMON, TOO.
SMASH
YEAH...
SHE'S...
WE HAVE TO KILL HER.
KILL HER.
KILL HER.

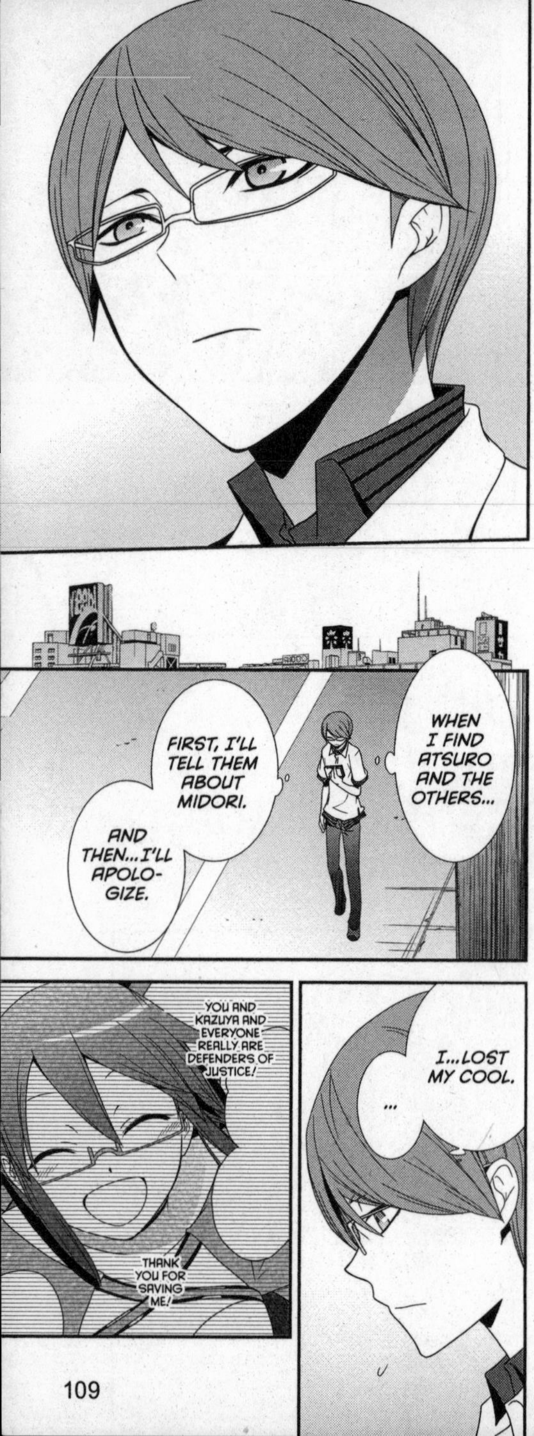
WHEN I FIND ATSURO AND THE OTHERS...
FIRST, I'LL TELL THEM ABOUT MIDORI.
AND THEN...I'LL APOLOGIZE.
I...LOST MY COOL.
...
YOU AND KAZUYA AND EVERYONE REALLY ARE DEFENDERS OF JUSTICE!
THANK YOU FOR SAVING ME!

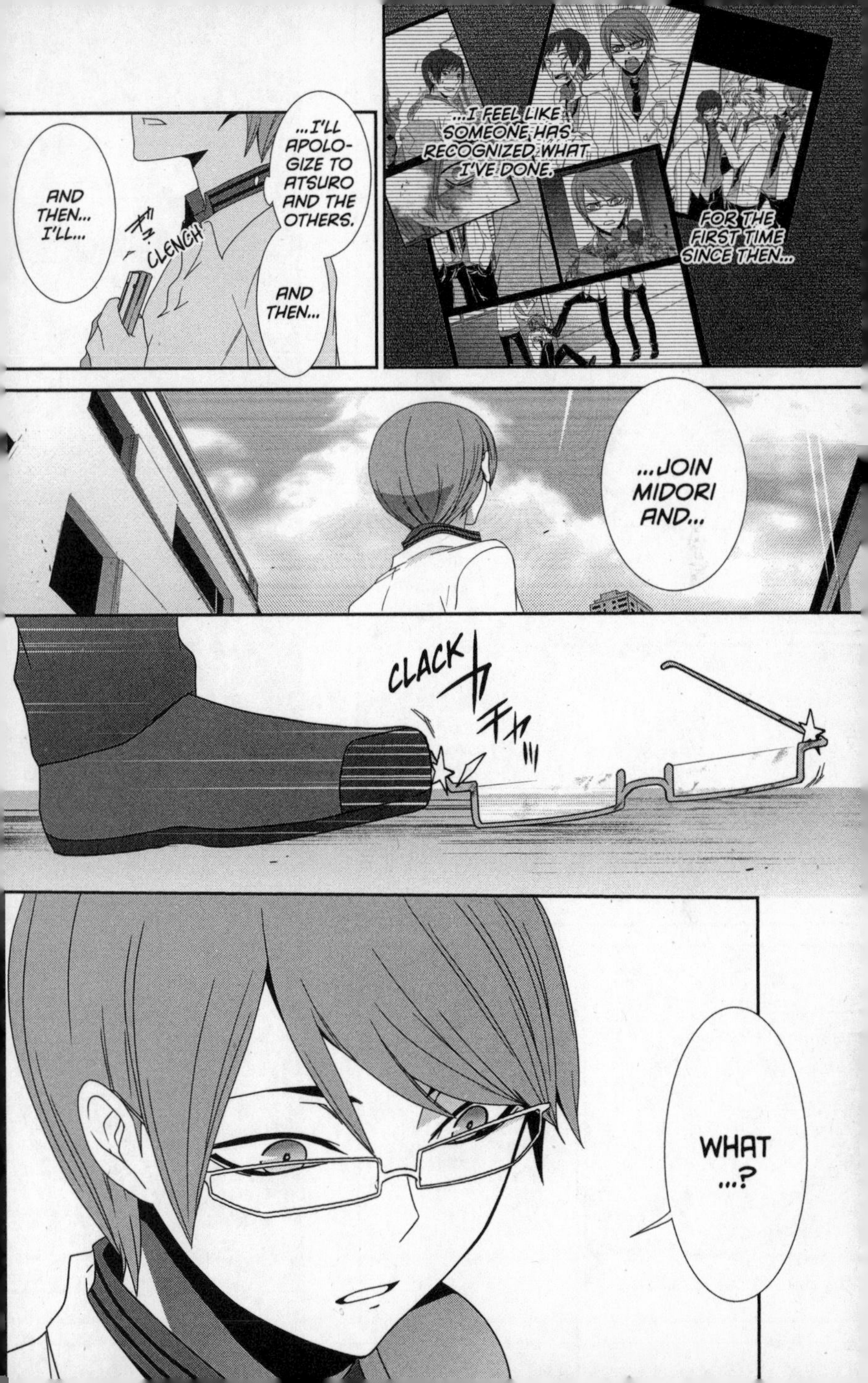

...I FEEL LIKE SOMEONE HAS RECOGNIZED WHAT I'VE DONE.
FOR THE FIRST TIME SINCE THEN...
...I'LL APOLOGIZE TO ATSURO AND THE OTHERS.
AND THEN...
CLENCH
AND THEN... I'LL...
...JOIN MIDORI AND...
CLACK
WHAT ...?

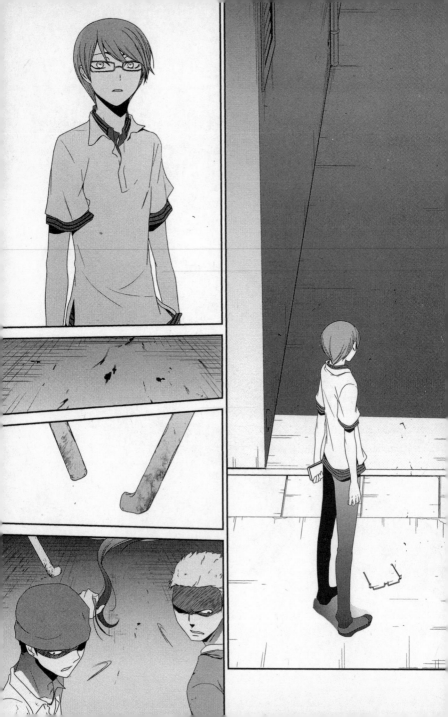

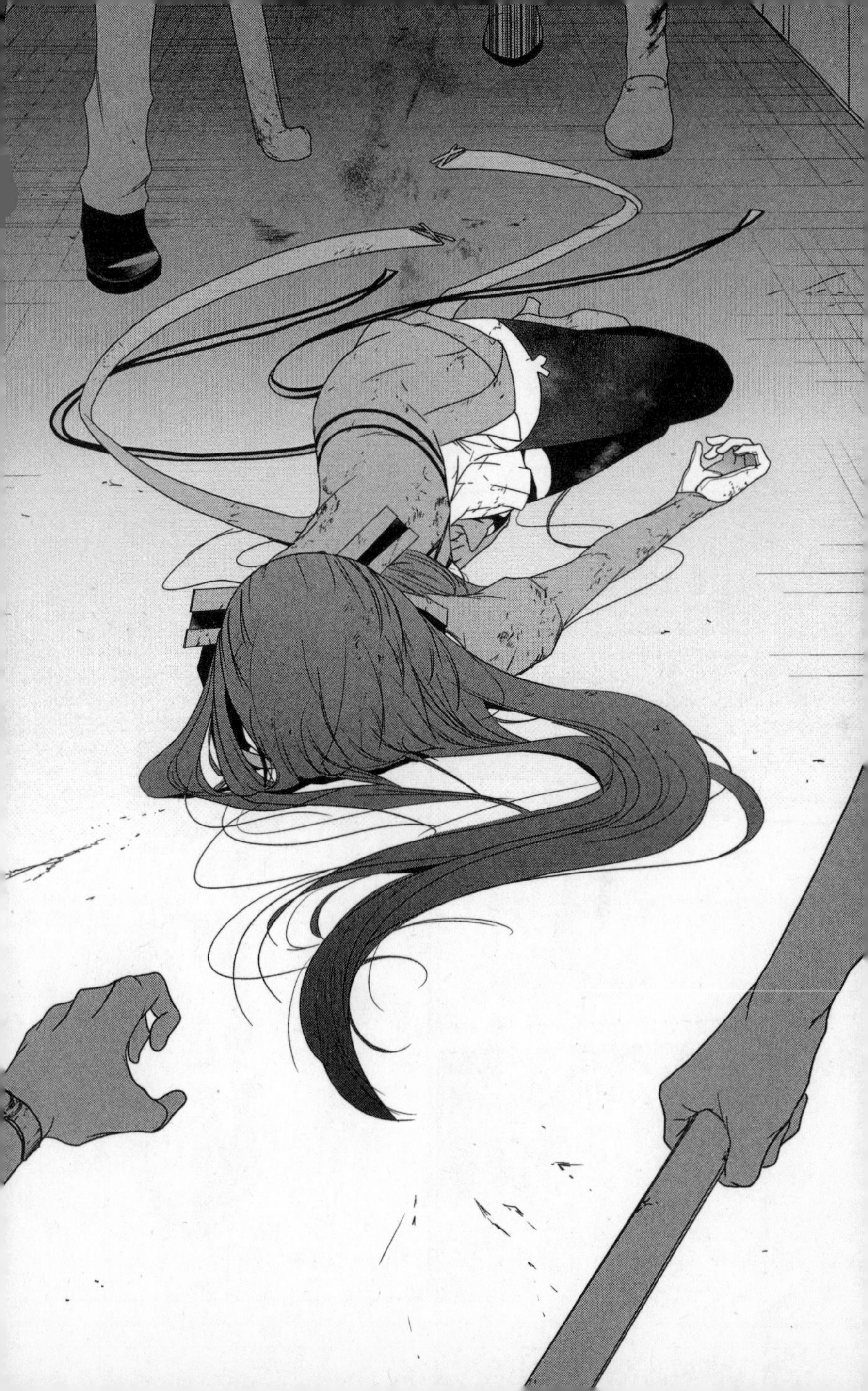

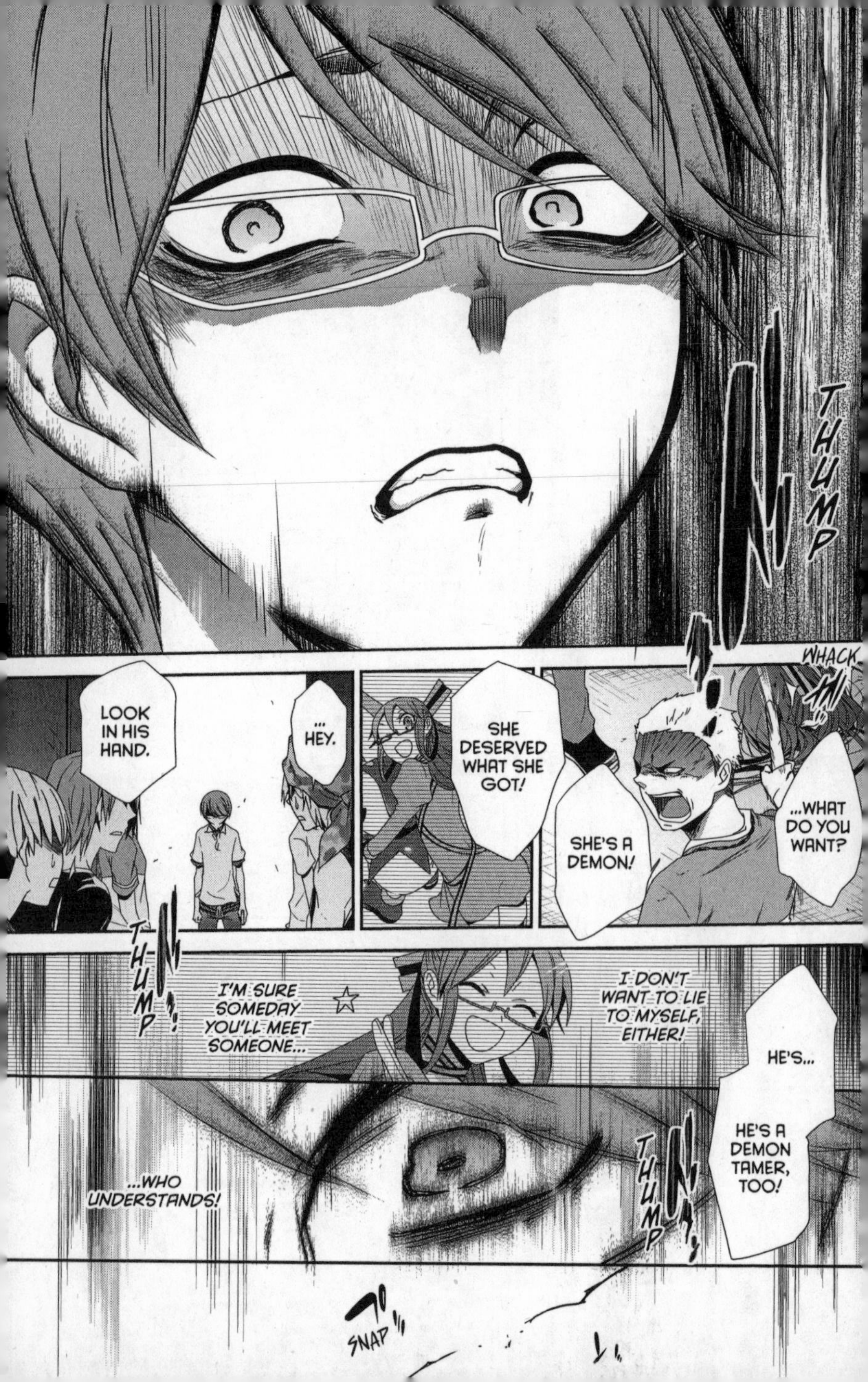
THUMP
WHACK
...WHAT DO YOU WANT?
SHE'S A DEMON!
SHE DESERVED WHAT SHE GOT!
...HEY.
LOOK IN HIS HAND.
THUMP
I DON'T WANT TO LIE TO MYSELF, EITHER!
I'M SURE SOMEDAY YOU'LL MEET SOMEONE...
HE'S...
HE'S A DEMON TAMER, TOO!
THUMP
...WHO UNDERSTANDS!
SNAP

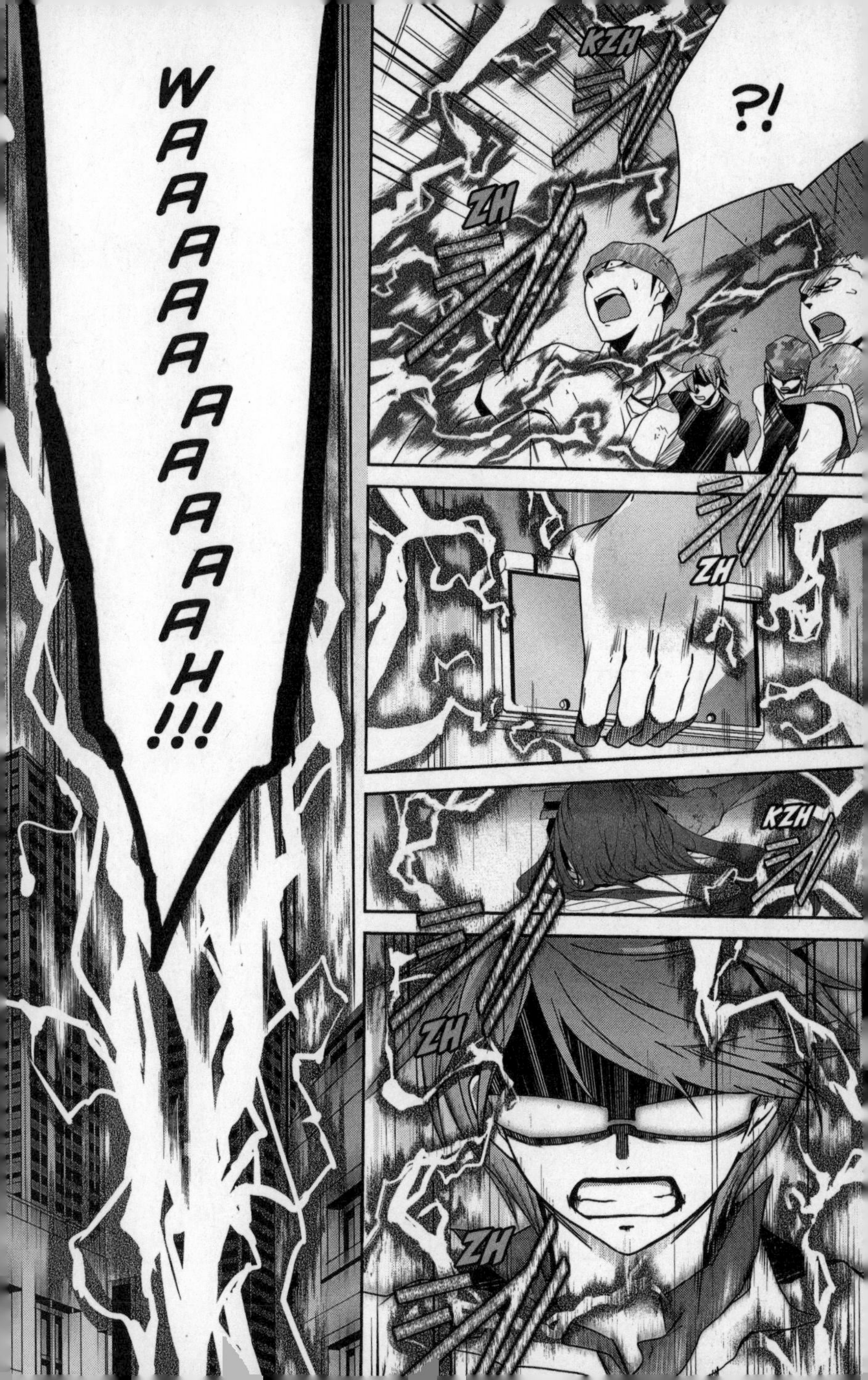
KZH
?!
ZH
ZH
KZH
ZH
ZH
WAAAAAAAAAAH!!!

DEVIL SURVIVOR

デビルサバイバー

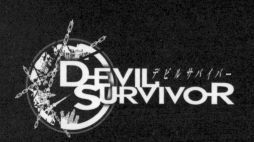

DEVIL SURVIVOR
デビルサバイバー

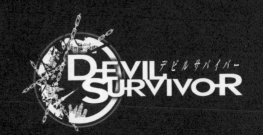

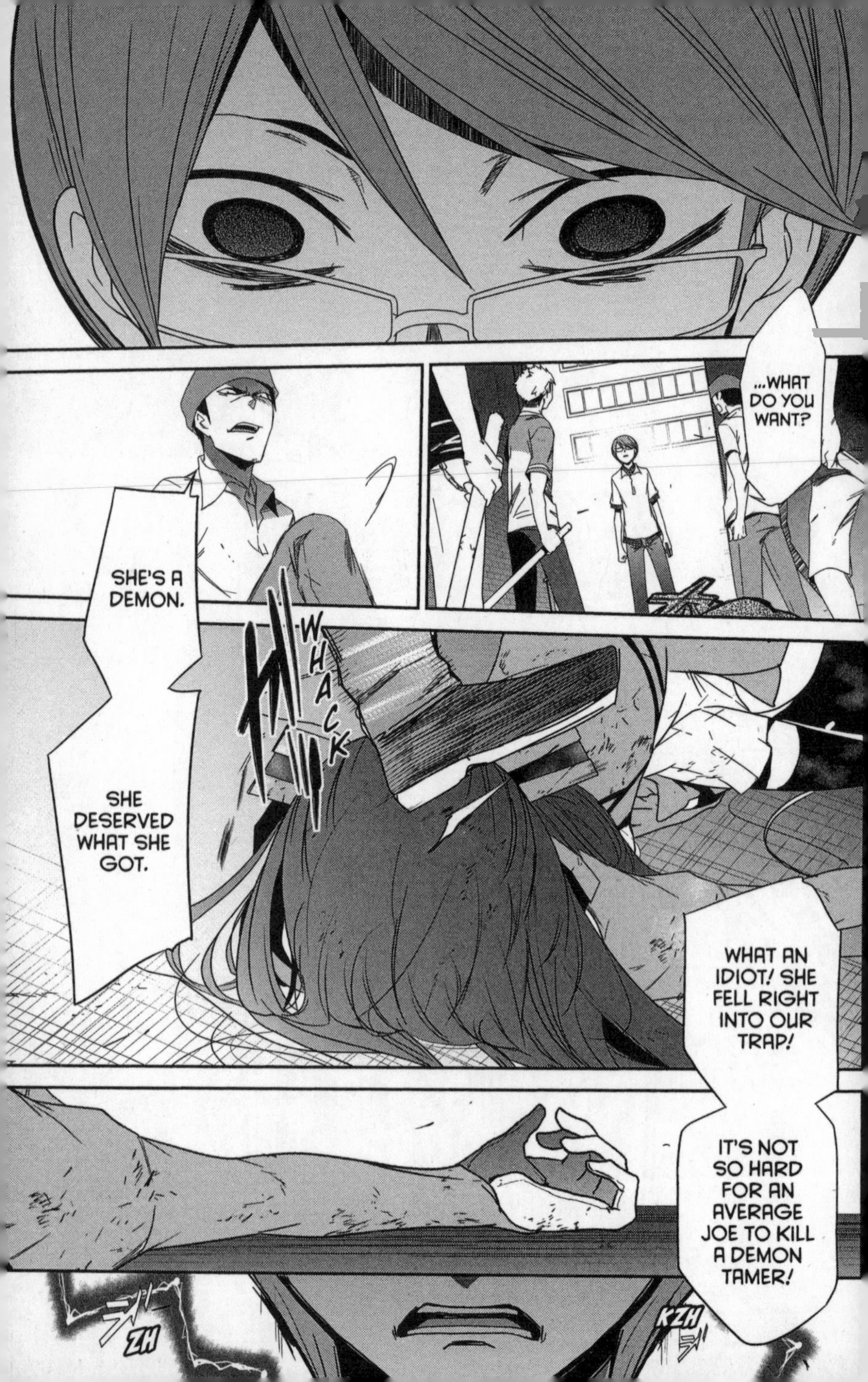
...WHAT DO YOU WANT?
SHE'S A DEMON.
WHACK
SHE DESERVED WHAT SHE GOT.
WHAT AN IDIOT! SHE FELL RIGHT INTO OUR TRAP!
IT'S NOT SO HARD FOR AN AVERAGE JOE TO KILL A DEMON TAMER!
KZH
ZH

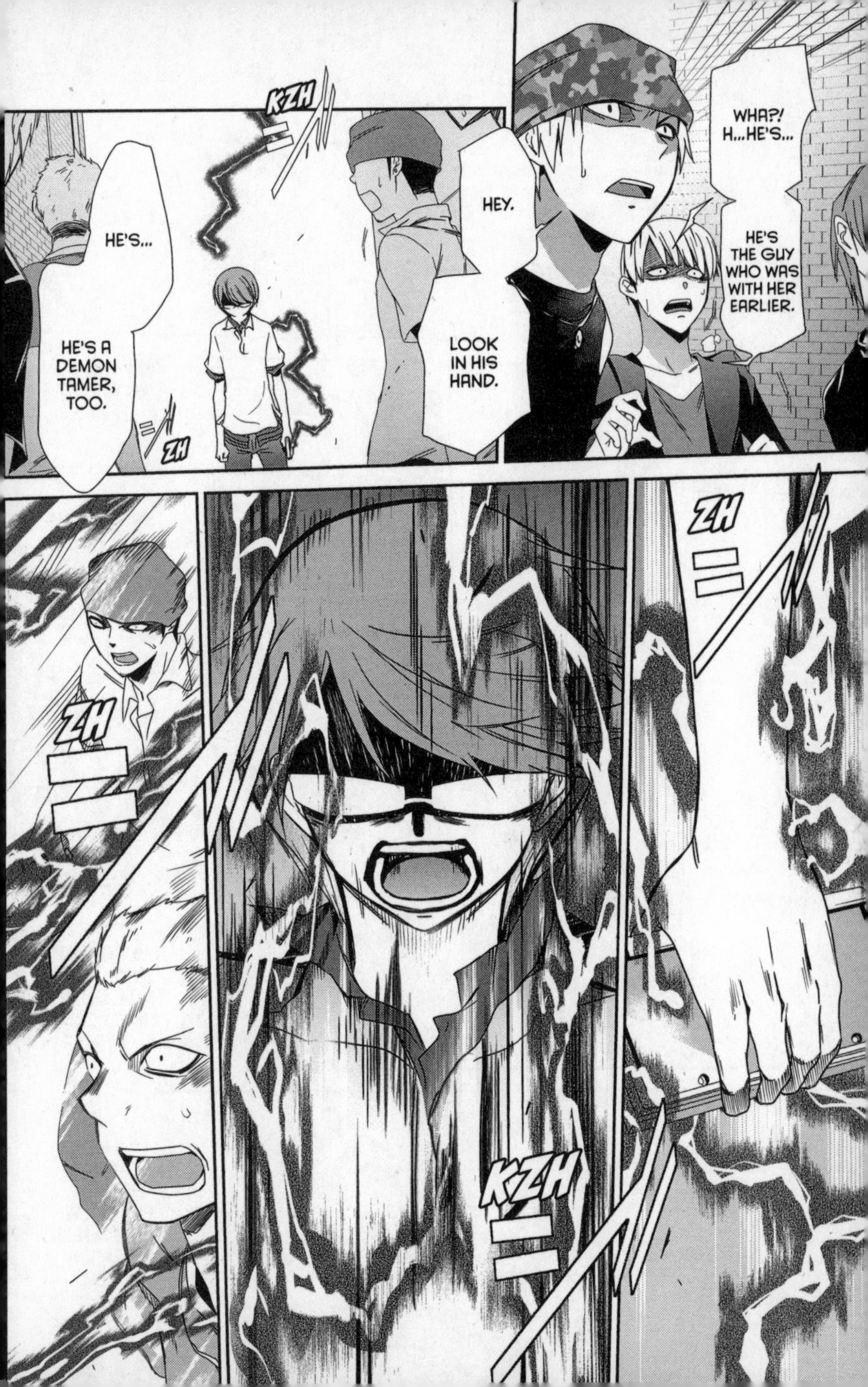
WHA?! H...HE'S...
HE'S THE GUY WHO WAS WITH HER EARLIER.
HEY.
LOOK IN HIS HAND.
KZH
HE'S...
HE'S A DEMON TAMER, TOO.
ZH
ZH
KZH
ZH

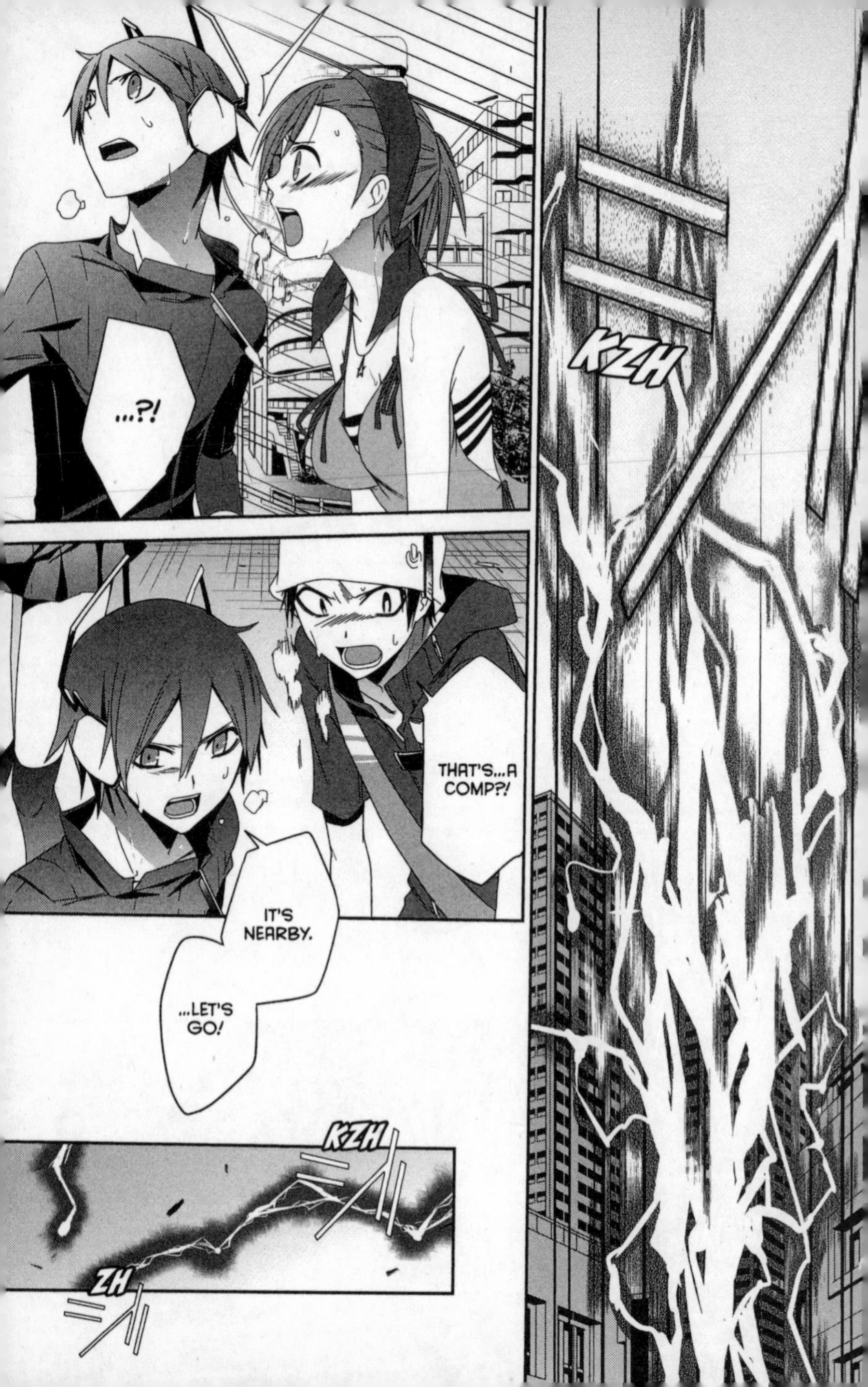
KZH
...?!
THAT'S...A COMP?!
IT'S NEARBY.
...LET'S GO!
KZH
ZH

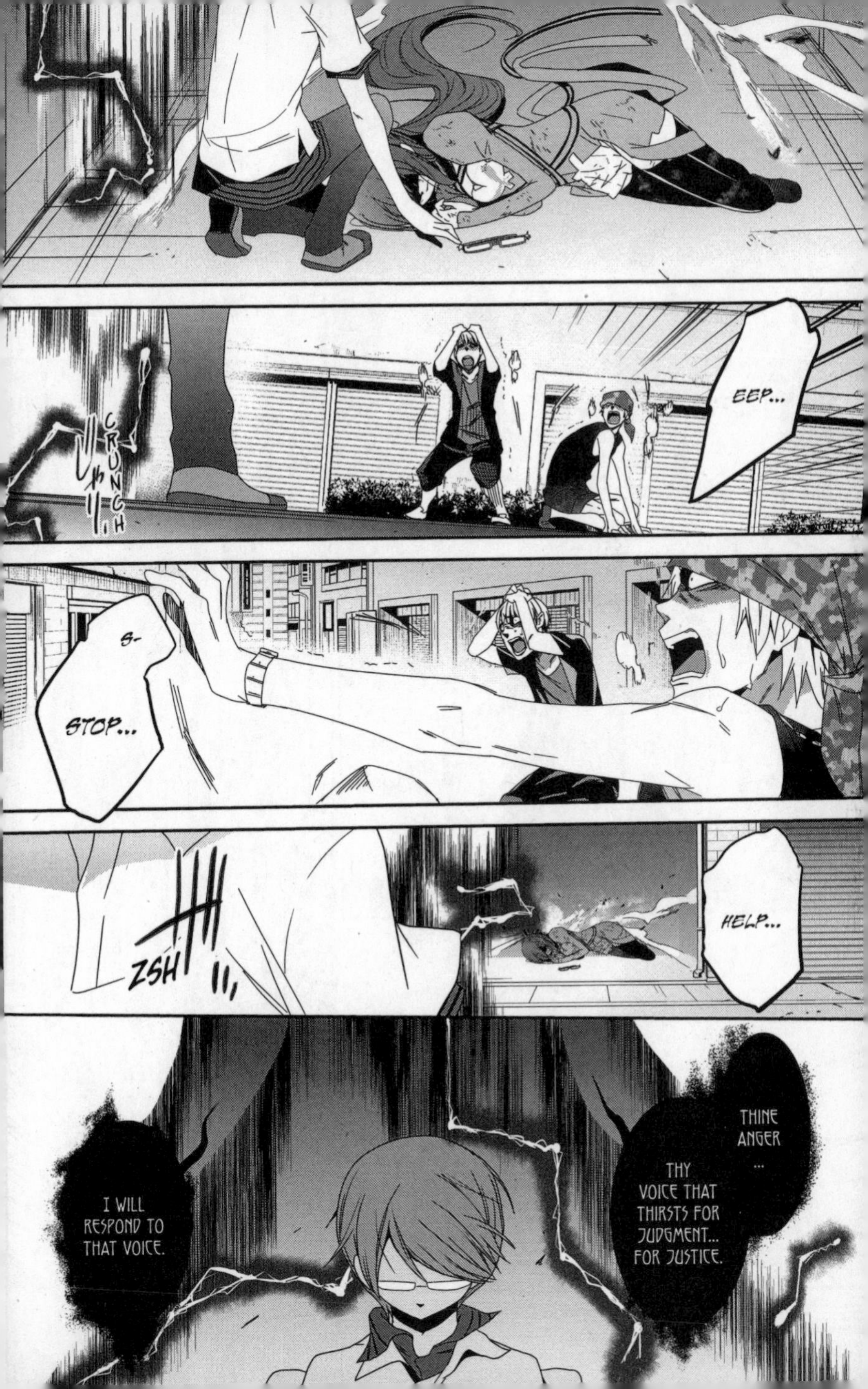
EEP...
CRUNCH
S-
STOP...
HELP...
ZSH
THINE ANGER...
THY VOICE THAT THIRSTS FOR JUDGMENT... FOR JUSTICE.
I WILL RESPOND TO THAT VOICE.

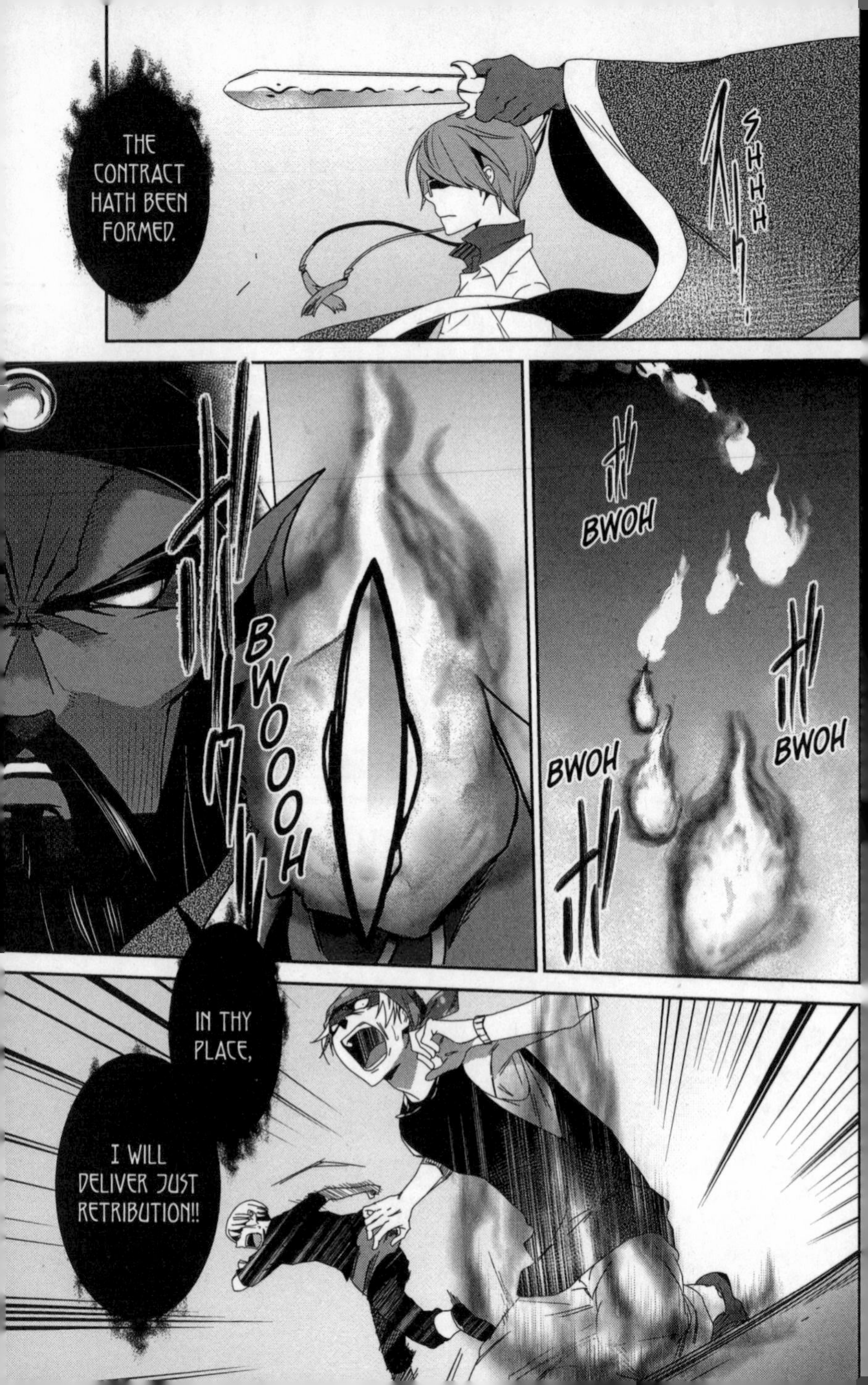
THE CONTRACT HATH BEEN FORMED.
SHHHH
BWOH
BWOH
BWOH
BWOOOOH
IN THY PLACE,
I WILL DELIVER JUST RETRIBUTION!!

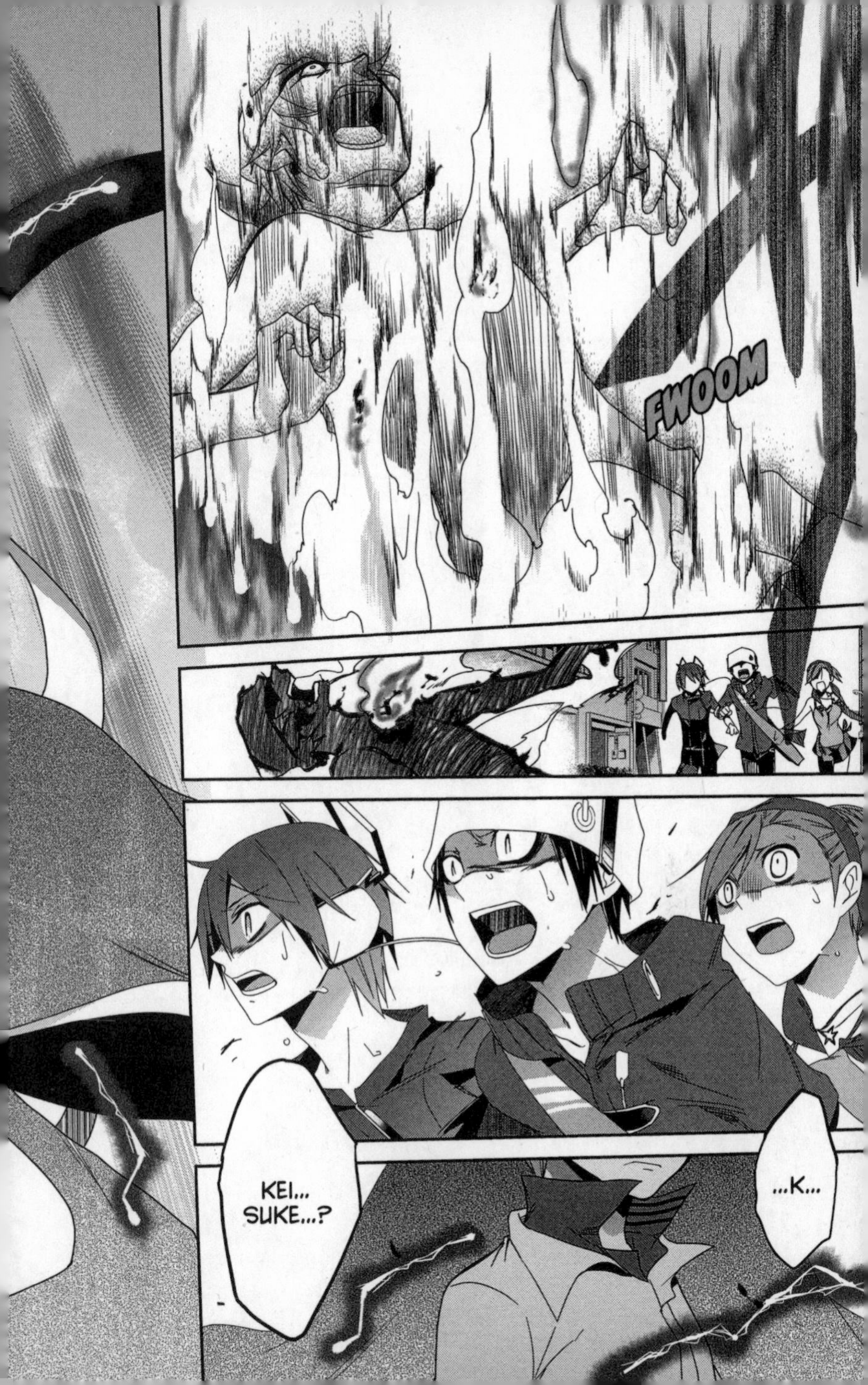
FWOOM
...K...
KEI... SUKE...?

SURVIVAL:19 COLD JUSTICE

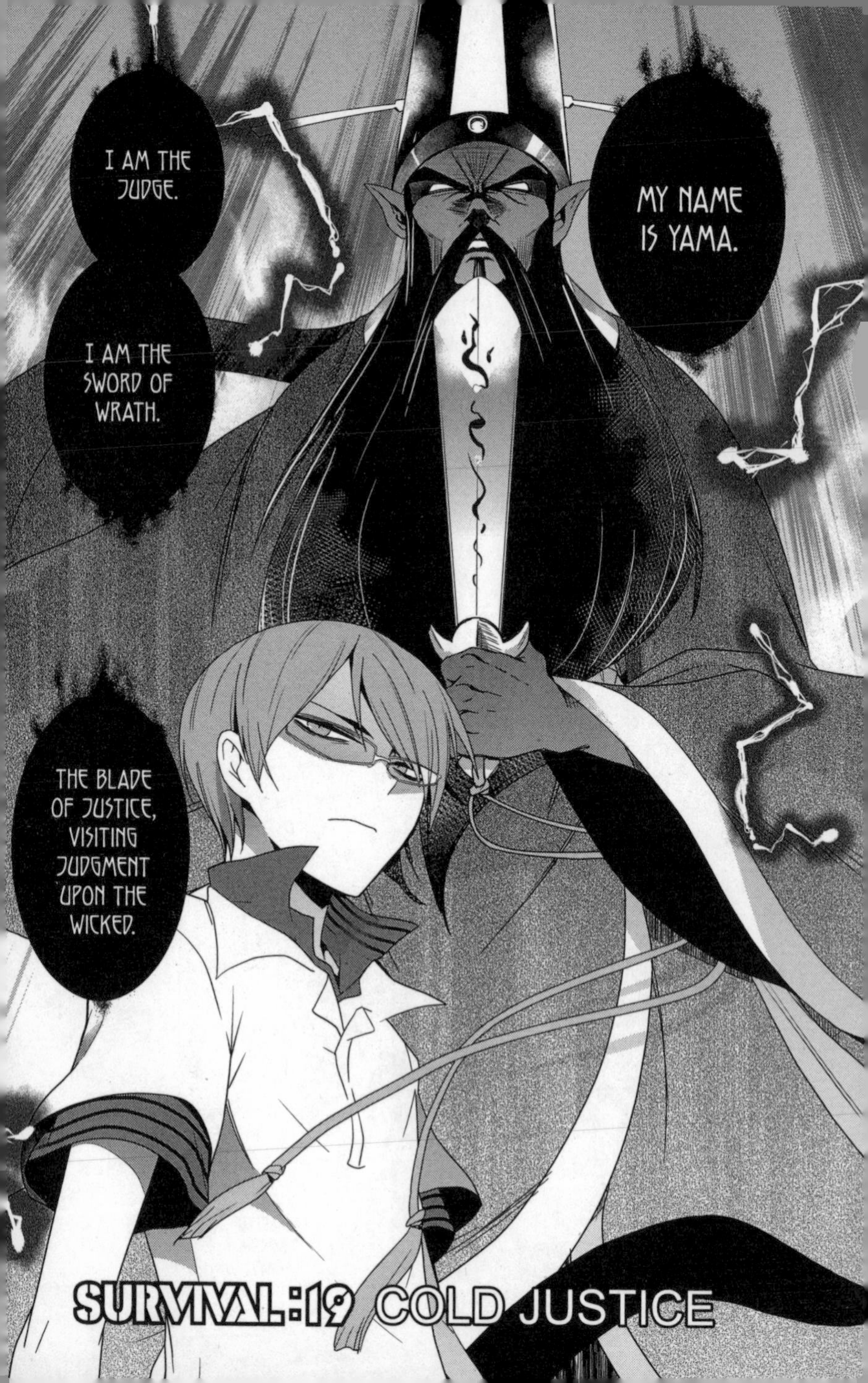
MY NAME IS YAMA.
I AM THE JUDGE.
I AM THE SWORD OF WRATH.
THE BLADE OF JUSTICE, VISITING JUDGMENT UPON THE WICKED.

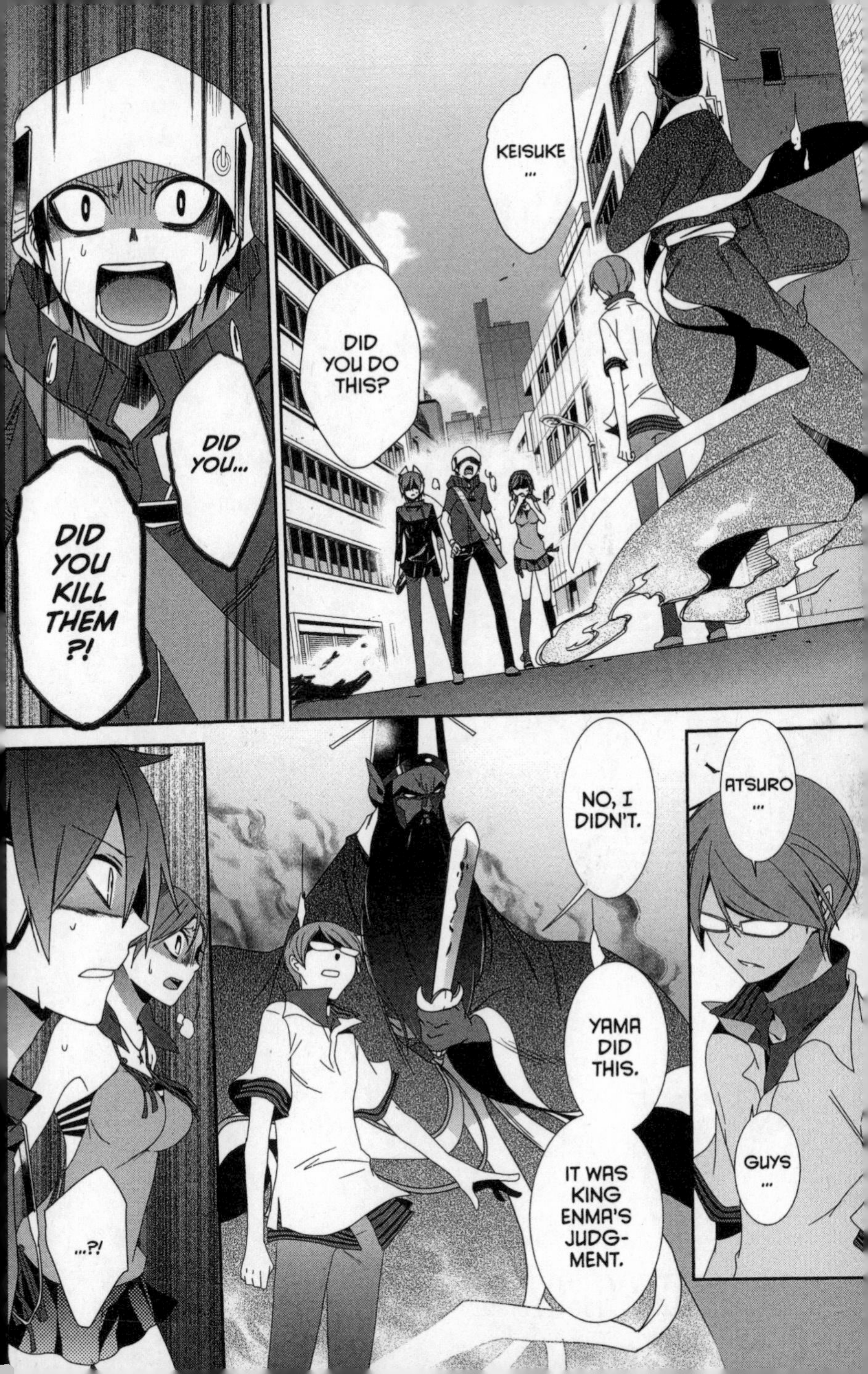
KEISUKE ...
DID YOU DO THIS?
DID YOU...
DID YOU KILL THEM ?!
ATSURO ...
GUYS ...
NO, I DIDN'T.
YAMA DID THIS.
IT WAS KING ENMA'S JUDG-MENT.
...?!

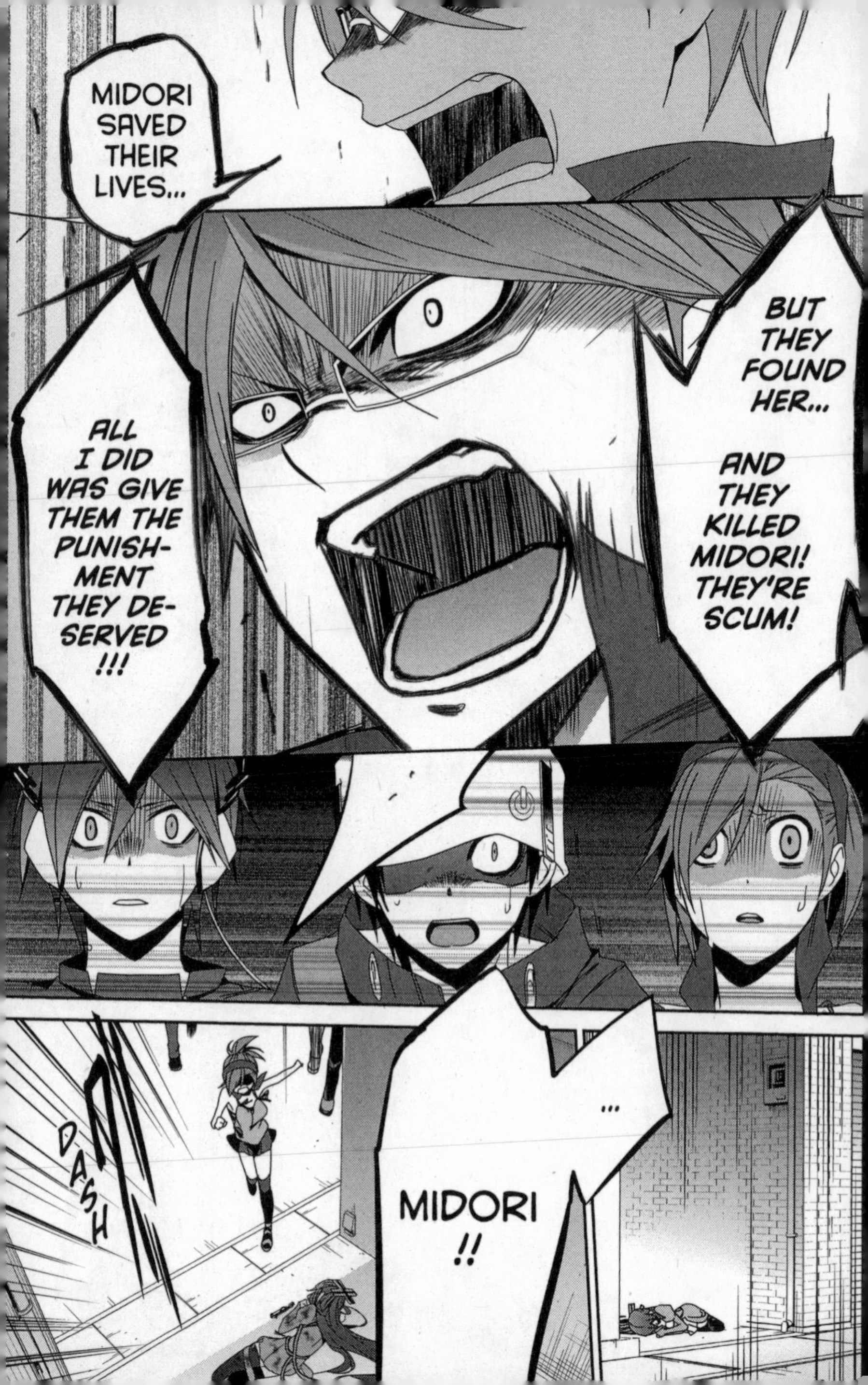
MIDORI SAVED THEIR LIVES...
BUT THEY FOUND HER...
AND THEY KILLED MIDORI! THEY'RE SCUM!
ALL I DID WAS GIVE THEM THE PUNISHMENT THEY DESERVED!!!
...
MIDORI !!
DASH

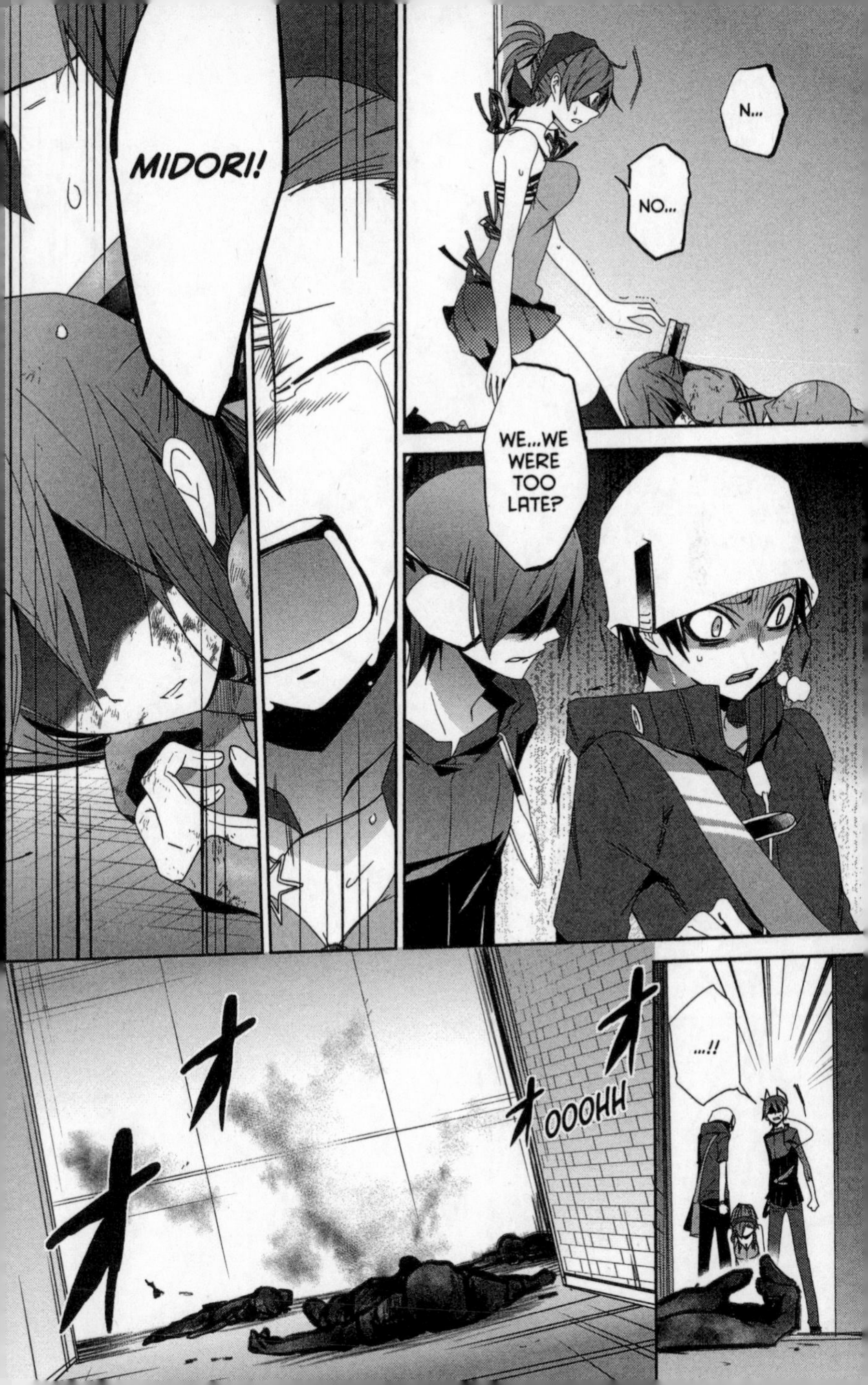
N...
NO...
WE...WE WERE TOO LATE?
MIDORI!
...!!
OOOHH

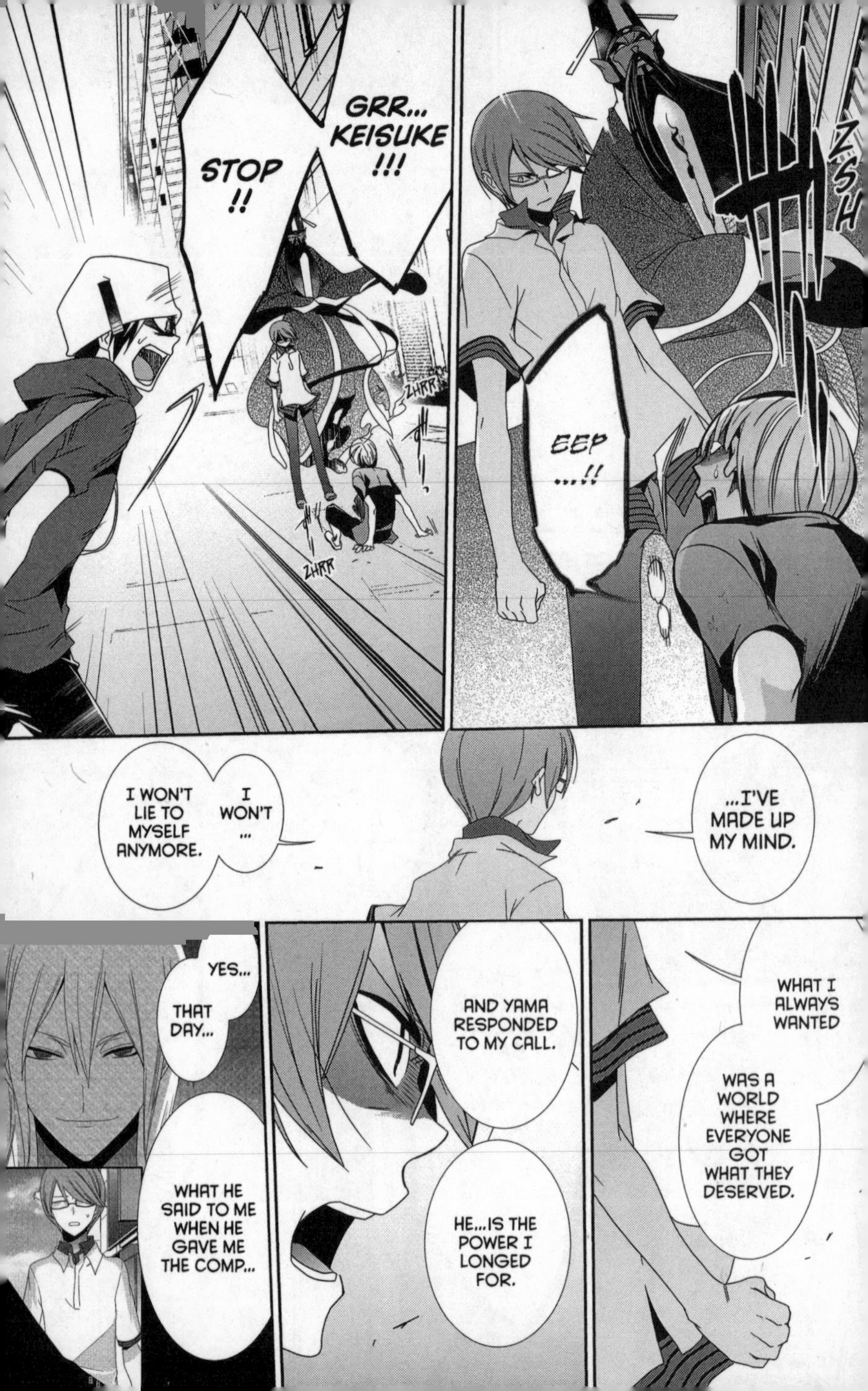
ZSH
EEP ...!!
GRR... KEISUKE !!!
STOP !!
ZHRR
ZHRR
...I'VE MADE UP MY MIND.
I WON'T ...
I WON'T LIE TO MYSELF ANYMORE.
WHAT I ALWAYS WANTED
WAS A WORLD WHERE EVERYONE GOT WHAT THEY DESERVED.
AND YAMA RESPONDED TO MY CALL.
HE...IS THE POWER I LONGED FOR.
YES...
THAT DAY...
WHAT HE SAID TO ME WHEN HE GAVE ME THE COMP...

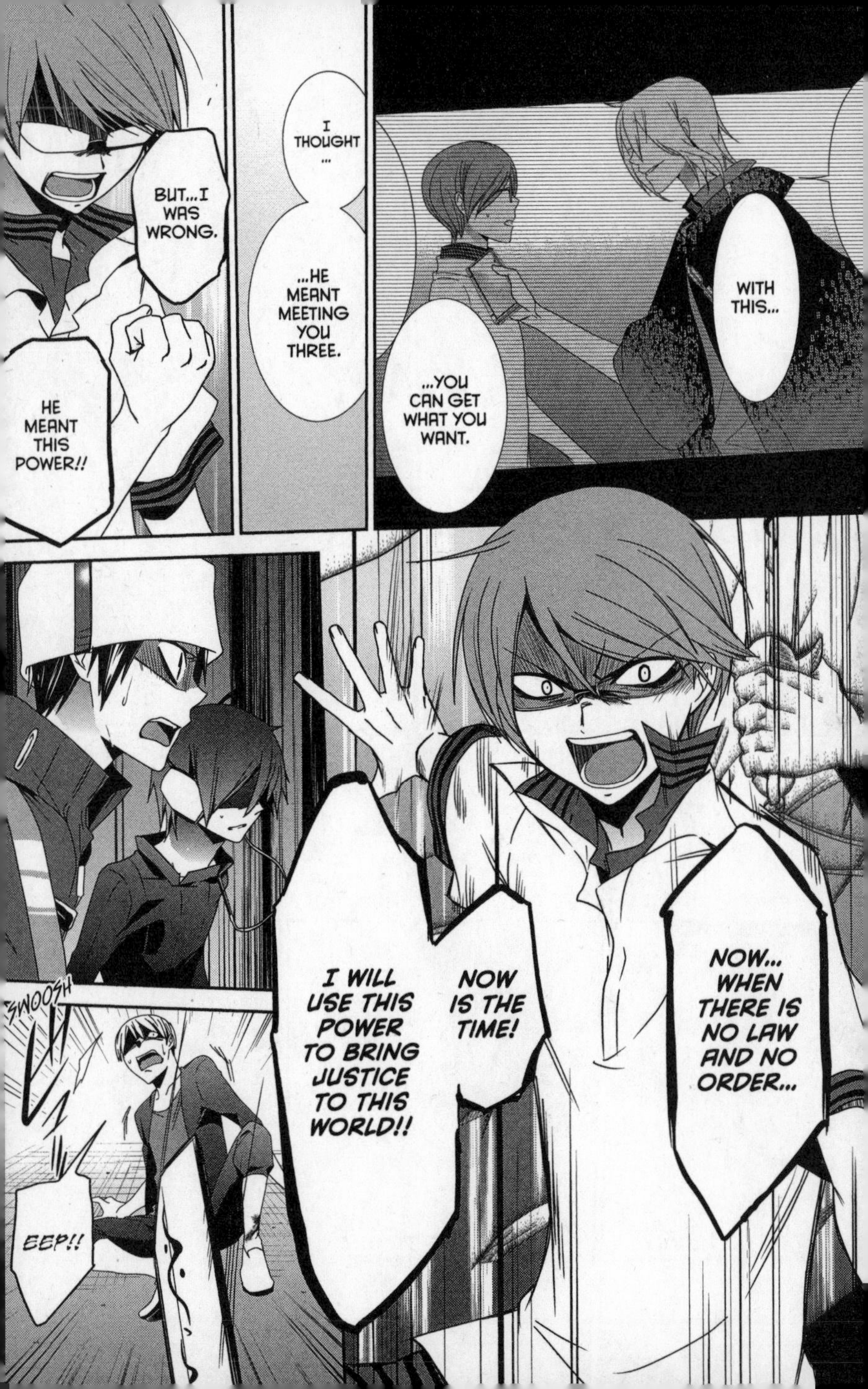
WITH THIS...
...YOU CAN GET WHAT YOU WANT.
I THOUGHT ...
...HE MEANT MEETING YOU THREE.
BUT...I WAS WRONG.
HE MEANT THIS POWER!!
NOW... WHEN THERE IS NO LAW AND NO ORDER...
NOW IS THE TIME!
I WILL USE THIS POWER TO BRING JUSTICE TO THIS WORLD!!
SWOOSH
EEP!!

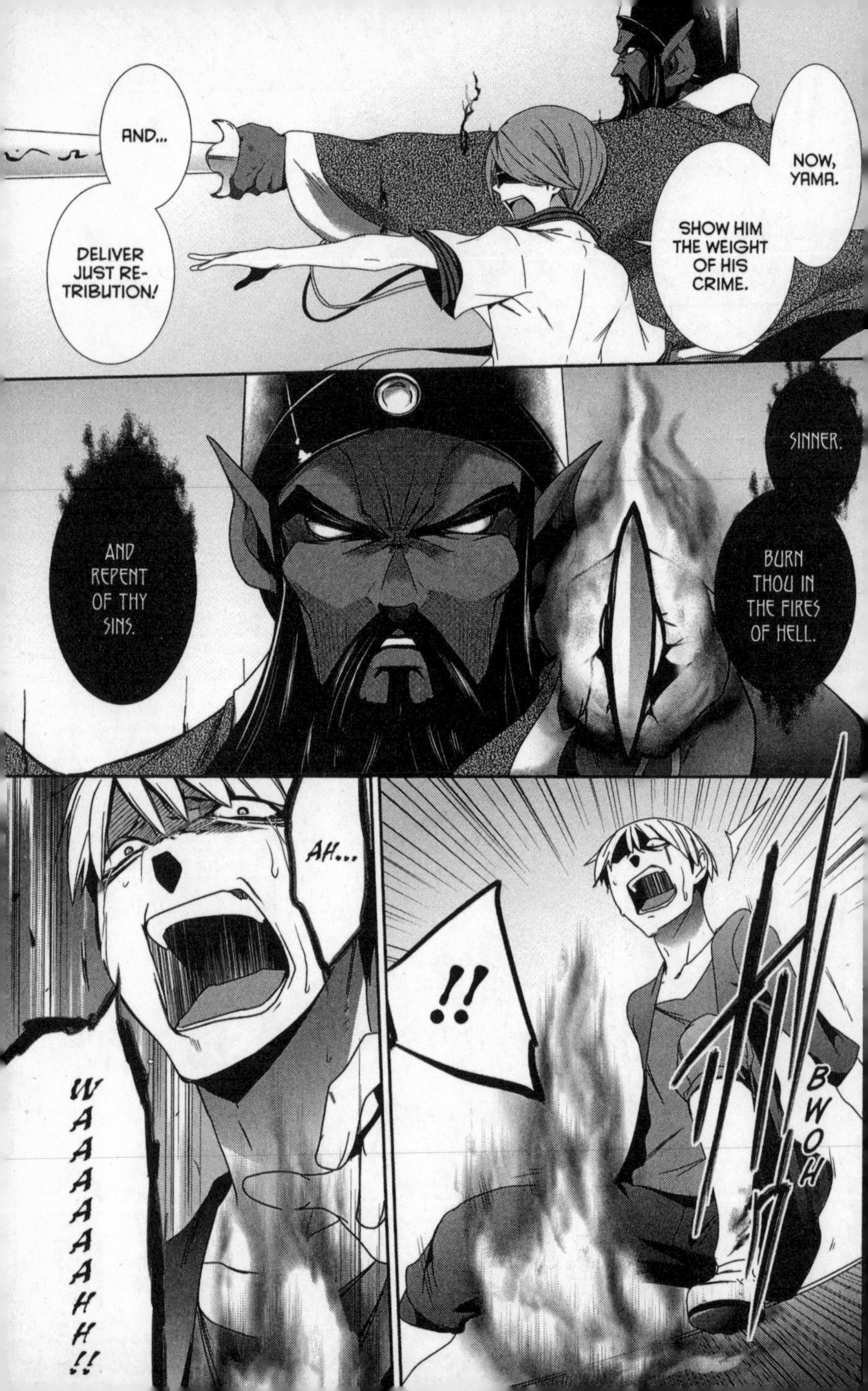
NOW, YAMA.
SHOW HIM THE WEIGHT OF HIS CRIME.
AND...
DELIVER JUST RE-TRIBUTION!
SINNER.
BURN THOU IN THE FIRES OF HELL.
AND REPENT OF THY SINS.
!!
BWOH
AH...
WAAAAAAHH!!

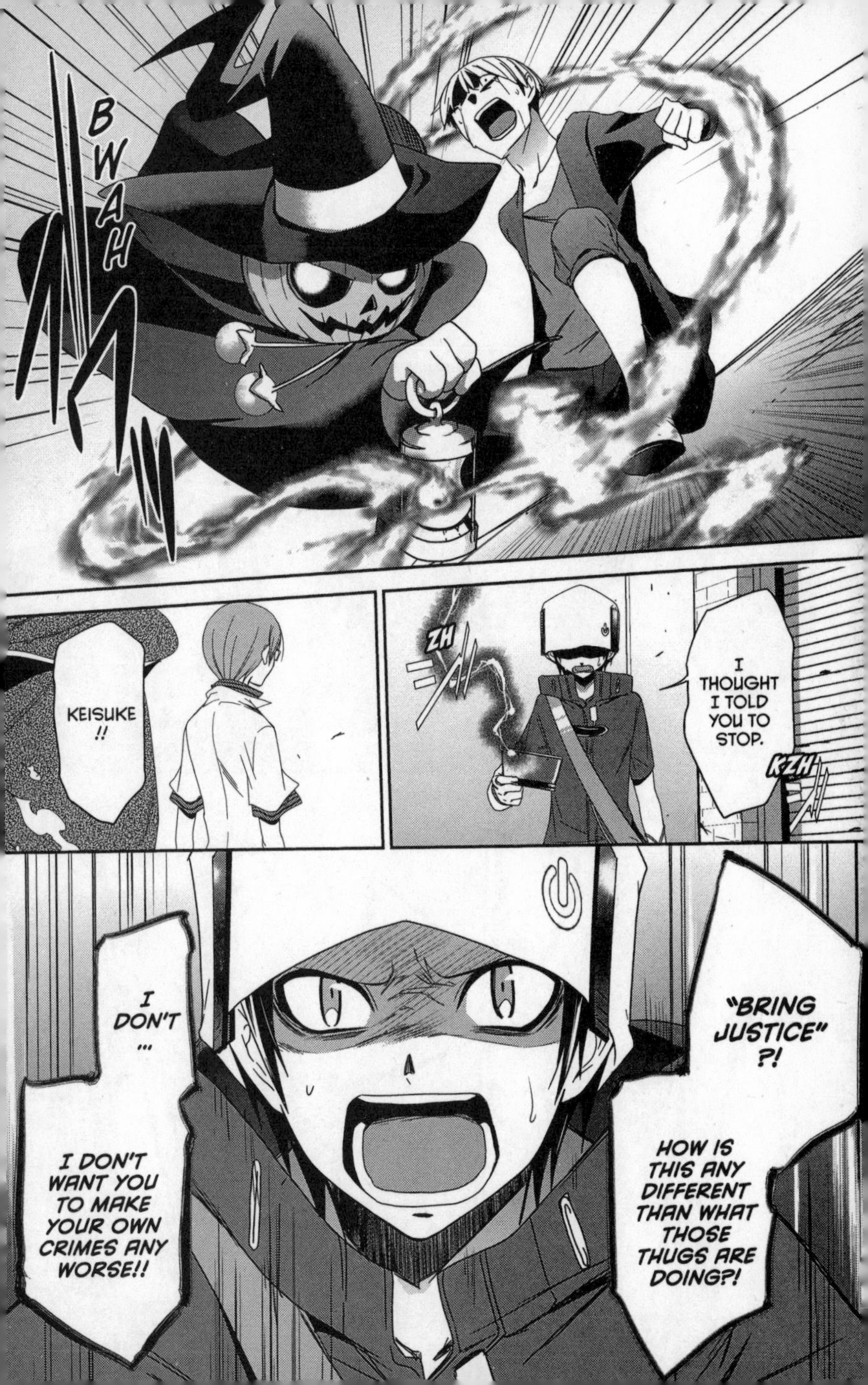
BWAH
I THOUGHT I TOLD YOU TO STOP.
ZH
KZH
KEISUKE !!
"BRING JUSTICE" ?!
HOW IS THIS ANY DIFFERENT THAN WHAT THOSE THUGS ARE DOING?!
I DON'T ...
I DON'T WANT YOU TO MAKE YOUR OWN CRIMES ANY WORSE!!

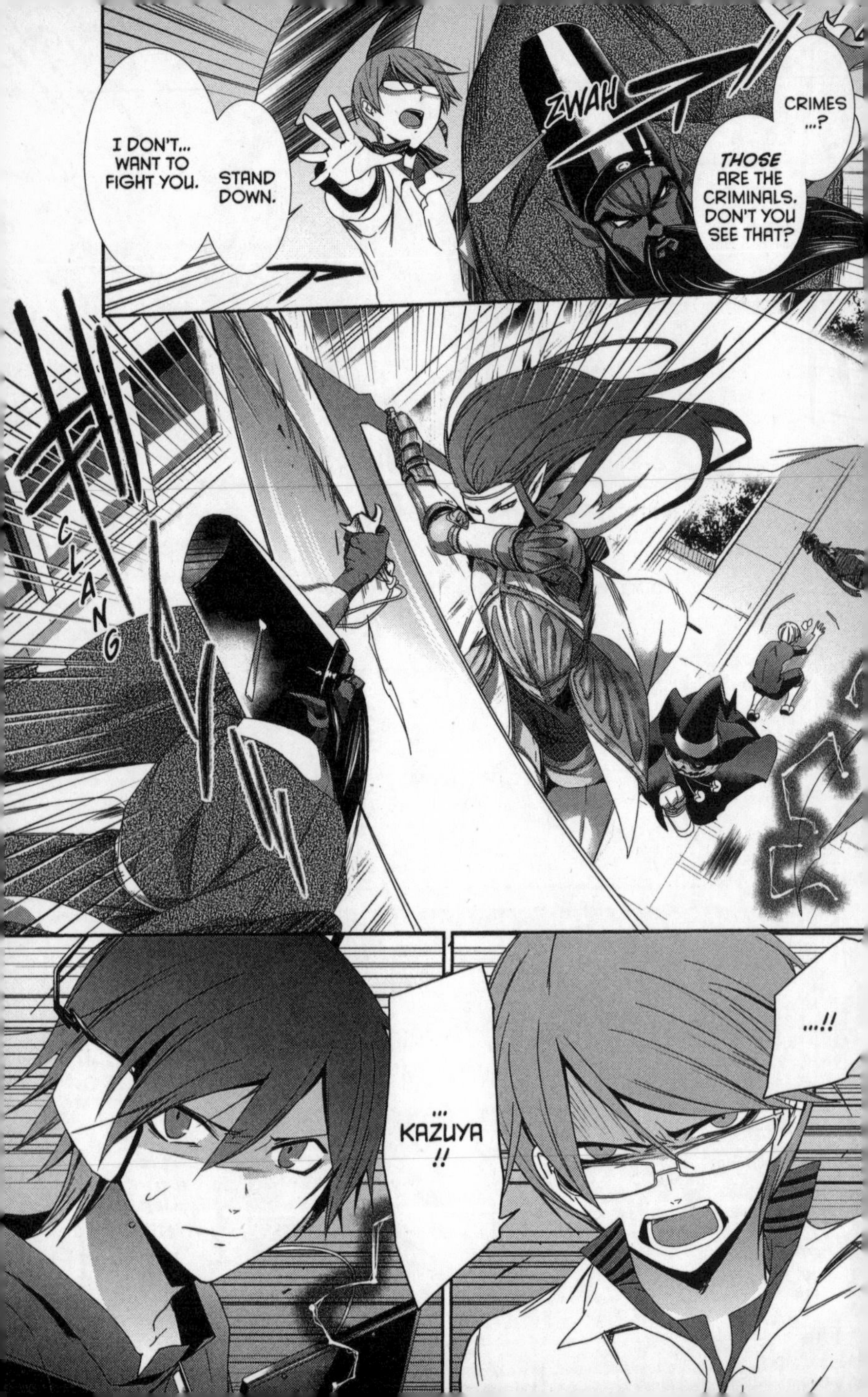
ZWAH
CRIMES ...?
THOSE ARE THE CRIMINALS. DON'T YOU SEE THAT?
STAND DOWN.
I DON'T... WANT TO FIGHT YOU.
CLANG
...!!
... KAZUYA !!

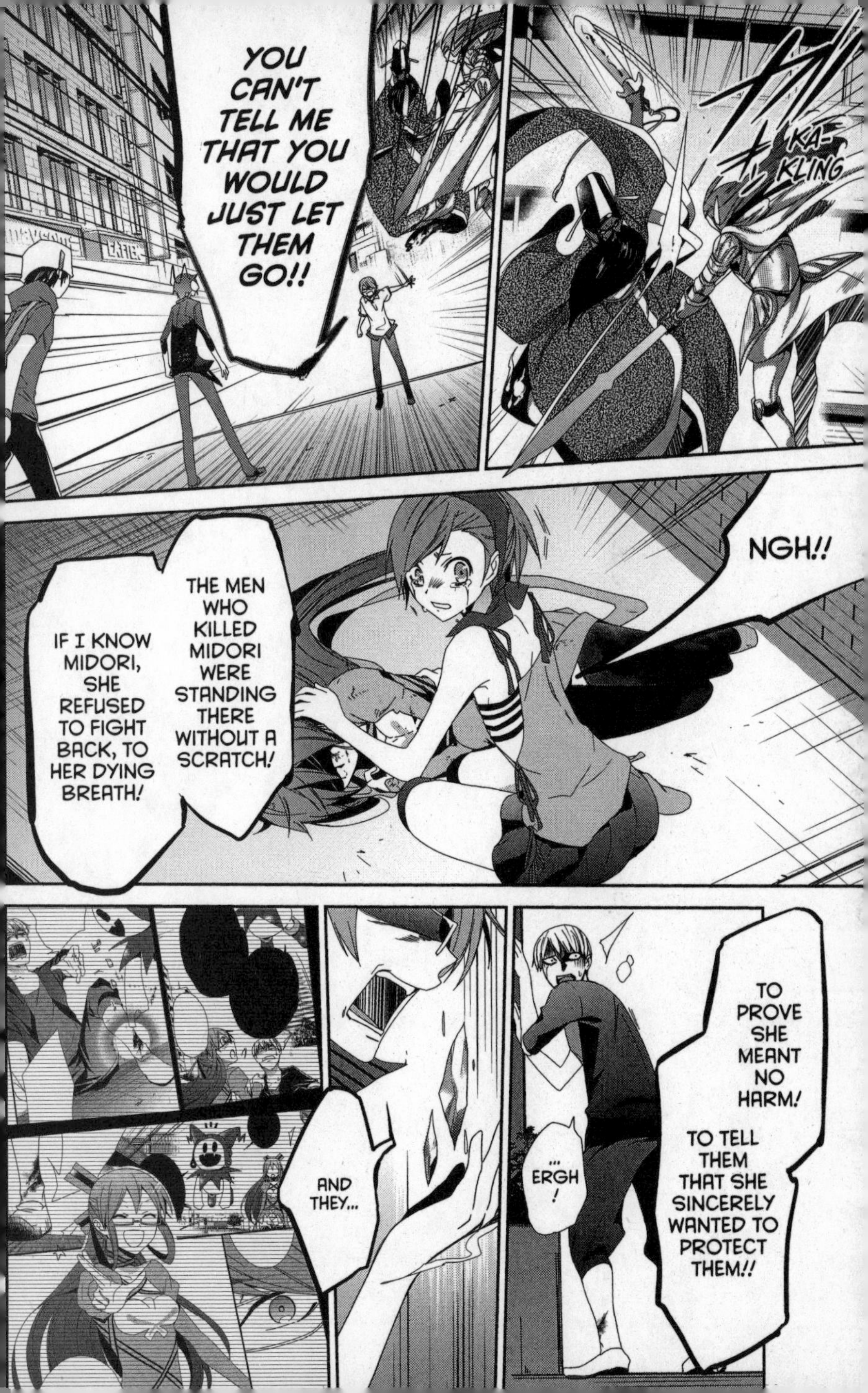
KA-KLING
YOU CAN'T TELL ME THAT YOU WOULD JUST LET THEM GO!!
NGH!!
THE MEN WHO KILLED MIDORI WERE STANDING THERE WITHOUT A SCRATCH!
IF I KNOW MIDORI, SHE REFUSED TO FIGHT BACK, TO HER DYING BREATH!
TO PROVE SHE MEANT NO HARM!
TO TELL THEM THAT SHE SINCERELY WANTED TO PROTECT THEM!!
...ERGH!
AND THEY...

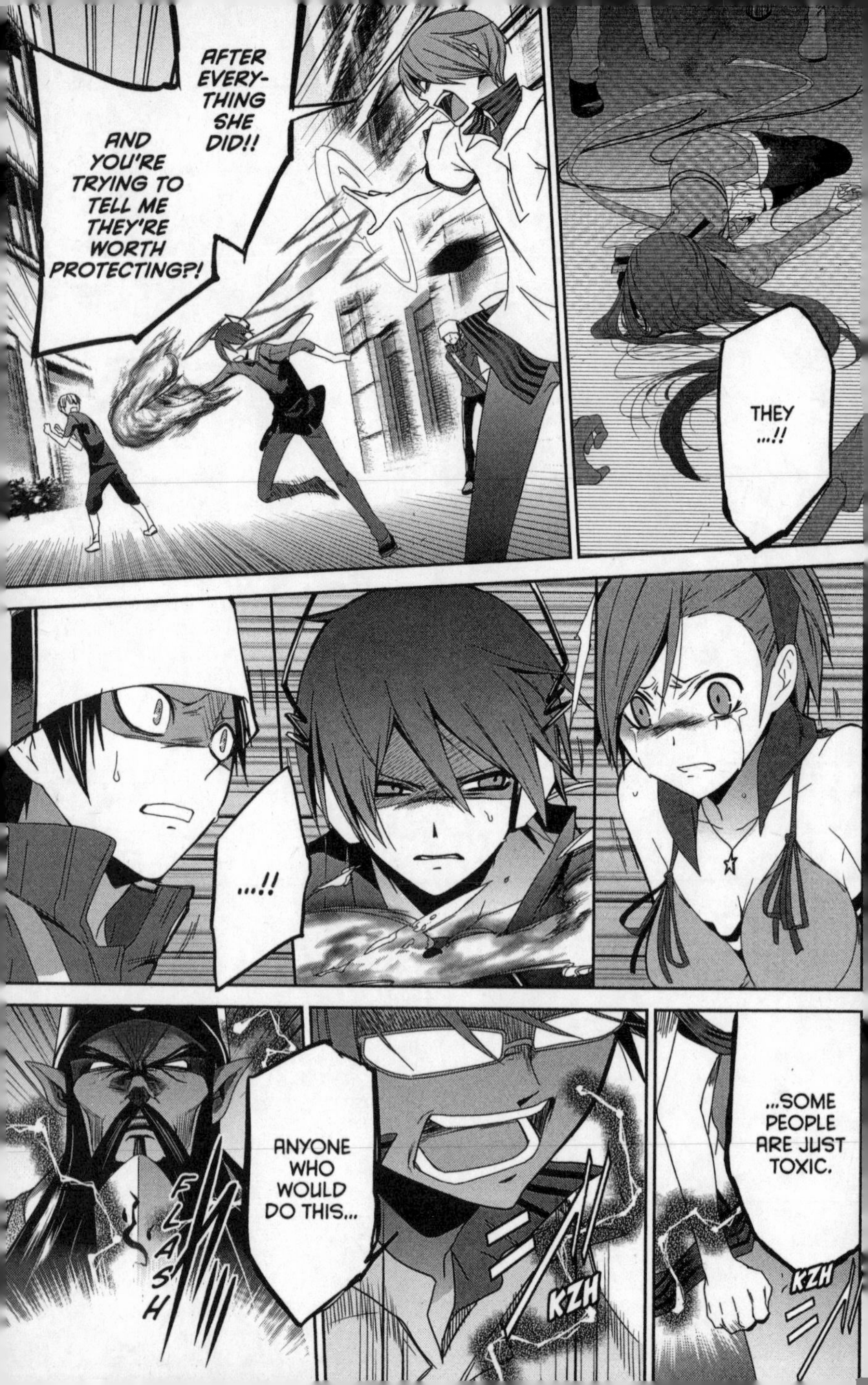
THEY ...!!
AFTER EVERY-THING SHE DID!!
AND YOU'RE TRYING TO TELL ME THEY'RE WORTH PROTECTING?!
...!!
...SOME PEOPLE ARE JUST TOXIC.
KZH
ANYONE WHO WOULD DO THIS...
KZH
FLASH

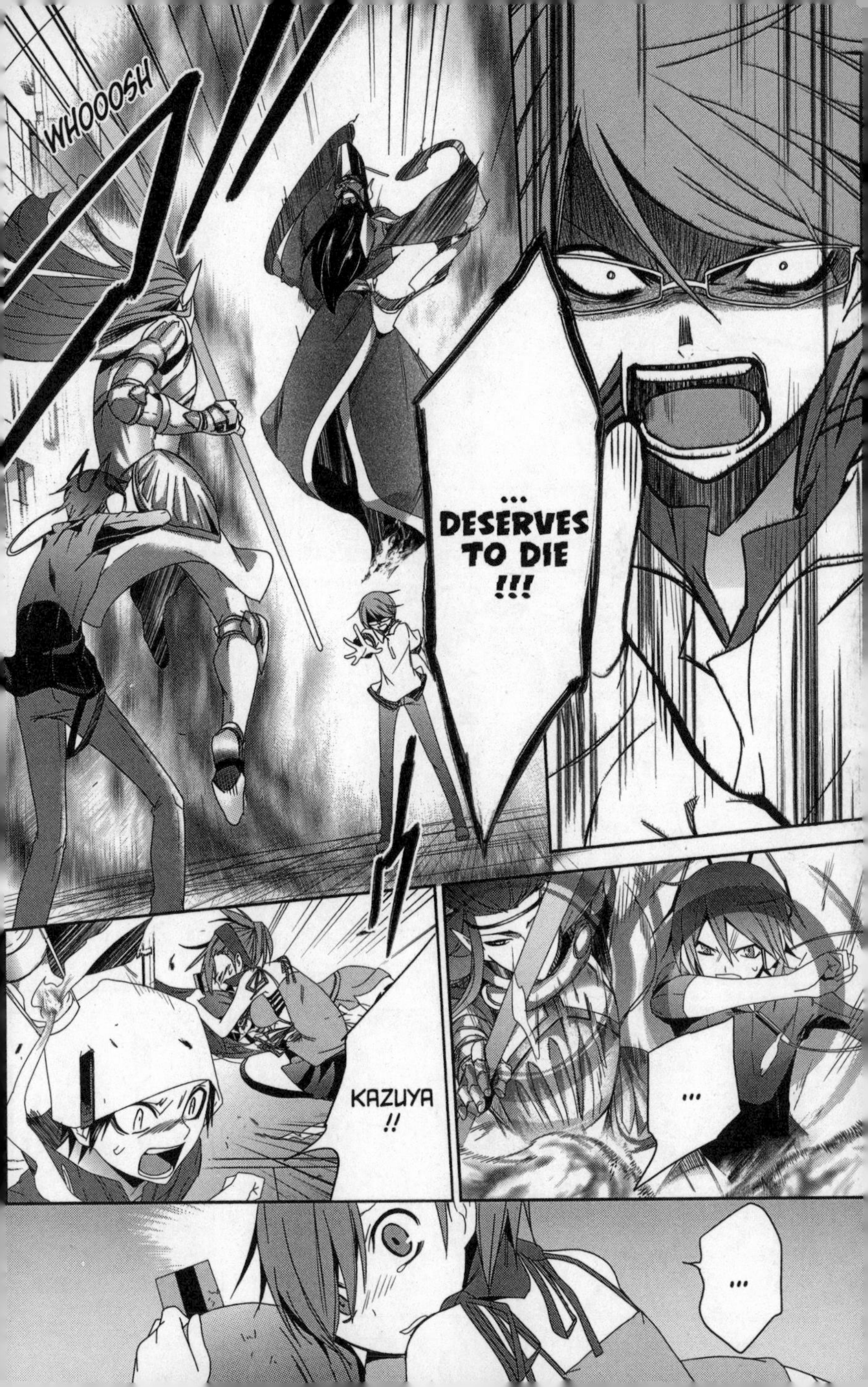
...DESERVES TO DIE!!!
WHOOOSH
...
KAZUYA!!
...

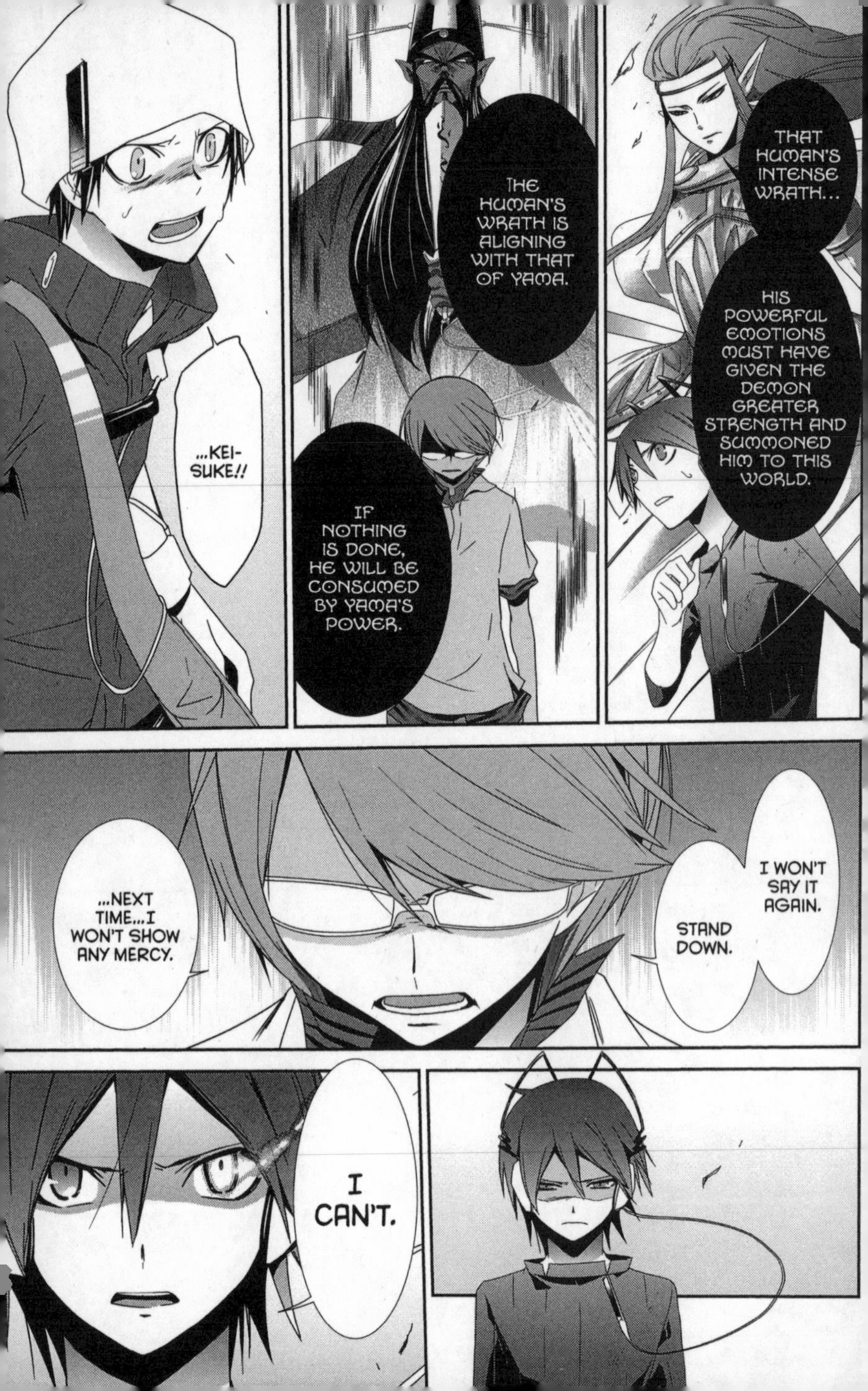
THAT HUMAN'S INTENSE WRATH...
HIS POWERFUL EMOTIONS MUST HAVE GIVEN THE DEMON GREATER STRENGTH AND SUMMONED HIM TO THIS WORLD.
THE HUMAN'S WRATH IS ALIGNING WITH THAT OF YAMA.
IF NOTHING IS DONE, HE WILL BE CONSUMED BY YAMA'S POWER.
...KEI-SUKE!!
I WON'T SAY IT AGAIN.
STAND DOWN.
...NEXT TIME...I WON'T SHOW ANY MERCY.
I CAN'T.

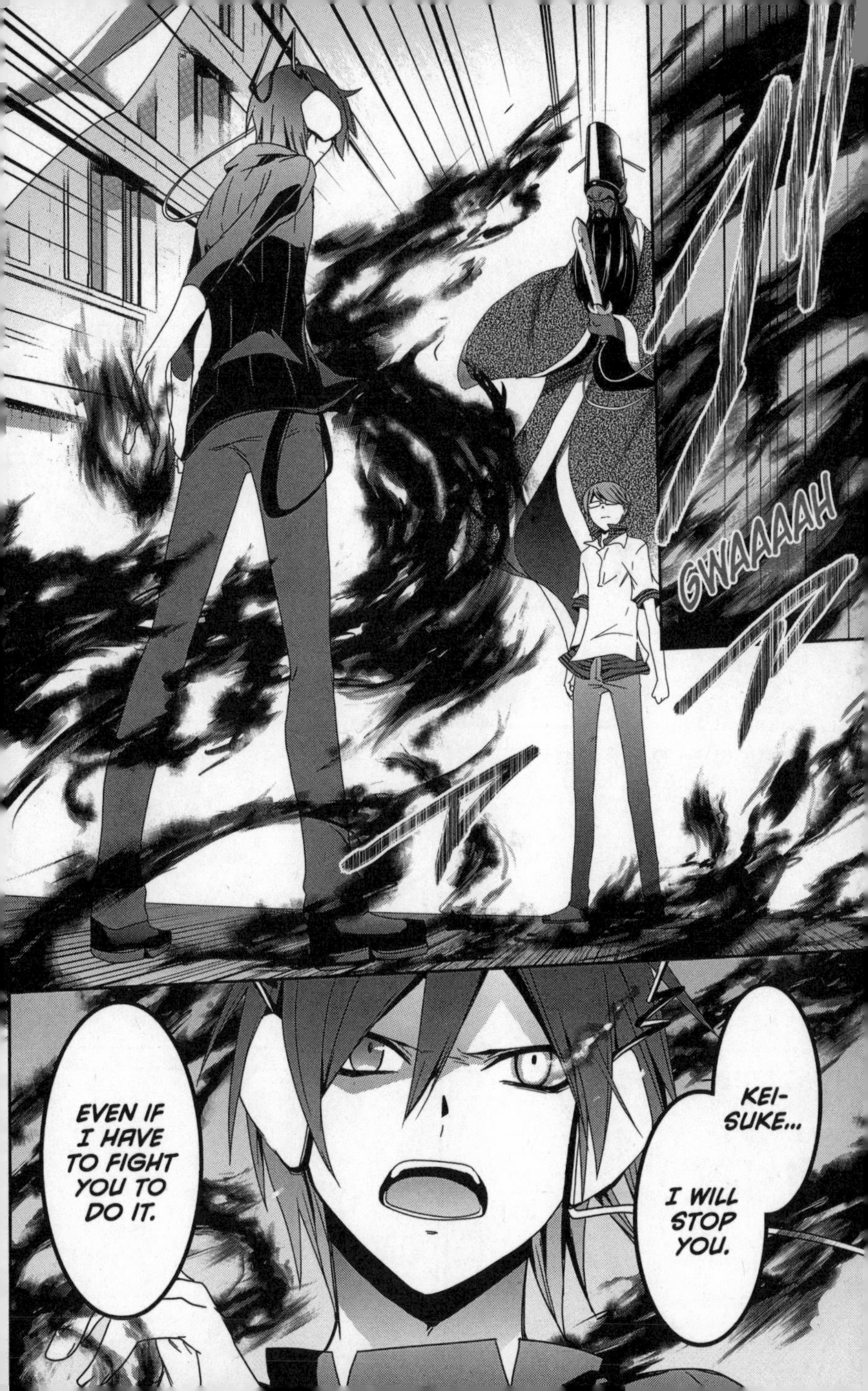
GWAAAAH
KEI-SUKE...
I WILL STOP YOU.
EVEN IF I HAVE TO FIGHT YOU TO DO IT.

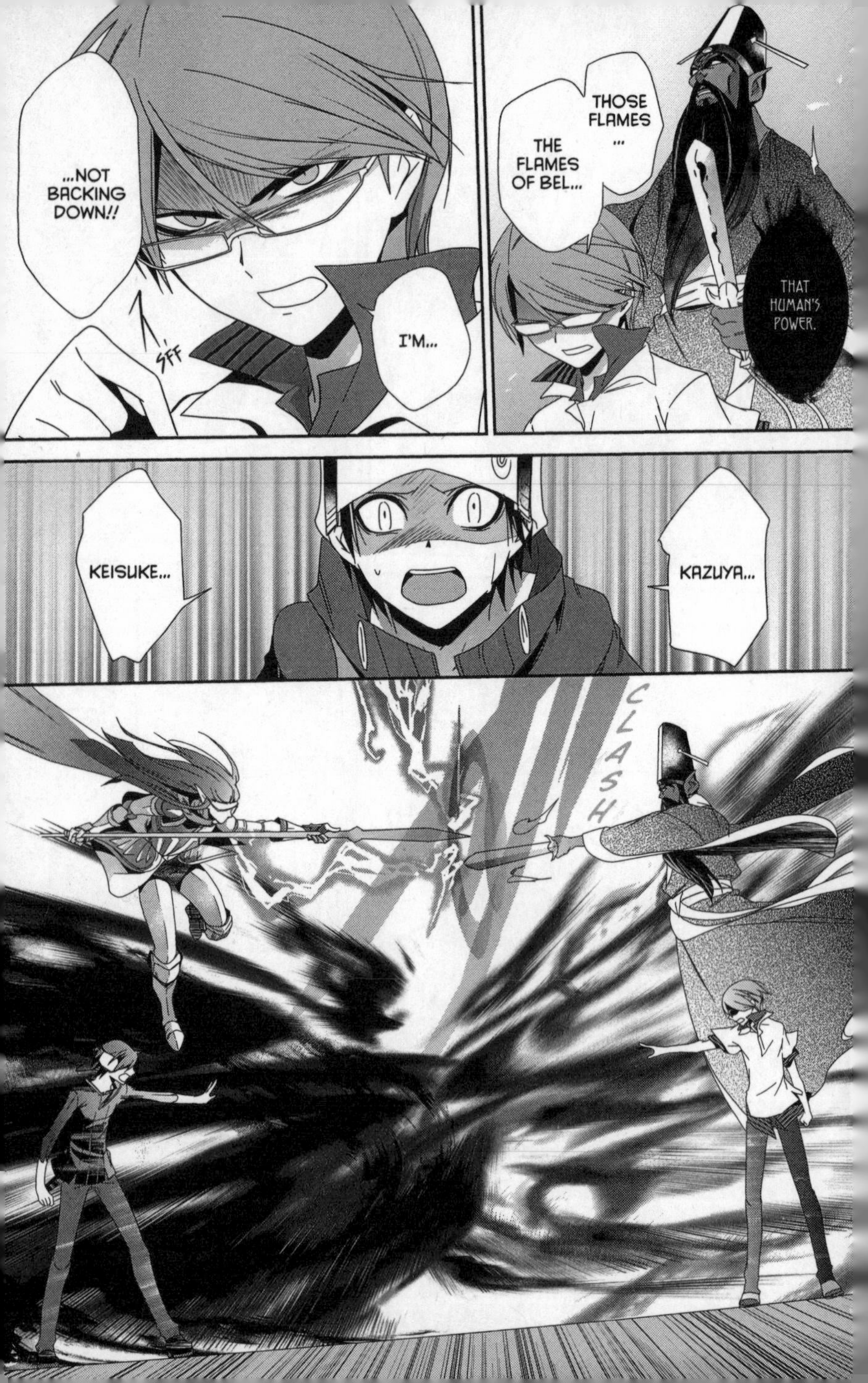
THOSE FLAMES ...
THE FLAMES OF BEL...
THAT HUMAN'S POWER.
I'M...
...NOT BACKING DOWN!!
SFF
KAZUYA...
KEISUKE...
CLASH

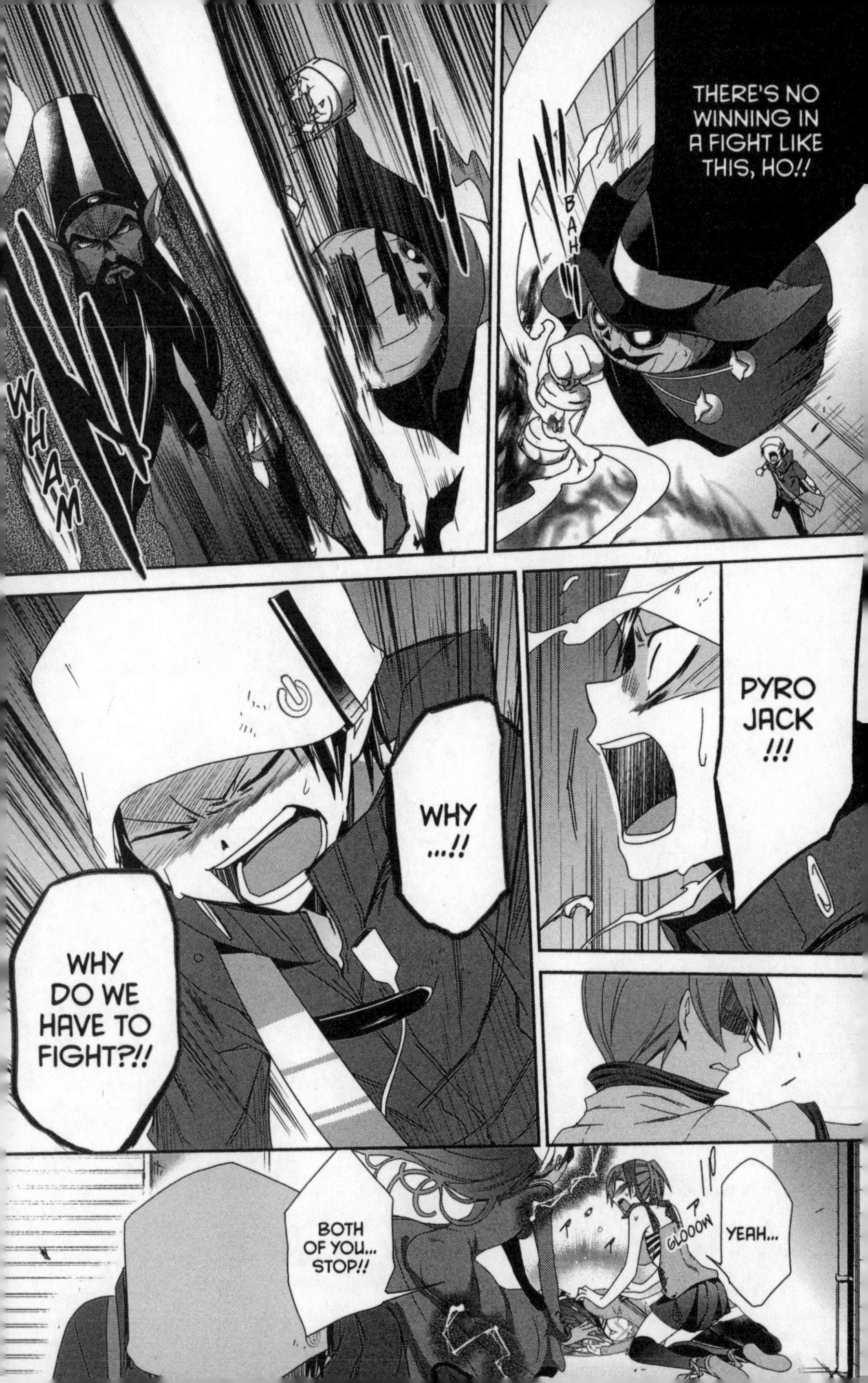
THERE'S NO WINNING IN A FIGHT LIKE THIS, HO!!
BAH
WHAM
PYRO JACK !!!
WHY ...!!
WHY DO WE HAVE TO FIGHT?!!
YEAH...
GLOOOW
BOTH OF YOU... STOP!!

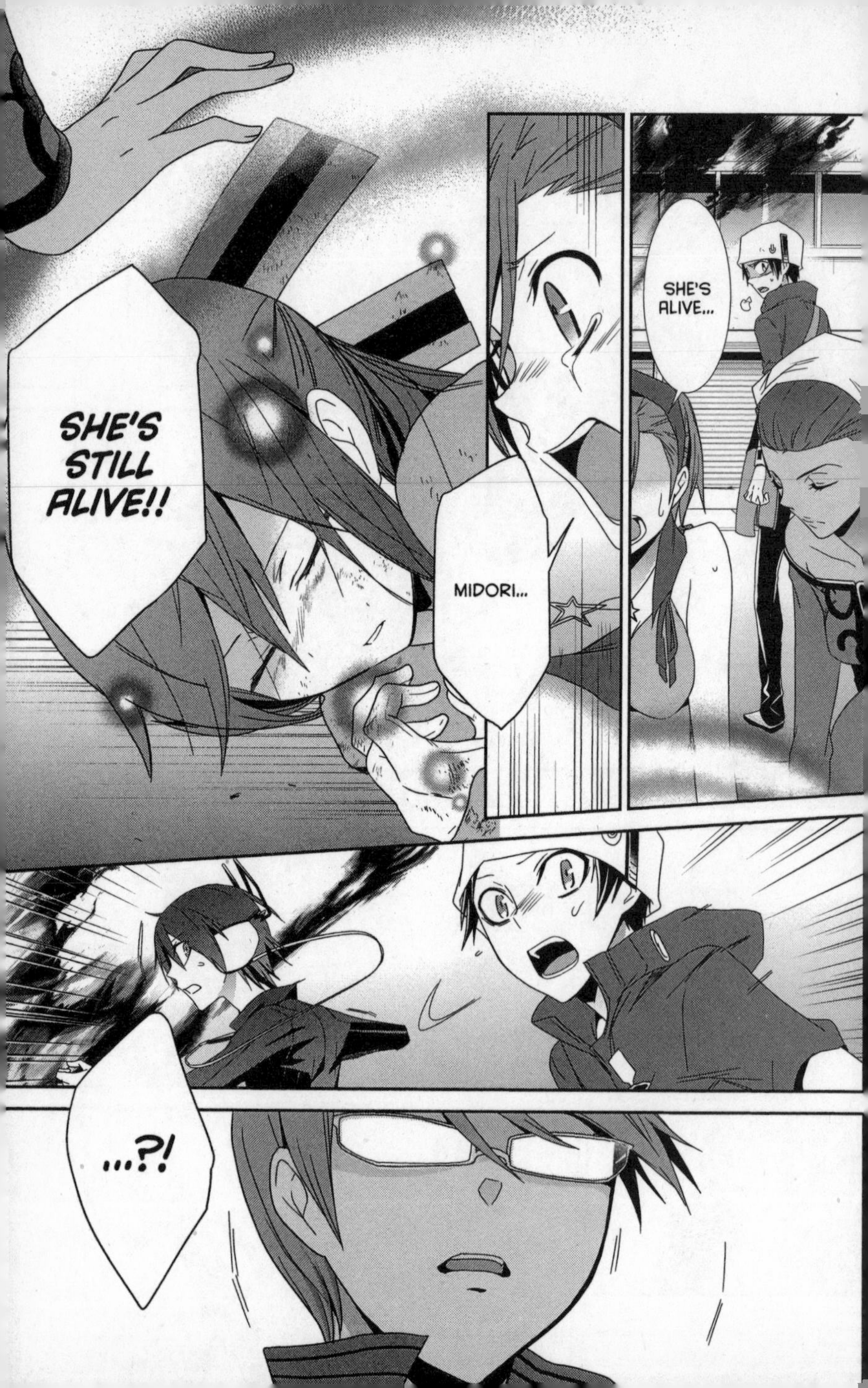
SHE'S ALIVE...
MIDORI...
SHE'S STILL ALIVE!!
...?!

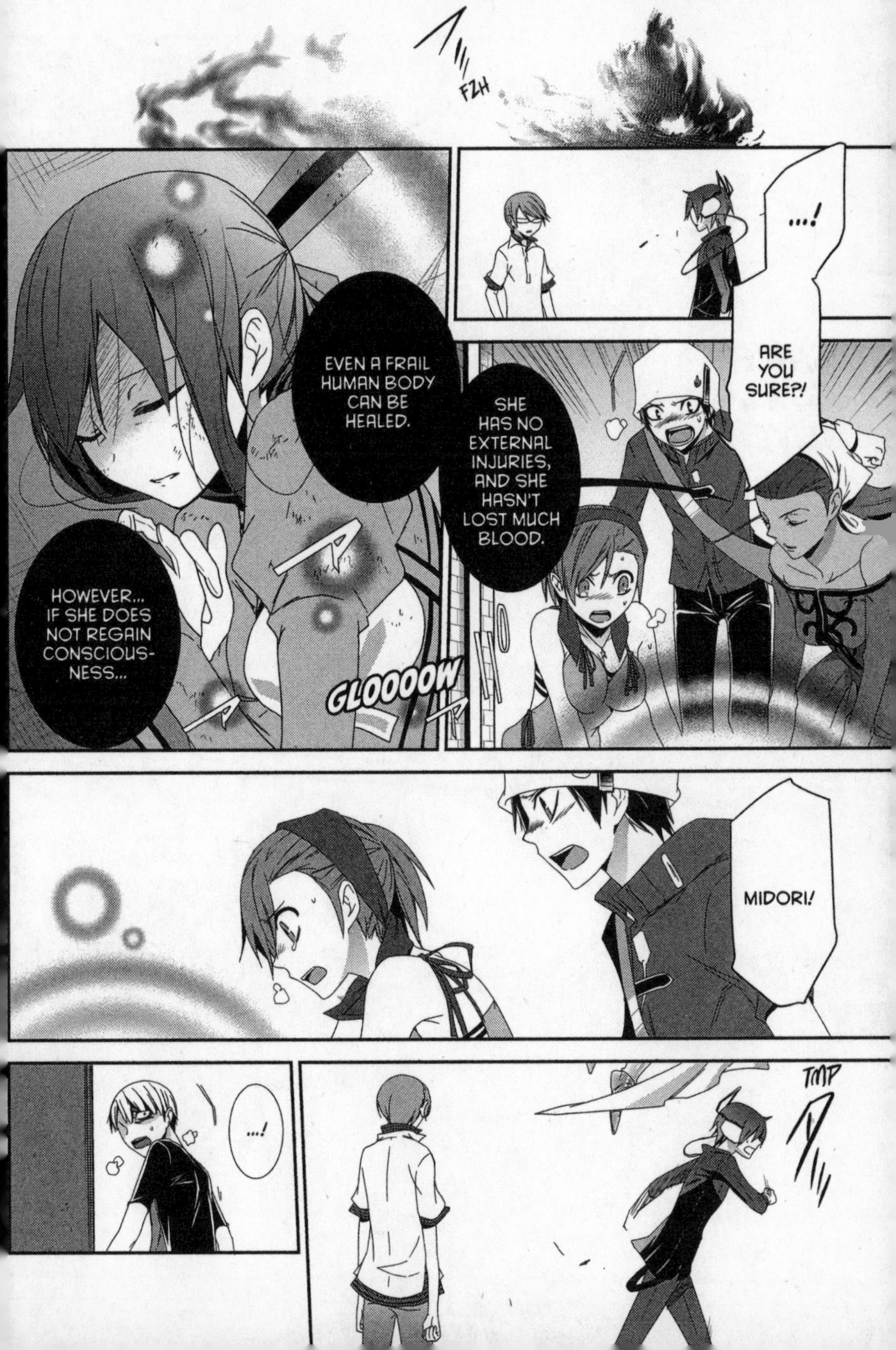
FZH
...!
ARE YOU SURE?!
SHE HAS NO EXTERNAL INJURIES, AND SHE HASN'T LOST MUCH BLOOD.
EVEN A FRAIL HUMAN BODY CAN BE HEALED.
HOWEVER... IF SHE DOES NOT REGAIN CONSCIOUS- NESS...
GLOOOOW
MIDORI!
TMP
...!

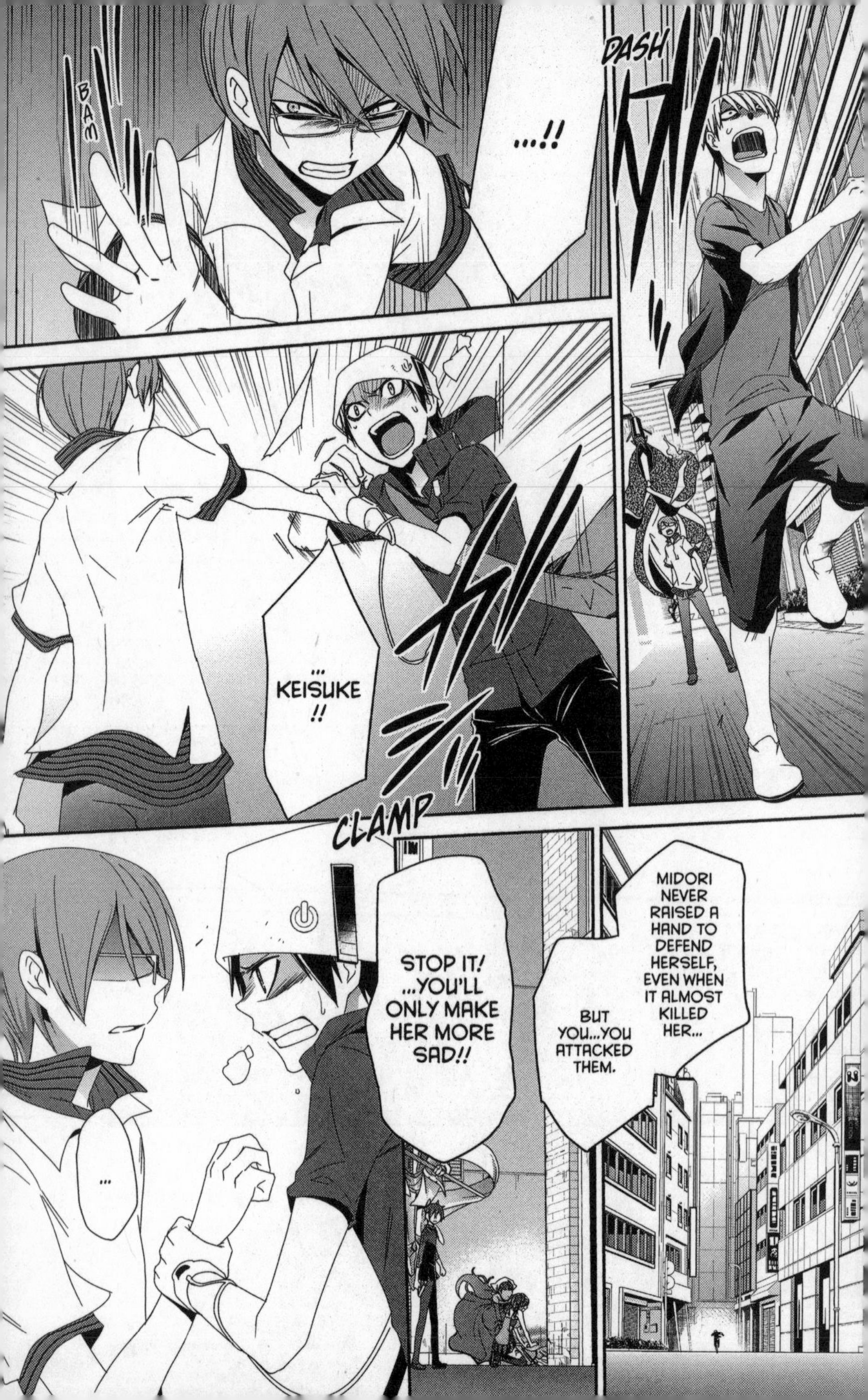
DASH
BAM
...!!
...KEISUKE!!
CLAMP
MIDORI NEVER RAISED A HAND TO DEFEND HERSELF, EVEN WHEN IT ALMOST KILLED HER...
BUT YOU...YOU ATTACKED THEM.
STOP IT! ...YOU'LL ONLY MAKE HER MORE SAD!!
...

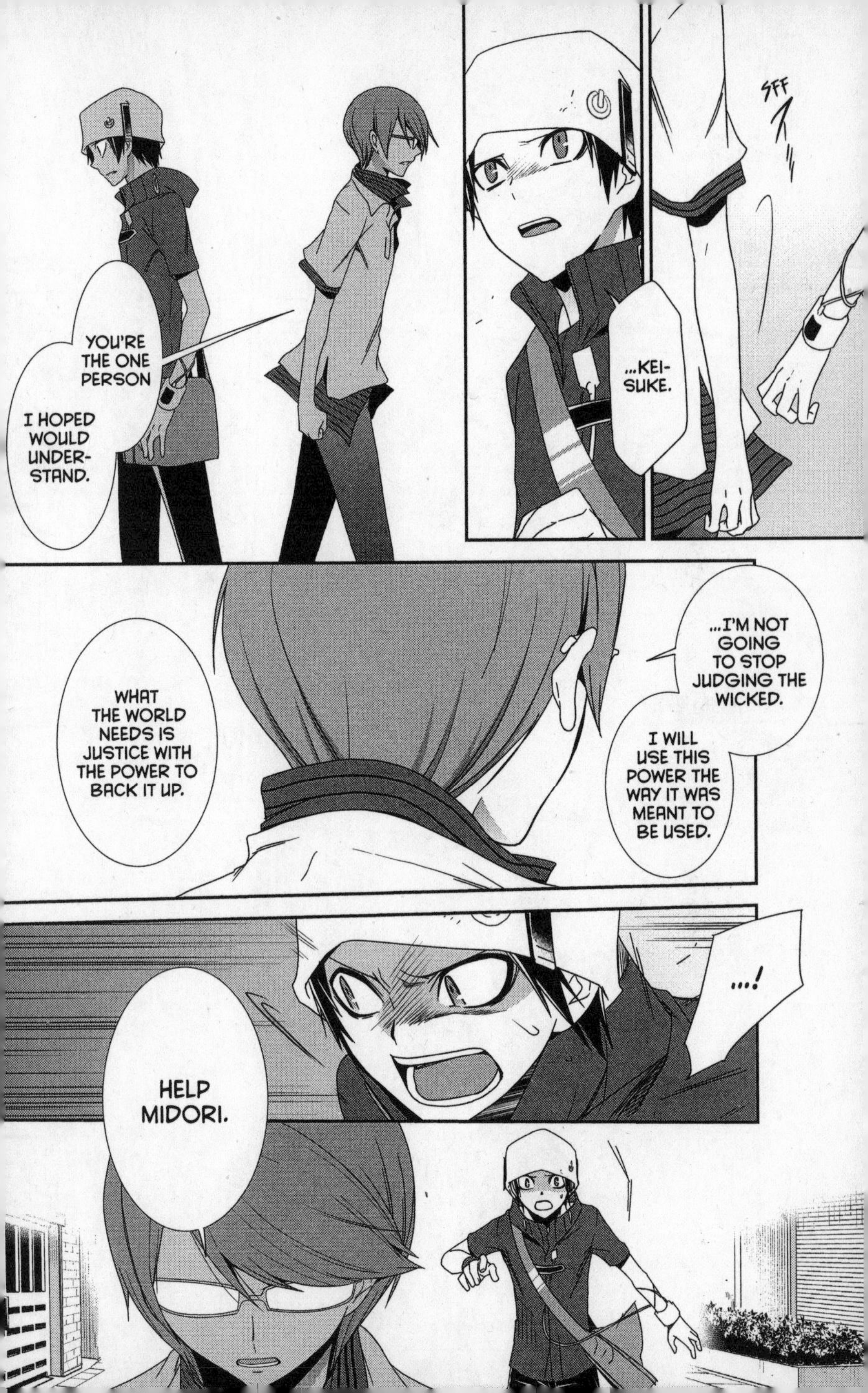
SFF
...KEI-SUKE.
YOU'RE THE ONE PERSON
I HOPED WOULD UNDER-STAND.
...I'M NOT GOING TO STOP JUDGING THE WICKED.
I WILL USE THIS POWER THE WAY IT WAS MEANT TO BE USED.
WHAT THE WORLD NEEDS IS JUSTICE WITH THE POWER TO BACK IT UP.
...!
HELP MIDORI.

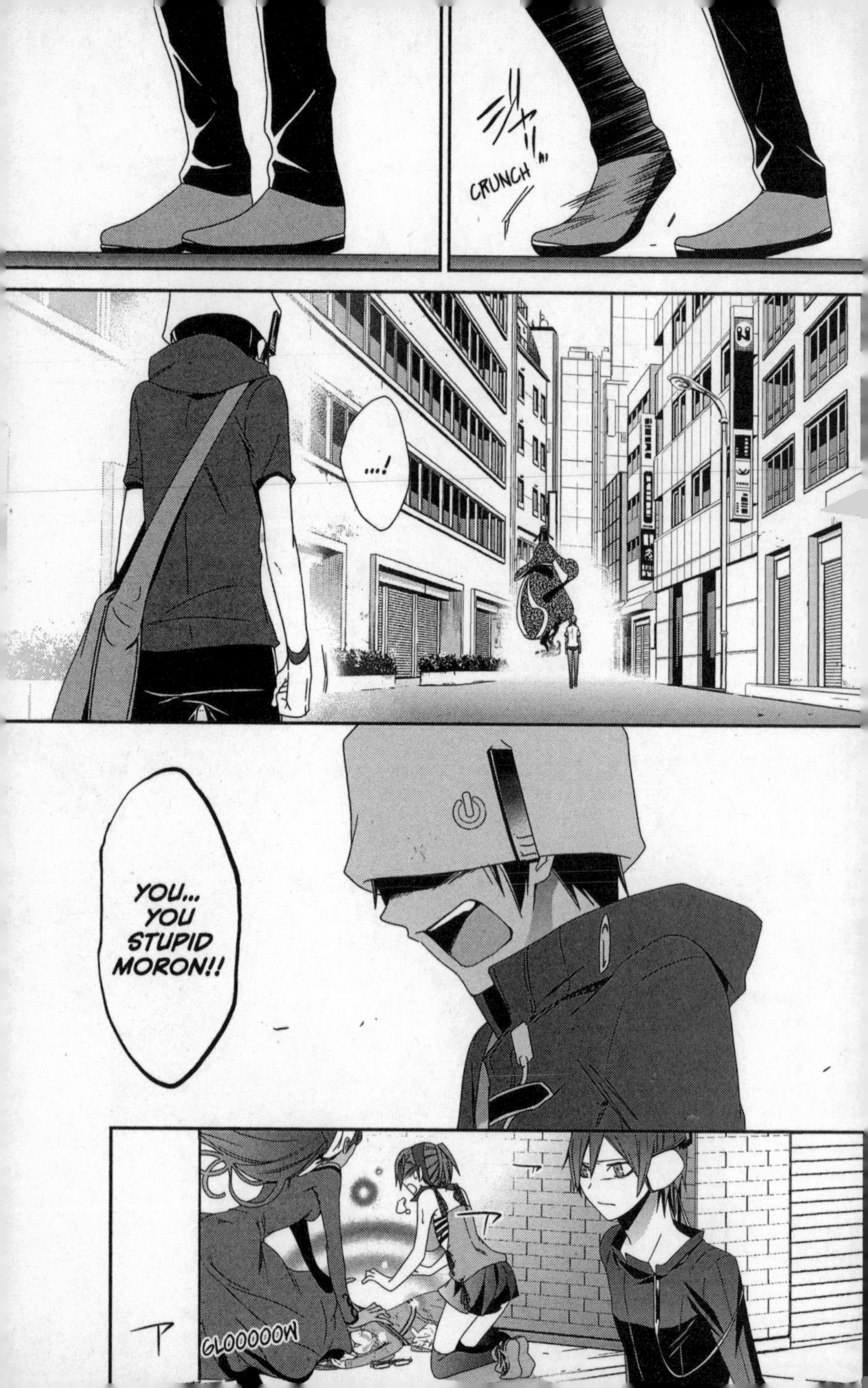
CRUNCH
...!
YOU... YOU STUPID MORON!!
GLOOOOOW

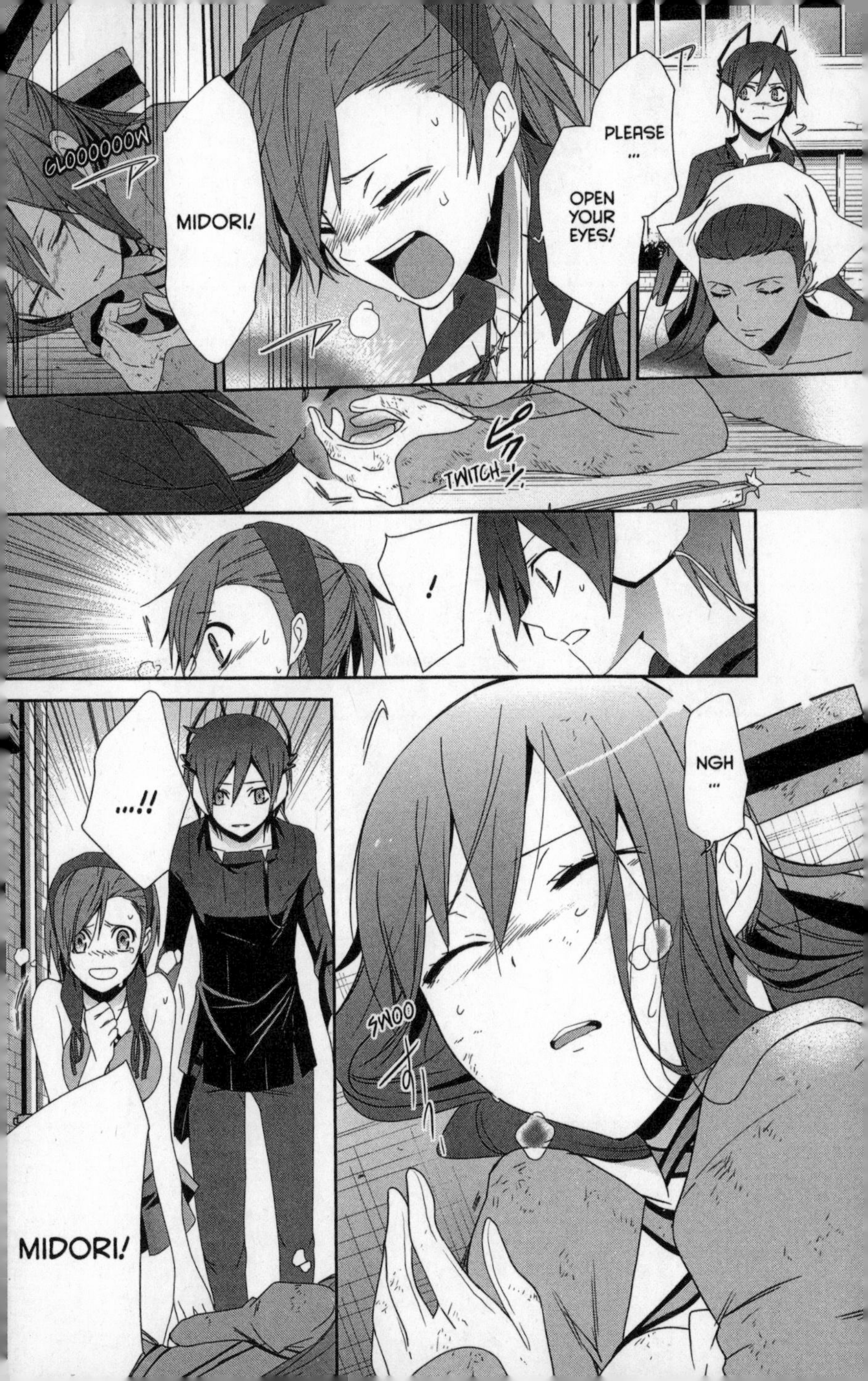
PLEASE ...
OPEN YOUR EYES!
MIDORI!
GLOOOOOOM
TWITCH
!
NGH ...
SWOO
...!!
MIDORI!

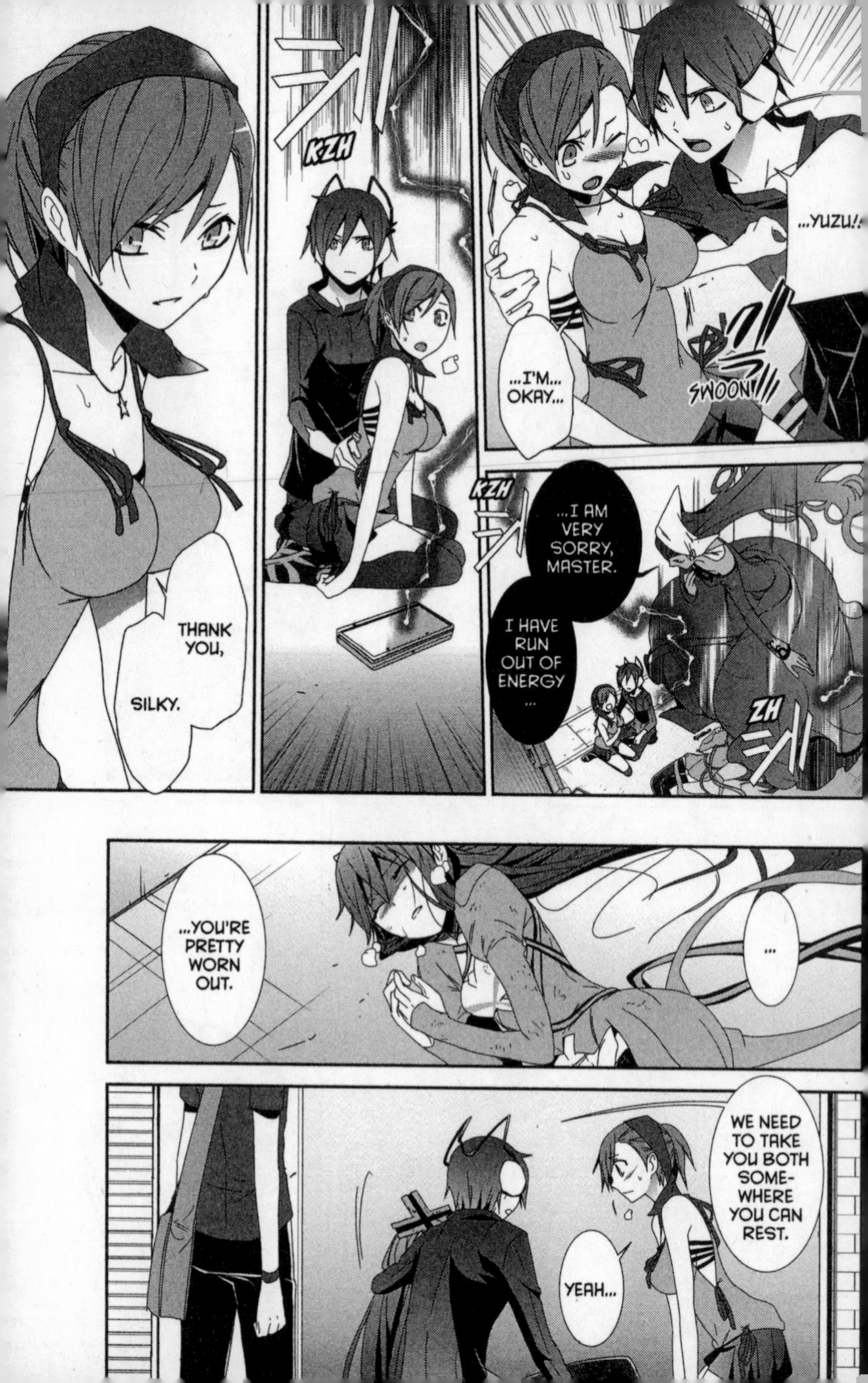
...YUZU!
...I'M... OKAY...
SWOON!!
KZH
...I AM VERY SORRY, MASTER.
I HAVE RUN OUT OF ENERGY ...
ZH
KZH
THANK YOU,
SILKY.
...
...YOU'RE PRETTY WORN OUT.
WE NEED TO TAKE YOU BOTH SOME-WHERE YOU CAN REST.
YEAH...

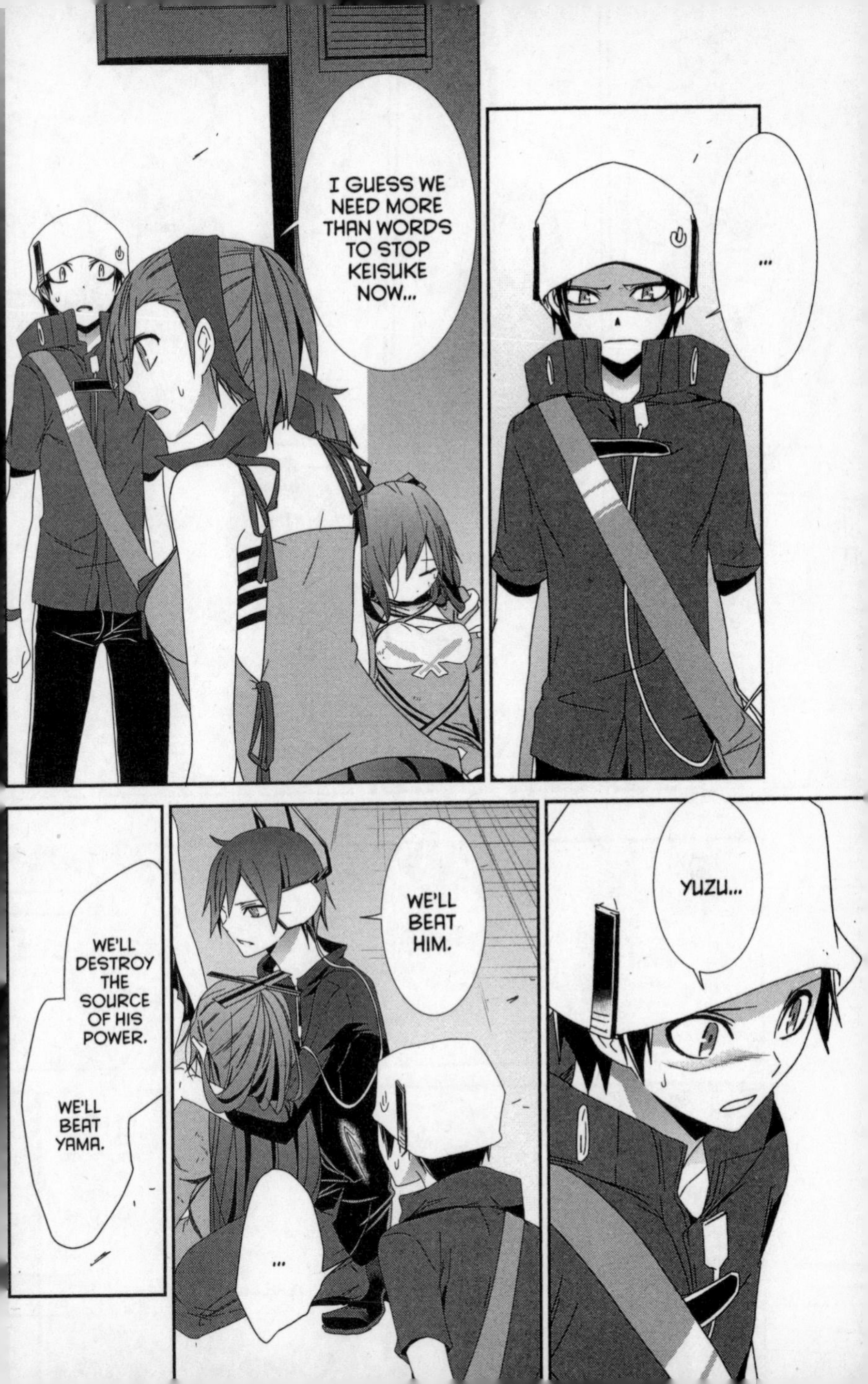
...
I GUESS WE NEED MORE THAN WORDS TO STOP KEISUKE NOW...
YUZU...
WE'LL BEAT HIM.
...
WE'LL DESTROY THE SOURCE OF HIS POWER.
WE'LL BEAT YAMA.

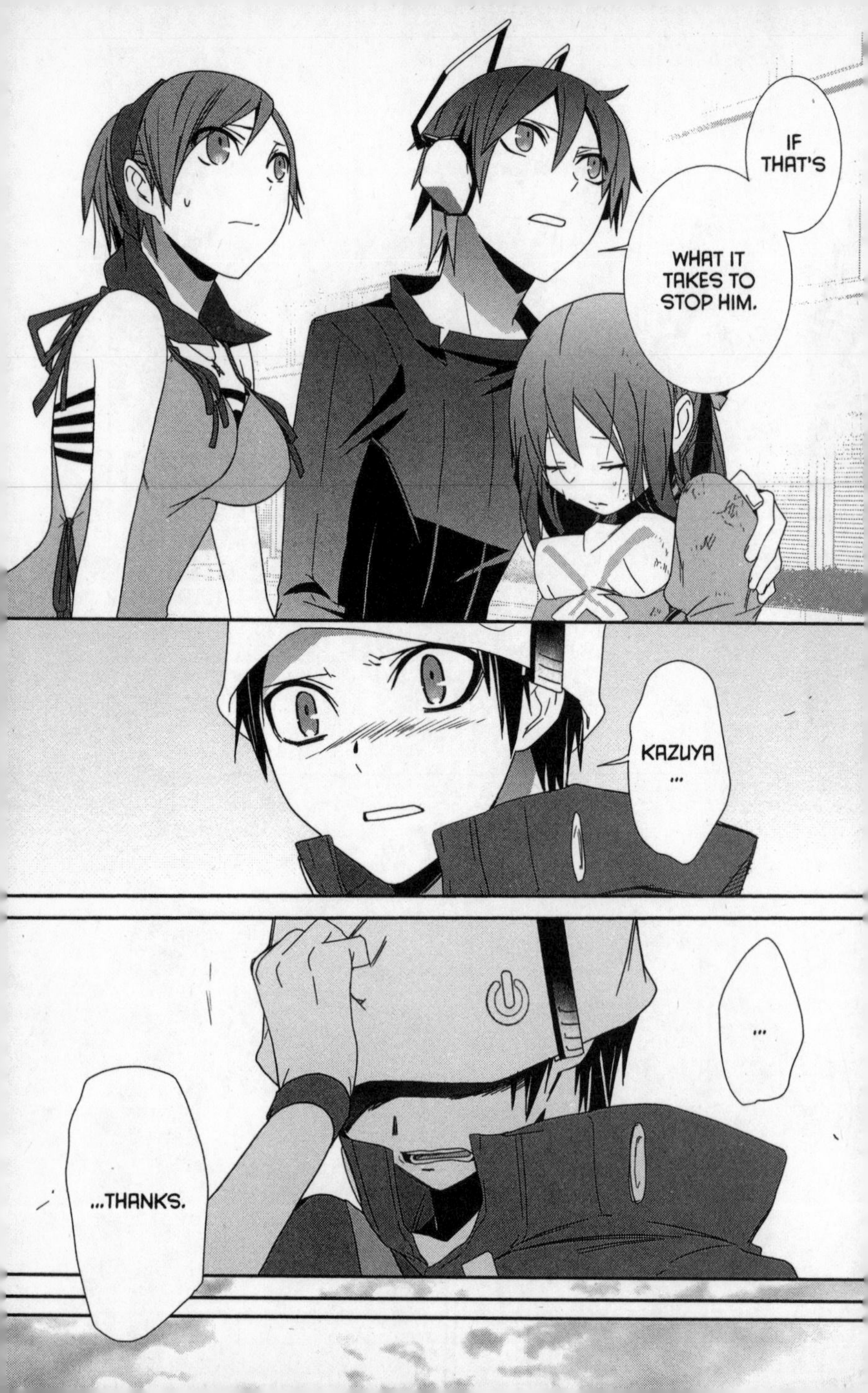
IF THAT'S
WHAT IT TAKES TO STOP HIM.
KAZUYA ...
...
...THANKS.

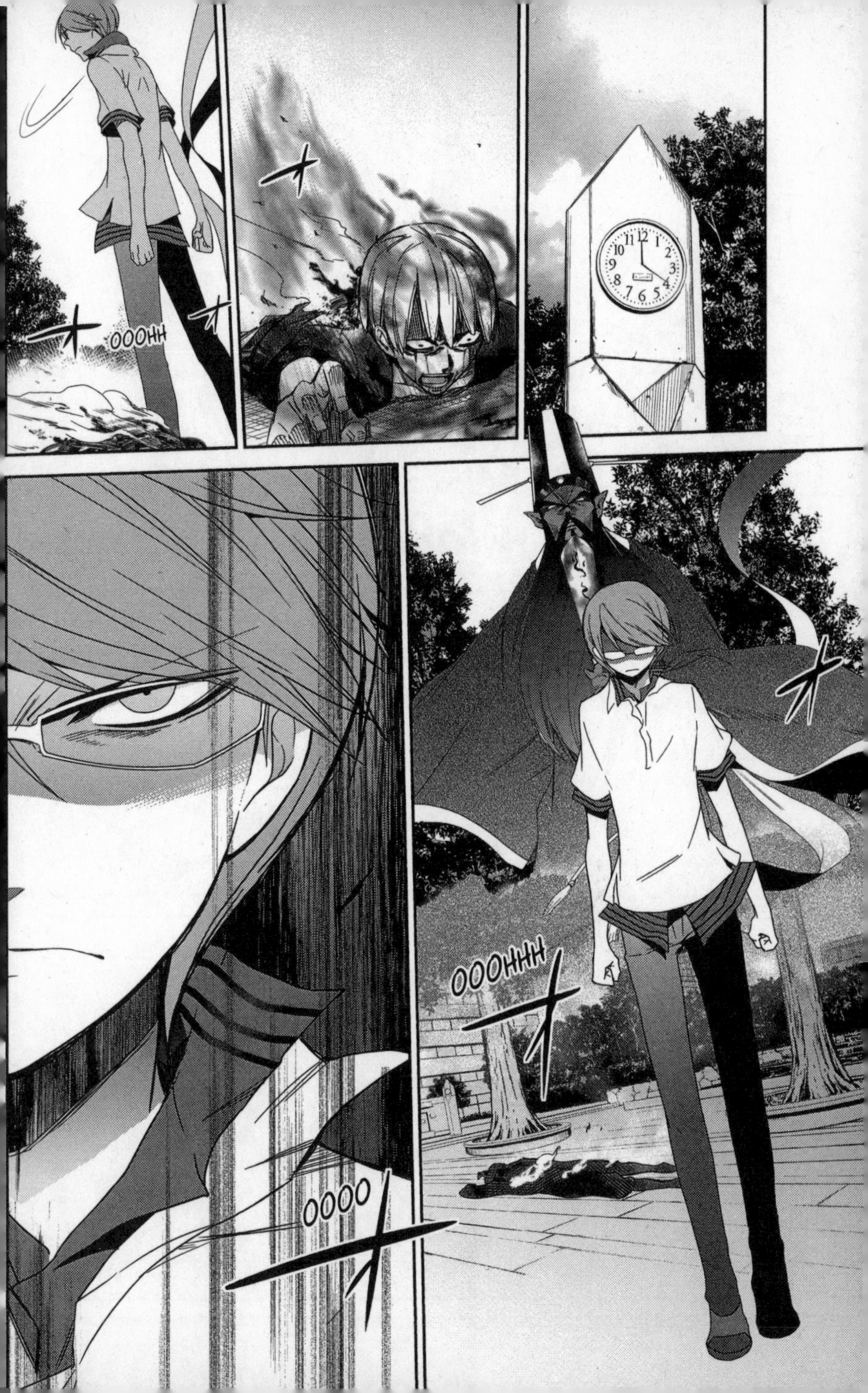
OOOHH
OOOHHH
OOOO

PROFILE

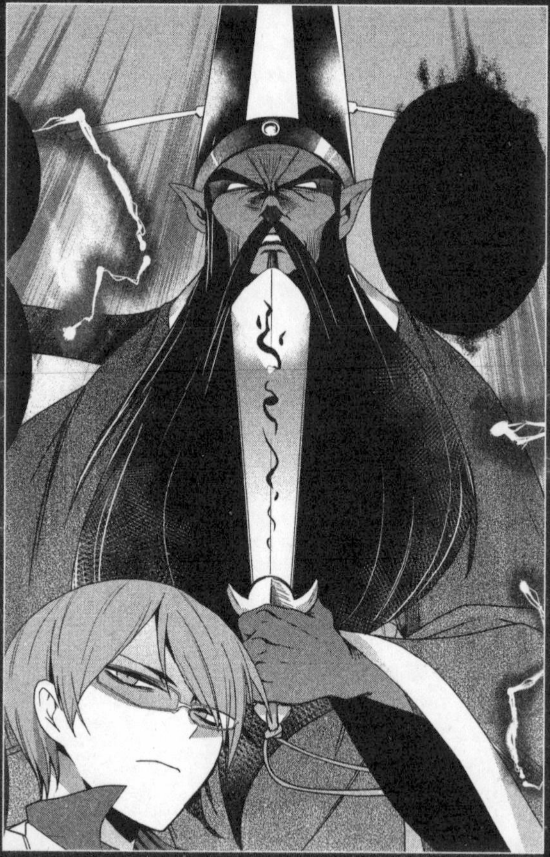

YAMA

A HINDU DEITY WHO OVERSEES HELL. HE HAS BEEN INCORPORATED INTO BUDDHISM AND IS WELL KNOWN AS KING ENMA. AS THE FIRST PERSON TO EVER DIE, YAMA WAS GIVEN THE ROLE OF GUIDING THE DECEASED TO THE LAND OF THE DEAD, BUT EVENTUALLY HE BEGAN PUNISHING THEM FOR THEIR DEEDS IN LIFE. ORIGINALLY, THE LAND OF THE DEAD CONSISTED ONLY OF HEAVEN, BUT THROUGH YAMA'S WORK, HELL WAS BORN AND HE BECAME ITS OVERSEER.

DEVIL SURVIVOR
デビルサバイバー

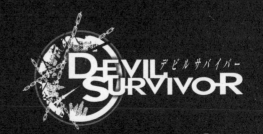

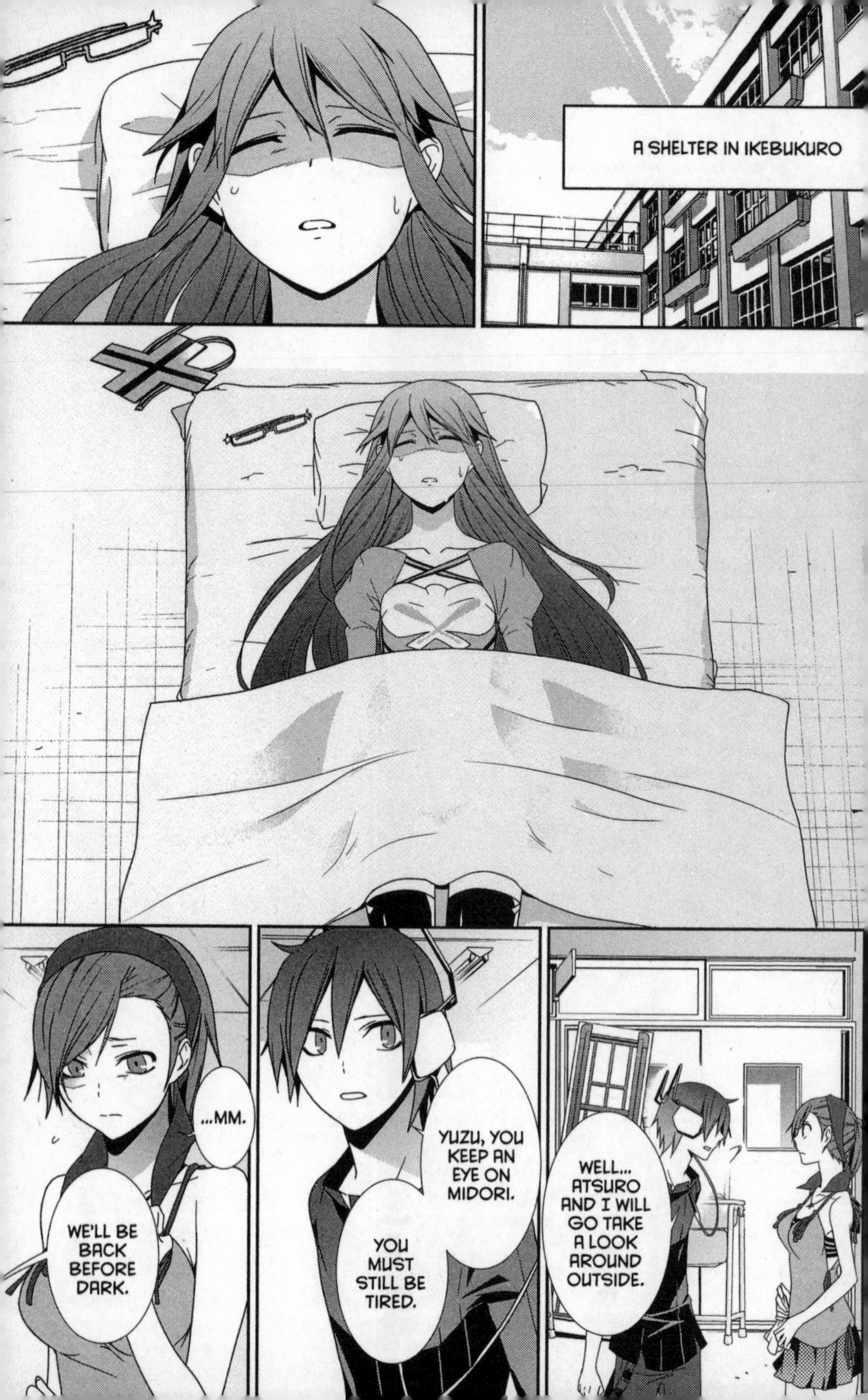
A SHELTER IN IKEBUKURO
WELL... ATSURO AND I WILL GO TAKE A LOOK AROUND OUTSIDE.
YUZU, YOU KEEP AN EYE ON MIDORI.
YOU MUST STILL BE TIRED.
...MM.
WE'LL BE BACK BEFORE DARK.

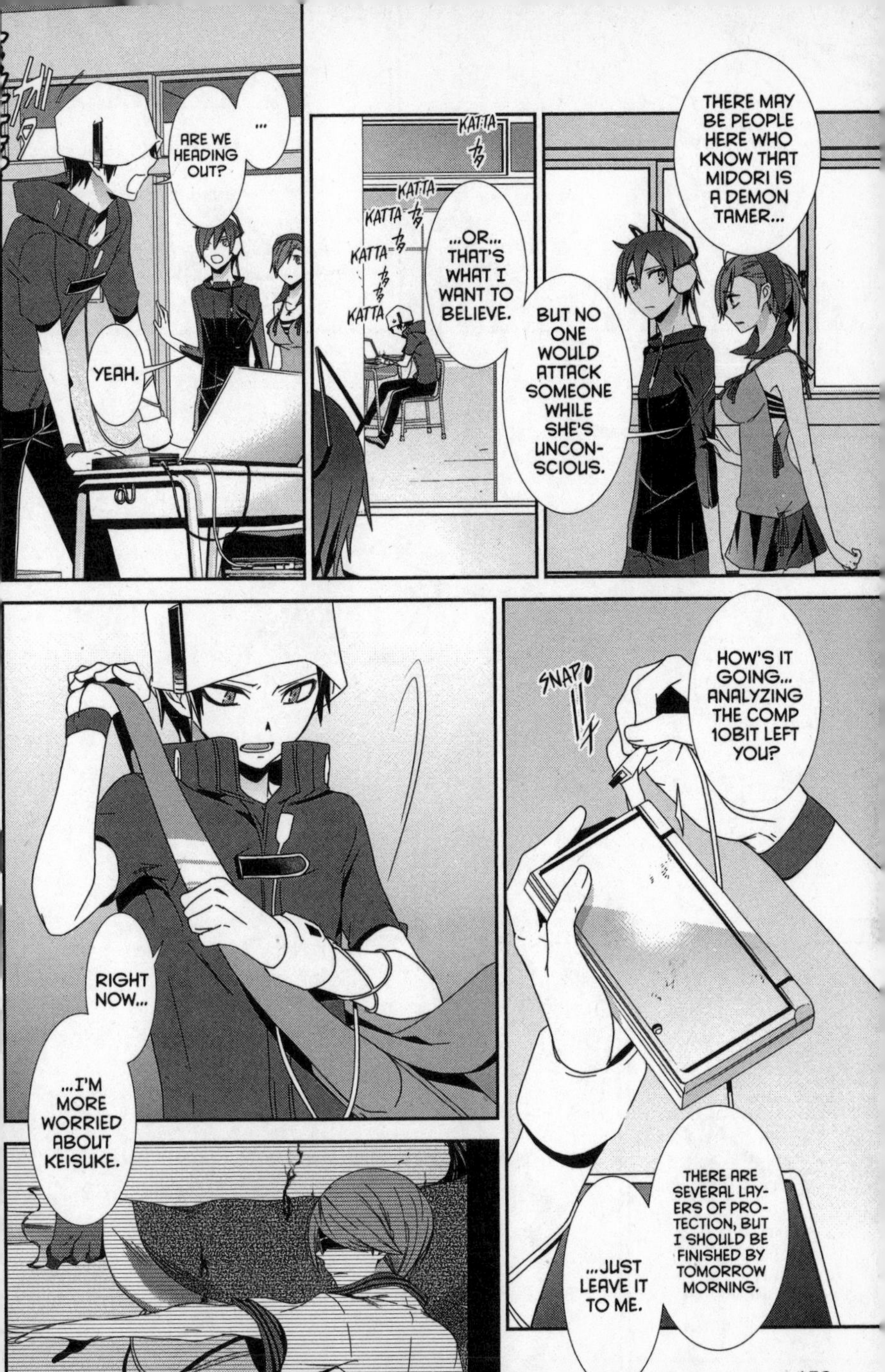
THERE MAY BE PEOPLE HERE WHO KNOW THAT MIDORI IS A DEMON TAMER...
BUT NO ONE WOULD ATTACK SOMEONE WHILE SHE'S UNCONSCIOUS.
KATTA
KATTA
KATTA
KATTA
KATTA
...OR... THAT'S WHAT I WANT TO BELIEVE.
...
ARE WE HEADING OUT?
YEAH.
SNAP
HOW'S IT GOING... ANALYZING THE COMP 10BIT LEFT YOU?
THERE ARE SEVERAL LAYERS OF PROTECTION, BUT I SHOULD BE FINISHED BY TOMORROW MORNING.
...JUST LEAVE IT TO ME.
RIGHT NOW...
...I'M MORE WORRIED ABOUT KEISUKE.

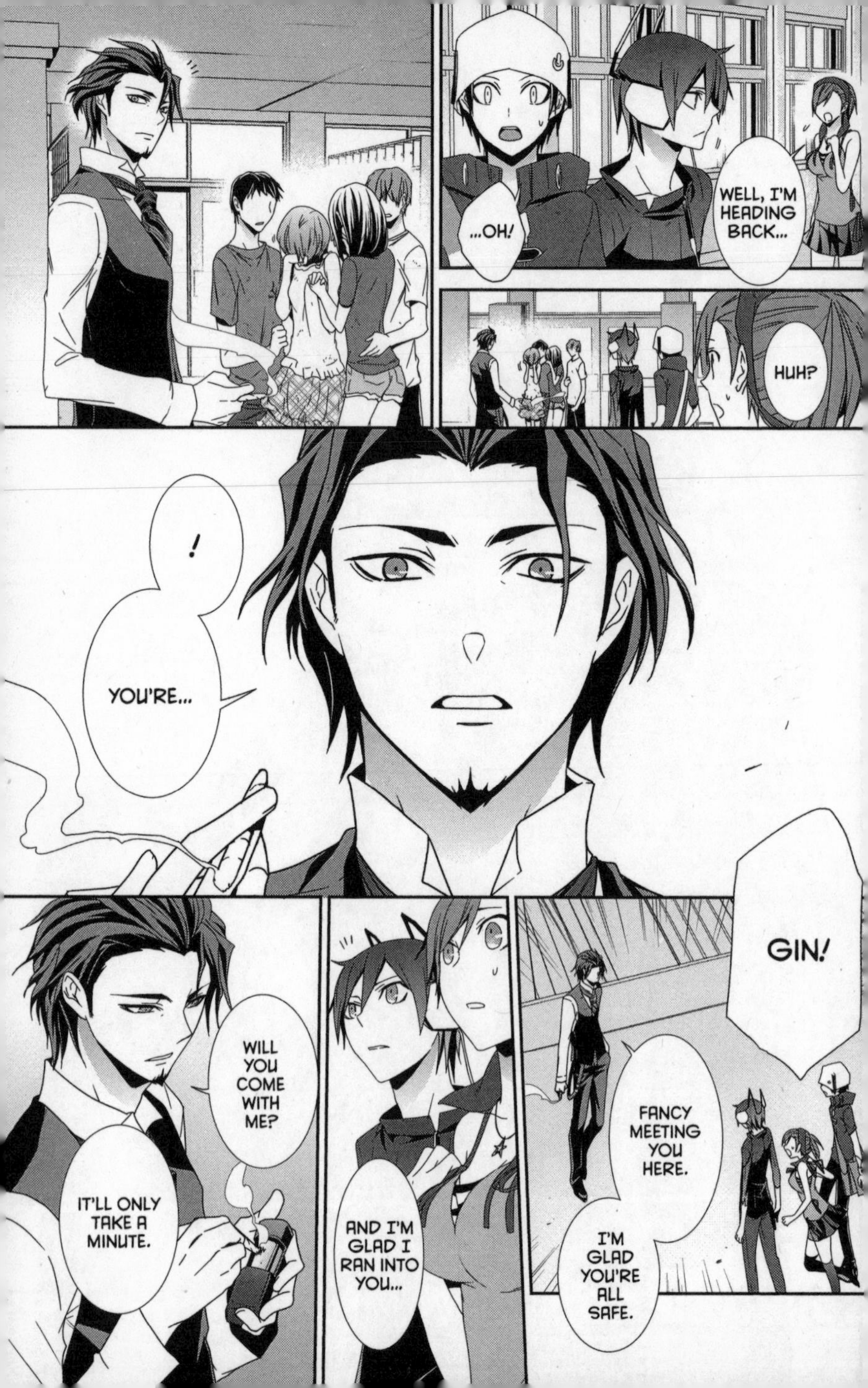
WELL, I'M HEADING BACK...
...OH!
HUH?
!
YOU'RE...
GIN!
FANCY MEETING YOU HERE.
I'M GLAD YOU'RE ALL SAFE.
AND I'M GLAD I RAN INTO YOU...
WILL YOU COME WITH ME?
IT'LL ONLY TAKE A MINUTE.

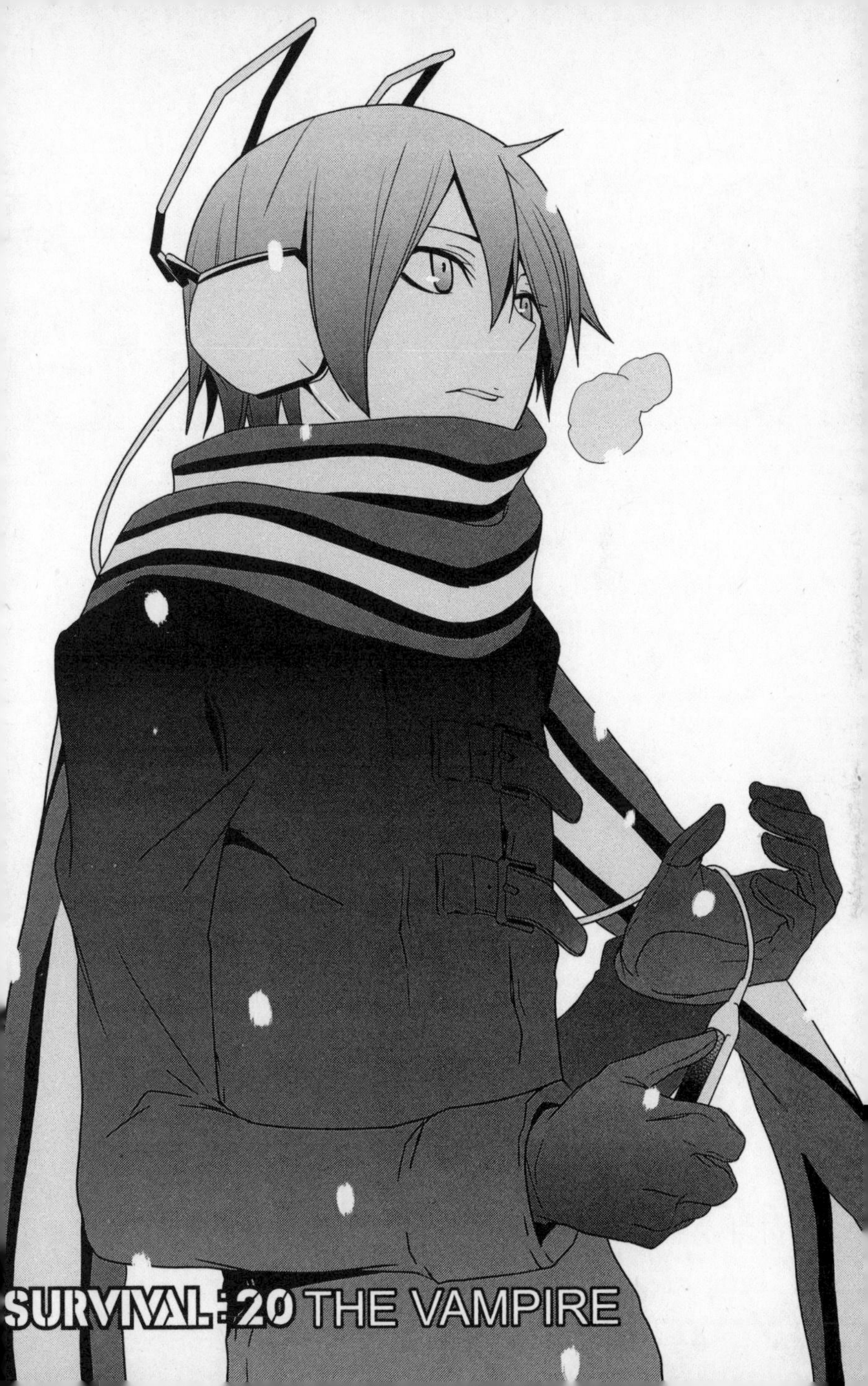

SURVIVAL : 20 THE VAMPIRE

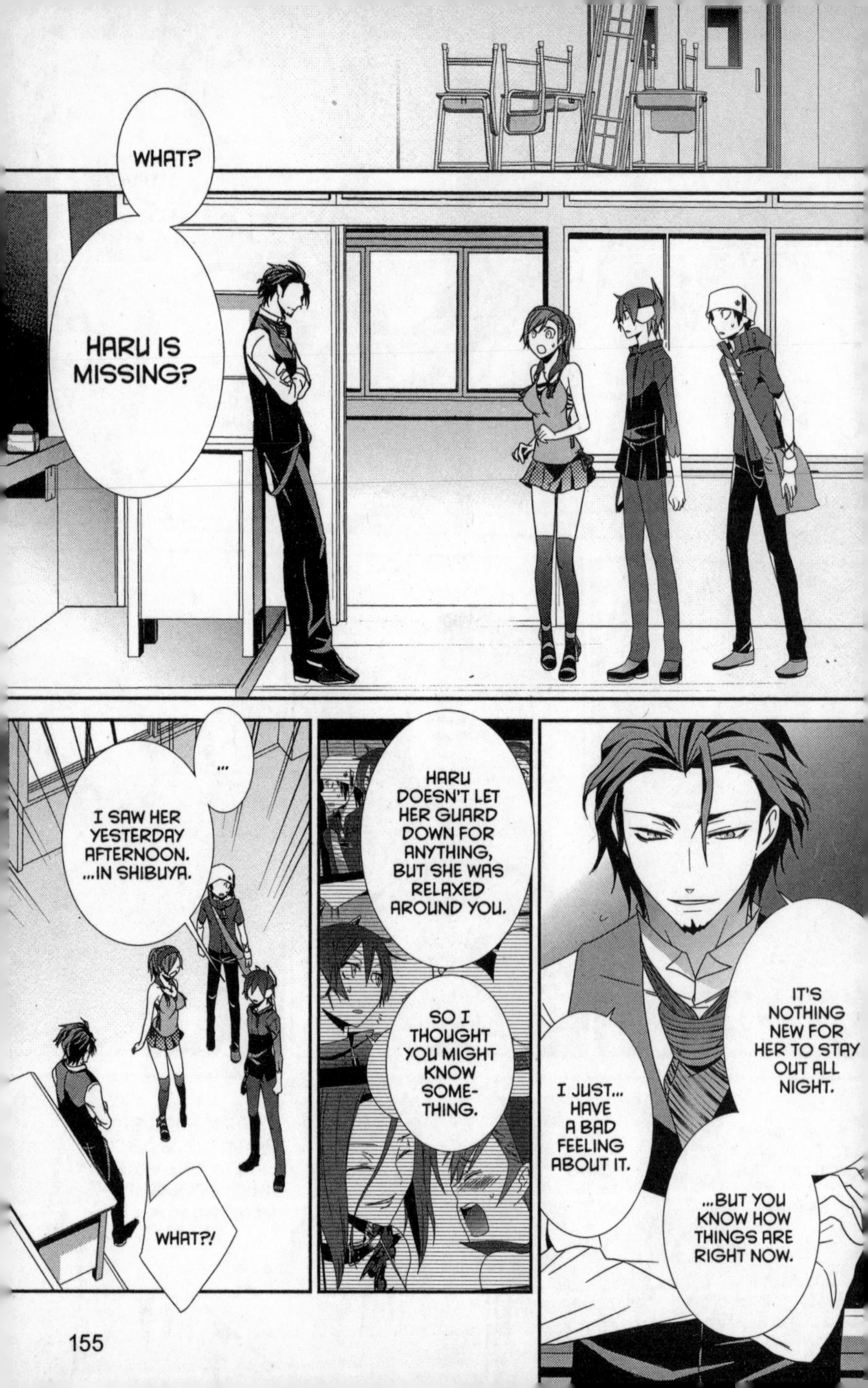
WHAT?
HARU IS MISSING?
IT'S NOTHING NEW FOR HER TO STAY OUT ALL NIGHT.
...BUT YOU KNOW HOW THINGS ARE RIGHT NOW.
I JUST... HAVE A BAD FEELING ABOUT IT.
HARU DOESN'T LET HER GUARD DOWN FOR ANYTHING, BUT SHE WAS RELAXED AROUND YOU.
SO I THOUGHT YOU MIGHT KNOW SOME-THING.
...
I SAW HER YESTERDAY AFTERNOON. ...IN SHIBUYA.
WHAT?!

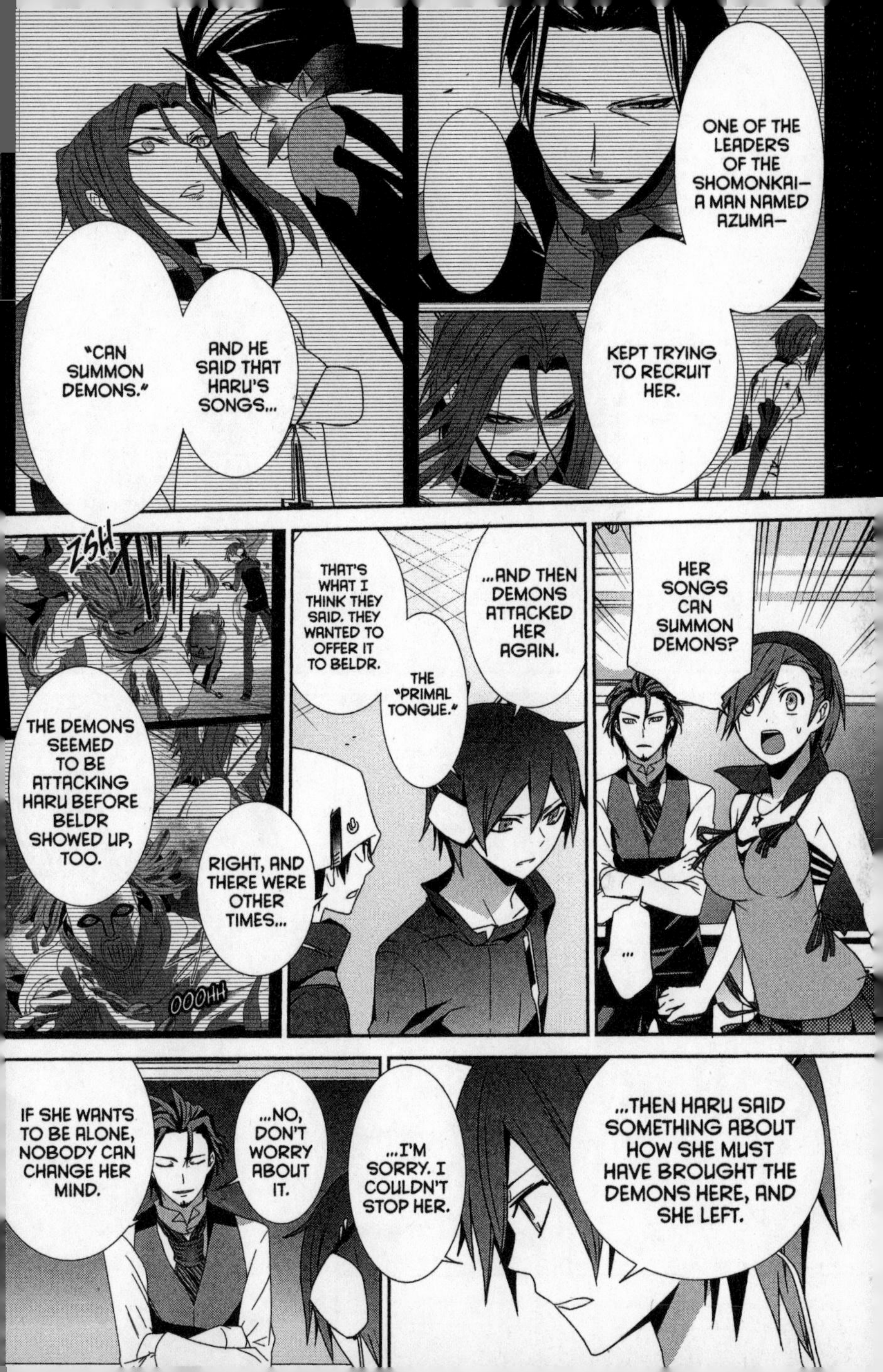
ONE OF THE LEADERS OF THE SHOMONKAI— A MAN NAMED AZUMA—
KEPT TRYING TO RECRUIT HER.
AND HE SAID THAT HARU'S SONGS...
"CAN SUMMON DEMONS."
HER SONGS CAN SUMMON DEMONS?
...
...AND THEN DEMONS ATTACKED HER AGAIN.
THAT'S WHAT I THINK THEY SAID. THEY WANTED TO OFFER IT TO BELDR.
THE "PRIMAL TONGUE."
RIGHT, AND THERE WERE OTHER TIMES...
ZSH
THE DEMONS SEEMED TO BE ATTACKING HARU BEFORE BELDR SHOWED UP, TOO.
OOOHH
...THEN HARU SAID SOMETHING ABOUT HOW SHE MUST HAVE BROUGHT THE DEMONS HERE, AND SHE LEFT.
...I'M SORRY. I COULDN'T STOP HER.
...NO, DON'T WORRY ABOUT IT.
IF SHE WANTS TO BE ALONE, NOBODY CAN CHANGE HER MIND.

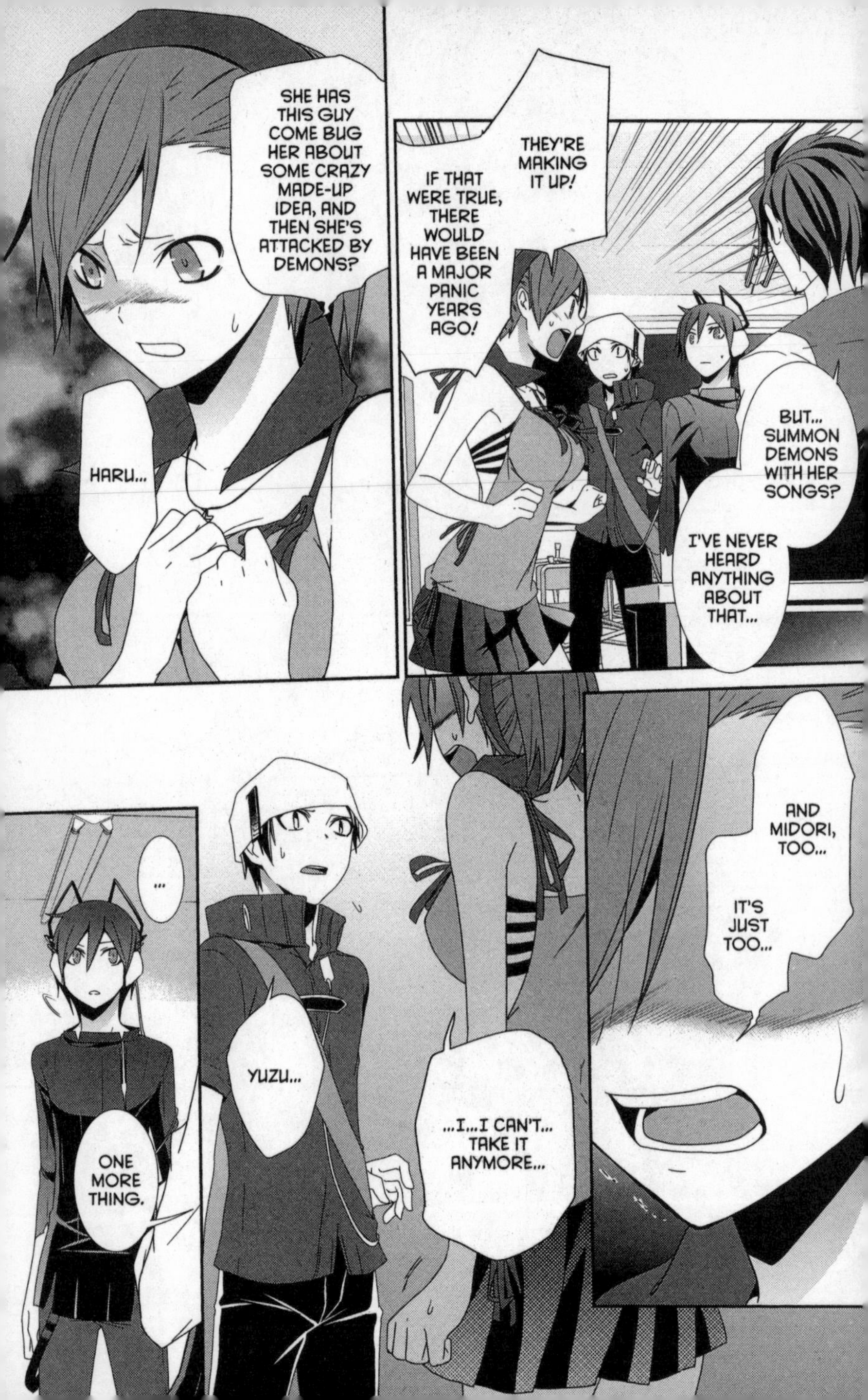
THEY'RE MAKING IT UP!
IF THAT WERE TRUE, THERE WOULD HAVE BEEN A MAJOR PANIC YEARS AGO!
BUT... SUMMON DEMONS WITH HER SONGS?
I'VE NEVER HEARD ANYTHING ABOUT THAT...
SHE HAS THIS GUY COME BUG HER ABOUT SOME CRAZY MADE-UP IDEA, AND THEN SHE'S ATTACKED BY DEMONS?
HARU...
AND MIDORI, TOO...
IT'S JUST TOO...
...I...I CAN'T... TAKE IT ANYMORE...
...
YUZU...
ONE MORE THING.

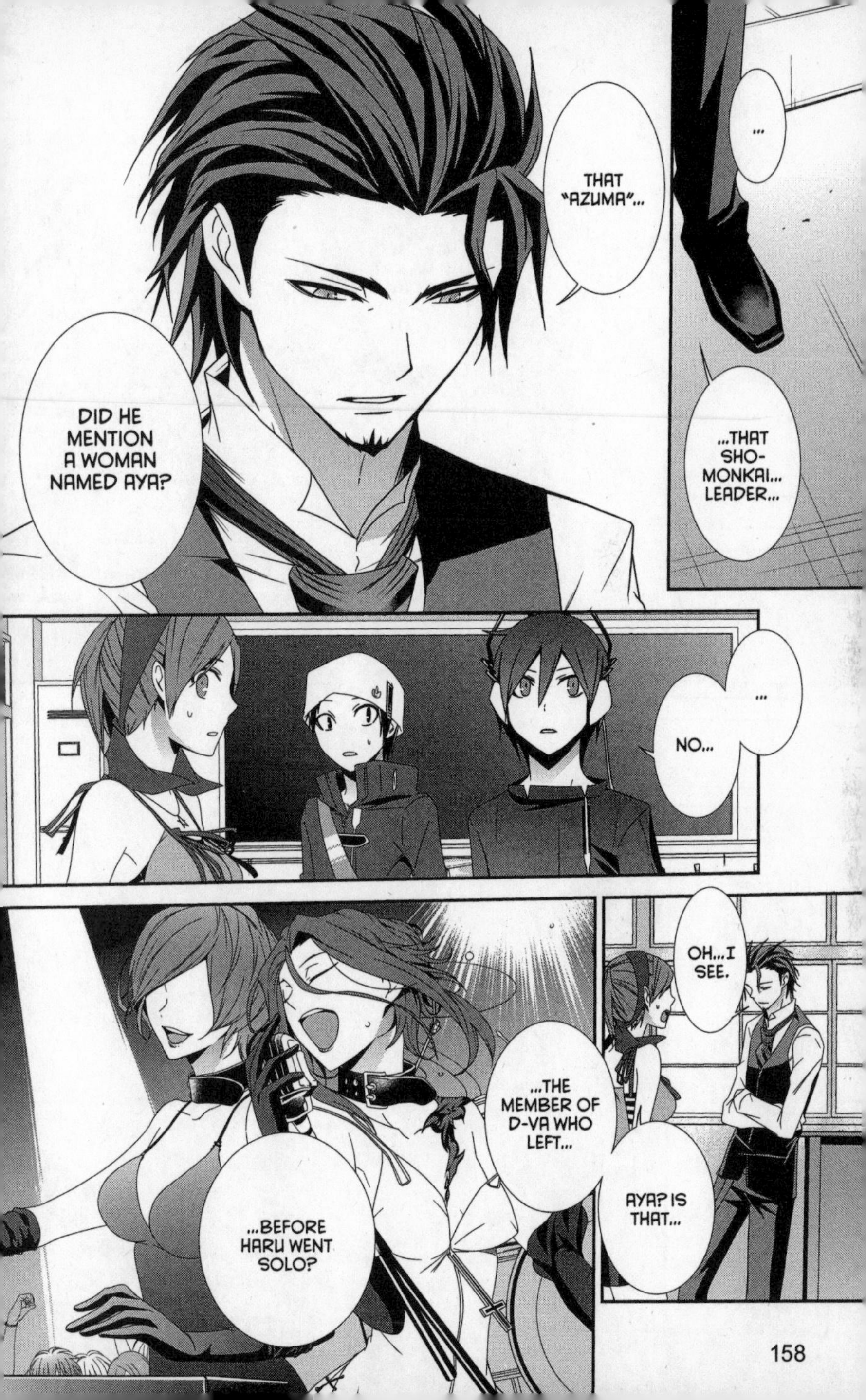
...
...THAT SHO-MONKAI... LEADER...
THAT "AZUMA"...
DID HE MENTION A WOMAN NAMED AYA?
...
NO...
OH...I SEE.
AYA? IS THAT...
...THE MEMBER OF D-VA WHO LEFT...
...BEFORE HARU WENT SOLO?

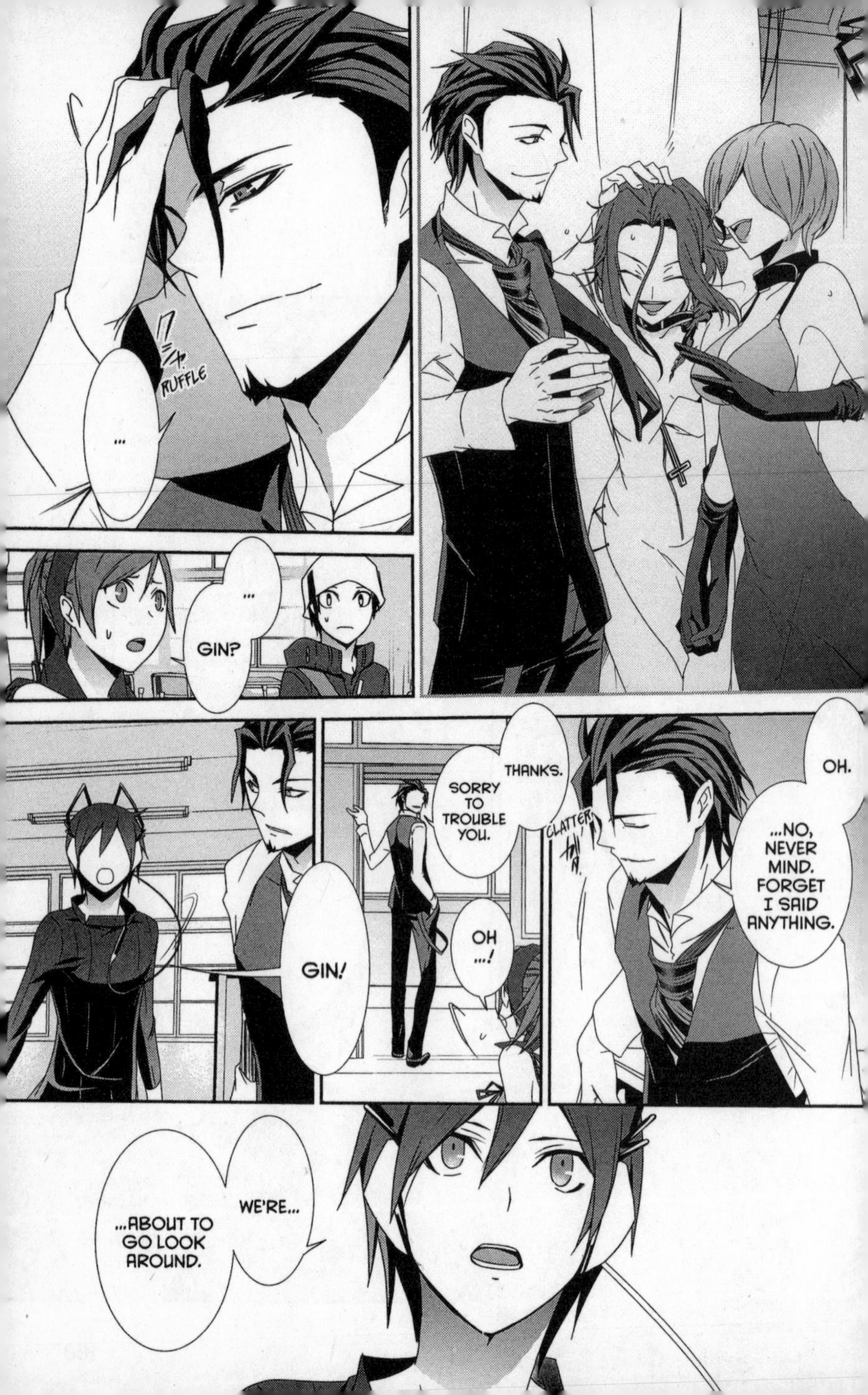
RUFFLE
...
...
GIN?
OH.
...NO, NEVER MIND. FORGET I SAID ANYTHING.
CLATTER
THANKS.
SORRY TO TROUBLE YOU.
OH ...!
GIN!
WE'RE...
...ABOUT TO GO LOOK AROUND.

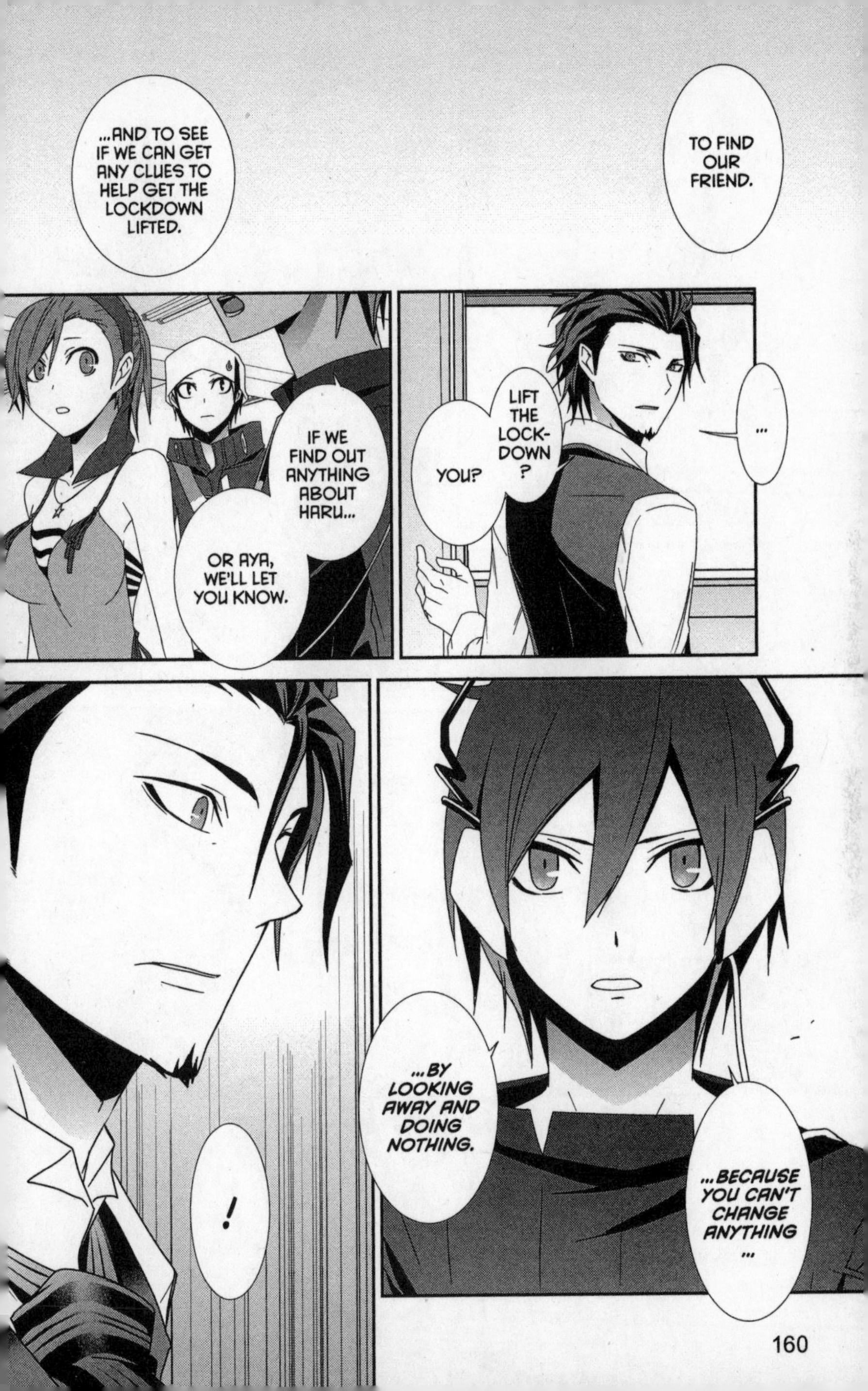
TO FIND OUR FRIEND.
...AND TO SEE IF WE CAN GET ANY CLUES TO HELP GET THE LOCKDOWN LIFTED.
...
LIFT THE LOCK-DOWN?
YOU?
IF WE FIND OUT ANYTHING ABOUT HARU...
OR AYA, WE'LL LET YOU KNOW.
...BECAUSE YOU CAN'T CHANGE ANYTHING...
...BY LOOKING AWAY AND DOING NOTHING.
!

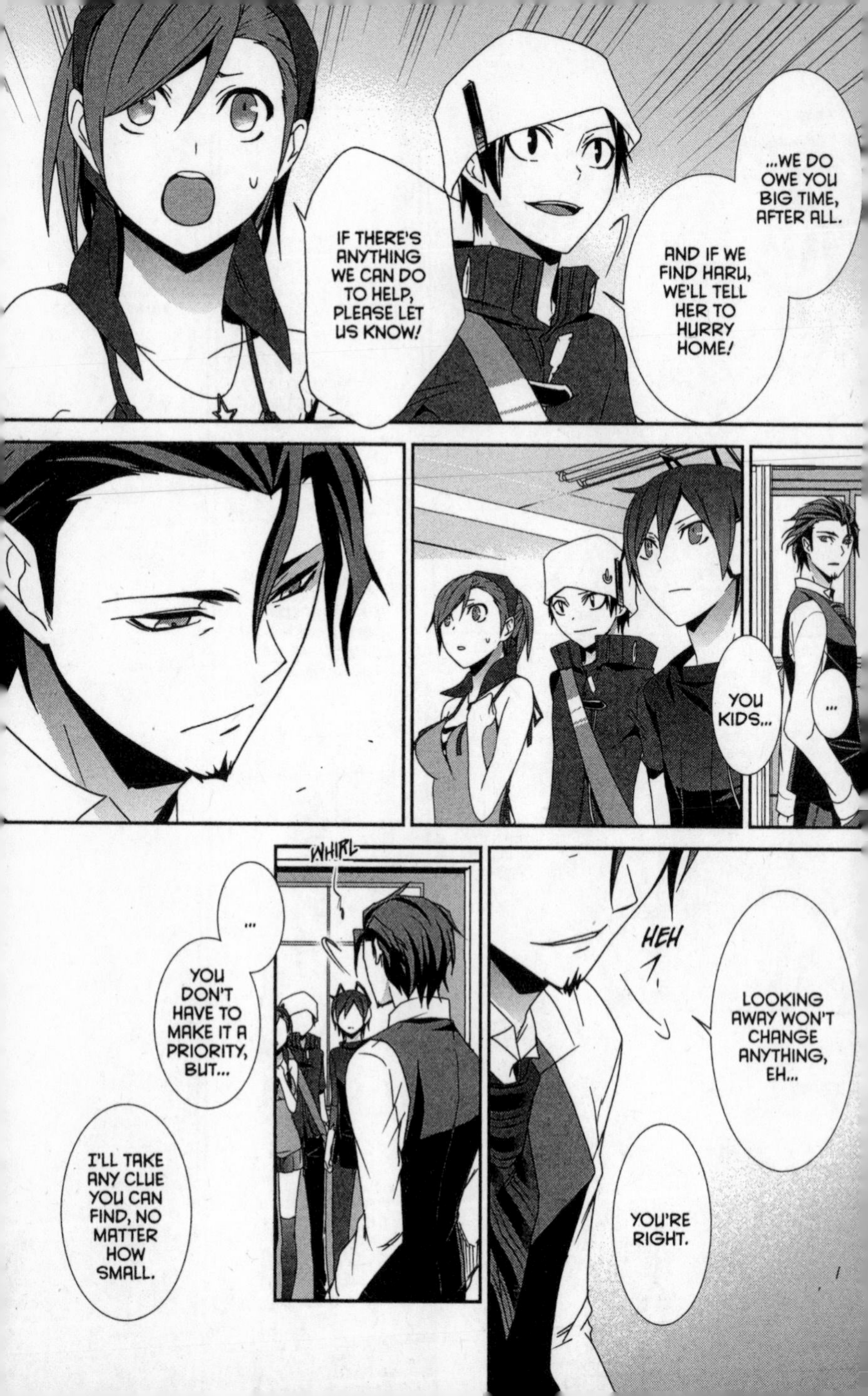
...WE DO OWE YOU BIG TIME, AFTER ALL.
AND IF WE FIND HARU, WE'LL TELL HER TO HURRY HOME!
IF THERE'S ANYTHING WE CAN DO TO HELP, PLEASE LET US KNOW!
...
YOU KIDS...
HEH
LOOKING AWAY WON'T CHANGE ANYTHING, EH...
YOU'RE RIGHT.
WHIRL
...
YOU DON'T HAVE TO MAKE IT A PRIORITY, BUT...
I'LL TAKE ANY CLUE YOU CAN FIND, NO MATTER HOW SMALL.

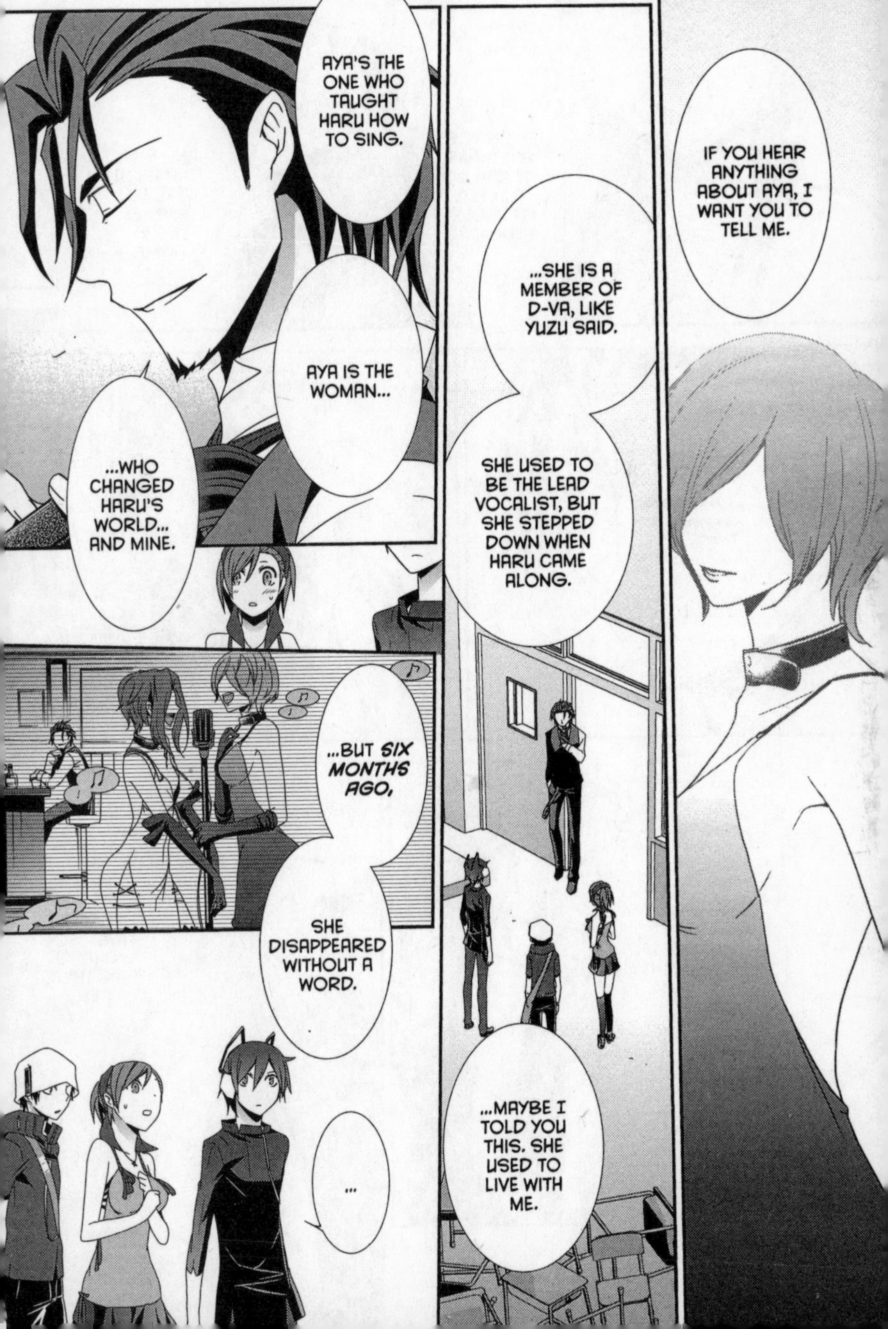
IF YOU HEAR ANYTHING ABOUT AYA, I WANT YOU TO TELL ME.
...SHE IS A MEMBER OF D-VA, LIKE YUZU SAID.
SHE USED TO BE THE LEAD VOCALIST, BUT SHE STEPPED DOWN WHEN HARU CAME ALONG.
...MAYBE I TOLD YOU THIS. SHE USED TO LIVE WITH ME.
AYA'S THE ONE WHO TAUGHT HARU HOW TO SING.
AYA IS THE WOMAN...
...WHO CHANGED HARU'S WORLD... AND MINE.
...BUT *SIX MONTHS AGO,*
SHE DISAPPEARED WITHOUT A WORD.
...

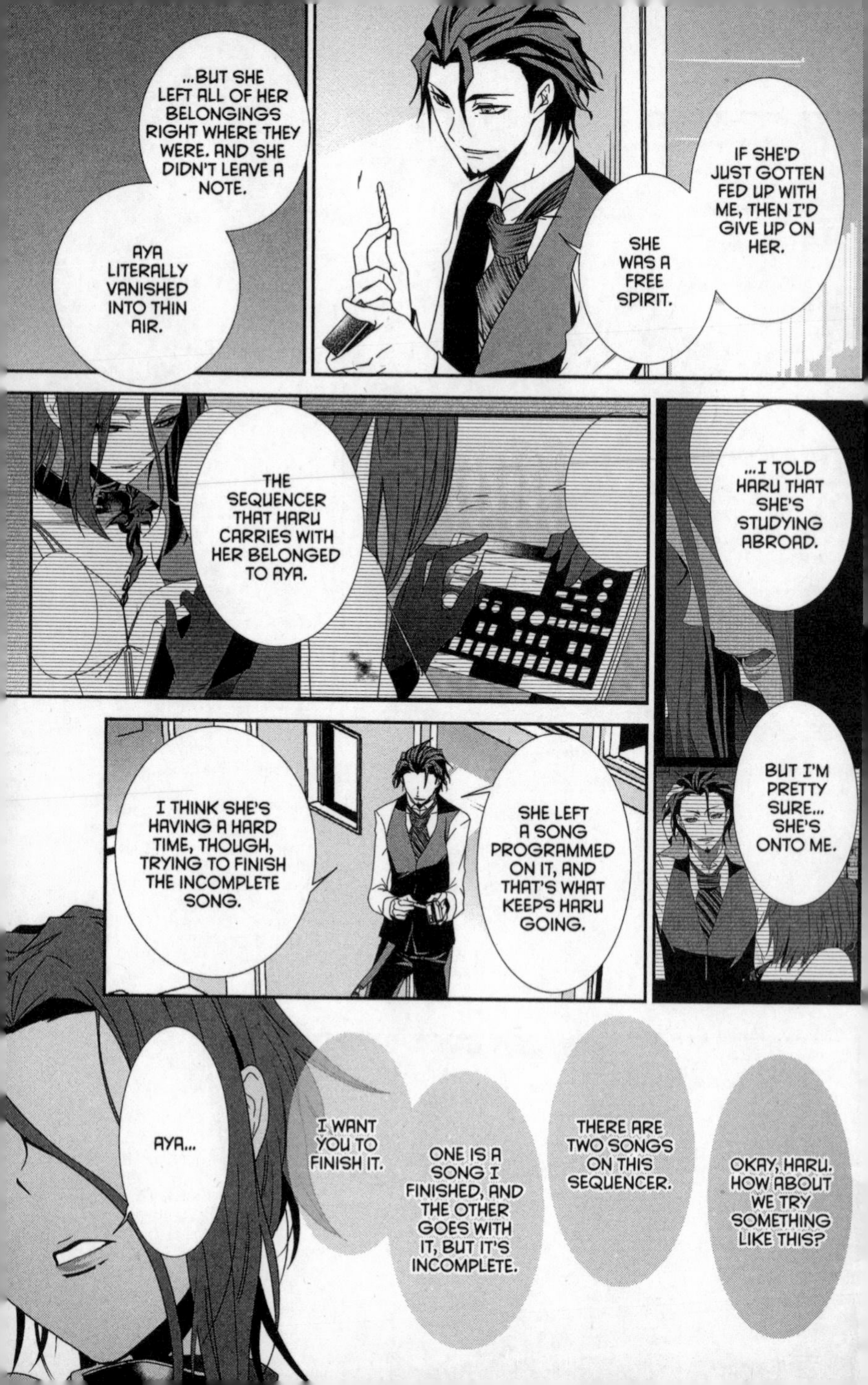
IF SHE'D JUST GOTTEN FED UP WITH ME, THEN I'D GIVE UP ON HER.
SHE WAS A FREE SPIRIT.
...BUT SHE LEFT ALL OF HER BELONGINGS RIGHT WHERE THEY WERE. AND SHE DIDN'T LEAVE A NOTE.
AYA LITERALLY VANISHED INTO THIN AIR.
...I TOLD HARU THAT SHE'S STUDYING ABROAD.
THE SEQUENCER THAT HARU CARRIES WITH HER BELONGED TO AYA.
SHE LEFT A SONG PROGRAMMED ON IT, AND THAT'S WHAT KEEPS HARU GOING.
I THINK SHE'S HAVING A HARD TIME, THOUGH, TRYING TO FINISH THE INCOMPLETE SONG.
BUT I'M PRETTY SURE... SHE'S ONTO ME.
OKAY, HARU. HOW ABOUT WE TRY SOMETHING LIKE THIS?
THERE ARE TWO SONGS ON THIS SEQUENCER.
ONE IS A SONG I FINISHED, AND THE OTHER GOES WITH IT, BUT IT'S INCOMPLETE.
I WANT YOU TO FINISH IT.
AYA...

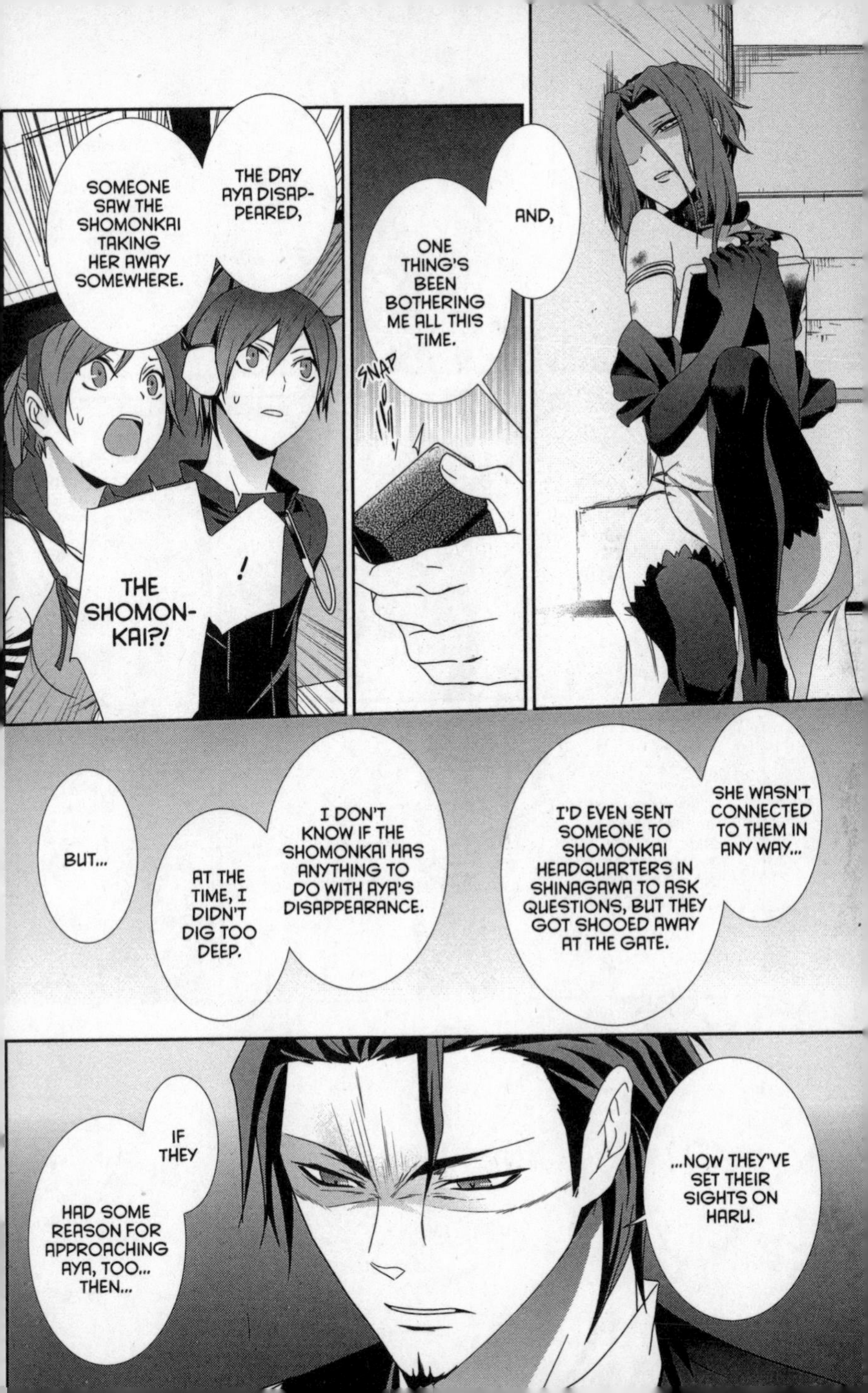
AND,
ONE THING'S BEEN BOTHERING ME ALL THIS TIME.
SNAP
THE DAY AYA DISAP-PEARED,
SOMEONE SAW THE SHOMONKAI TAKING HER AWAY SOMEWHERE.
!
THE SHOMON-KAI?!
SHE WASN'T CONNECTED TO THEM IN ANY WAY...
I'D EVEN SENT SOMEONE TO SHOMONKAI HEADQUARTERS IN SHINAGAWA TO ASK QUESTIONS, BUT THEY GOT SHOOED AWAY AT THE GATE.
I DON'T KNOW IF THE SHOMONKAI HAS ANYTHING TO DO WITH AYA'S DISAPPEARANCE.
AT THE TIME, I DIDN'T DIG TOO DEEP.
BUT...
IF THEY
HAD SOME REASON FOR APPROACHING AYA, TOO... THEN...
...NOW THEY'VE SET THEIR SIGHTS ON HARU.

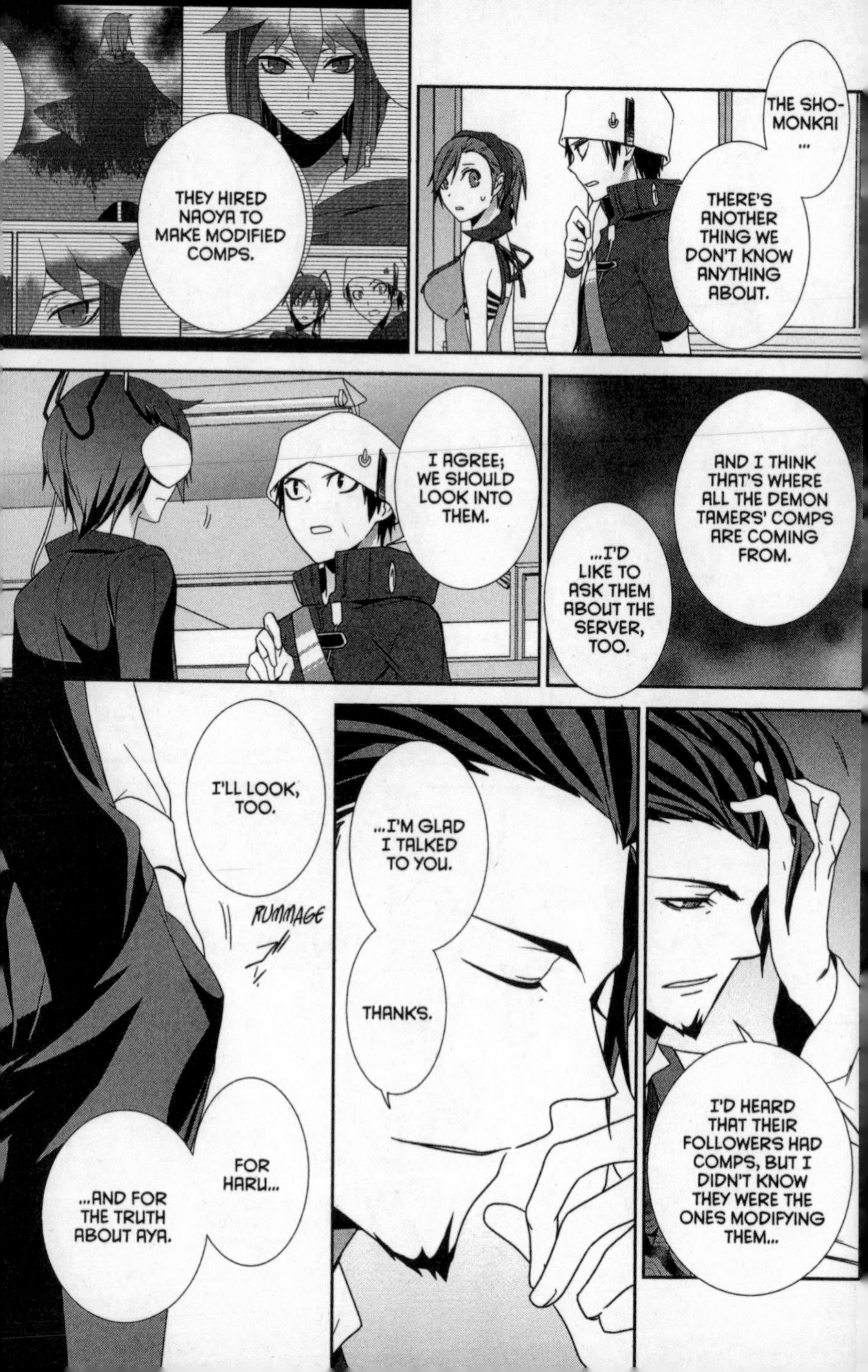
THE SHO-MONKAI...
THERE'S ANOTHER THING WE DON'T KNOW ANYTHING ABOUT.
THEY HIRED NAOYA TO MAKE MODIFIED COMPS.
AND I THINK THAT'S WHERE ALL THE DEMON TAMERS' COMPS ARE COMING FROM.
...I'D LIKE TO ASK THEM ABOUT THE SERVER, TOO.
I AGREE; WE SHOULD LOOK INTO THEM.
I'D HEARD THAT THEIR FOLLOWERS HAD COMPS, BUT I DIDN'T KNOW THEY WERE THE ONES MODIFYING THEM...
...I'M GLAD I TALKED TO YOU.
THANKS.
I'LL LOOK, TOO.
RUMMAGE
FOR HARU...
...AND FOR THE TRUTH ABOUT AYA.

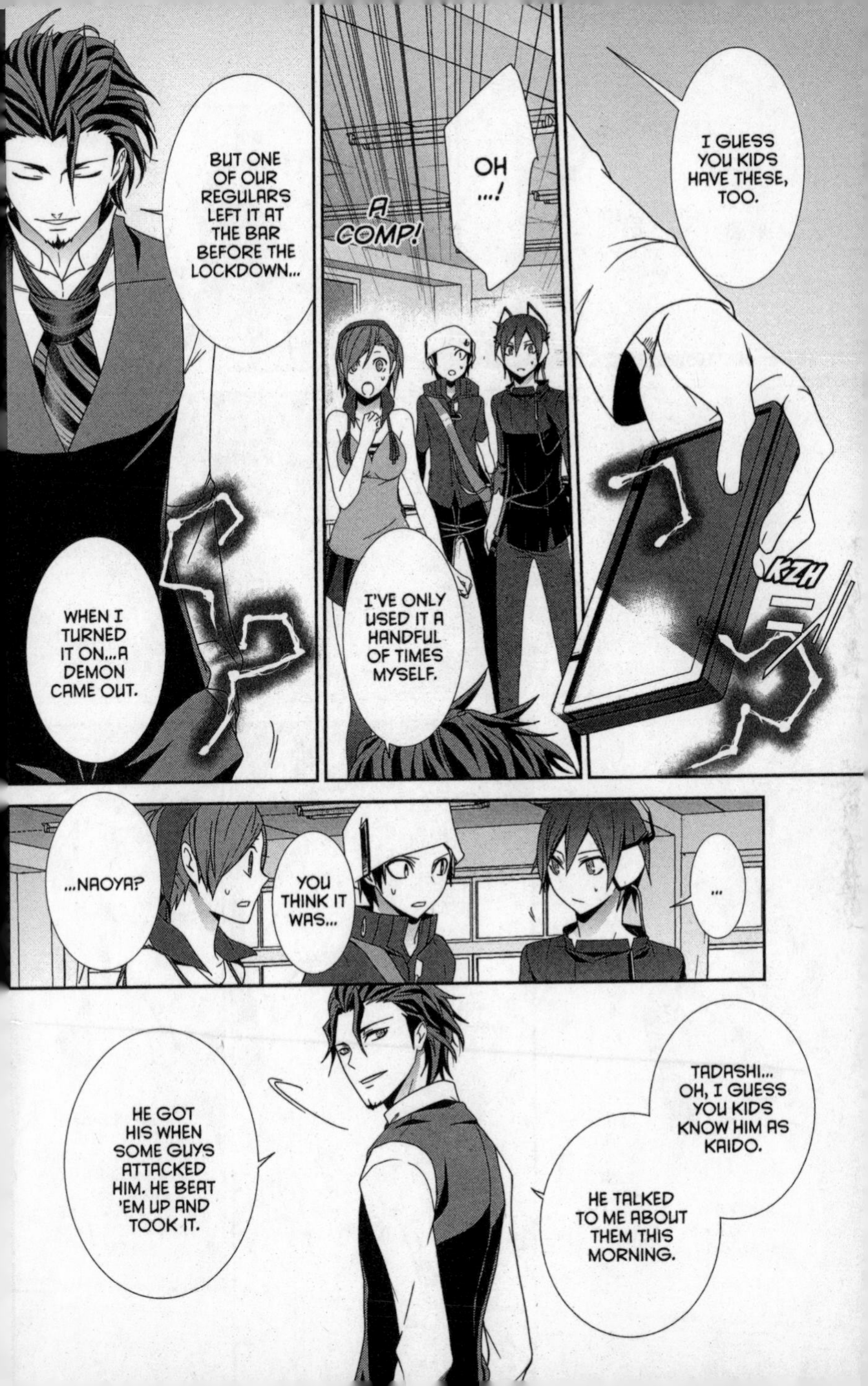
I GUESS YOU KIDS HAVE THESE, TOO.
KZH
OH ...!
A COMP!
I'VE ONLY USED IT A HANDFUL OF TIMES MYSELF.
BUT ONE OF OUR REGULARS LEFT IT AT THE BAR BEFORE THE LOCKDOWN...
WHEN I TURNED IT ON...A DEMON CAME OUT.
...
YOU THINK IT WAS...
...NAOYA?
TADASHI... OH, I GUESS YOU KIDS KNOW HIM AS KAIDO.
HE TALKED TO ME ABOUT THEM THIS MORNING.
HE GOT HIS WHEN SOME GUYS ATTACKED HIM. HE BEAT 'EM UP AND TOOK IT.

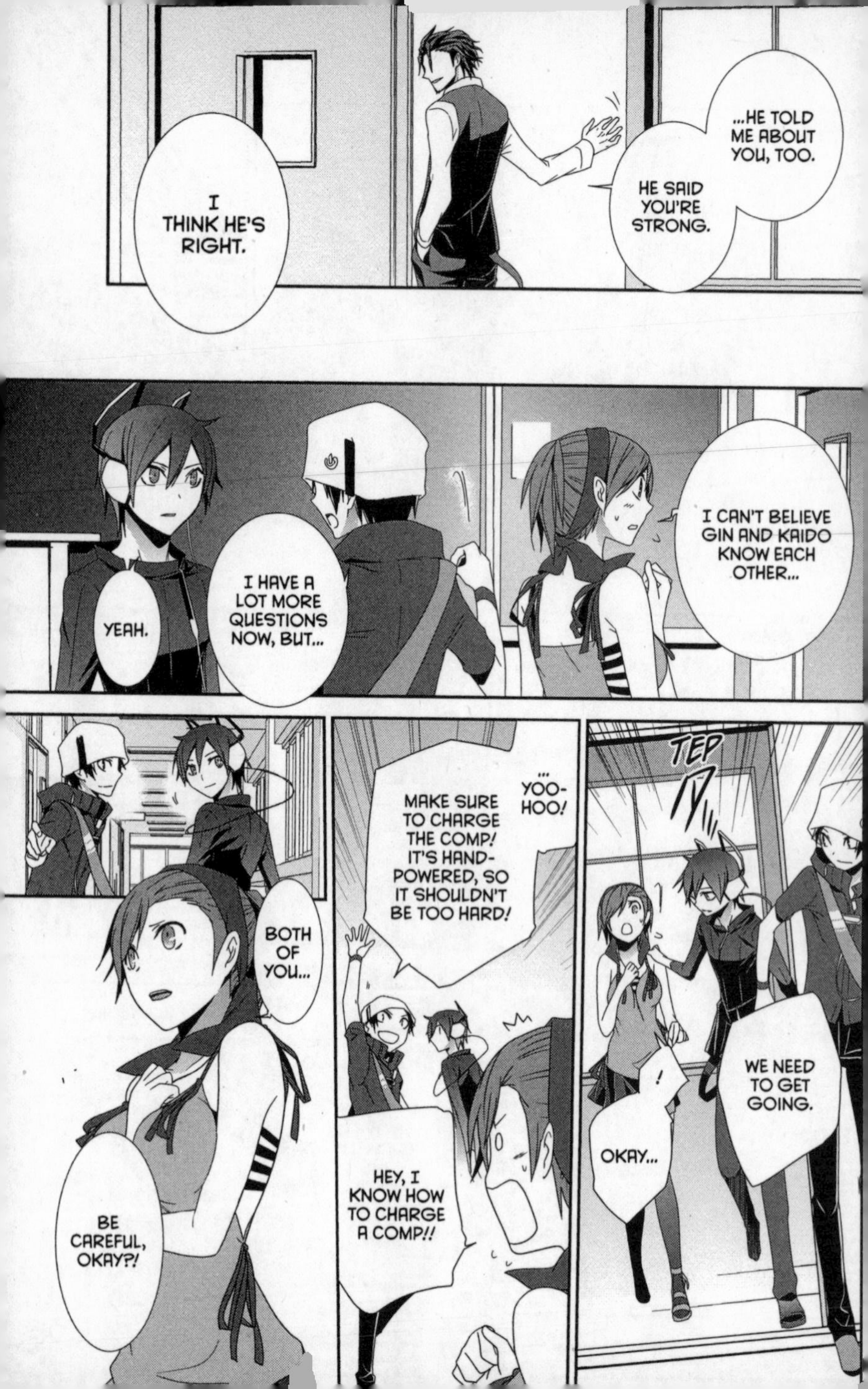
...HE TOLD ME ABOUT YOU, TOO.
HE SAID YOU'RE STRONG.
I THINK HE'S RIGHT.
I CAN'T BELIEVE GIN AND KAIDO KNOW EACH OTHER...
I HAVE A LOT MORE QUESTIONS NOW, BUT...
YEAH.
TEP
WE NEED TO GET GOING.
OKAY...
...YOO-HOO!
MAKE SURE TO CHARGE THE COMP! IT'S HAND-POWERED, SO IT SHOULDN'T BE TOO HARD!
HEY, I KNOW HOW TO CHARGE A COMP!!
BOTH OF YOU...
BE CAREFUL, OKAY?!

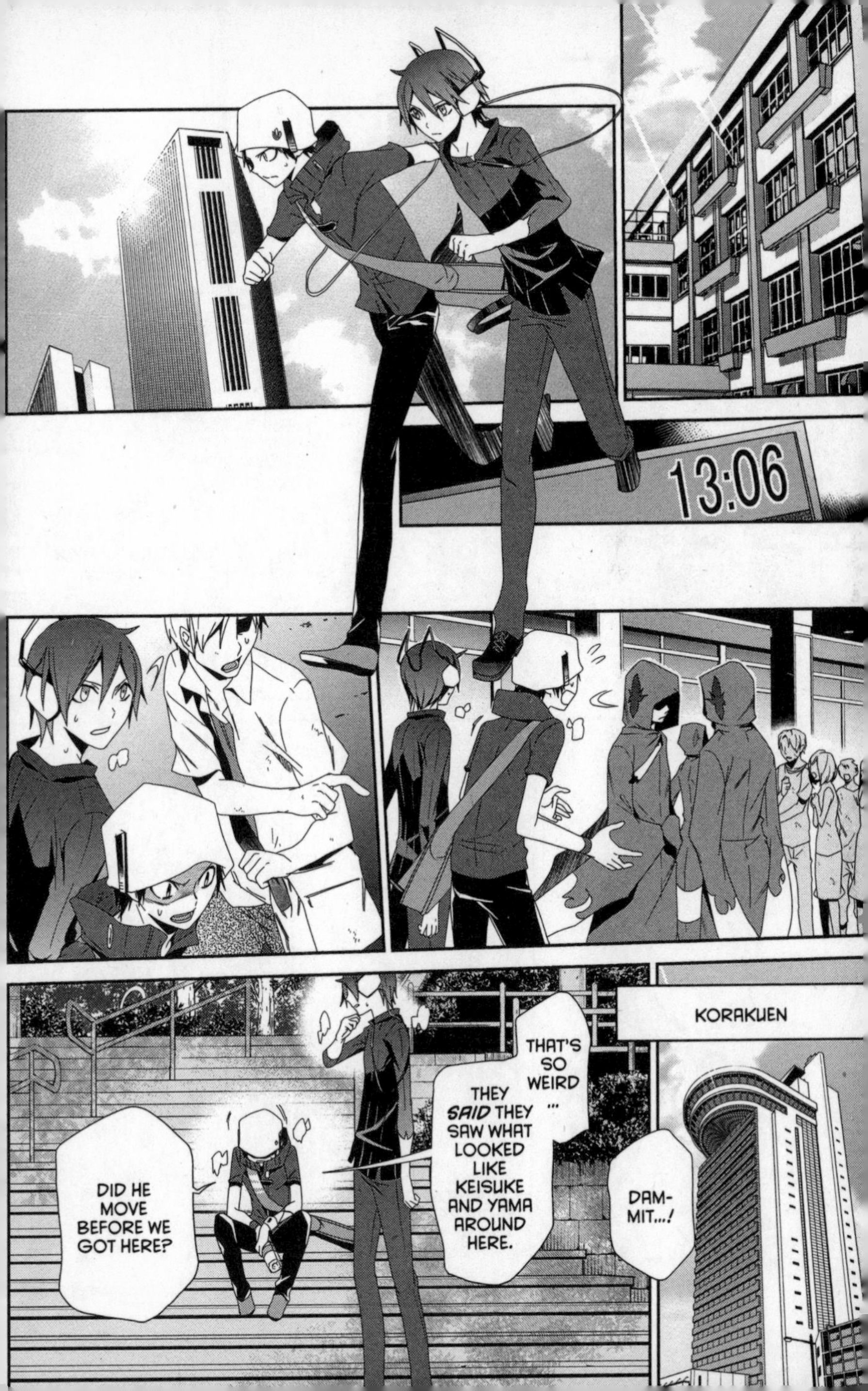
13:06
KORAKUEN
DAM-MIT...!
THAT'S SO WEIRD ...
THEY *SAID* THEY SAW WHAT LOOKED LIKE KEISUKE AND YAMA AROUND HERE.
DID HE MOVE BEFORE WE GOT HERE?

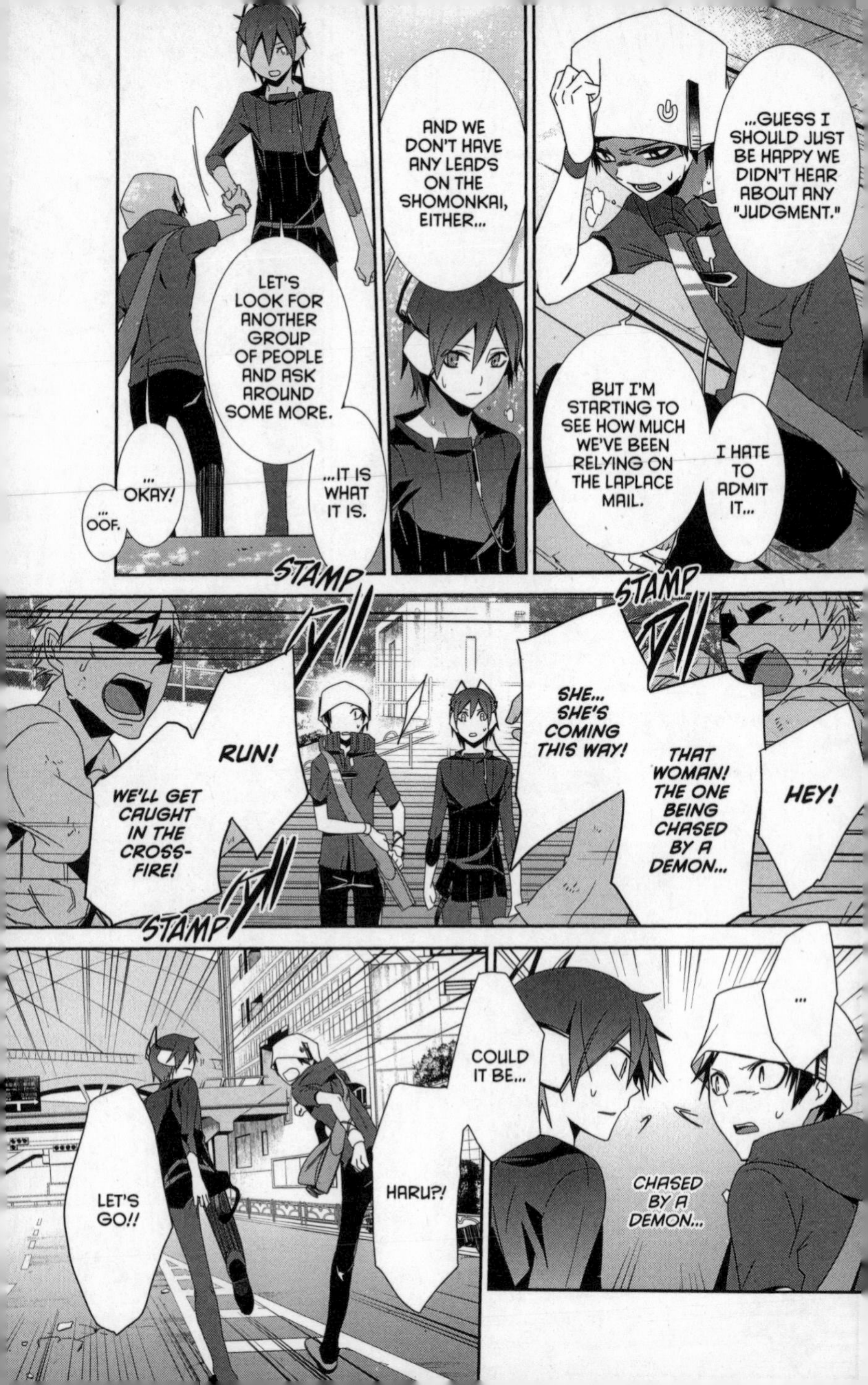
...GUESS I SHOULD JUST BE HAPPY WE DIDN'T HEAR ABOUT ANY "JUDGMENT."
I HATE TO ADMIT IT...
BUT I'M STARTING TO SEE HOW MUCH WE'VE BEEN RELYING ON THE LAPLACE MAIL.
AND WE DON'T HAVE ANY LEADS ON THE SHOMONKAI, EITHER...
LET'S LOOK FOR ANOTHER GROUP OF PEOPLE AND ASK AROUND SOME MORE.
...IT IS WHAT IT IS.
... OKAY!
... OOF.
STAMP
STAMP
HEY!
THAT WOMAN! THE ONE BEING CHASED BY A DEMON...
SHE... SHE'S COMING THIS WAY!
RUN!
WE'LL GET CAUGHT IN THE CROSS-FIRE!
STAMP
...
COULD IT BE...
CHASED BY A DEMON...
HARU?!
LET'S GO!!

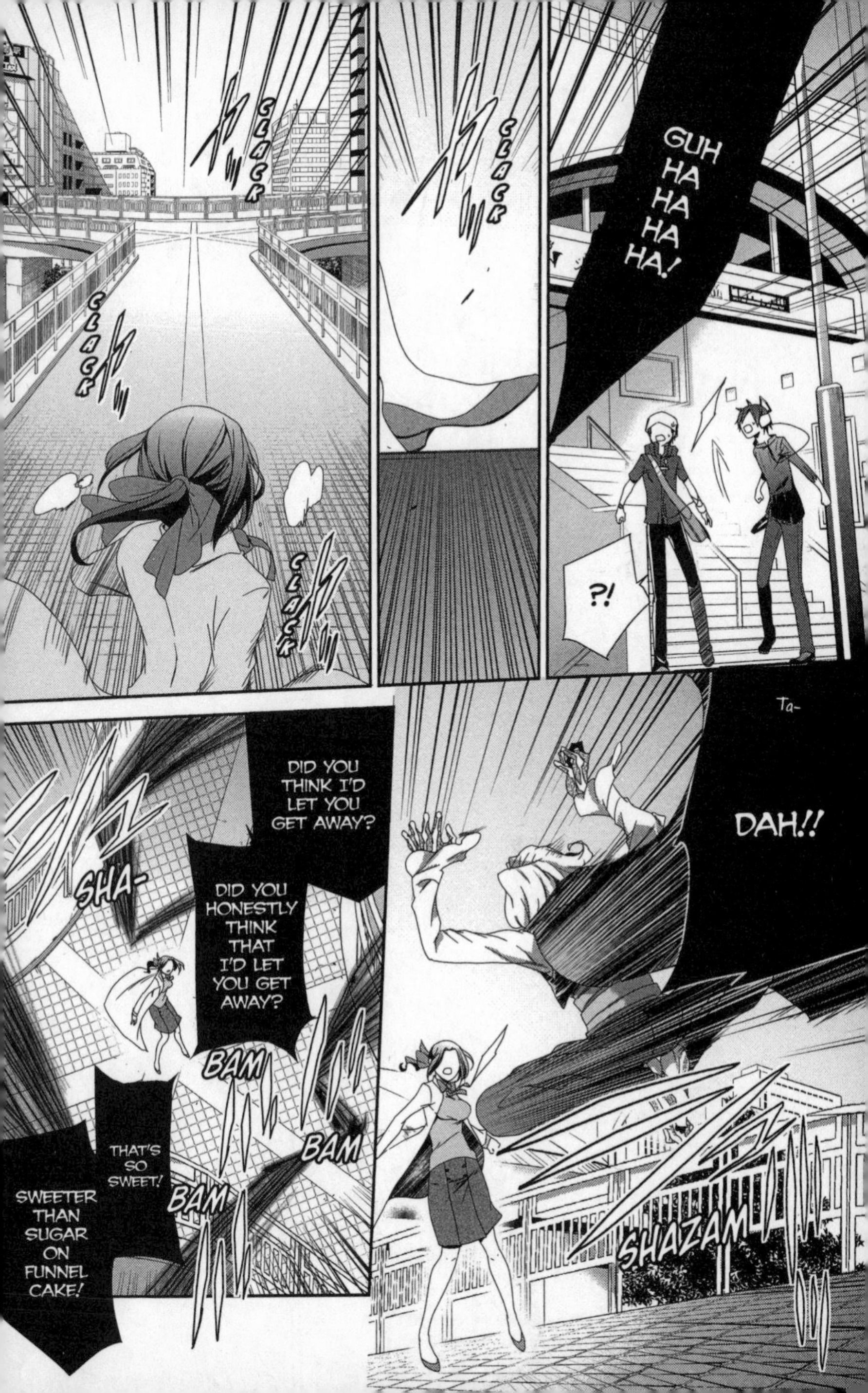
GUH HA HA HA HA!
?!
CLACK
CLACK
CLACK
CLACK
Ta-
DAH!!
SHAZAM
DID YOU THINK I'D LET YOU GET AWAY?
SHA-
DID YOU HONESTLY THINK THAT I'D LET YOU GET AWAY?
BAM
THAT'S SO SWEET!
BAM
BAM
SWEETER THAN SUGAR ON FUNNEL CAKE!

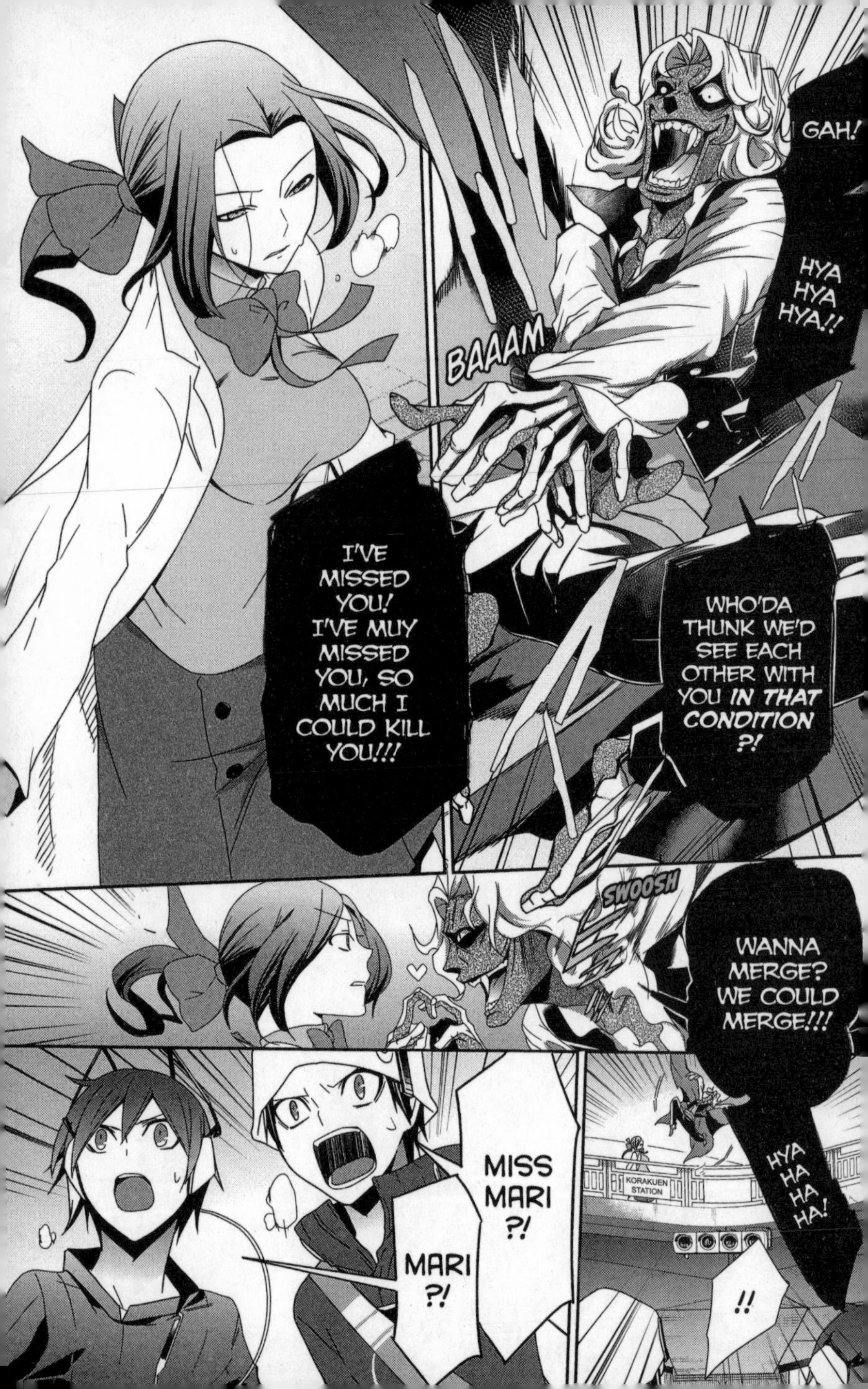

GAH!
HYA HYA HYA!!
BAAAM
WHO'DA THUNK WE'D SEE EACH OTHER WITH YOU *IN THAT CONDITION* ?!
I'VE MISSED YOU! I'VE MUY MISSED YOU, SO MUCH I COULD KILL YOU!!!
SWOOSH
WANNA MERGE? WE COULD MERGE!!!
KORAKUEN STATION
HYA HA HA HA!
!!
MISS MARI ?!
MARI ?!

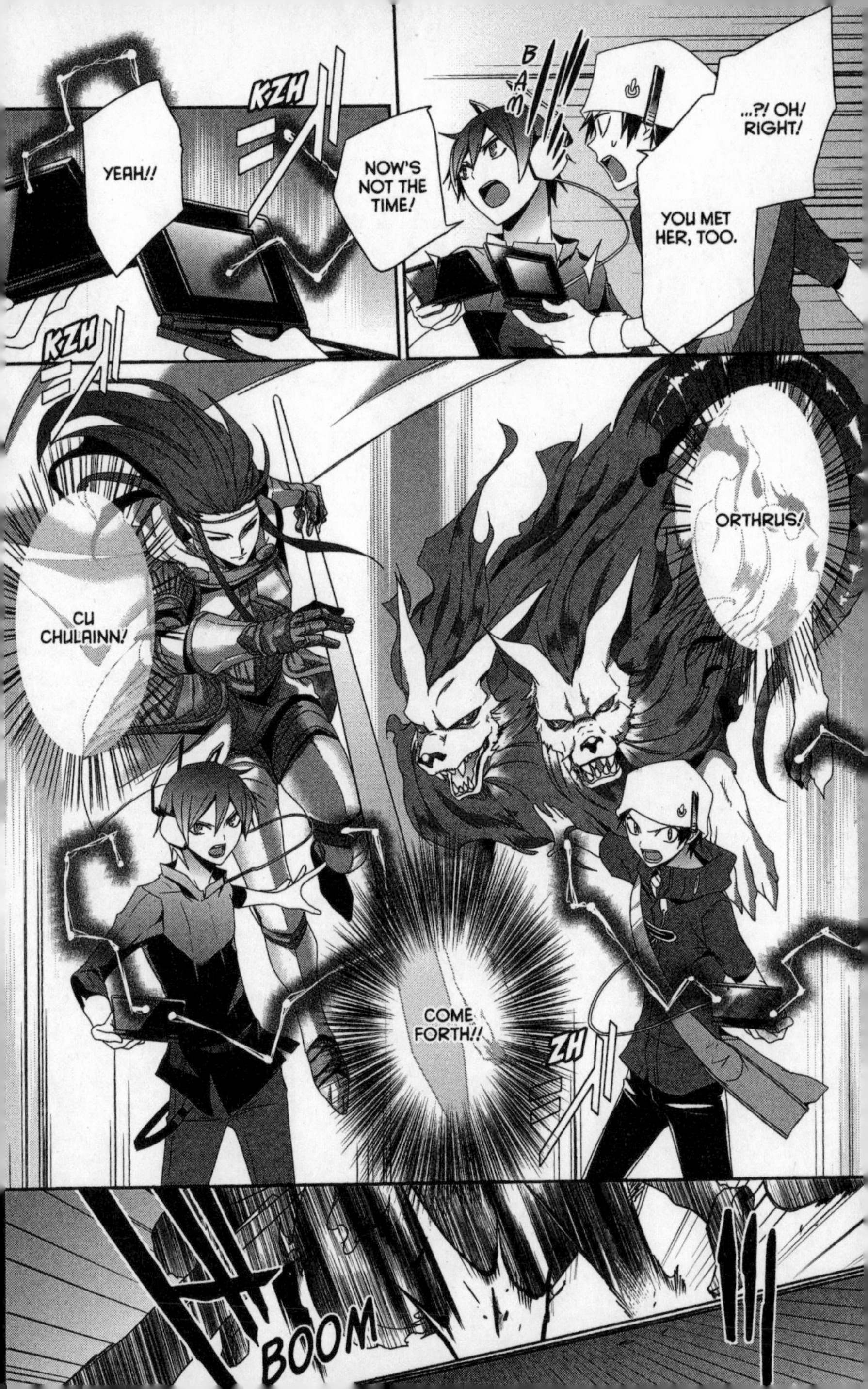

...?! OH! RIGHT!
YOU MET HER, TOO.
BAM
NOW'S NOT THE TIME!
KZH
YEAH!!
KZH
ORTHRUS!
CU CHULAINN!
COME FORTH!!
ZH
BOOM

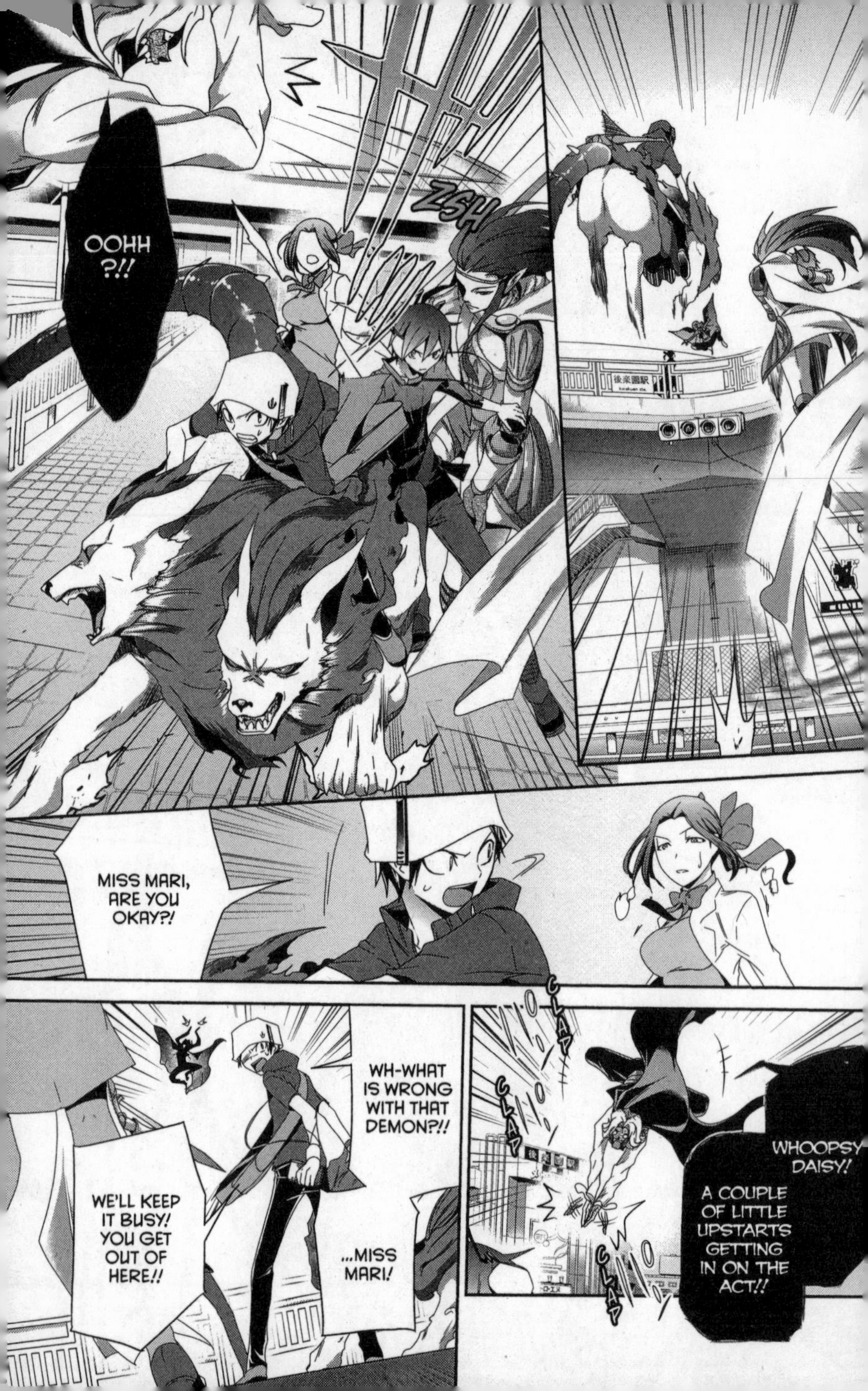
ZSH
OOHH ?!!
MISS MARI, ARE YOU OKAY?!
CLAP
CLAP
CLAP
CLAP
WHOOPSY DAISY!
A COUPLE OF LITTLE UPSTARTS GETTING IN ON THE ACT!!
WH-WHAT IS WRONG WITH THAT DEMON?!!
...MISS MARI!
WE'LL KEEP IT BUSY! YOU GET OUT OF HERE!!

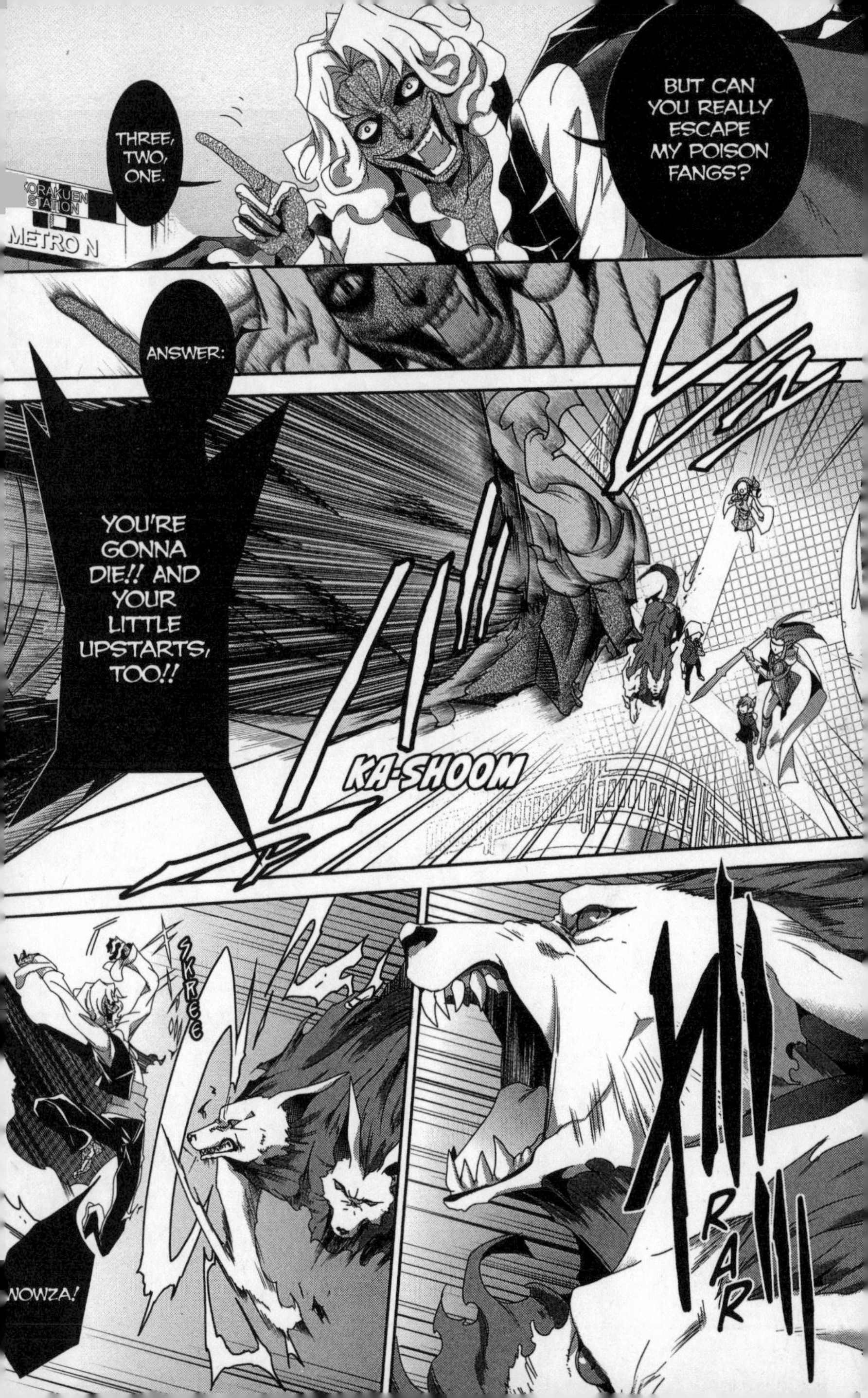
BUT CAN YOU REALLY ESCAPE MY POISON FANGS?
THREE, TWO, ONE.
KORAKUEN STATION
METRO N
ANSWER:
YOU'RE GONNA DIE!! AND YOUR LITTLE UPSTARTS, TOO!!
KA-SHOOM
RAR
SKREE
NOWZA!

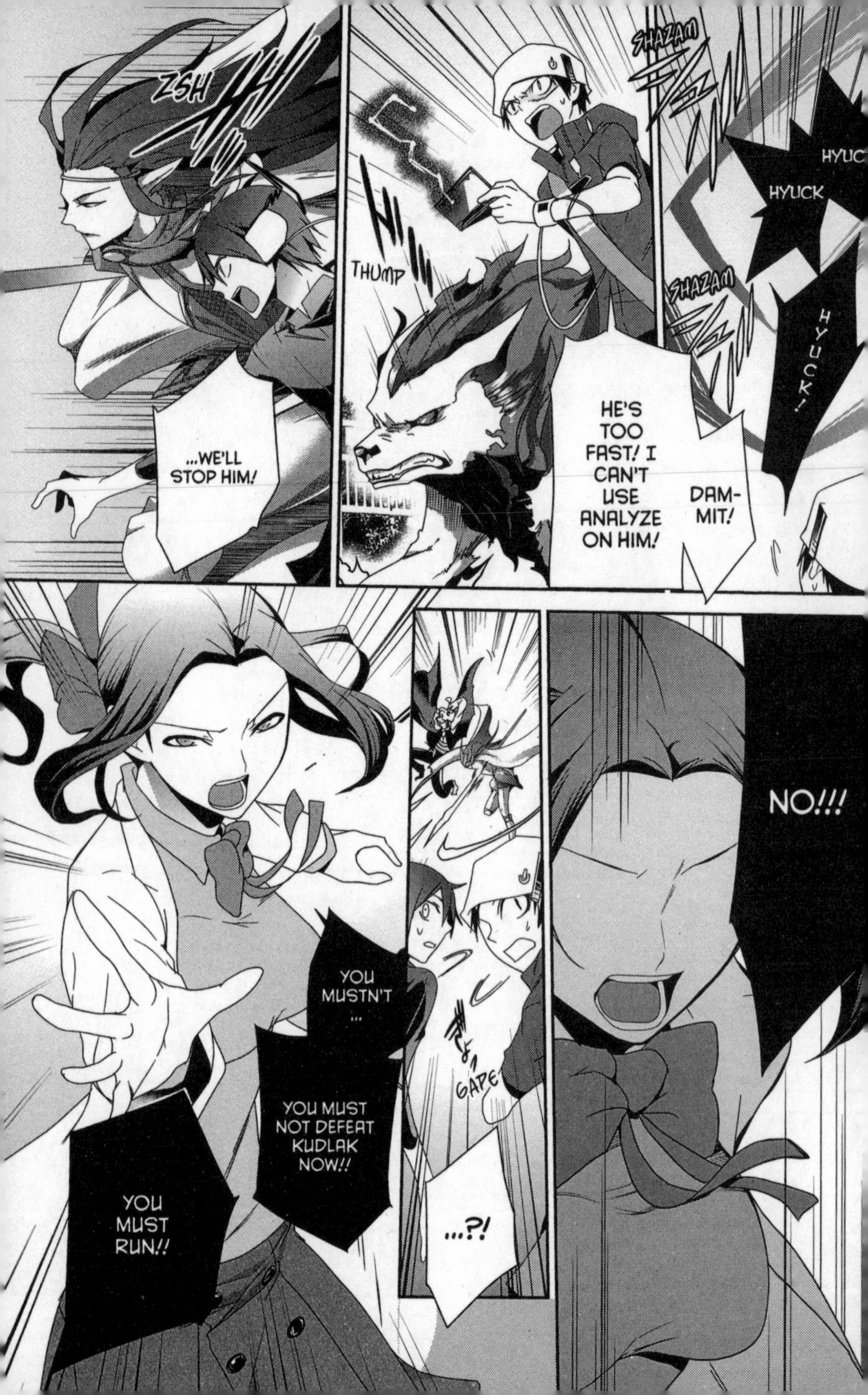
SHAZAM
HYUCK
HYUCK
SHAZAM
HYUCK!
DAM-
MIT!
HE'S TOO FAST! I CAN'T USE ANALYZE ON HIM!
THUMP
ZSH
...WE'LL STOP HIM!
NO!!!
...?!
GAPE
YOU MUSTN'T ...
YOU MUST NOT DEFEAT KUDLAK NOW!!
YOU MUST RUN!!

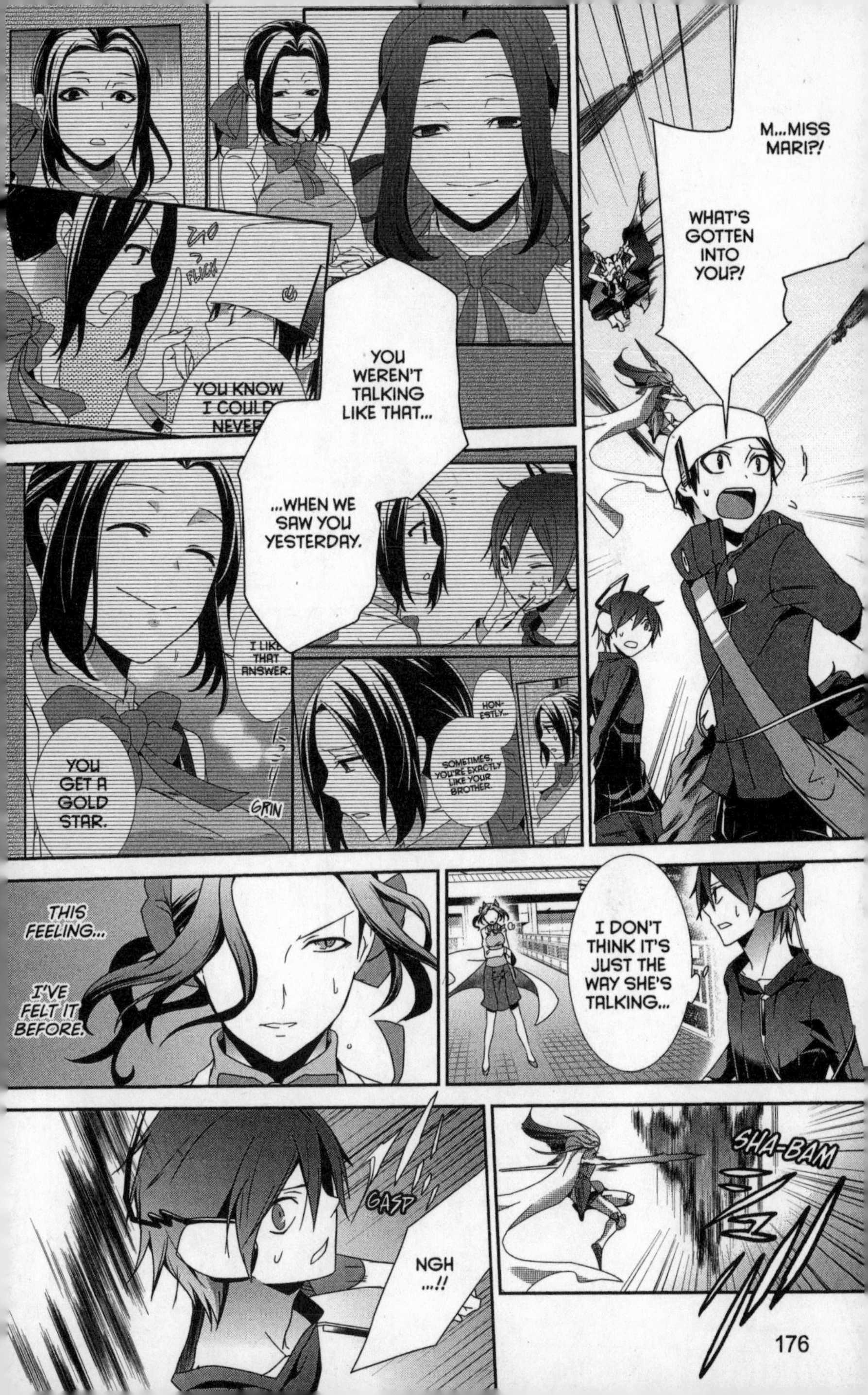
M...MISS MARI?!
WHAT'S GOTTEN INTO YOU?!
YOU WEREN'T TALKING LIKE THAT...
...WHEN WE SAW YOU YESTERDAY.
FLICK
YOU KNOW I COULD NEVER
HON-ESTLY...
SOMETIMES, YOU'RE EXACTLY LIKE YOUR BROTHER
I LIKE THAT ANSWER.
GRIN
YOU GET A GOLD STAR.
I DON'T THINK IT'S JUST THE WAY SHE'S TALKING...
THIS FEELING...
I'VE FELT IT BEFORE.
SHA-BAM
GASP
NGH ...!!

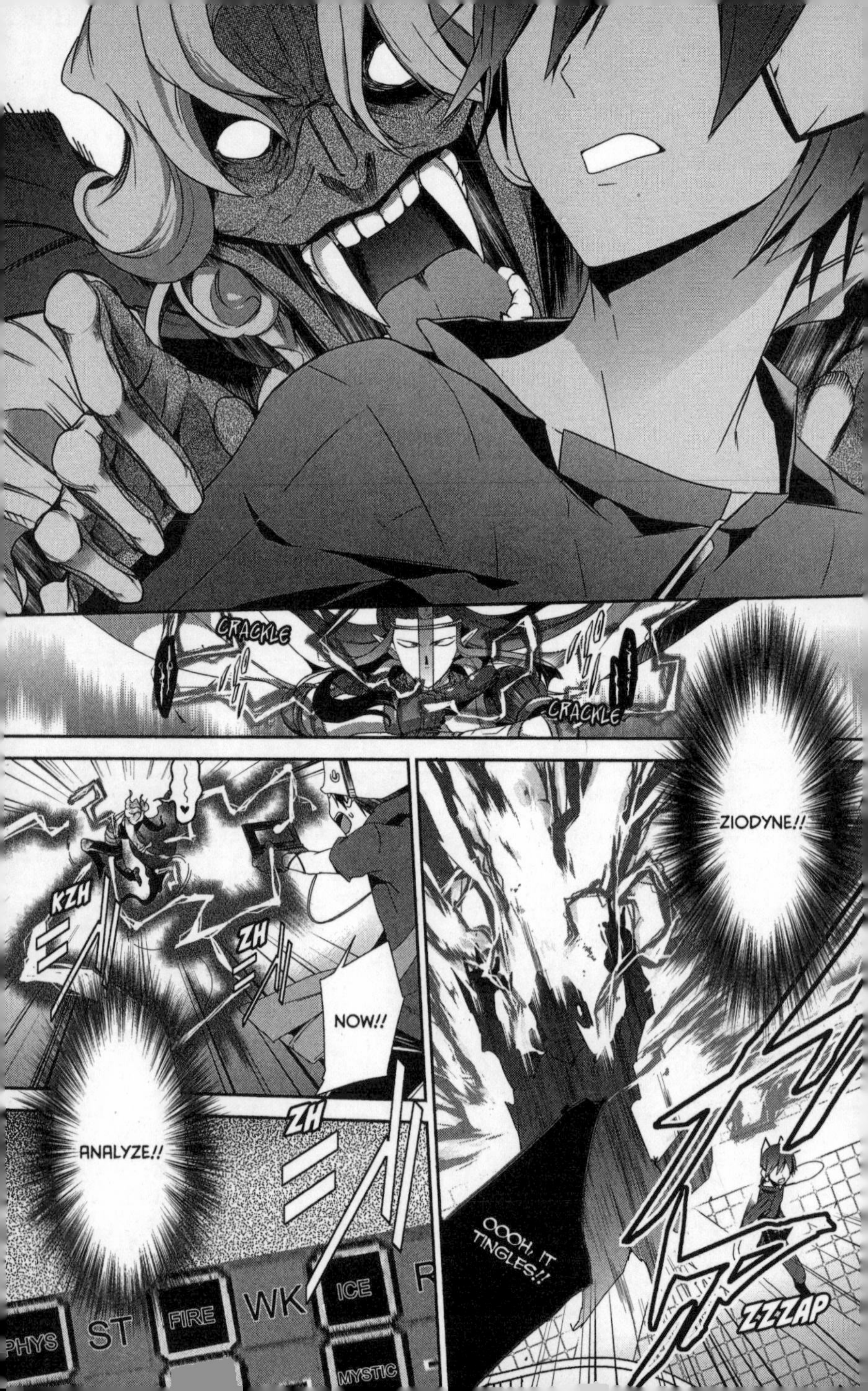
CRACKLE
CRACKLE
ZIODYNE!!
OOOH, IT TINGLES!!
Z-Z-ZAP
NOW!!
KZH
ZH
ZH
ANALYZE!!
PHYS
ST
FIRE
WK
ICE
R
MYSTIC

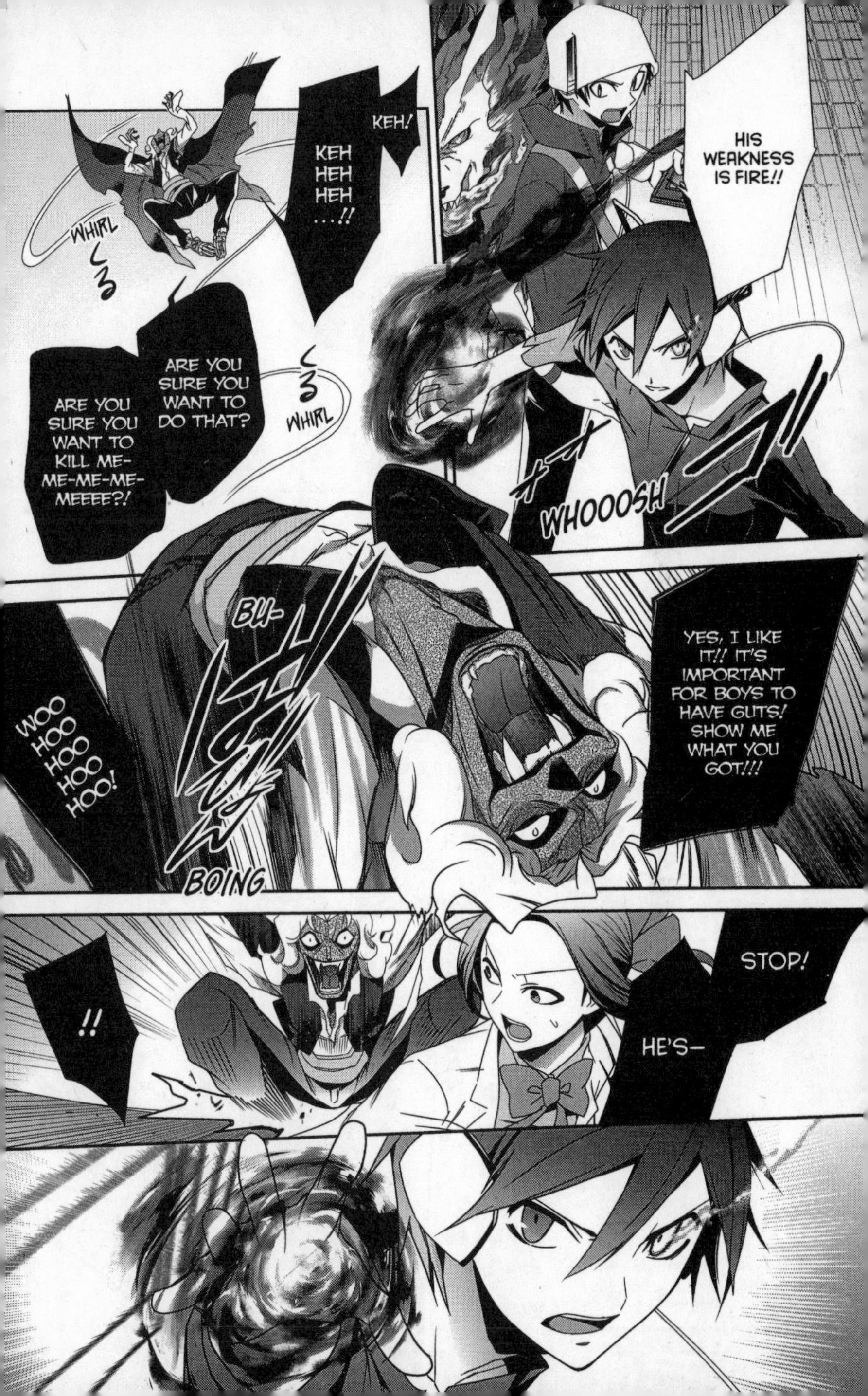
HIS WEAKNESS IS FIRE!!
WHOOOSH
KEH!
KEH HEH HEH ...!!
WHIRL
ARE YOU SURE YOU WANT TO DO THAT?
ARE YOU SURE YOU WANT TO KILL ME-ME-ME-ME-MEEEE?!
WHIRL
YES, I LIKE IT!! IT'S IMPORTANT FOR BOYS TO HAVE GUTS! SHOW ME WHAT YOU GOT!!!
BU-
BOING
WOO HOO HOO HOO HOO!
STOP!
HE'S—
!!

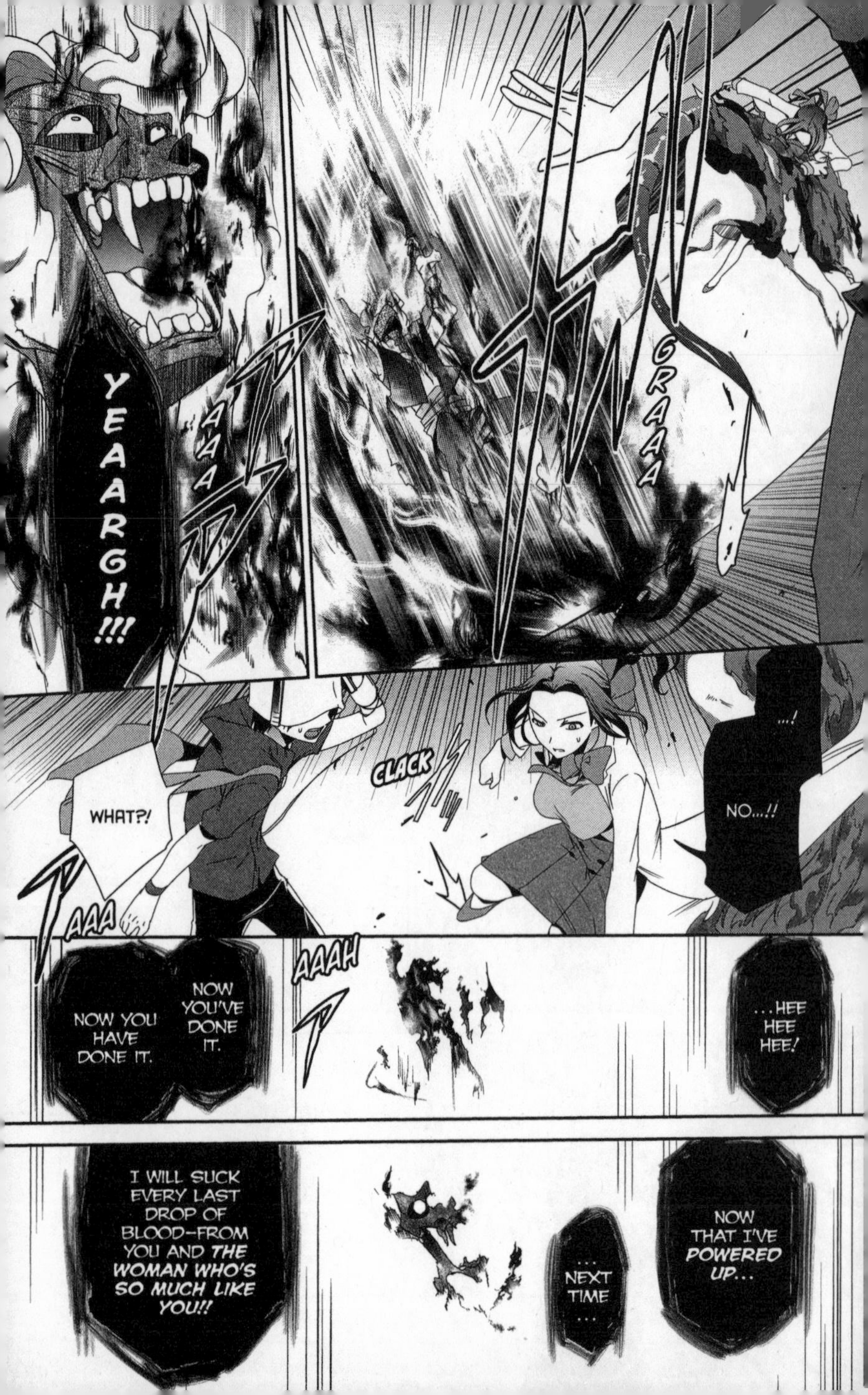
GRAAAA
AAAA
YEAAARGH!!!
...!
NO...!!
CLACK
WHAT?!
AAA
...HEE HEE HEE!
AAAH
NOW YOU'VE DONE IT.
NOW YOU HAVE DONE IT.
NOW THAT I'VE *POWERED UP*...
...NEXT TIME...
I WILL SUCK EVERY LAST DROP OF BLOOD—FROM YOU AND *THE WOMAN WHO'S SO MUCH LIKE YOU!!*

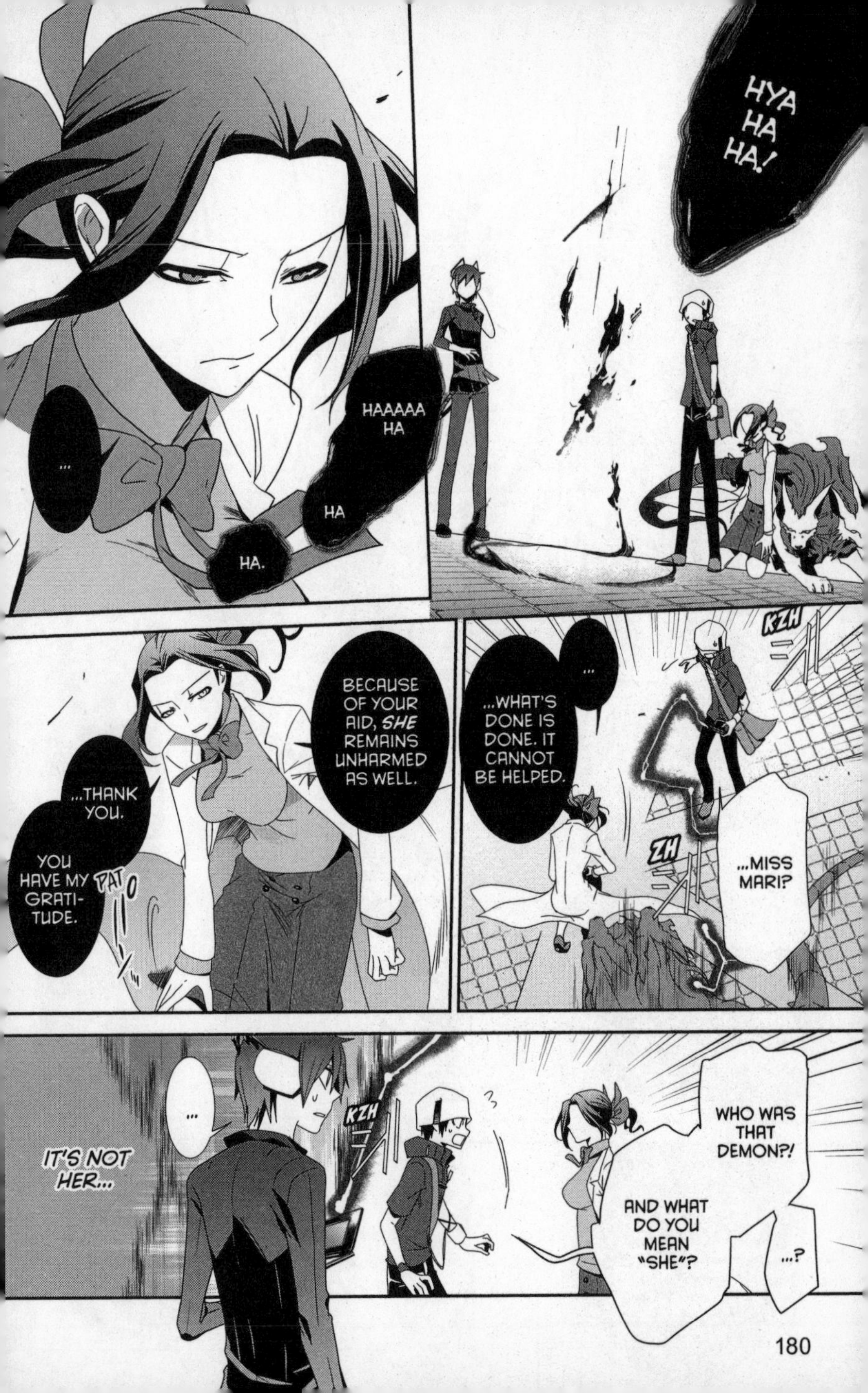
HYA HA HA!
HAAAAA HA
HA
HA.
...
KZH
...
...WHAT'S DONE IS DONE. IT CANNOT BE HELPED.
ZH
...MISS MARI?
BECAUSE OF YOUR AID, *SHE* REMAINS UNHARMED AS WELL.
...THANK YOU.
YOU HAVE MY GRATITUDE.
PAT
WHO WAS THAT DEMON?!
AND WHAT DO YOU MEAN "SHE"?
...?
KZH
...
IT'S NOT HER...

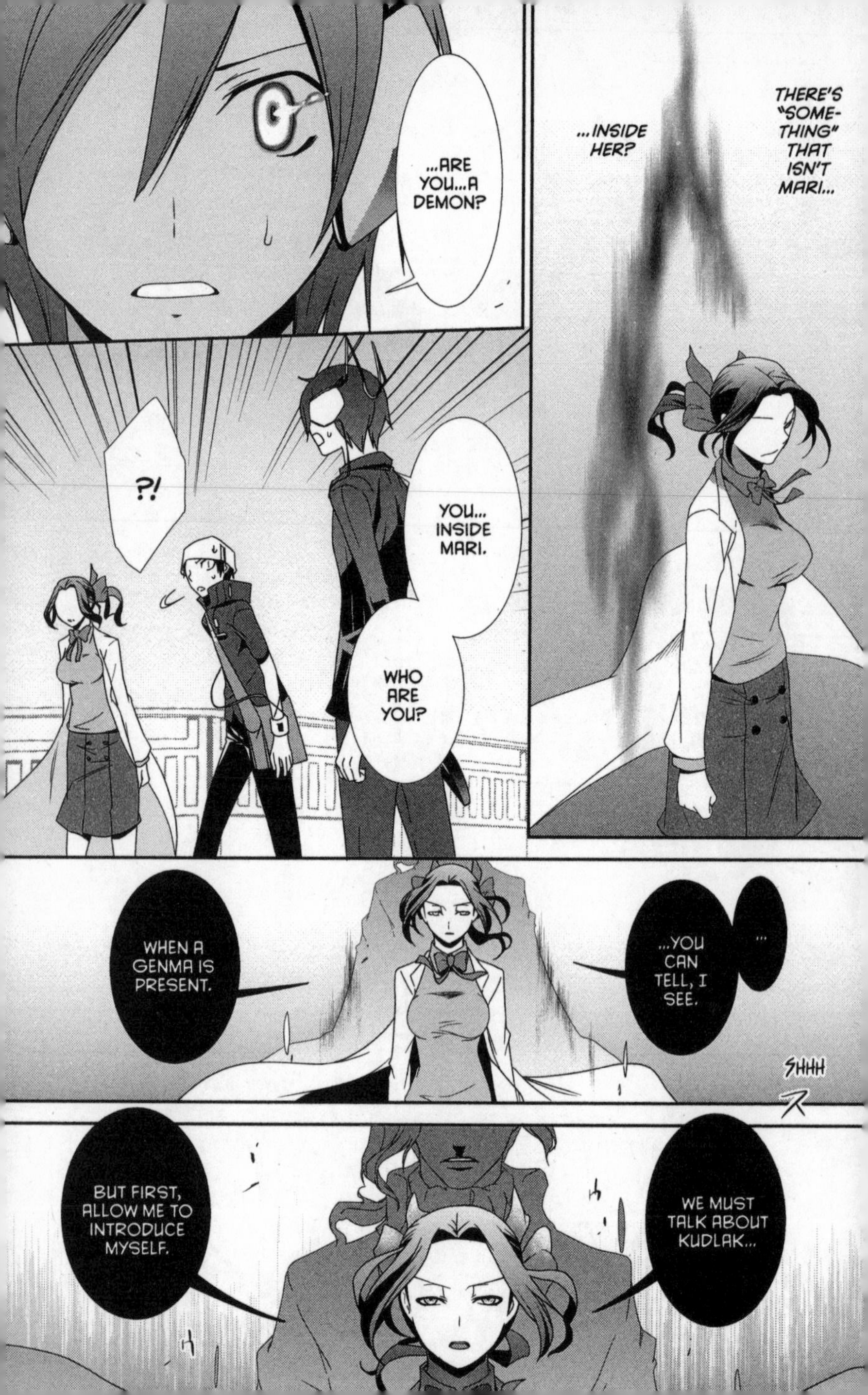
THERE'S "SOMETHING" THAT ISN'T MARI...
...INSIDE HER?
...ARE YOU...A DEMON?
YOU... INSIDE MARI.
WHO ARE YOU?
?!
...
...YOU CAN TELL, I SEE.
WHEN A GENMA IS PRESENT.
SHHH
WE MUST TALK ABOUT KUDLAK...
BUT FIRST, ALLOW ME TO INTRODUCE MYSELF.

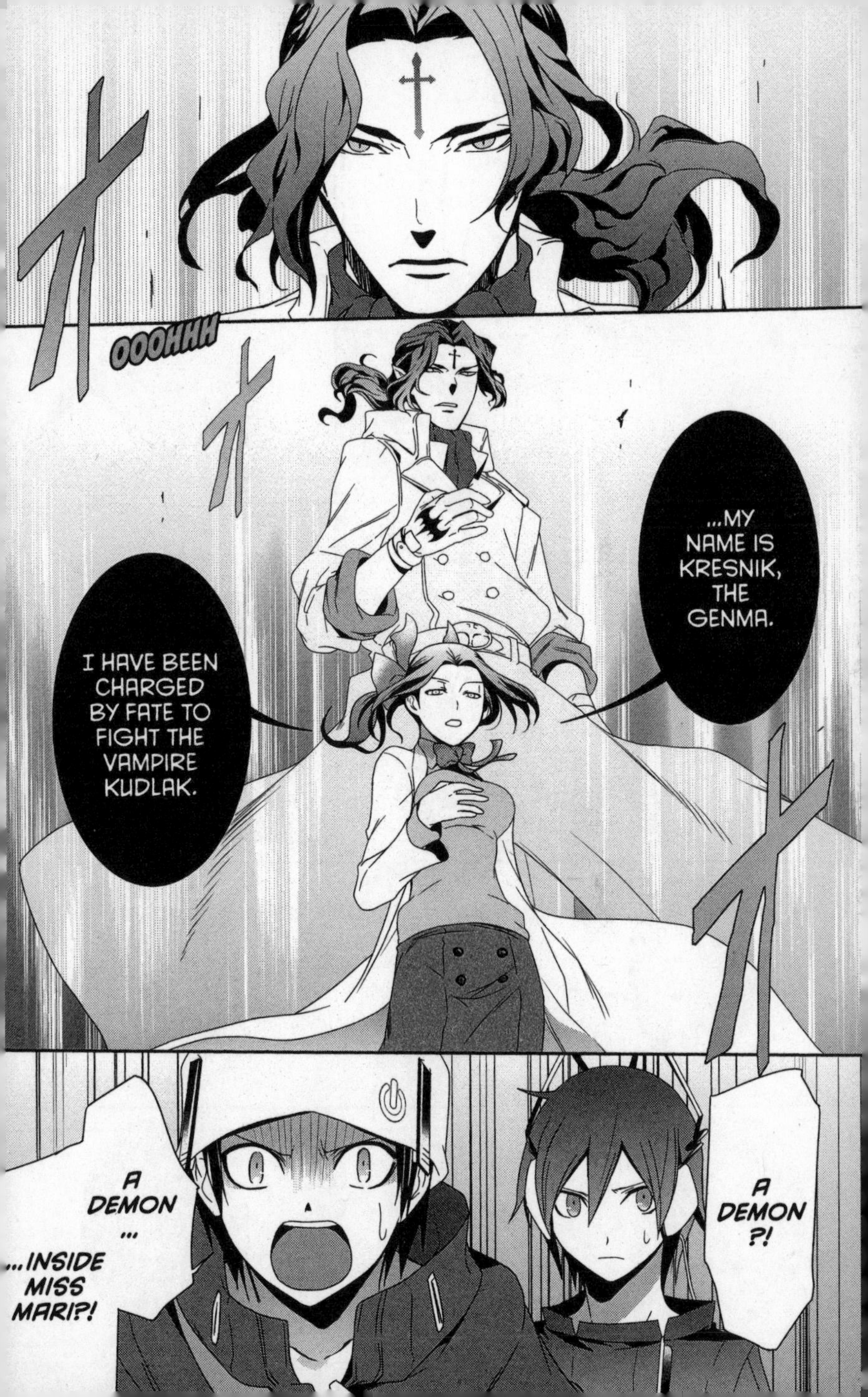
OOOHHH
...MY NAME IS KRESNIK, THE GENMA.
I HAVE BEEN CHARGED BY FATE TO FIGHT THE VAMPIRE KUDLAK.
A DEMON ?!
A DEMON ...
...INSIDE MISS MARI?!

PROFILE

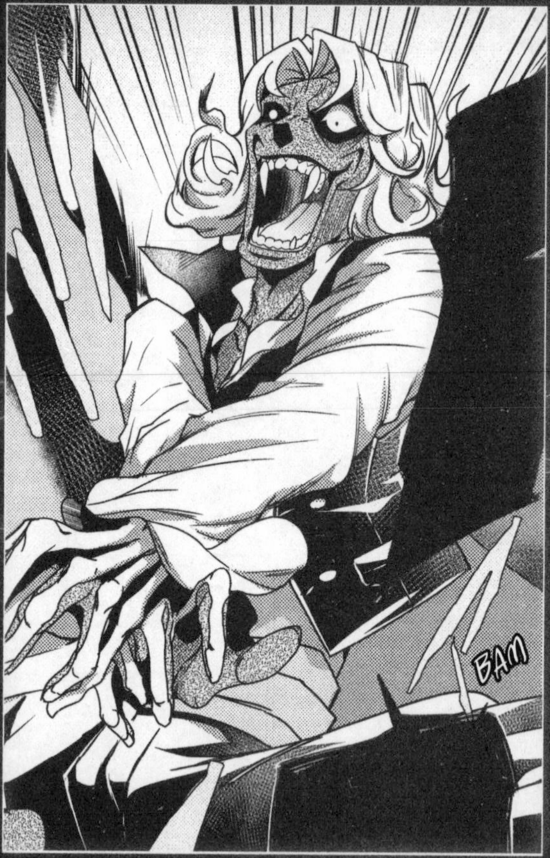
BAM

KUDLAK

A VAMPIRE SYMBOLIZING EVIL AND DARKNESS, HE IS IN STRONG OPPOSITION TO KRESNIK, AGENT OF GOD. IT IS BELIEVED THAT PESTILENCE, POOR HARVESTS, BAD LUCK, AND ALL MISFORTUNE THAT MAY BEFALL MORTALS ARE BROUGHT ABOUT BY KUDLAK. HE ALWAYS ATTACKS THE INNOCENT AND DEFENSELESS. WHEN FIGHTING KRESNIK, HE ASSUMES THE FORMS OF VARIOUS ANIMALS, SUCH AS A HORSE AND A PIG, BUT HIS COLOR IS ALWAYS BLACK, SYMBOLIZING DARKNESS.

DEVIL SURVIVOR
デビルサバイバー

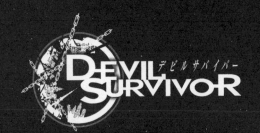

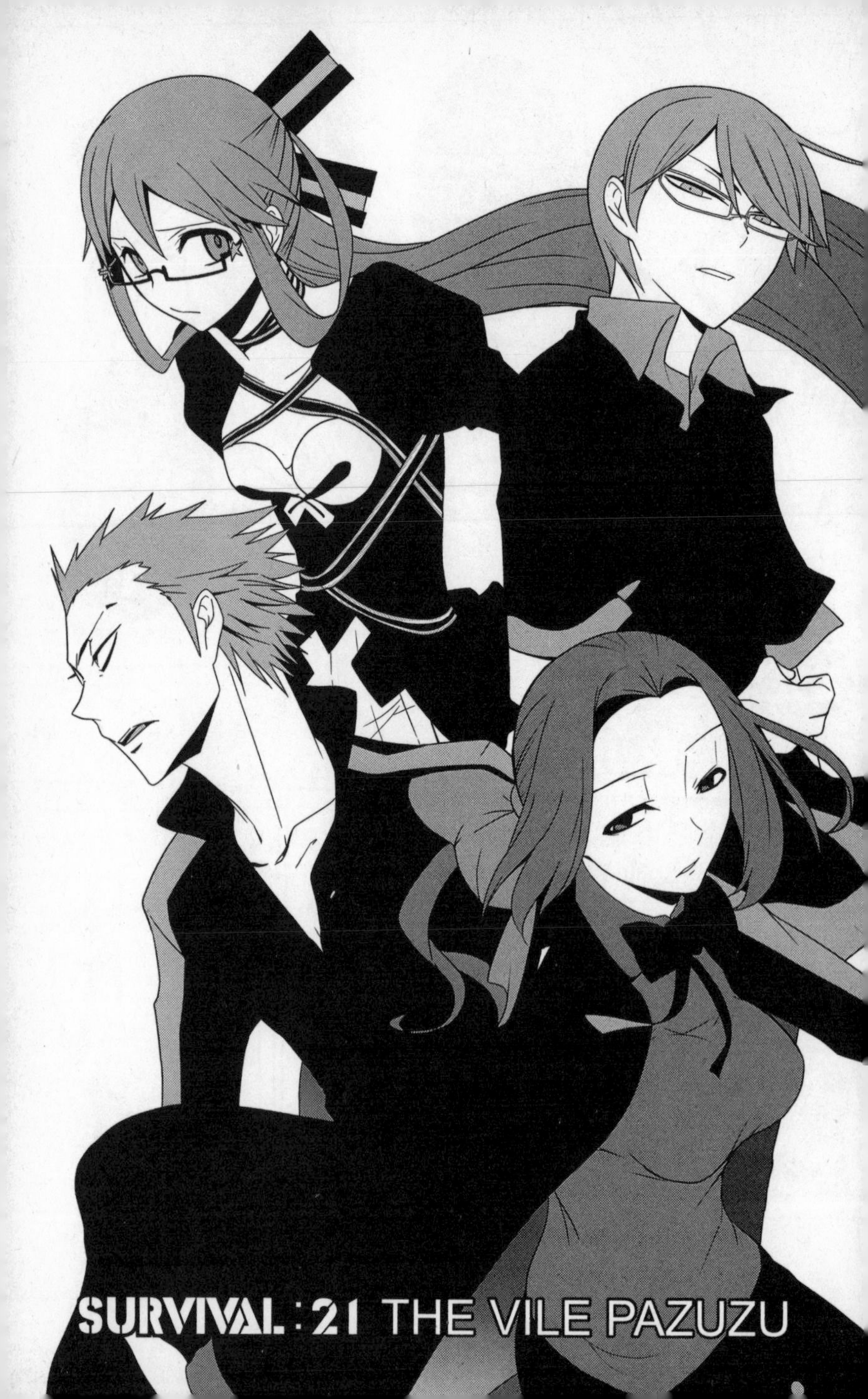

SURVIVAL : 21 THE VILE PAZUZU

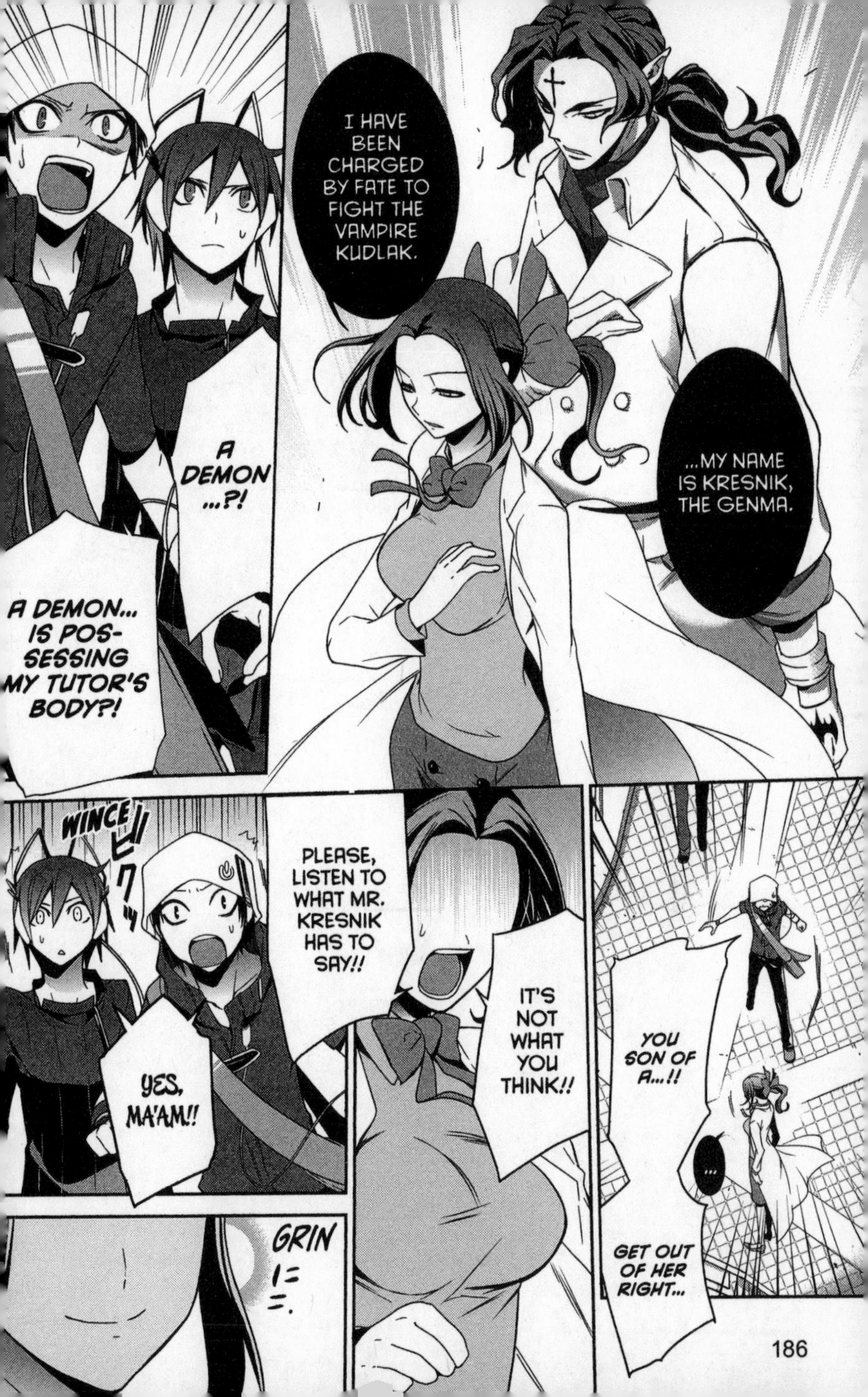
...MY NAME IS KRESNIK, THE GENMA.
I HAVE BEEN CHARGED BY FATE TO FIGHT THE VAMPIRE KUDLAK.
A DEMON ...?!
A DEMON... IS POSSESSING MY TUTOR'S BODY?!
YOU SON OF A...!!
...
GET OUT OF HER RIGHT...
IT'S NOT WHAT YOU THINK!!
PLEASE, LISTEN TO WHAT MR. KRESNIK HAS TO SAY!!
WINCE
YES, MA'AM!!
GRIN

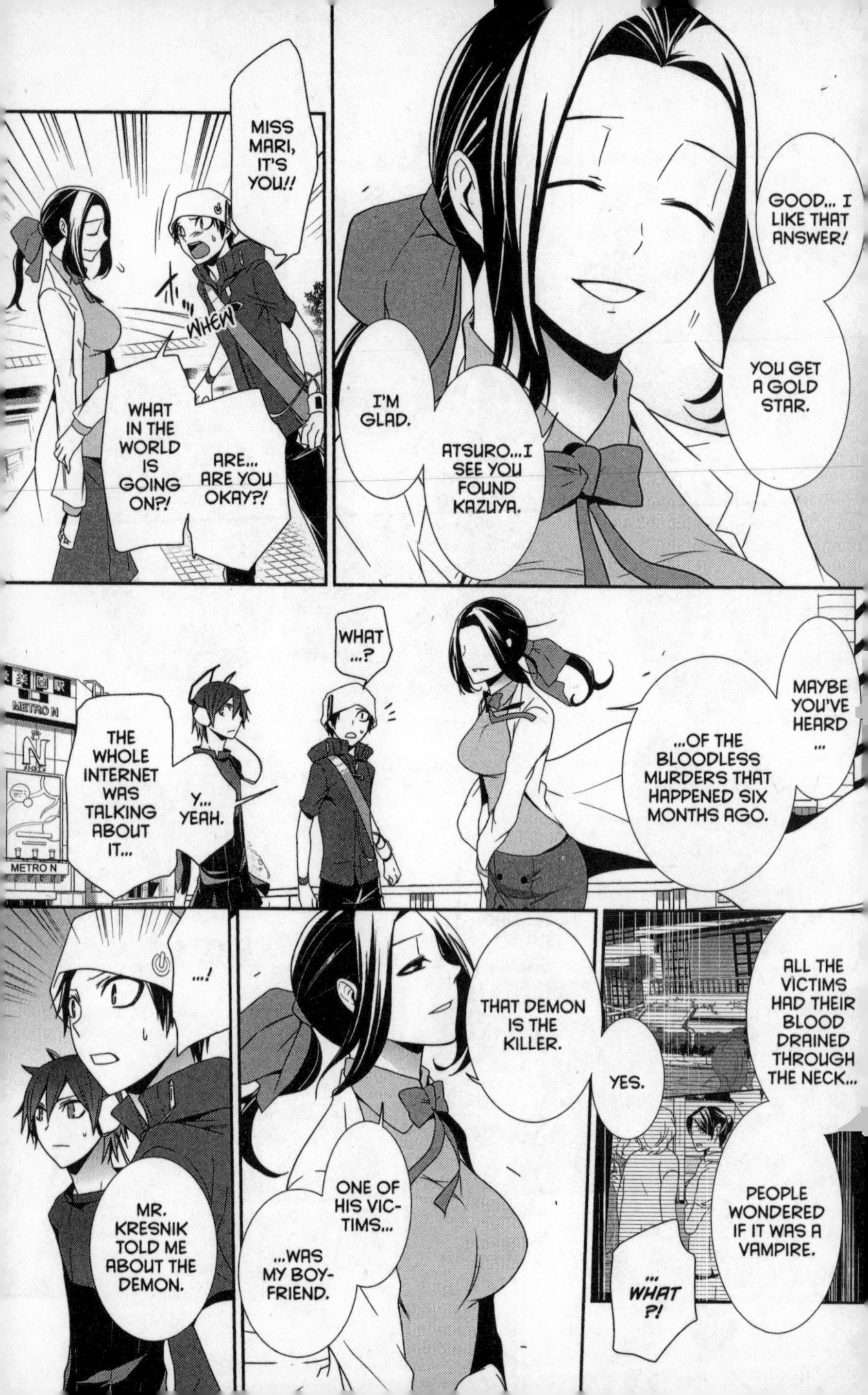
GOOD... I LIKE THAT ANSWER!
YOU GET A GOLD STAR.
ATSURO...I SEE YOU FOUND KAZUYA.
I'M GLAD.
MISS MARI, IT'S YOU!!
WHEW
ARE... ARE YOU OKAY?!
WHAT IN THE WORLD IS GOING ON?!
MAYBE YOU'VE HEARD...
...OF THE BLOODLESS MURDERS THAT HAPPENED SIX MONTHS AGO.
WHAT ...?
THE WHOLE INTERNET WAS TALKING ABOUT IT...
Y... YEAH.
METRO N
METRO N
ALL THE VICTIMS HAD THEIR BLOOD DRAINED THROUGH THE NECK...
PEOPLE WONDERED IF IT WAS A VAMPIRE.
...WHAT ?!
THAT DEMON IS THE KILLER.
YES.
ONE OF HIS VIC-TIMS...
...WAS MY BOY-FRIEND.
...!
MR. KRESNIK TOLD ME ABOUT THE DEMON.

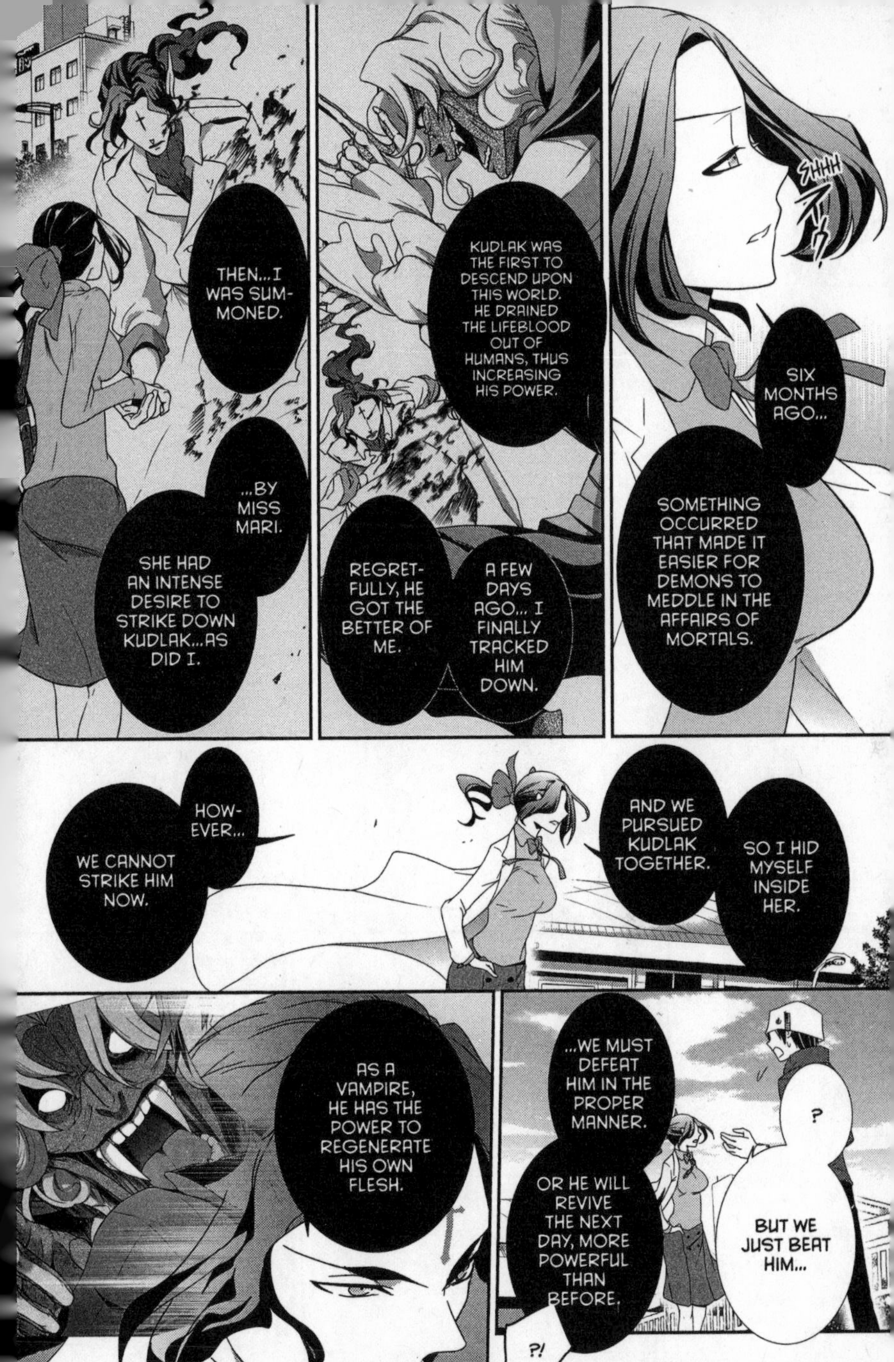
SHHH
SIX MONTHS AGO...
SOMETHING OCCURRED THAT MADE IT EASIER FOR DEMONS TO MEDDLE IN THE AFFAIRS OF MORTALS.
KUDLAK WAS THE FIRST TO DESCEND UPON THIS WORLD. HE DRAINED THE LIFEBLOOD OUT OF HUMANS, THUS INCREASING HIS POWER.
A FEW DAYS AGO... I FINALLY TRACKED HIM DOWN.
REGRETFULLY, HE GOT THE BETTER OF ME.
THEN...I WAS SUMMONED.
...BY MISS MARI.
SHE HAD AN INTENSE DESIRE TO STRIKE DOWN KUDLAK...AS DID I.
SO I HID MYSELF INSIDE HER.
AND WE PURSUED KUDLAK TOGETHER.
HOWEVER...
WE CANNOT STRIKE HIM NOW.
?
BUT WE JUST BEAT HIM...
AS A VAMPIRE, HE HAS THE POWER TO REGENERATE HIS OWN FLESH.
...WE MUST DEFEAT HIM IN THE PROPER MANNER.
OR HE WILL REVIVE THE NEXT DAY, MORE POWERFUL THAN BEFORE.
?!

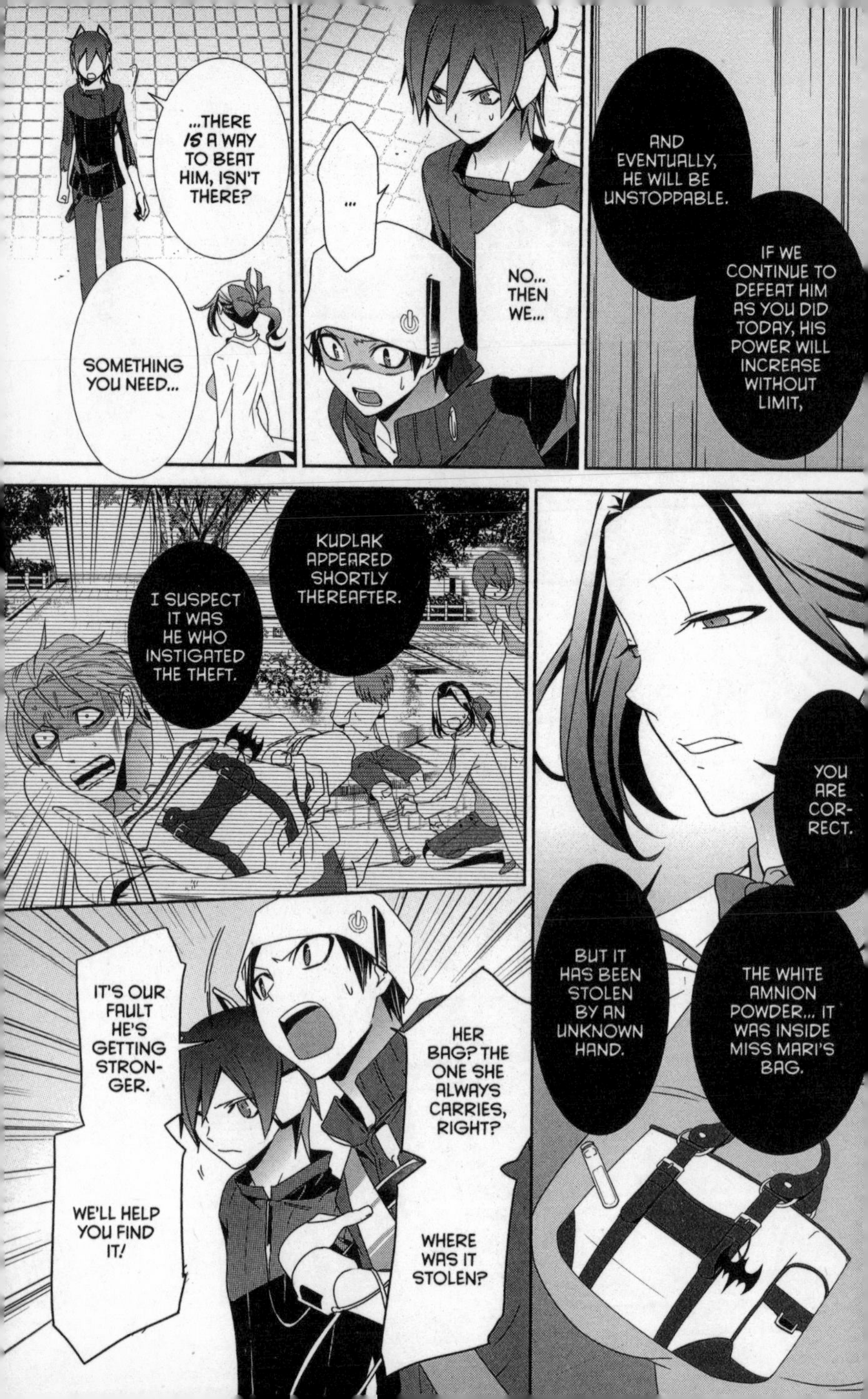
IF WE CONTINUE TO DEFEAT HIM AS YOU DID TODAY, HIS POWER WILL INCREASE WITHOUT LIMIT,
AND EVENTUALLY, HE WILL BE UNSTOPPABLE.
NO... THEN WE...
...
...THERE *IS* A WAY TO BEAT HIM, ISN'T THERE?
SOMETHING YOU NEED...
YOU ARE COR-RECT.
THE WHITE AMNION POWDER... IT WAS INSIDE MISS MARI'S BAG.
BUT IT HAS BEEN STOLEN BY AN UNKNOWN HAND.
KUDLAK APPEARED SHORTLY THEREAFTER.
I SUSPECT IT WAS HE WHO INSTIGATED THE THEFT.
HER BAG? THE ONE SHE ALWAYS CARRIES, RIGHT?
WHERE WAS IT STOLEN?
IT'S OUR FAULT HE'S GETTING STRON-GER.
WE'LL HELP YOU FIND IT!

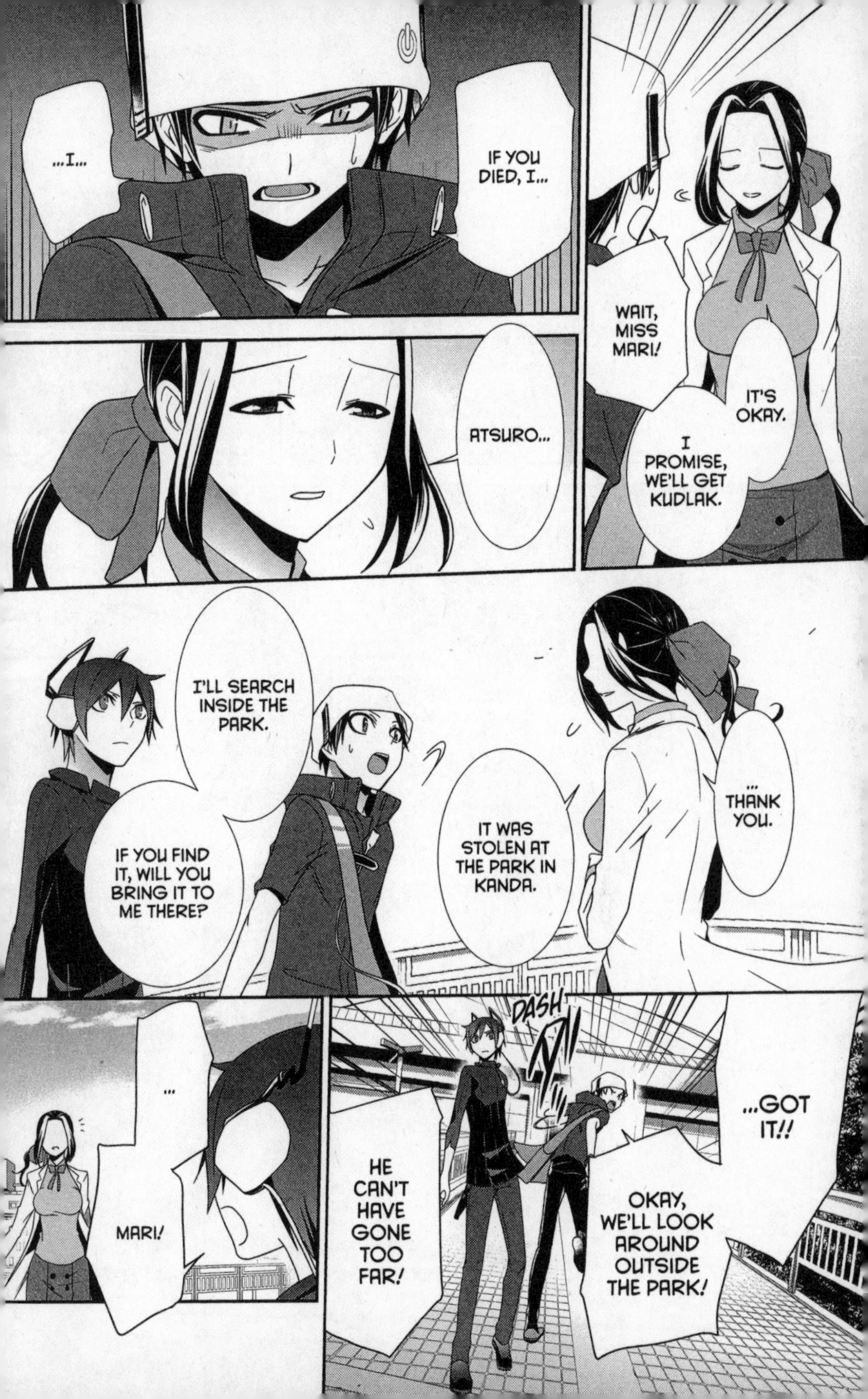
WAIT, MISS MARI!
IT'S OKAY.
I PROMISE, WE'LL GET KUDLAK.
IF YOU DIED, I...
...I...
ATSURO...
... THANK YOU.
IT WAS STOLEN AT THE PARK IN KANDA.
I'LL SEARCH INSIDE THE PARK.
IF YOU FIND IT, WILL YOU BRING IT TO ME THERE?
...GOT IT!!
OKAY, WE'LL LOOK AROUND OUTSIDE THE PARK!
DASH
HE CAN'T HAVE GONE TOO FAR!
...
MARI!

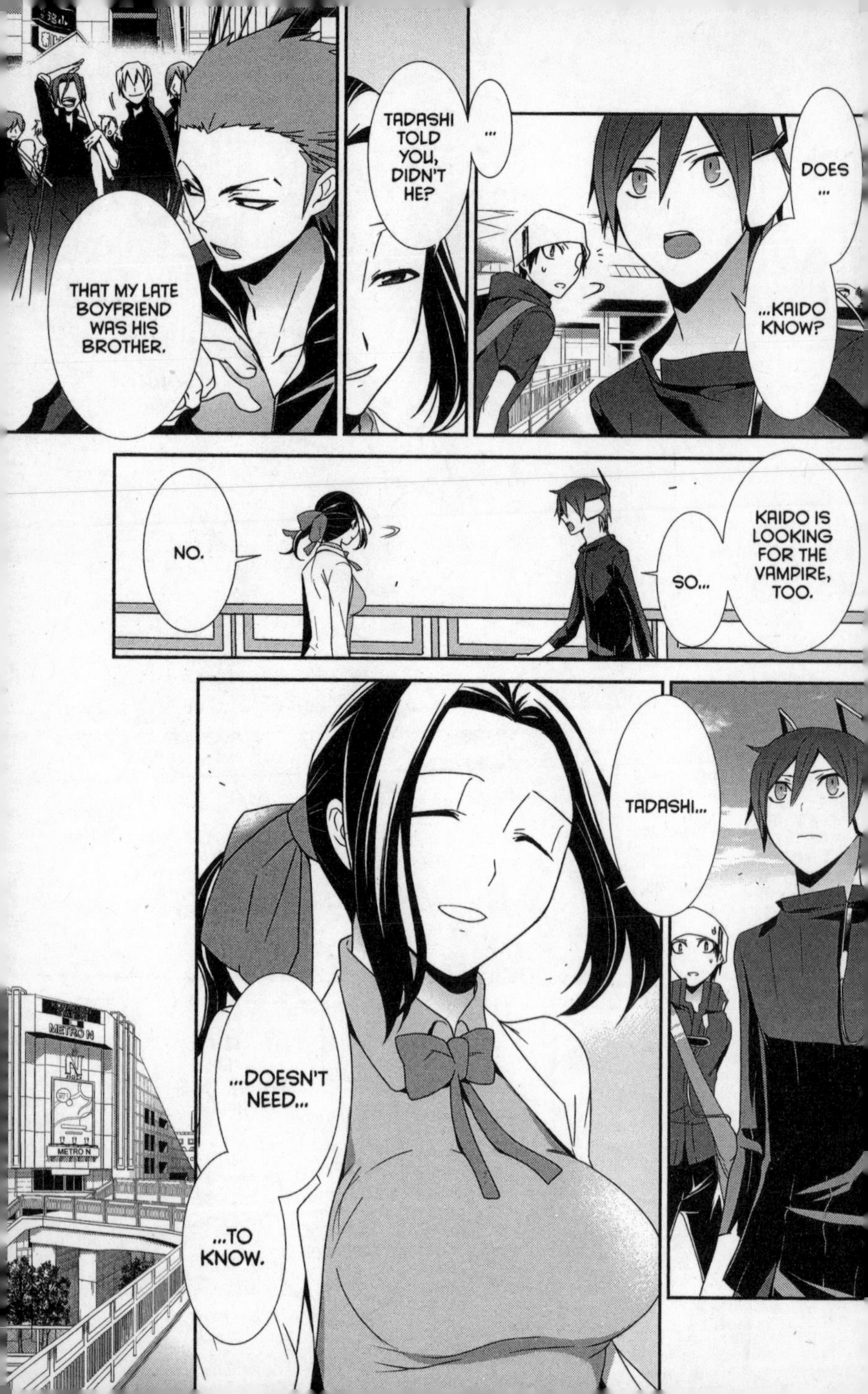
DOES ...
...KAIDO KNOW?
...
TADASHI TOLD YOU, DIDN'T HE?
THAT MY LATE BOYFRIEND WAS HIS BROTHER.
KAIDO IS LOOKING FOR THE VAMPIRE, TOO.
SO...
NO.
TADASHI...
...DOESN'T NEED...
...TO KNOW.
METRO N
METRO N

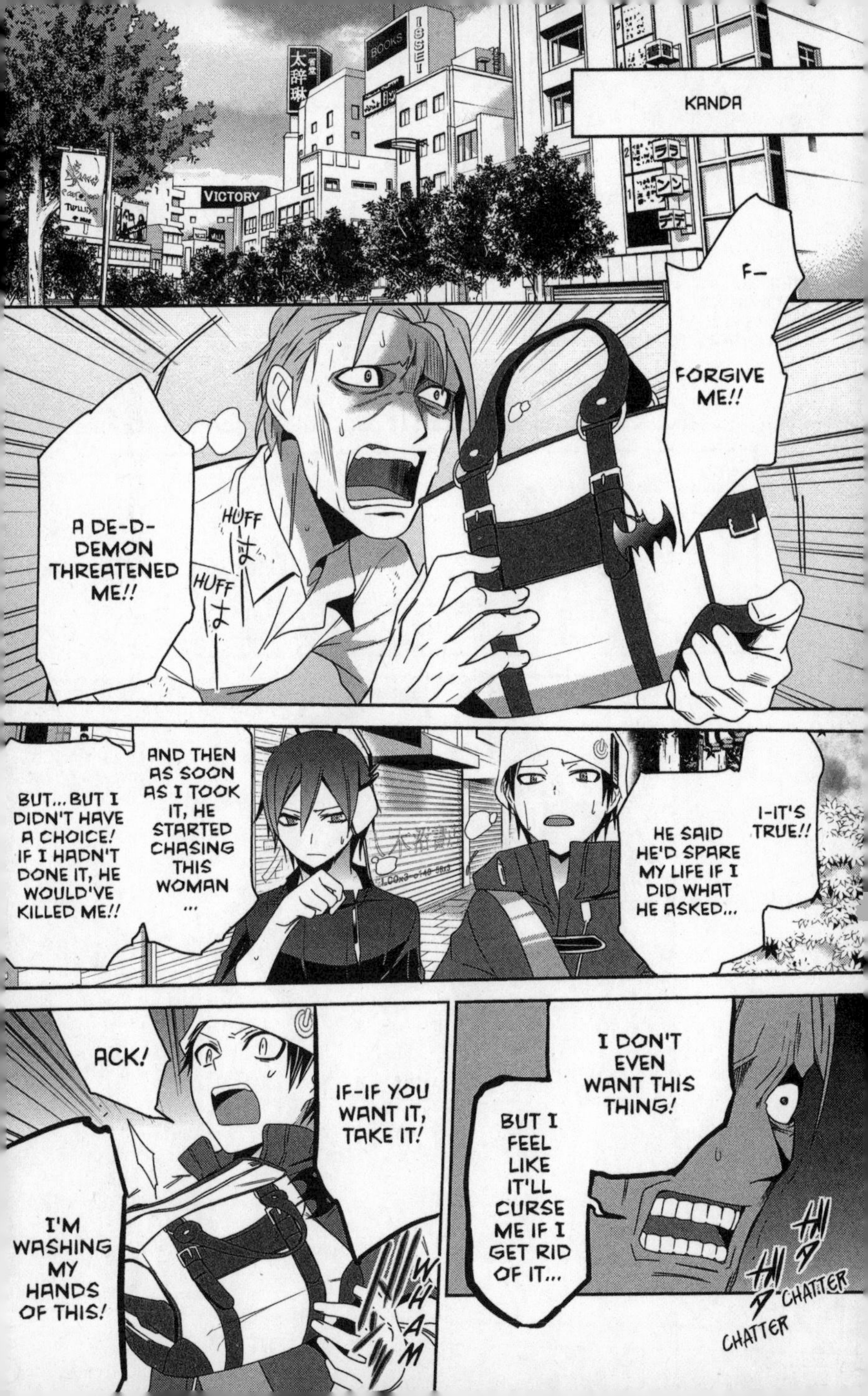

ISSEI
BOOKS
VICTORY
KANDA
F—
FORGIVE ME!!
A DE-D-DEMON THREATENED ME!!
HUFF
HUFF
I-IT'S TRUE!!
HE SAID HE'D SPARE MY LIFE IF I DID WHAT HE ASKED...
AND THEN AS SOON AS I TOOK IT, HE STARTED CHASING THIS WOMAN ...
BUT... BUT I DIDN'T HAVE A CHOICE! IF I HADN'T DONE IT, HE WOULD'VE KILLED ME!!
I DON'T EVEN WANT THIS THING!
BUT I FEEL LIKE IT'LL CURSE ME IF I GET RID OF IT...
CHATTER
CHATTER
ACK!
IF-IF YOU WANT IT, TAKE IT!
I'M WASHING MY HANDS OF THIS!
WHAM

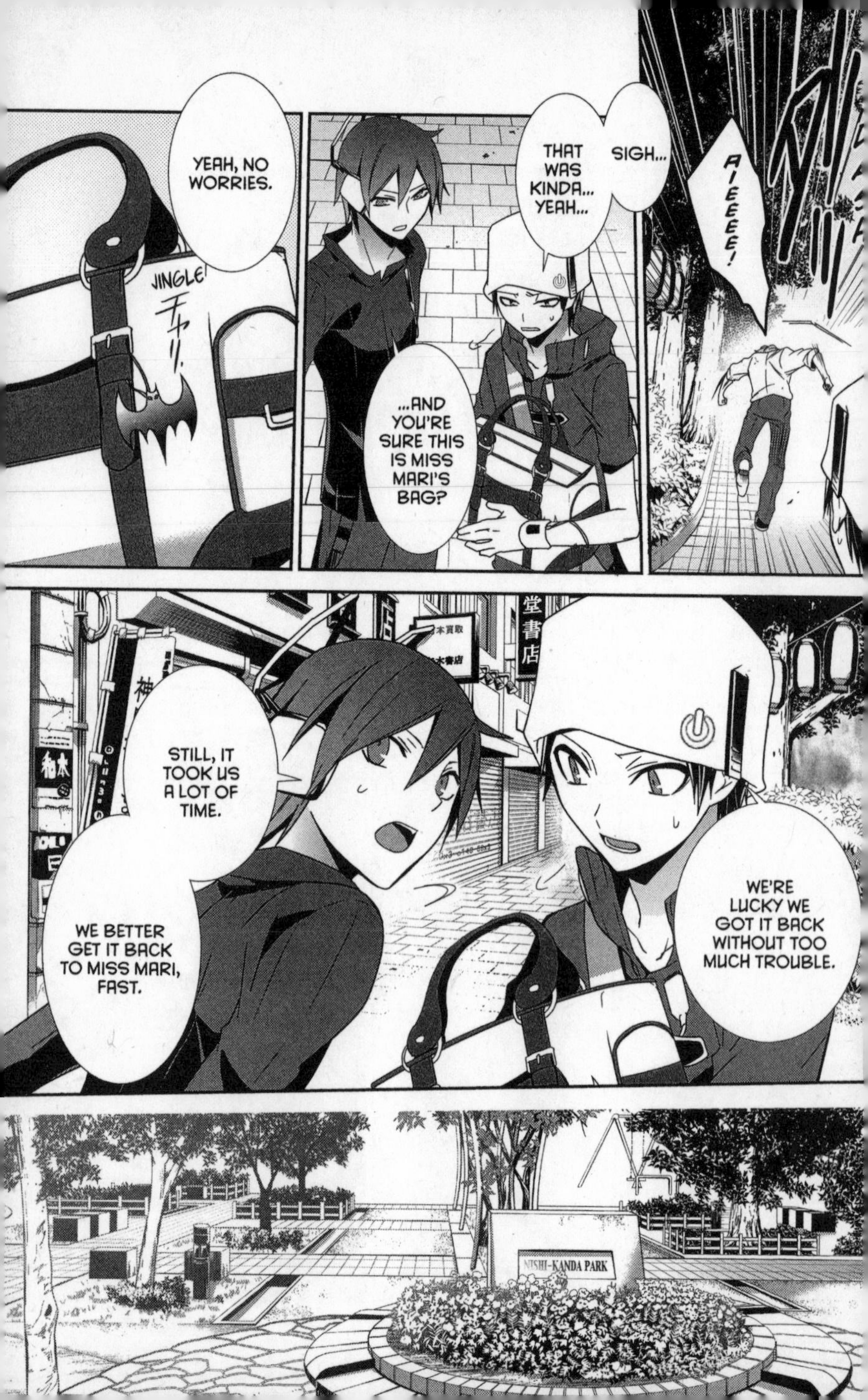
AIEEEEE!
SIGH...
THAT WAS KINDA... YEAH...
...AND YOU'RE SURE THIS IS MISS MARI'S BAG?
YEAH, NO WORRIES.
JINGLE
チャリ
WE'RE LUCKY WE GOT IT BACK WITHOUT TOO MUCH TROUBLE.
STILL, IT TOOK US A LOT OF TIME.
WE BETTER GET IT BACK TO MISS MARI, FAST.
NISHI-KANDA PARK

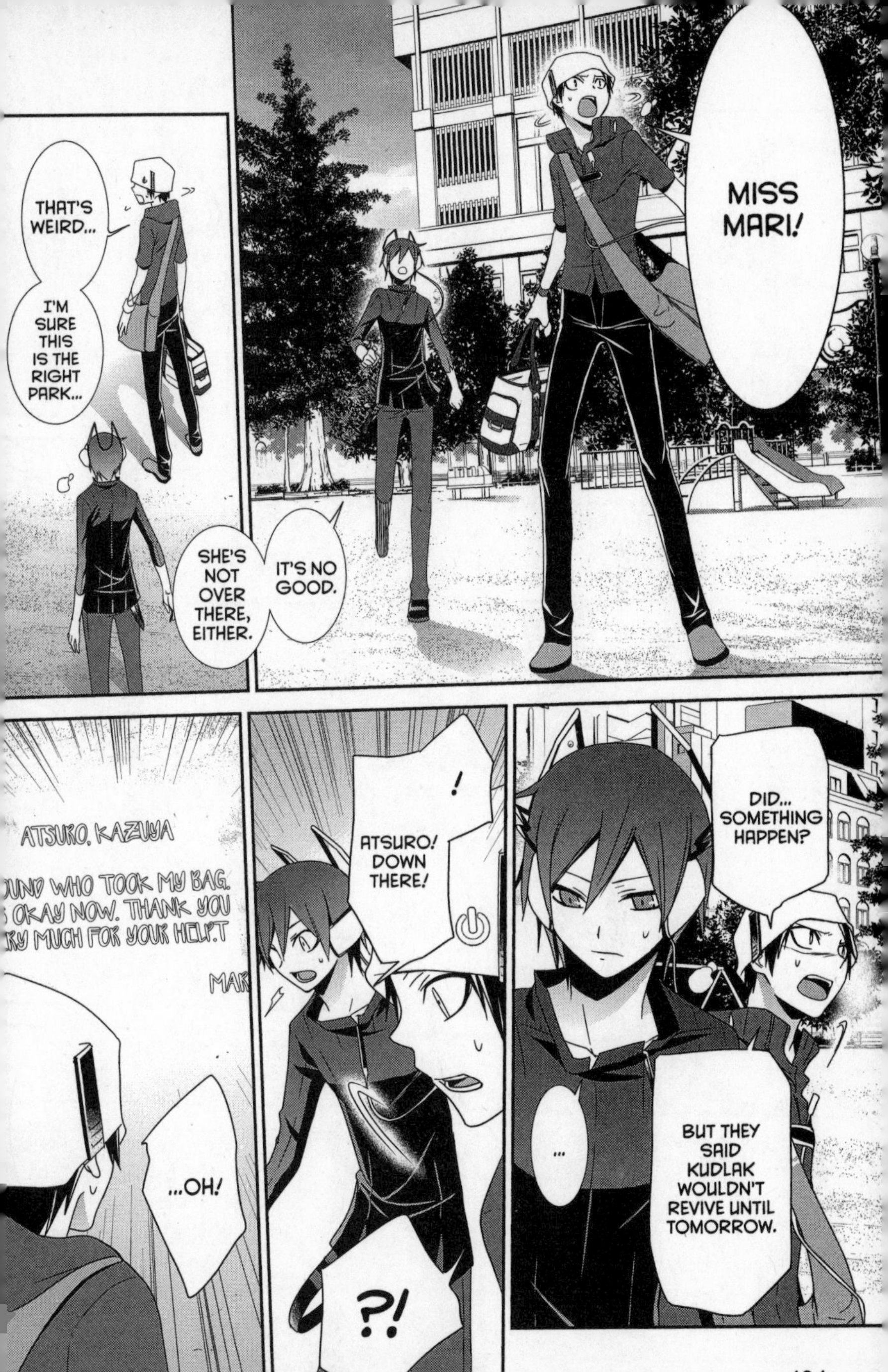
MISS MARI!
IT'S NO GOOD.
SHE'S NOT OVER THERE, EITHER.
THAT'S WEIRD...
I'M SURE THIS IS THE RIGHT PARK...
DID... SOMETHING HAPPEN?
...
BUT THEY SAID KUDLAK WOULDN'T REVIVE UNTIL TOMORROW.
!
ATSURO! DOWN THERE!
?!
ATSURO, KAZUYA
WHO TOOK MY BAG.
OKAY NOW. THANK YOU
MUCH FOR YOUR HELP.
...OH!

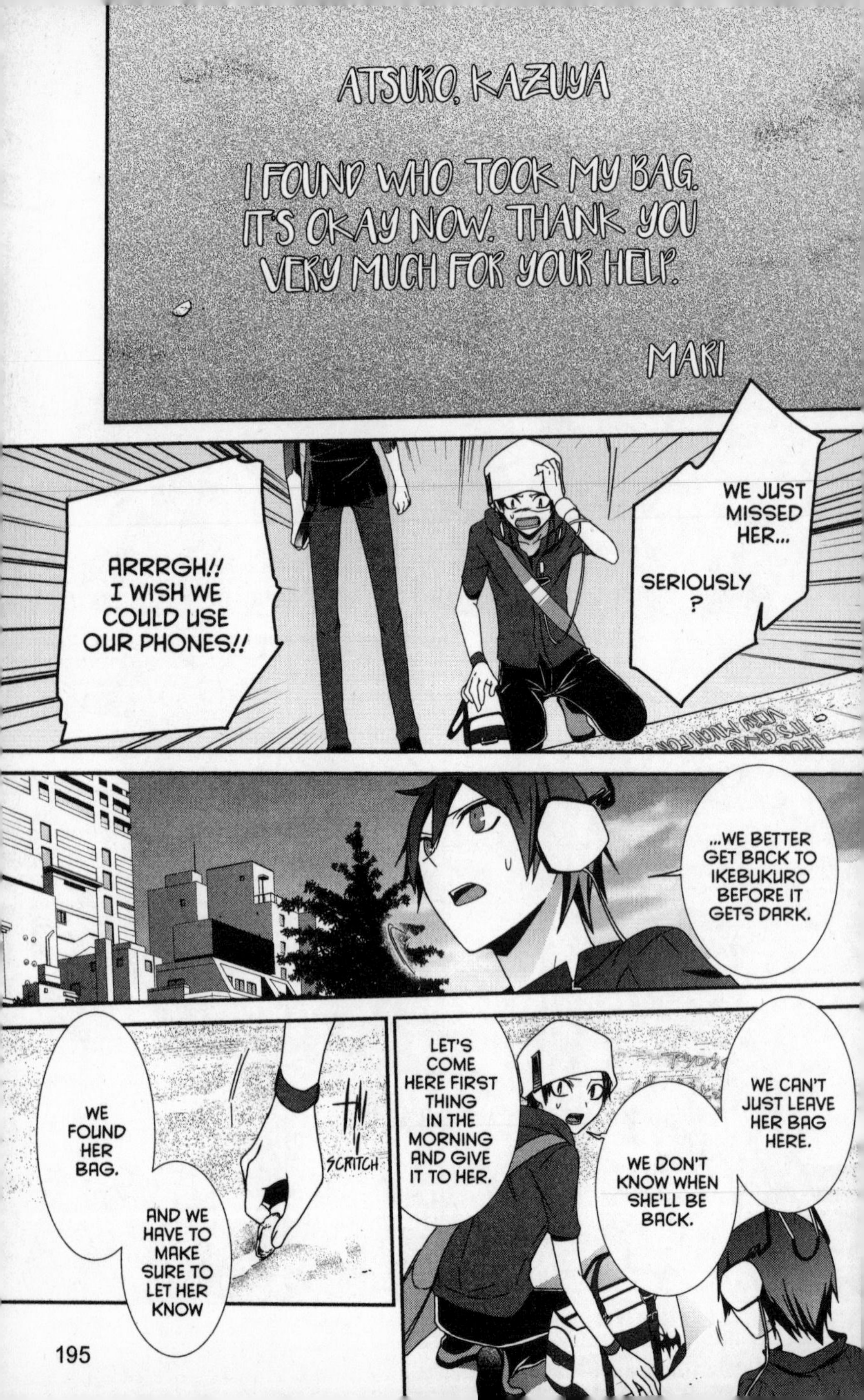
ATSURO, KAZUYA
I FOUND WHO TOOK MY BAG. IT'S OKAY NOW. THANK YOU VERY MUCH FOR YOUR HELP.
MARI
WE JUST MISSED HER...
SERIOUSLY?
ARRRGH!! I WISH WE COULD USE OUR PHONES!!
...WE BETTER GET BACK TO IKEBUKURO BEFORE IT GETS DARK.
WE CAN'T JUST LEAVE HER BAG HERE.
WE DON'T KNOW WHEN SHE'LL BE BACK.
LET'S COME HERE FIRST THING IN THE MORNING AND GIVE IT TO HER.
SCRITCH
WE FOUND HER BAG.
AND WE HAVE TO MAKE SURE TO LET HER KNOW

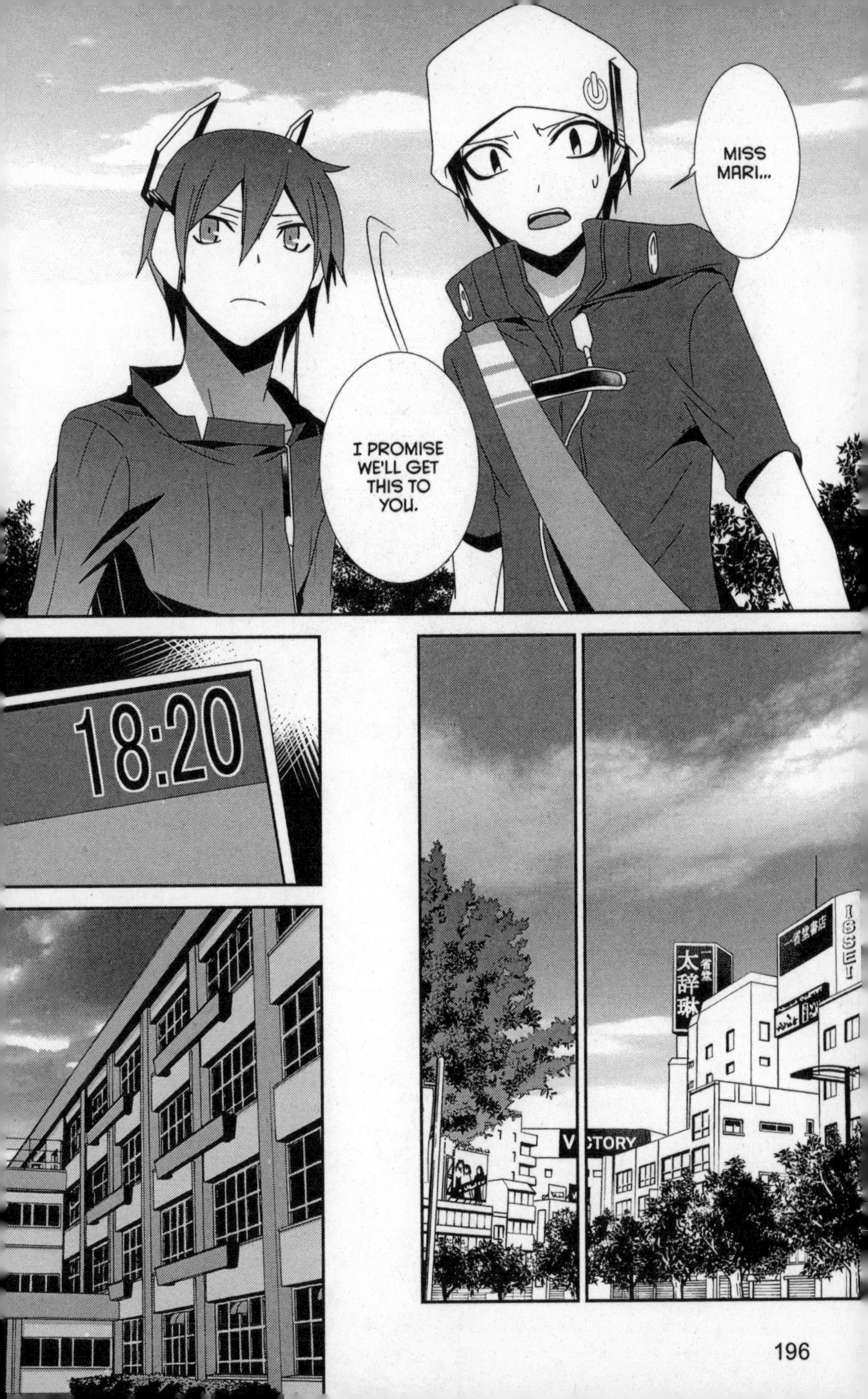
MISS MARI...
I PROMISE WE'LL GET THIS TO YOU.
18:20
ISSEI
VICTORY

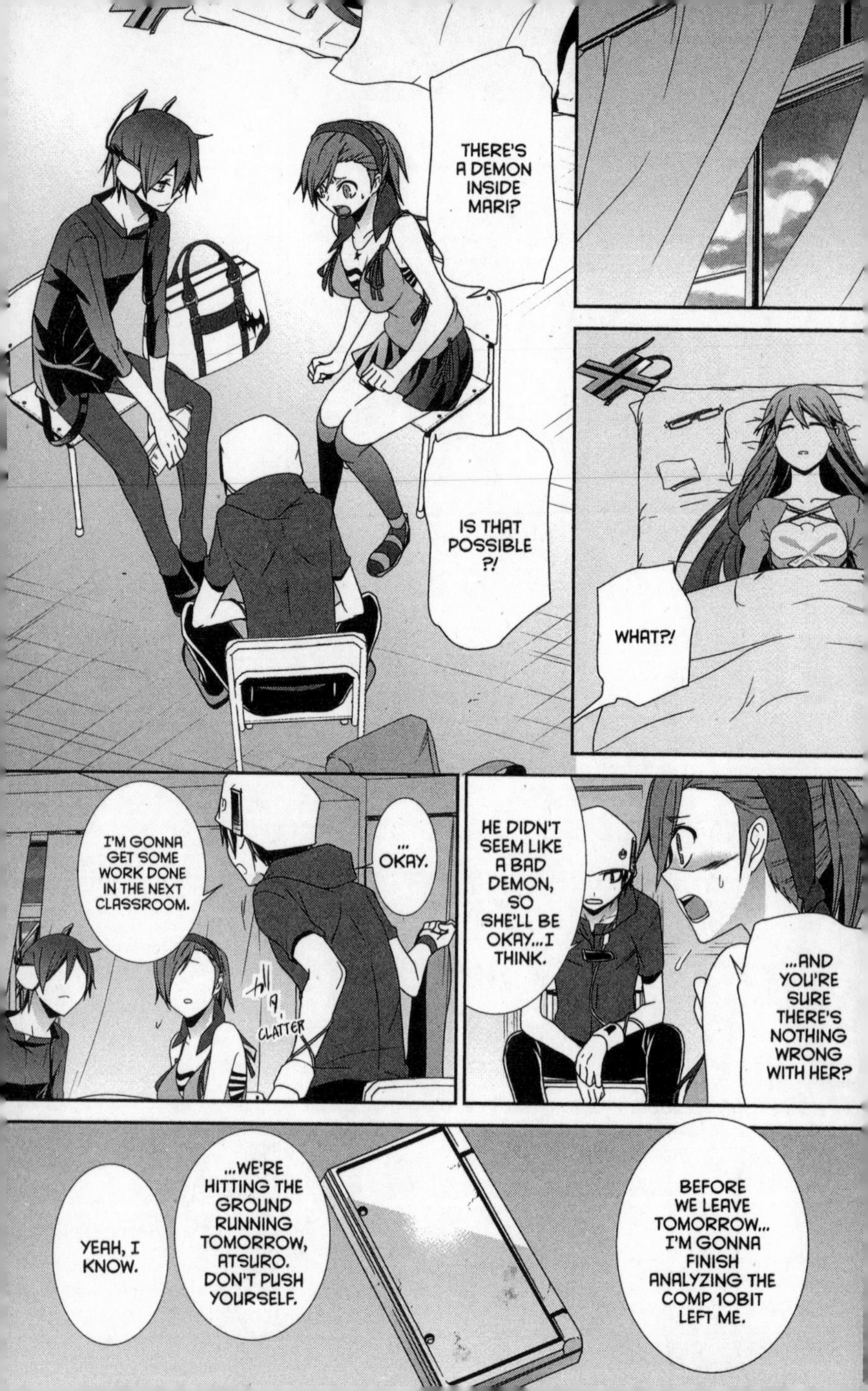
WHAT?!
THERE'S A DEMON INSIDE MARI?
IS THAT POSSIBLE?!
HE DIDN'T SEEM LIKE A BAD DEMON, SO SHE'LL BE OKAY...I THINK.
...AND YOU'RE SURE THERE'S NOTHING WRONG WITH HER?
I'M GONNA GET SOME WORK DONE IN THE NEXT CLASSROOM.
... OKAY.
CLATTER
BEFORE WE LEAVE TOMORROW... I'M GONNA FINISH ANALYZING THE COMP 10BIT LEFT ME.
...WE'RE HITTING THE GROUND RUNNING TOMORROW, ATSURO. DON'T PUSH YOURSELF.
YEAH, I KNOW.

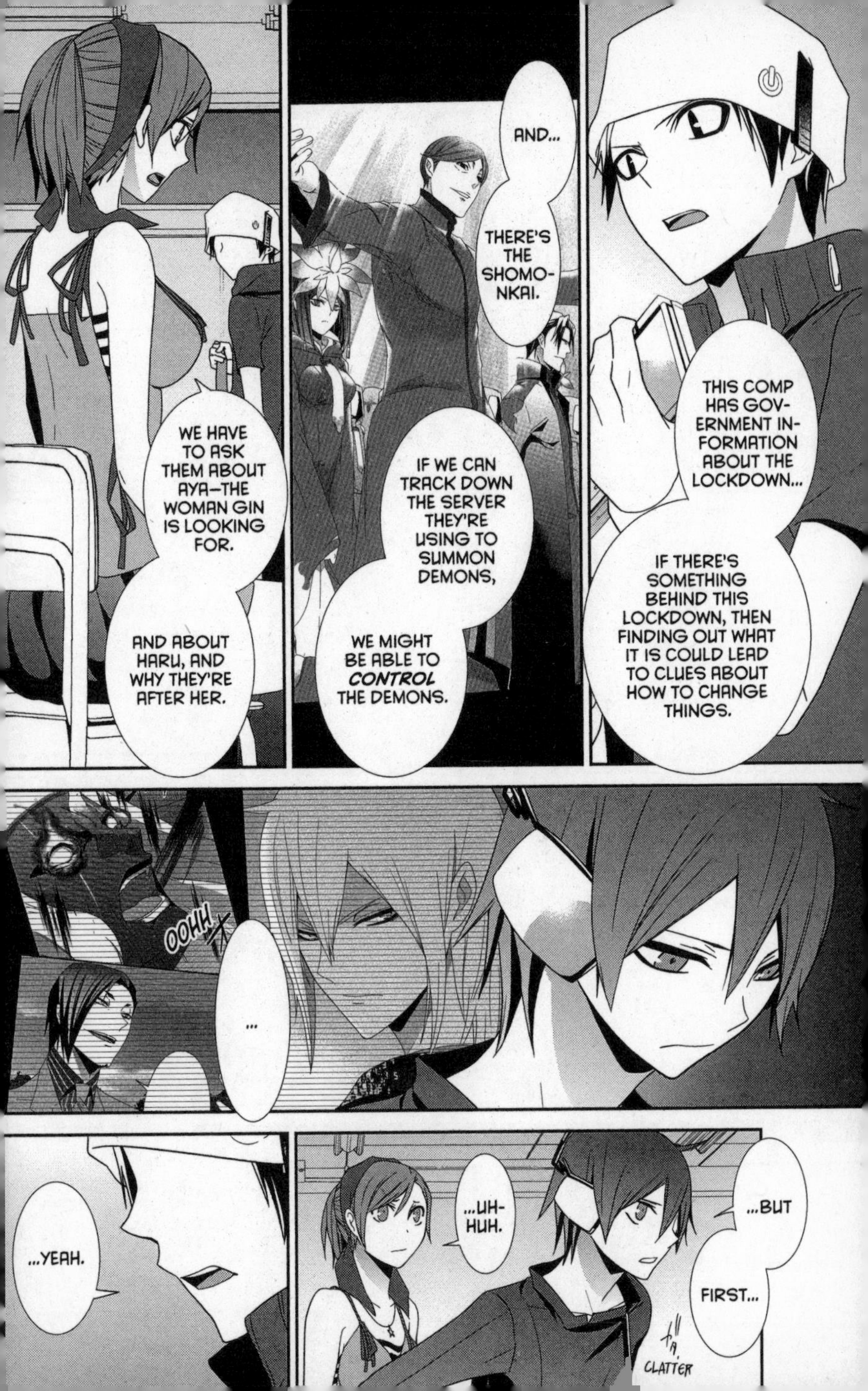

THIS COMP HAS GOVERNMENT INFORMATION ABOUT THE LOCKDOWN...
IF THERE'S SOMETHING BEHIND THIS LOCKDOWN, THEN FINDING OUT WHAT IT IS COULD LEAD TO CLUES ABOUT HOW TO CHANGE THINGS.
AND...
THERE'S THE SHOMONKAI.
IF WE CAN TRACK DOWN THE SERVER THEY'RE USING TO SUMMON DEMONS,
WE MIGHT BE ABLE TO *CONTROL* THE DEMONS.
WE HAVE TO ASK THEM ABOUT AYA—THE WOMAN GIN IS LOOKING FOR.
AND ABOUT HARU, AND WHY THEY'RE AFTER HER.
...
OOHH
...BUT
FIRST...
...UH-HUH.
CLATTER
...YEAH.

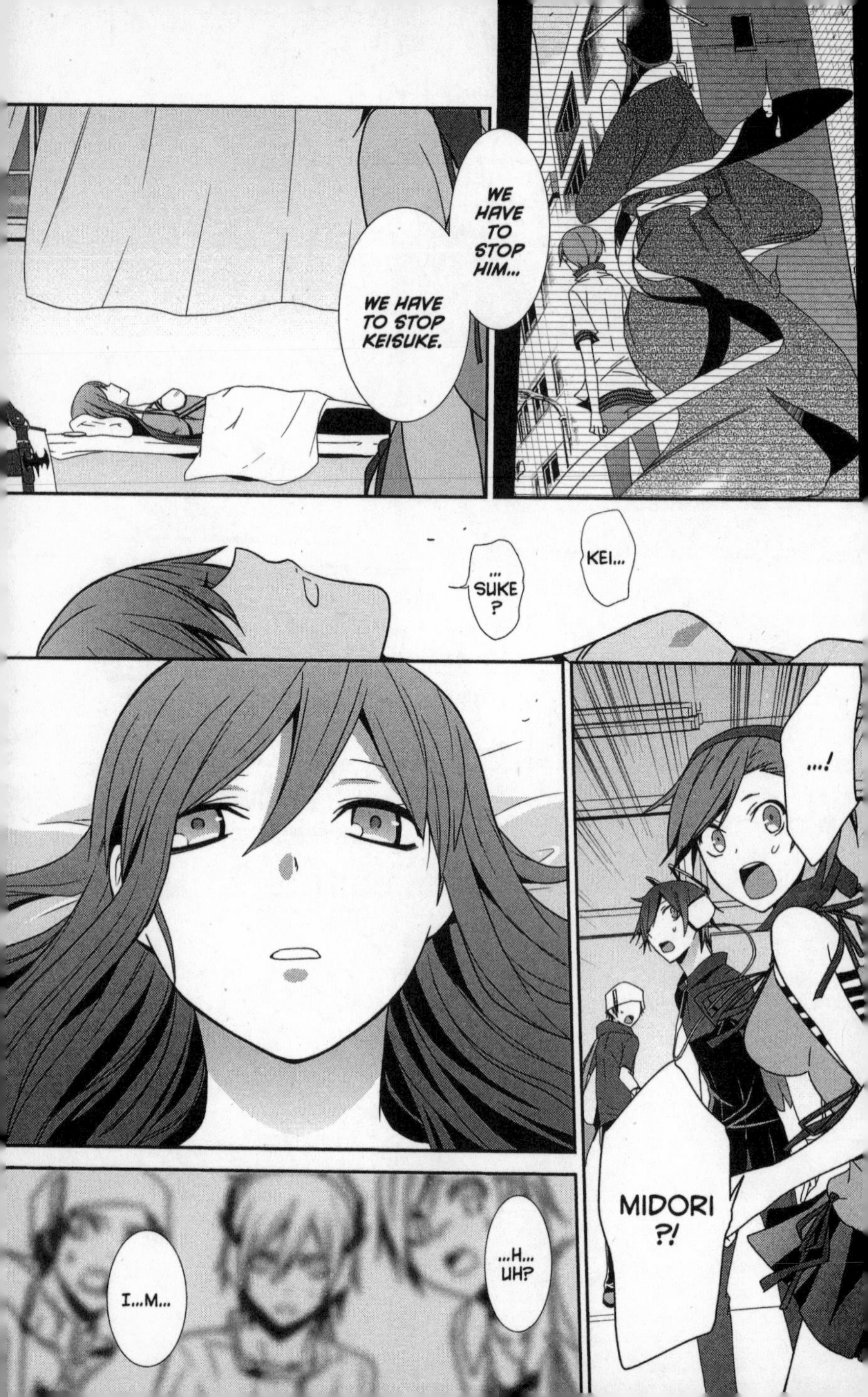
WE HAVE TO STOP HIM...
WE HAVE TO STOP KEISUKE.
KEI...
...SUKE?
...!
MIDORI?!
...H... UH?
I...M...

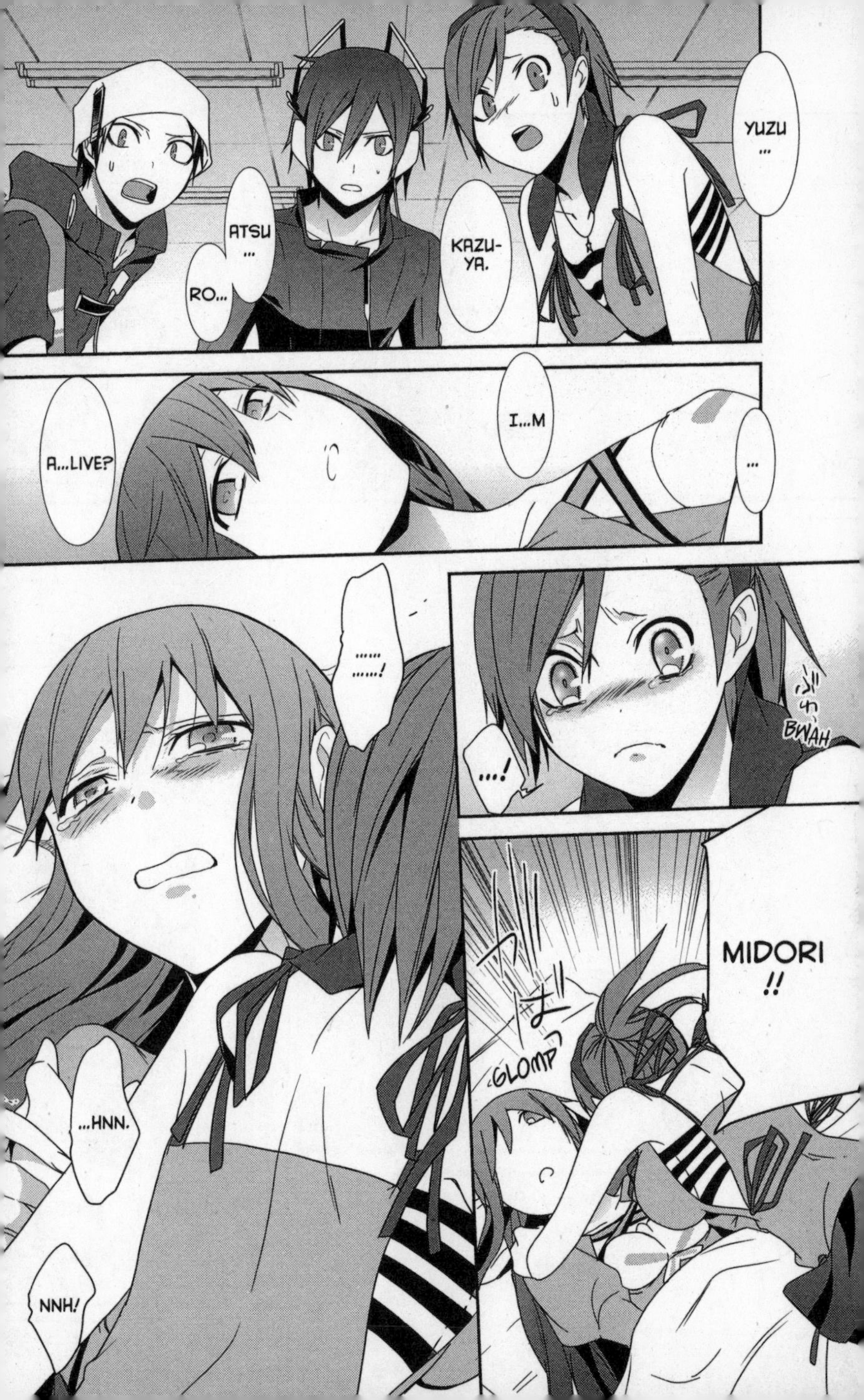
YUZU ...
KAZU-YA.
ATSU ...
RO...
...
I...M
A...LIVE?
ぶわ
BWAH
....!
MIDORI !!
GLOMP
....!
...HNN.
NNH!

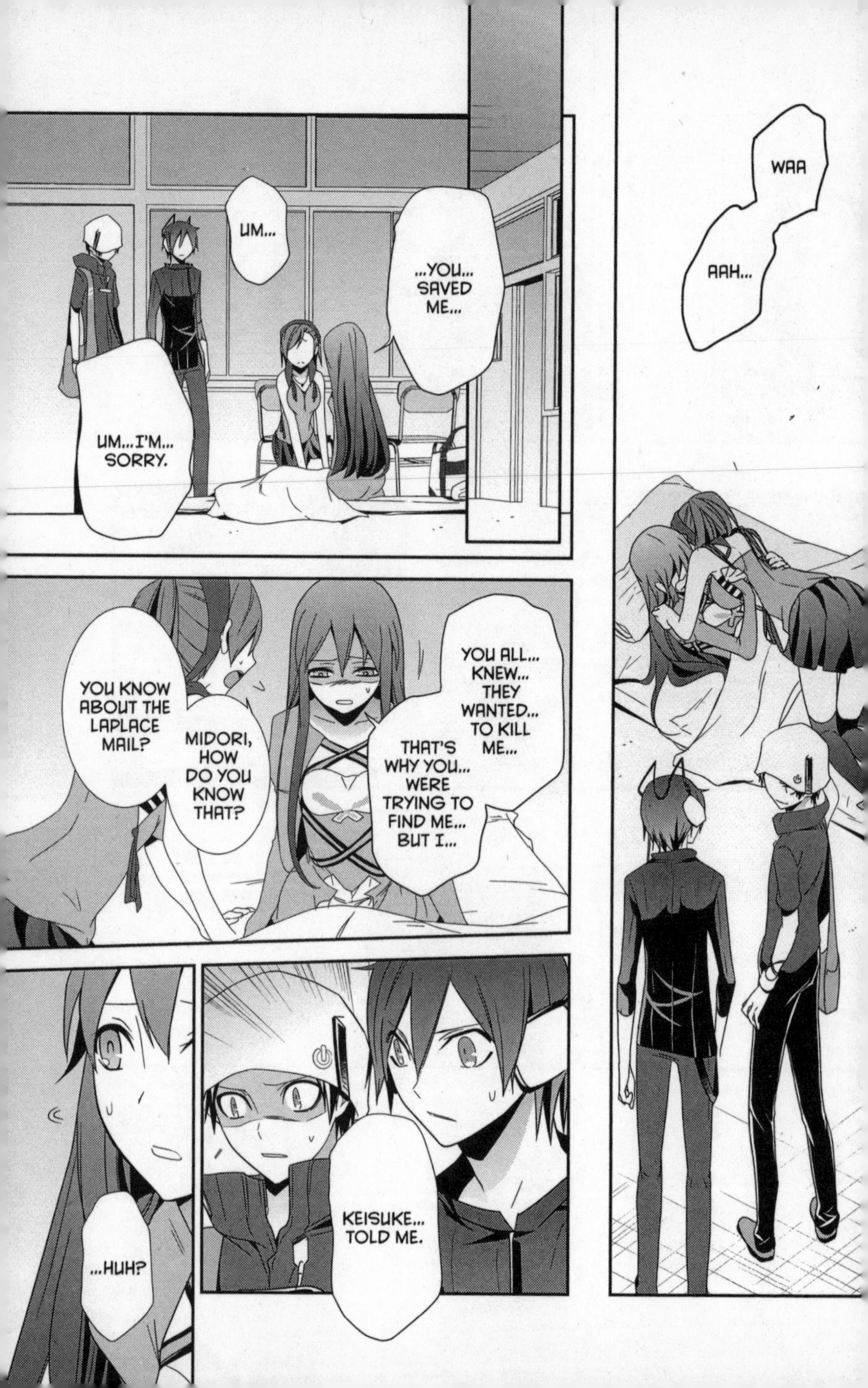
WAA
AAH...
...YOU... SAVED ME...
UM...
UM...I'M... SORRY.
YOU ALL... KNEW... THEY WANTED... TO KILL ME...
THAT'S WHY YOU... WERE TRYING TO FIND ME... BUT I...
MIDORI, HOW DO YOU KNOW THAT?
YOU KNOW ABOUT THE LAPLACE MAIL?
KEISUKE... TOLD ME.
...HUH?

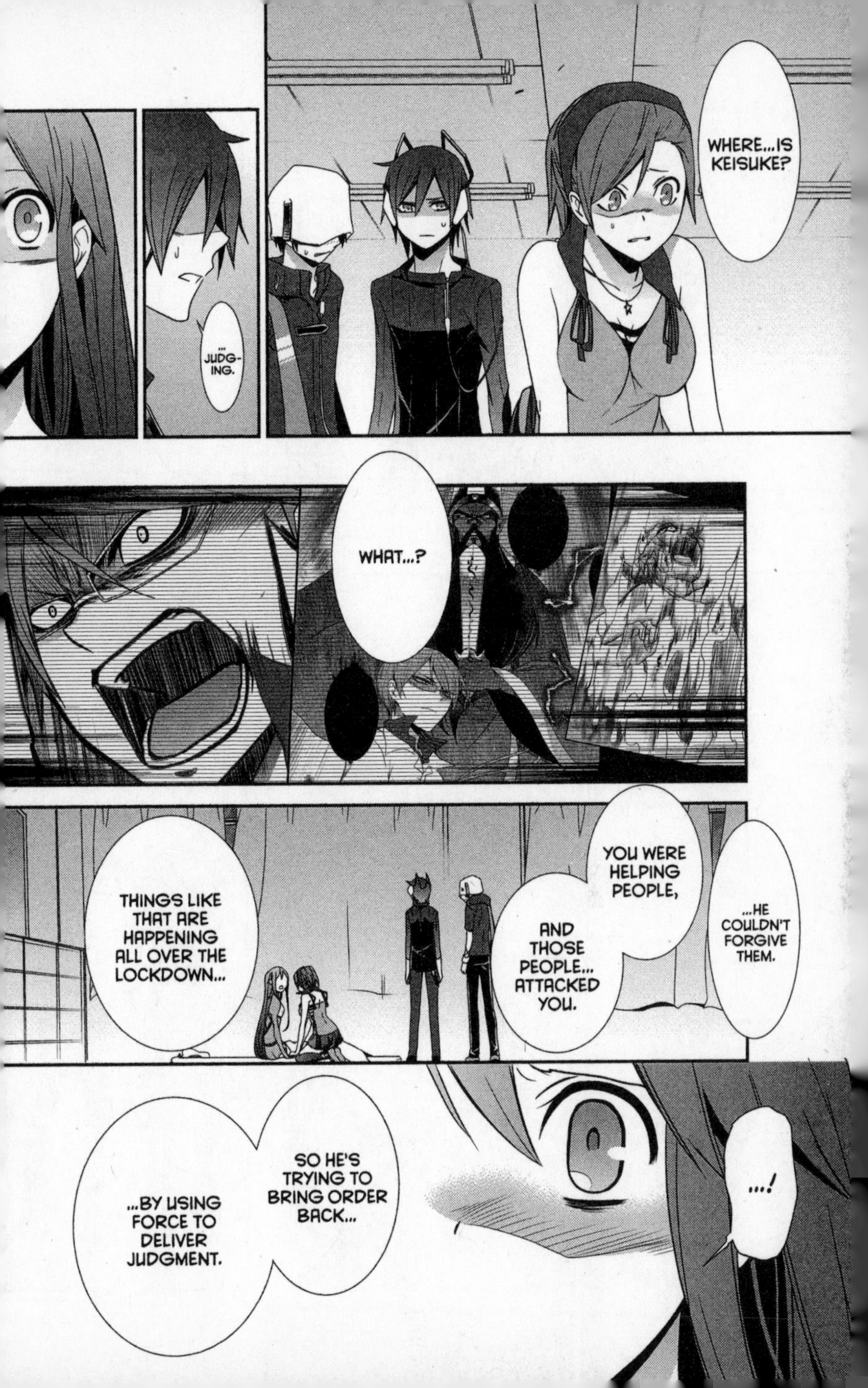
WHERE...IS KEISUKE?
...JUDG-ING.
WHAT...?
YOU WERE HELPING PEOPLE,
AND THOSE PEOPLE... ATTACKED YOU.
...HE COULDN'T FORGIVE THEM.
THINGS LIKE THAT ARE HAPPENING ALL OVER THE LOCKDOWN...
...!
SO HE'S TRYING TO BRING ORDER BACK...
...BY USING FORCE TO DELIVER JUDGMENT.

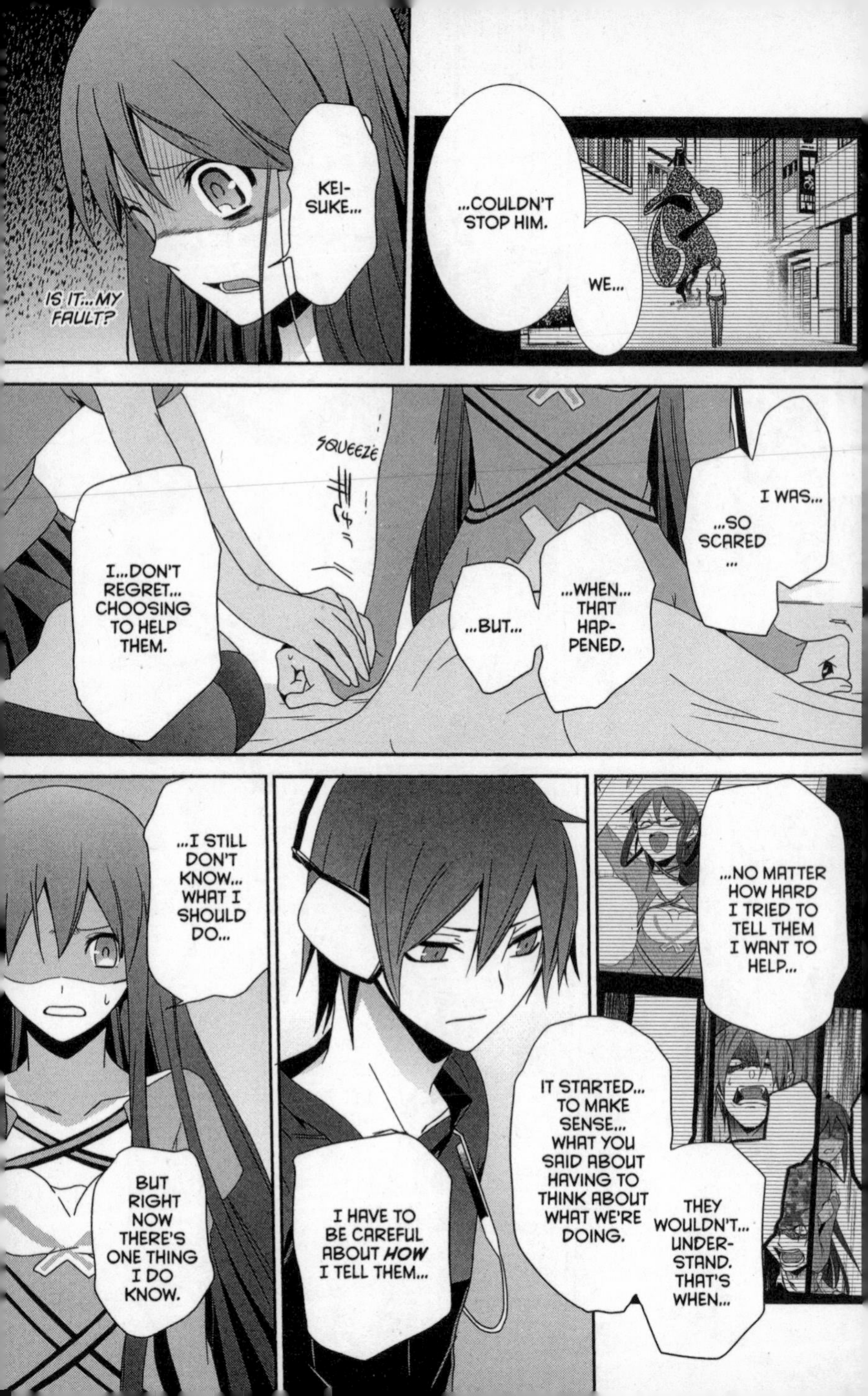
WE...
...COULDN'T STOP HIM.
KEI-SUKE...
IS IT...MY FAULT?
I WAS...
...SO SCARED ...
...WHEN... THAT HAP-PENED.
...BUT...
SQUEEZE
I...DON'T REGRET... CHOOSING TO HELP THEM.
...NO MATTER HOW HARD I TRIED TO TELL THEM I WANT TO HELP...
THEY WOULDN'T... UNDER-STAND. THAT'S WHEN...
IT STARTED... TO MAKE SENSE... WHAT YOU SAID ABOUT HAVING TO THINK ABOUT WHAT WE'RE DOING.
I HAVE TO BE CAREFUL ABOUT *HOW* I TELL THEM...
...I STILL DON'T KNOW... WHAT I SHOULD DO...
BUT RIGHT NOW THERE'S ONE THING I DO KNOW.

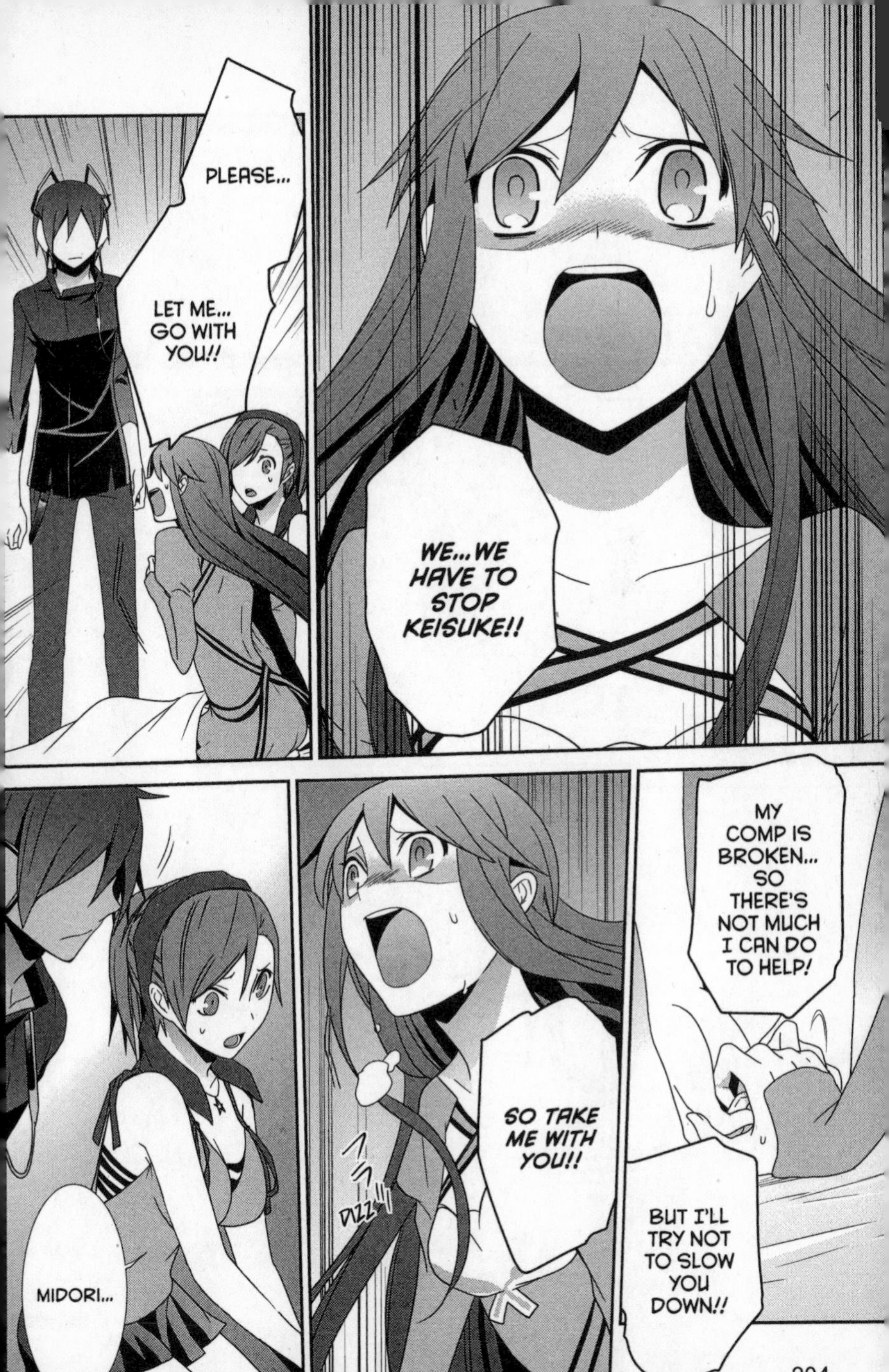
WE...WE HAVE TO STOP KEISUKE!!
PLEASE...
LET ME... GO WITH YOU!!
MY COMP IS BROKEN... SO THERE'S NOT MUCH I CAN DO TO HELP!
BUT I'LL TRY NOT TO SLOW YOU DOWN!!
SO TAKE ME WITH YOU!!
DIZZY
MIDORI...

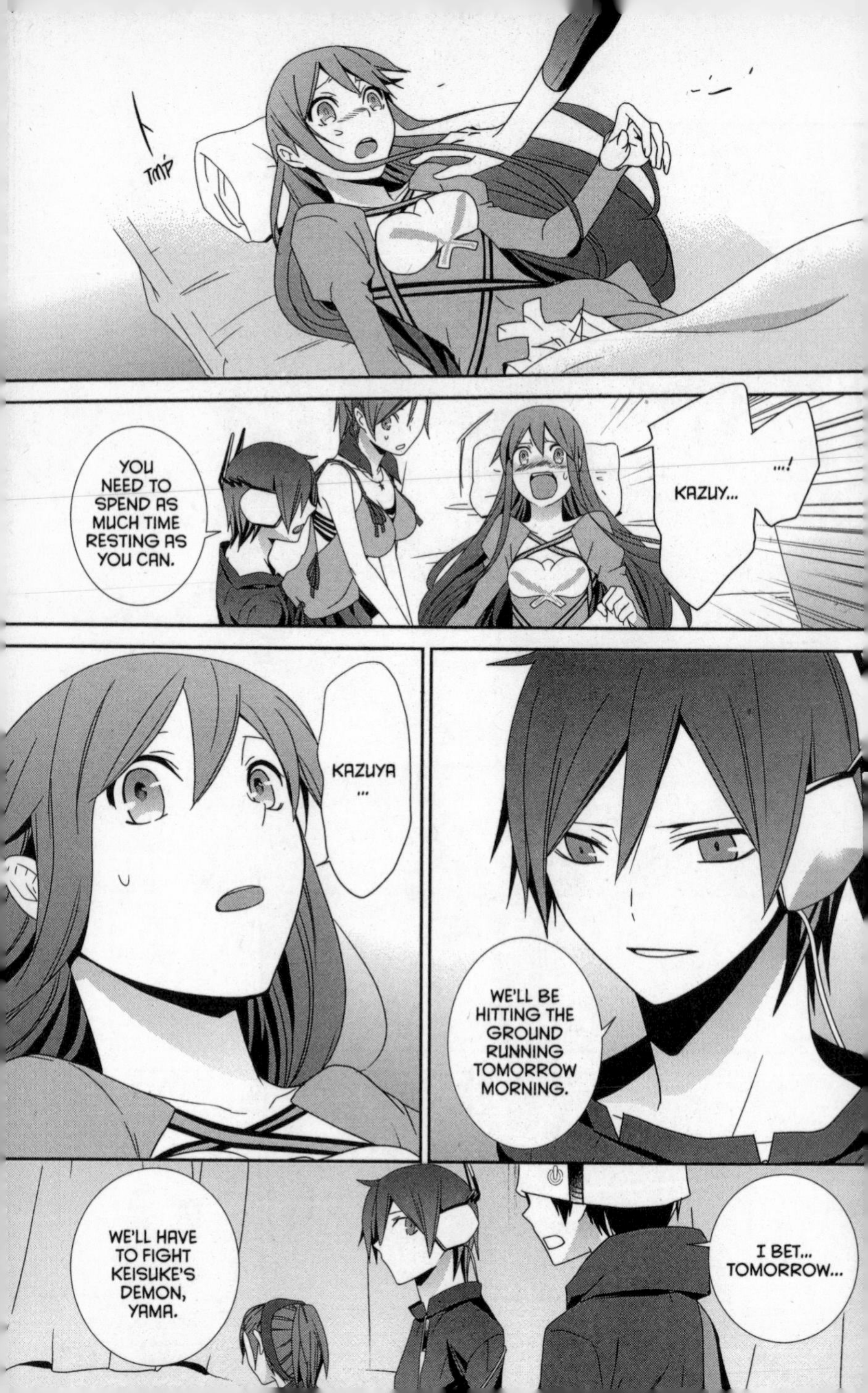
TMP
...!
KAZUY...
YOU NEED TO SPEND AS MUCH TIME RESTING AS YOU CAN.
WE'LL BE HITTING THE GROUND RUNNING TOMORROW MORNING.
KAZUYA ...
I BET... TOMORROW...
WE'LL HAVE TO FIGHT KEISUKE'S DEMON, YAMA.

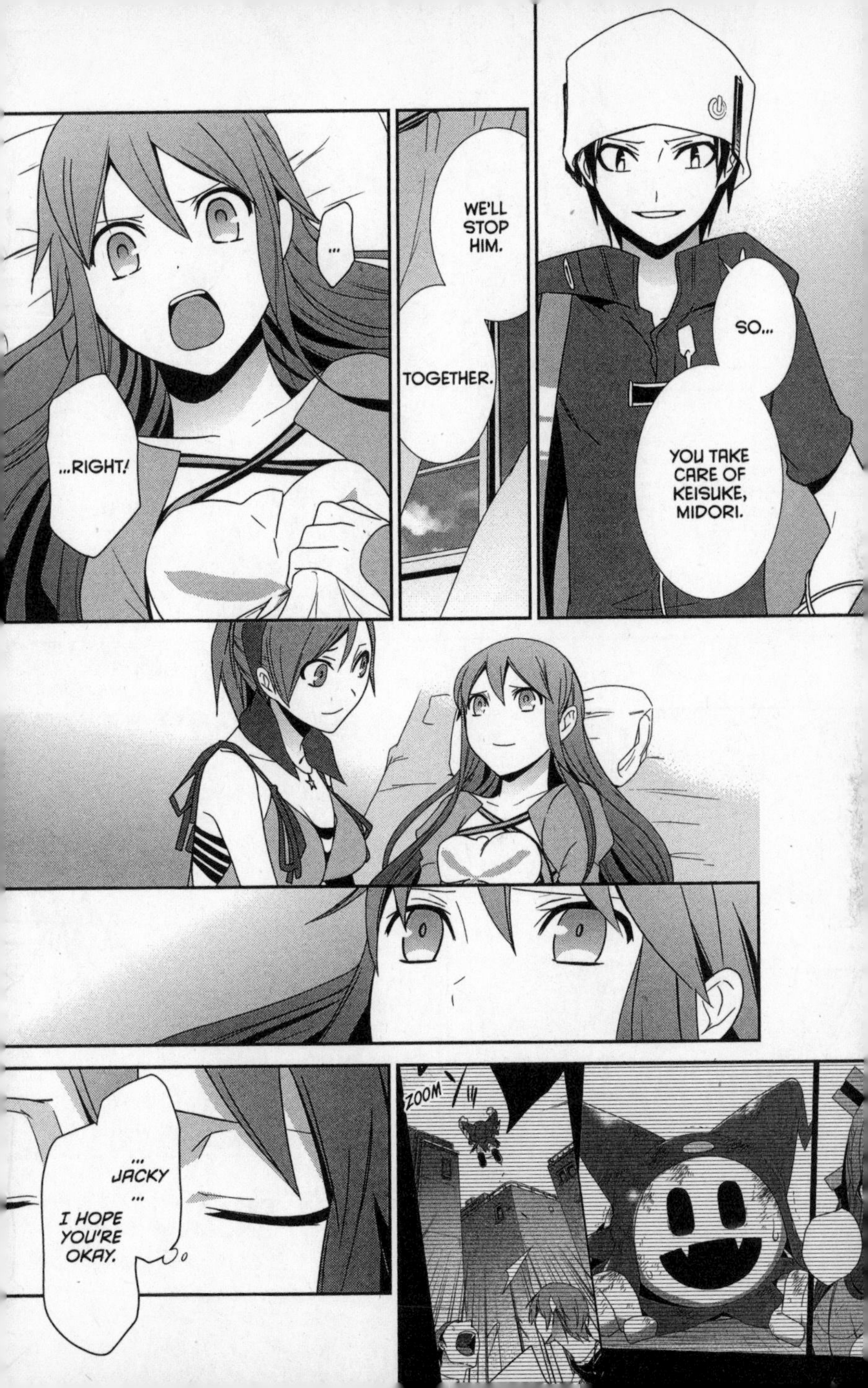
SO...
YOU TAKE CARE OF KEISUKE, MIDORI.
WE'LL STOP HIM.
TOGETHER.
...
...RIGHT!
ZOOM
... JACKY ... I HOPE YOU'RE OKAY.

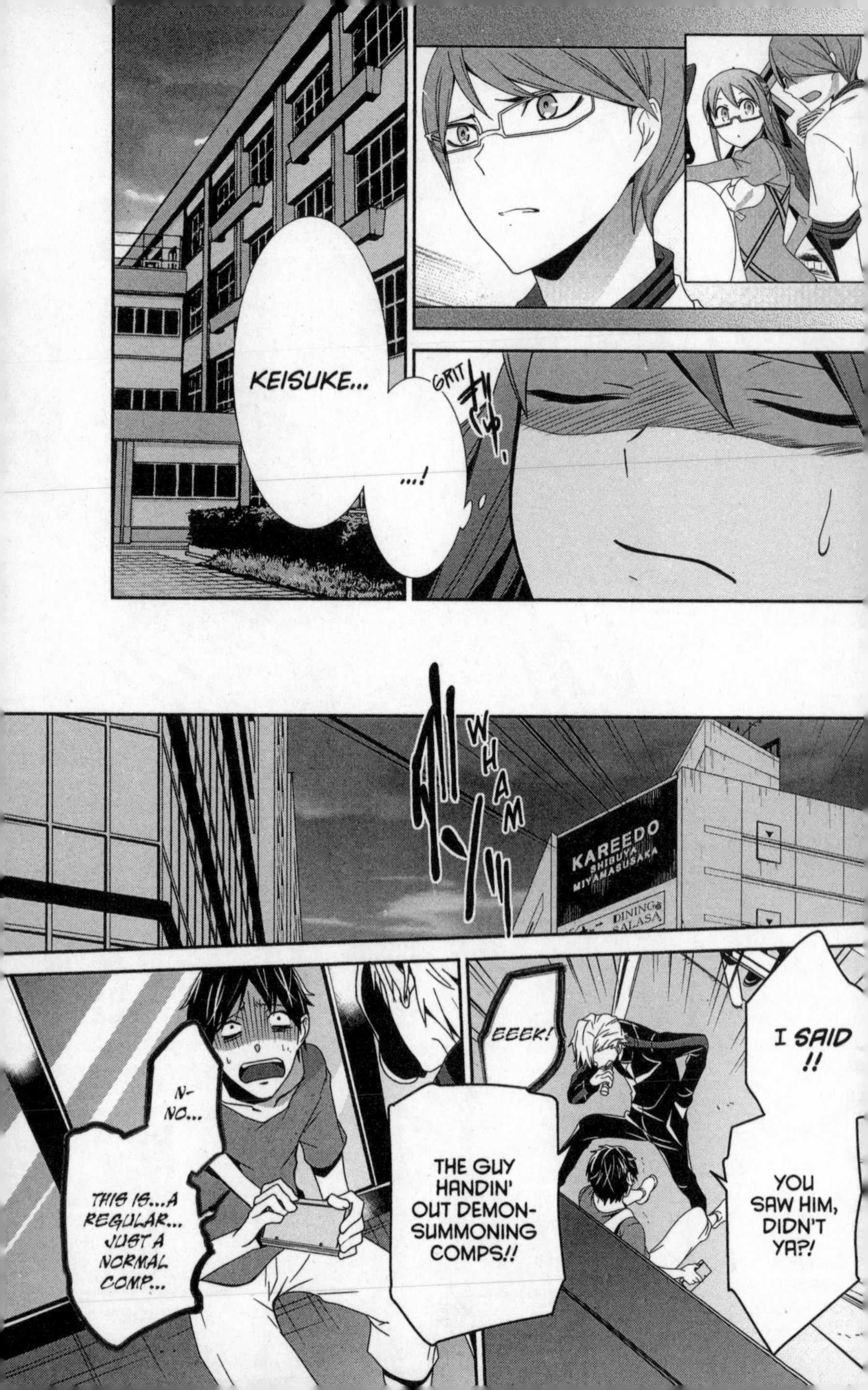
KEISUKE...
GRIT
...!
WHAM
KAREEDO
SHIBUYA
MIYAMASUSAKA
DINING
SALASA
I SAID!!
YOU SAW HIM, DIDN'T YA?!
EEEK!
THE GUY HANDIN' OUT DEMON-SUMMONING COMPS!!
N-NO...
THIS IS...A REGULAR... JUST A NORMAL COMP...

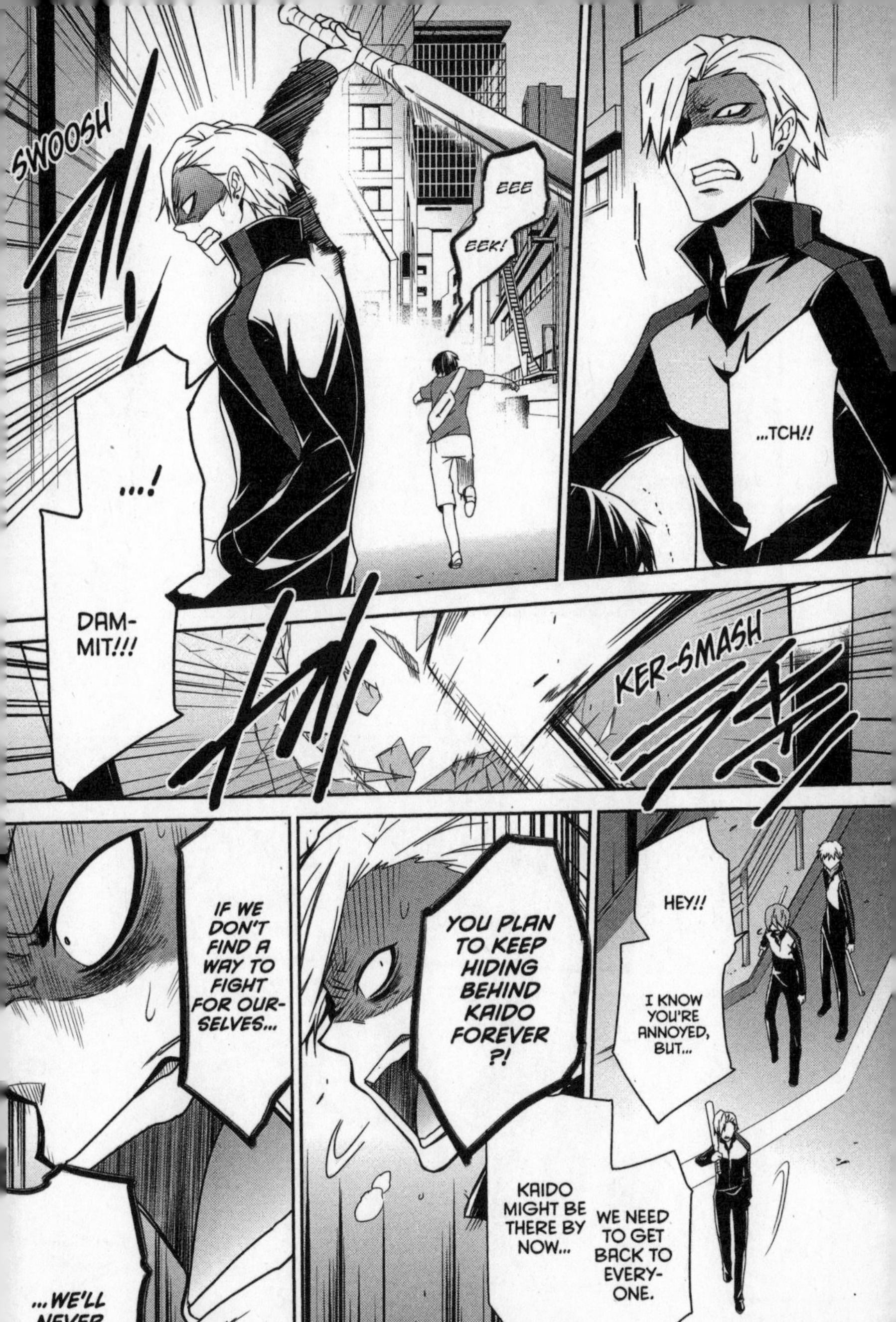
...TCH!!
EEE
EEK!
SWOOSH
...!
DAM-MIT!!!
KER-SMASH
HEY!!
I KNOW YOU'RE ANNOYED, BUT...
WE NEED TO GET BACK TO EVERY-ONE.
KAIDO MIGHT BE THERE BY NOW...
YOU PLAN TO KEEP HIDING BEHIND KAIDO FOREVER ?!
IF WE DON'T FIND A WAY TO FIGHT FOR OUR-SELVES...
...WE'LL NEVER SURVIVE!!

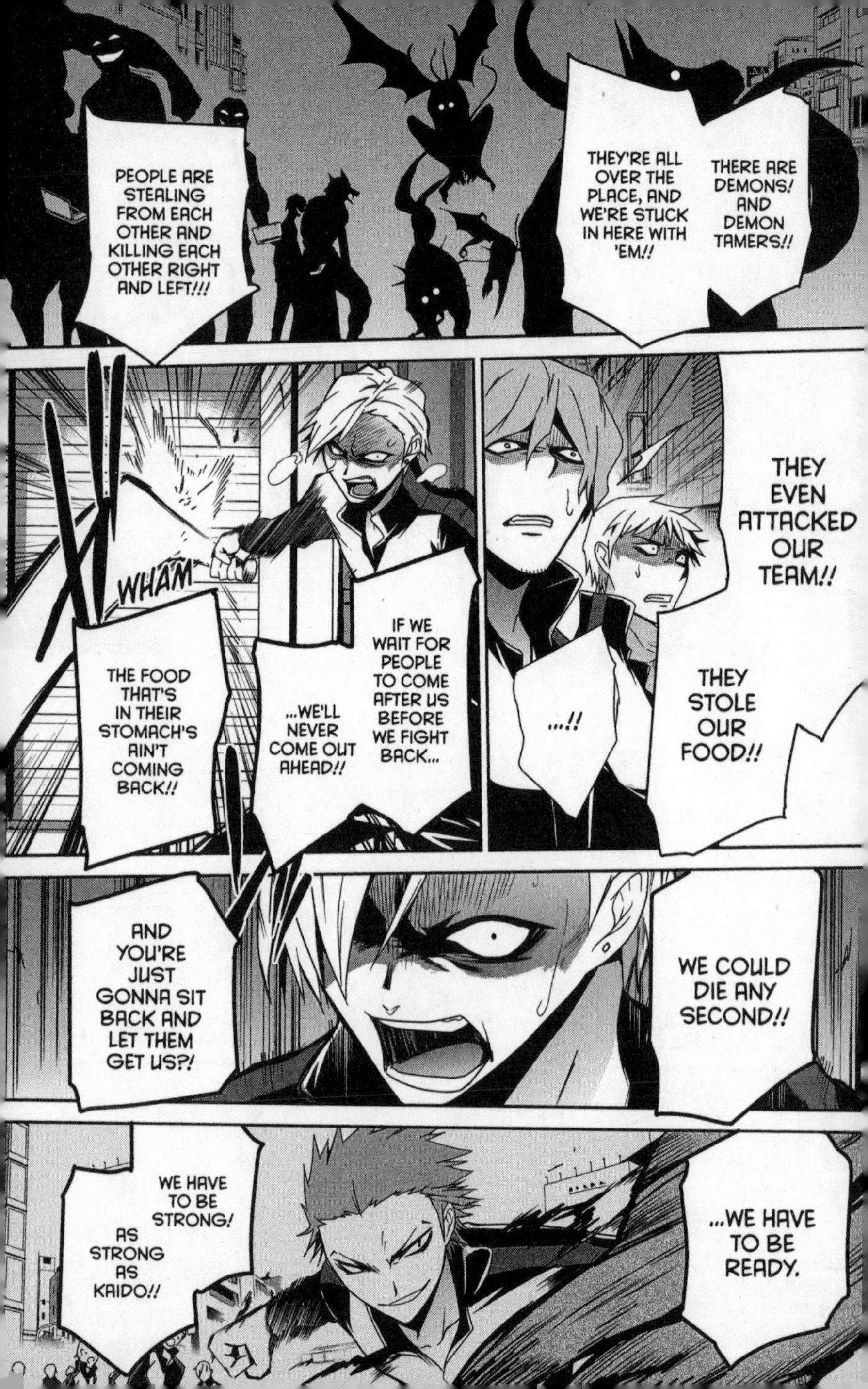
THERE ARE DEMONS! AND DEMON TAMERS!!
THEY'RE ALL OVER THE PLACE, AND WE'RE STUCK IN HERE WITH 'EM!!
PEOPLE ARE STEALING FROM EACH OTHER AND KILLING EACH OTHER RIGHT AND LEFT!!!
THEY EVEN ATTACKED OUR TEAM!!
THEY STOLE OUR FOOD!!
...!!
IF WE WAIT FOR PEOPLE TO COME AFTER US BEFORE WE FIGHT BACK...
...WE'LL NEVER COME OUT AHEAD!!
WHAM
THE FOOD THAT'S IN THEIR STOMACH'S AIN'T COMING BACK!!
WE COULD DIE ANY SECOND!!
AND YOU'RE JUST GONNA SIT BACK AND LET THEM GET US?!
...WE HAVE TO BE READY.
WE HAVE TO BE STRONG!
AS STRONG AS KAIDO!!

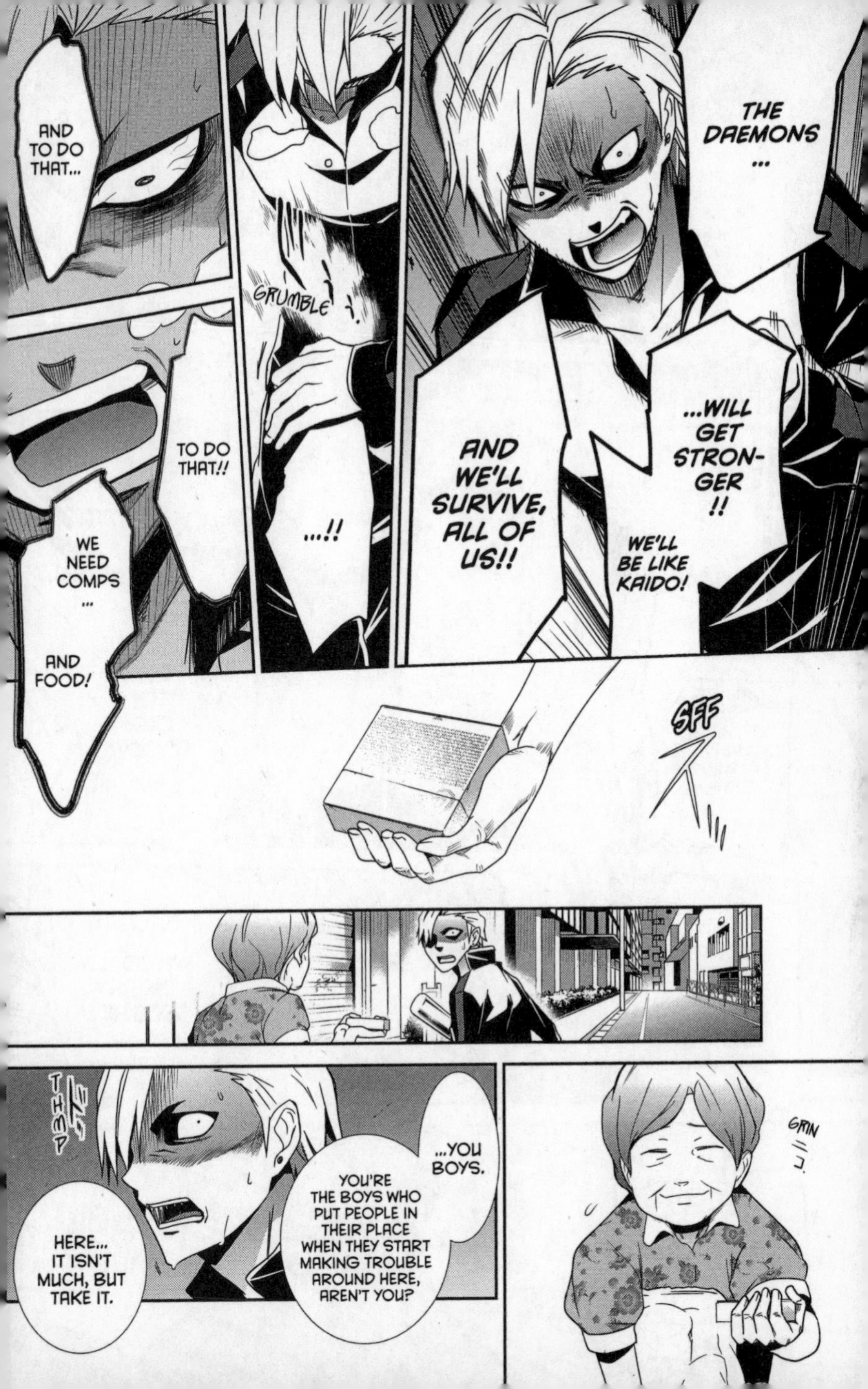
THE DAEMONS...
...WILL GET STRON-GER!!
WE'LL BE LIKE KAIDO!
AND WE'LL SURVIVE, ALL OF US!!
GRUMBLE
...!!
AND TO DO THAT...
TO DO THAT!!
WE NEED COMPS...
AND FOOD!
SFF
GRIN
...YOU BOYS.
YOU'RE THE BOYS WHO PUT PEOPLE IN THEIR PLACE WHEN THEY START MAKING TROUBLE AROUND HERE, AREN'T YOU?
HERE... IT ISN'T MUCH, BUT TAKE IT.
THMP

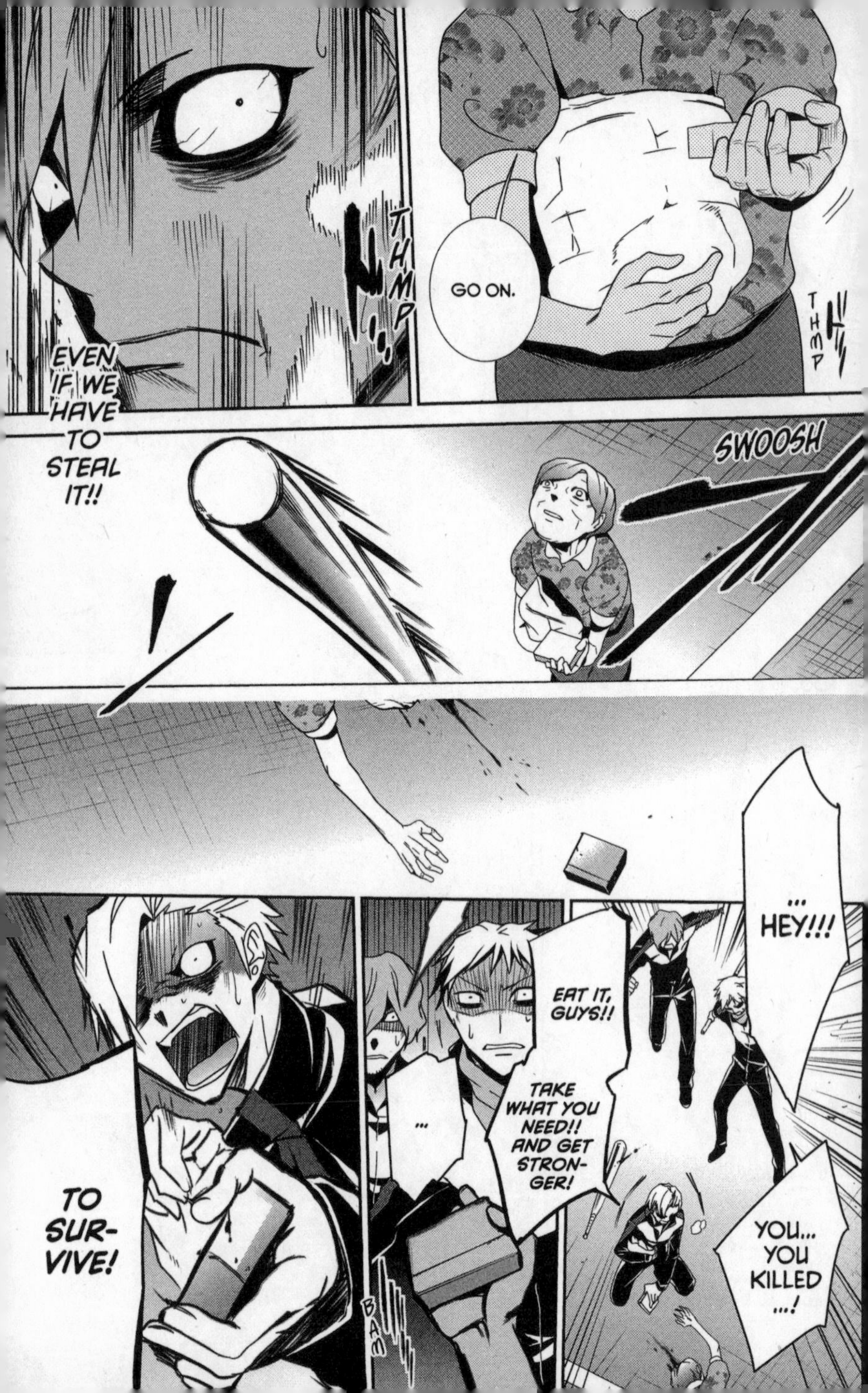
GO ON.
THMP
THMP
EVEN IF WE HAVE TO STEAL IT!!
SWOOSH
...HEY!!!
EAT IT, GUYS!!
TAKE WHAT YOU NEED!! AND GET STRONGER!
YOU... YOU KILLED ...!
...
BAM
TO SURVIVE!

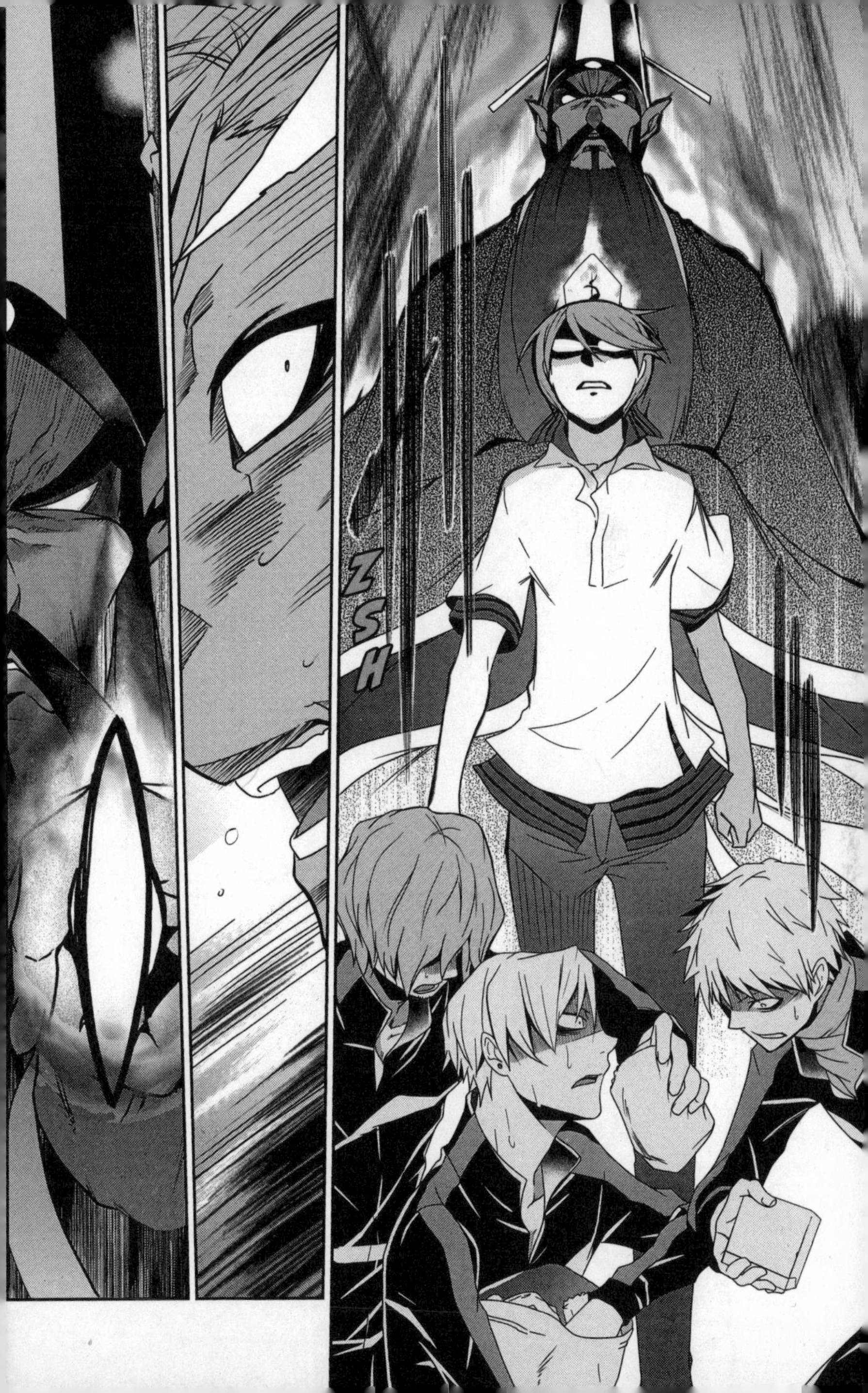
ZSH

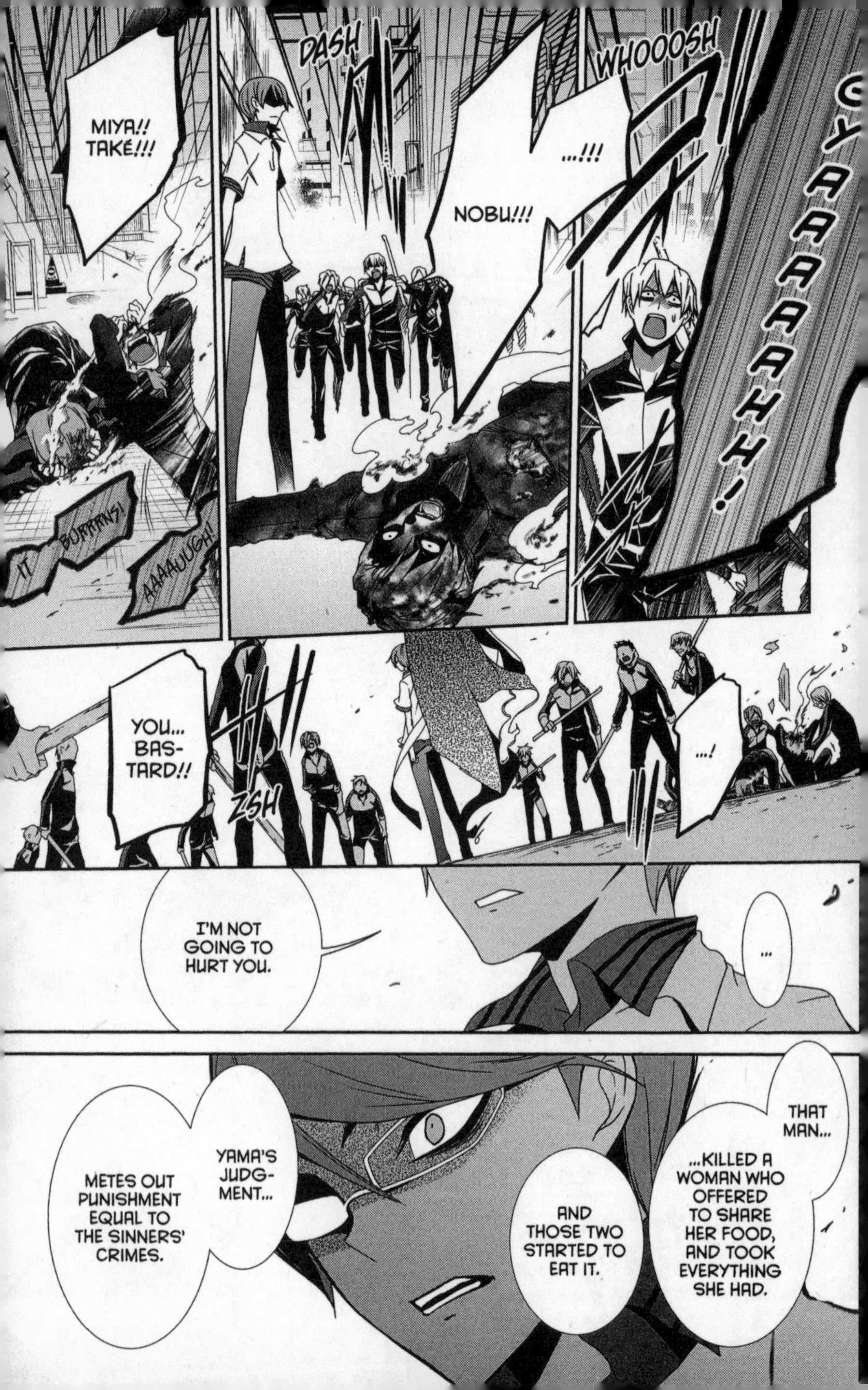
WHOOOSH
GYAAAAAAAHH!
DASH
...!!!
NOBU!!!
MIYA!! TAKÉ!!!
IT BURRRNS!
AAAAUUGH!
...!
YOU... BAS-TARD!!
ZSH
...
I'M NOT GOING TO HURT YOU.
THAT MAN...
...KILLED A WOMAN WHO OFFERED TO SHARE HER FOOD, AND TOOK EVERYTHING SHE HAD.
AND THOSE TWO STARTED TO EAT IT.
YAMA'S JUDG-MENT...
METES OUT PUNISHMENT EQUAL TO THE SINNERS' CRIMES.

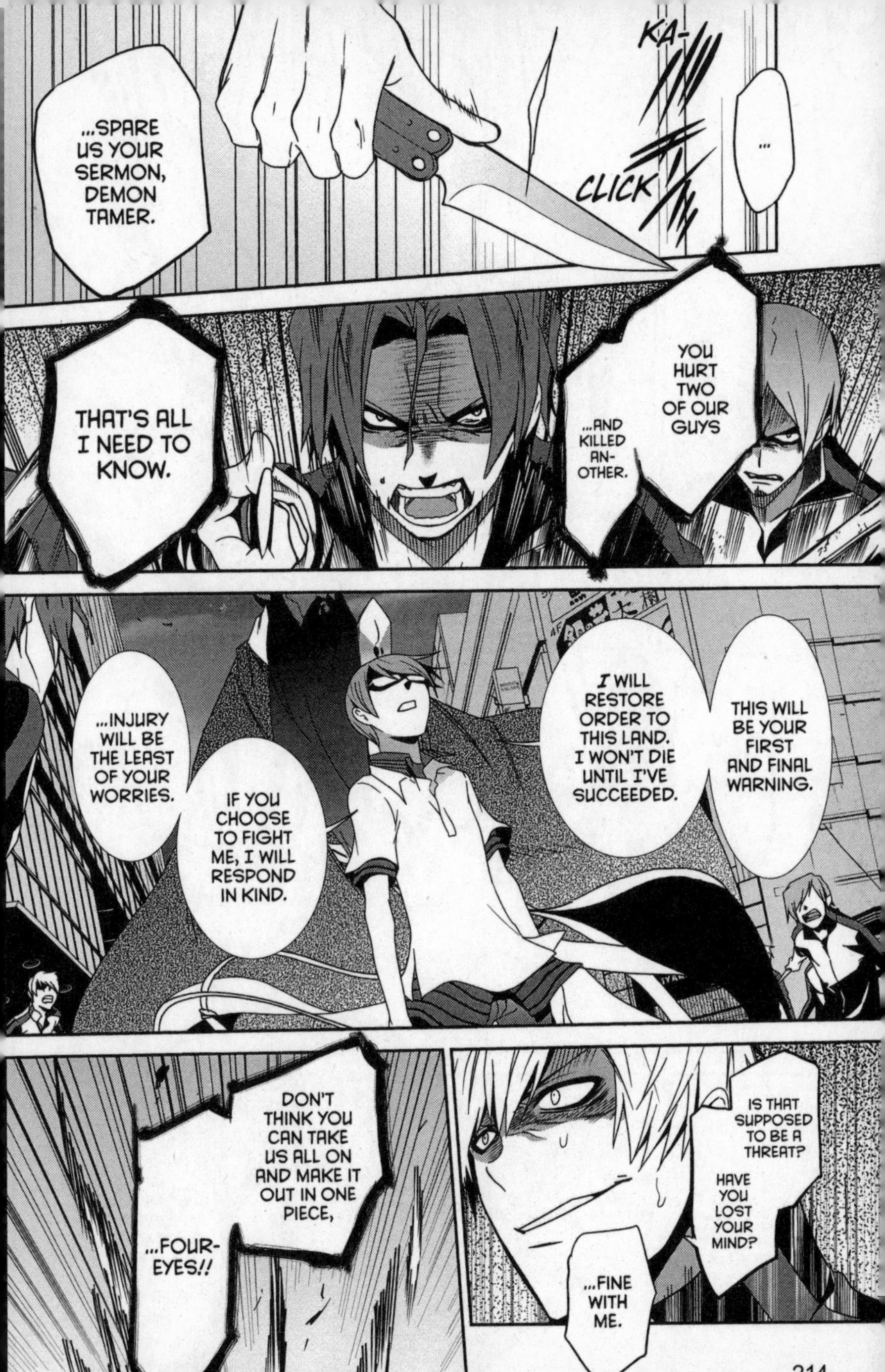
KA-
...
CLICK
...SPARE US YOUR SERMON, DEMON TAMER.
YOU HURT TWO OF OUR GUYS
...AND KILLED AN-OTHER.
THAT'S ALL I NEED TO KNOW.
THIS WILL BE YOUR FIRST AND FINAL WARNING.
I WILL RESTORE ORDER TO THIS LAND. I WON'T DIE UNTIL I'VE SUCCEEDED.
IF YOU CHOOSE TO FIGHT ME, I WILL RESPOND IN KIND.
...INJURY WILL BE THE LEAST OF YOUR WORRIES.
IS THAT SUPPOSED TO BE A THREAT?
HAVE YOU LOST YOUR MIND?
DON'T THINK YOU CAN TAKE US ALL ON AND MAKE IT OUT IN ONE PIECE,
...FOUR-EYES!!
...FINE WITH ME.

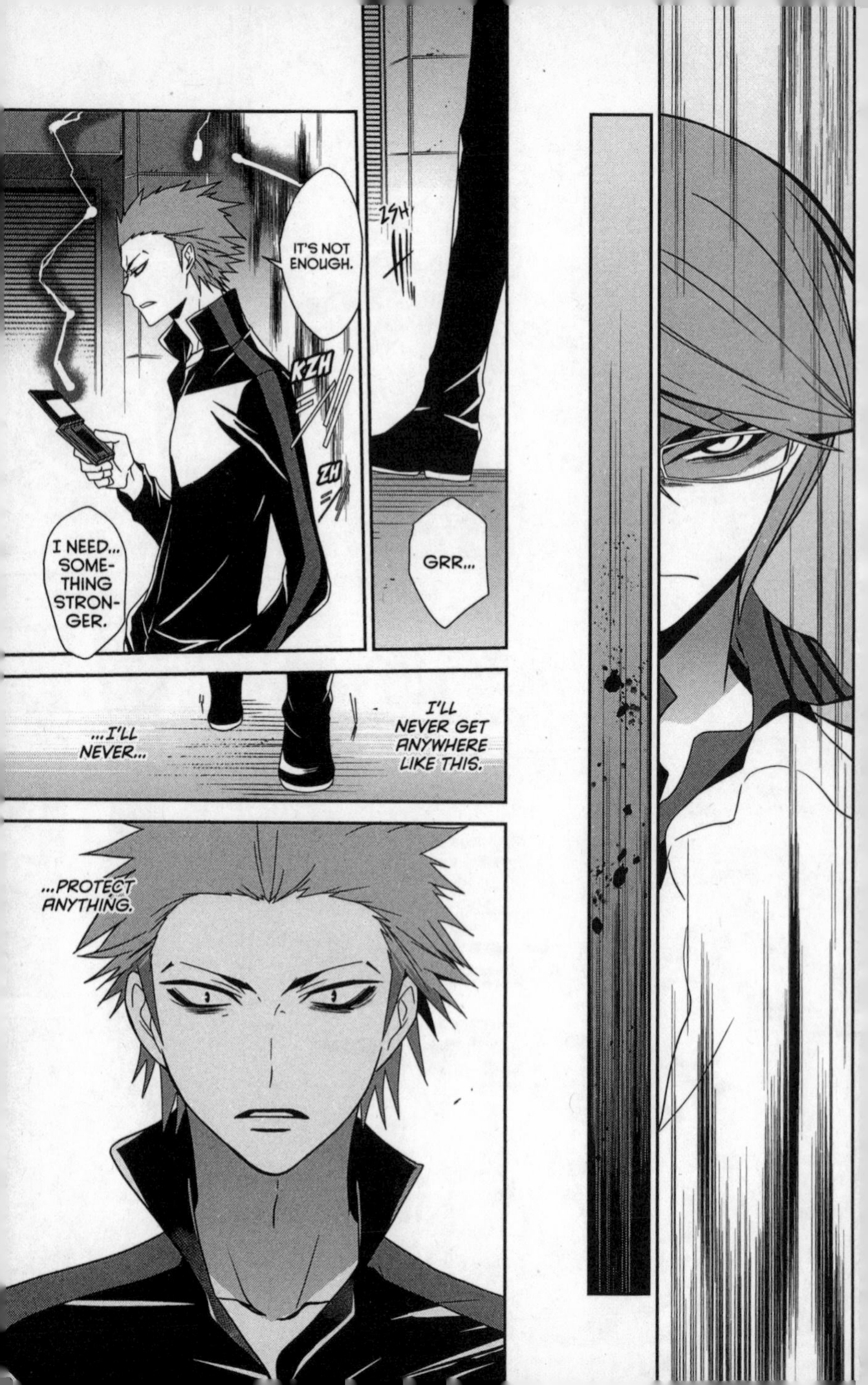
ZSH
GRR...
IT'S NOT ENOUGH.
KZH
ZH
I NEED... SOME-THING STRON-GER.
I'LL NEVER GET ANYWHERE LIKE THIS.
...I'LL NEVER...
...PROTECT ANYTHING.

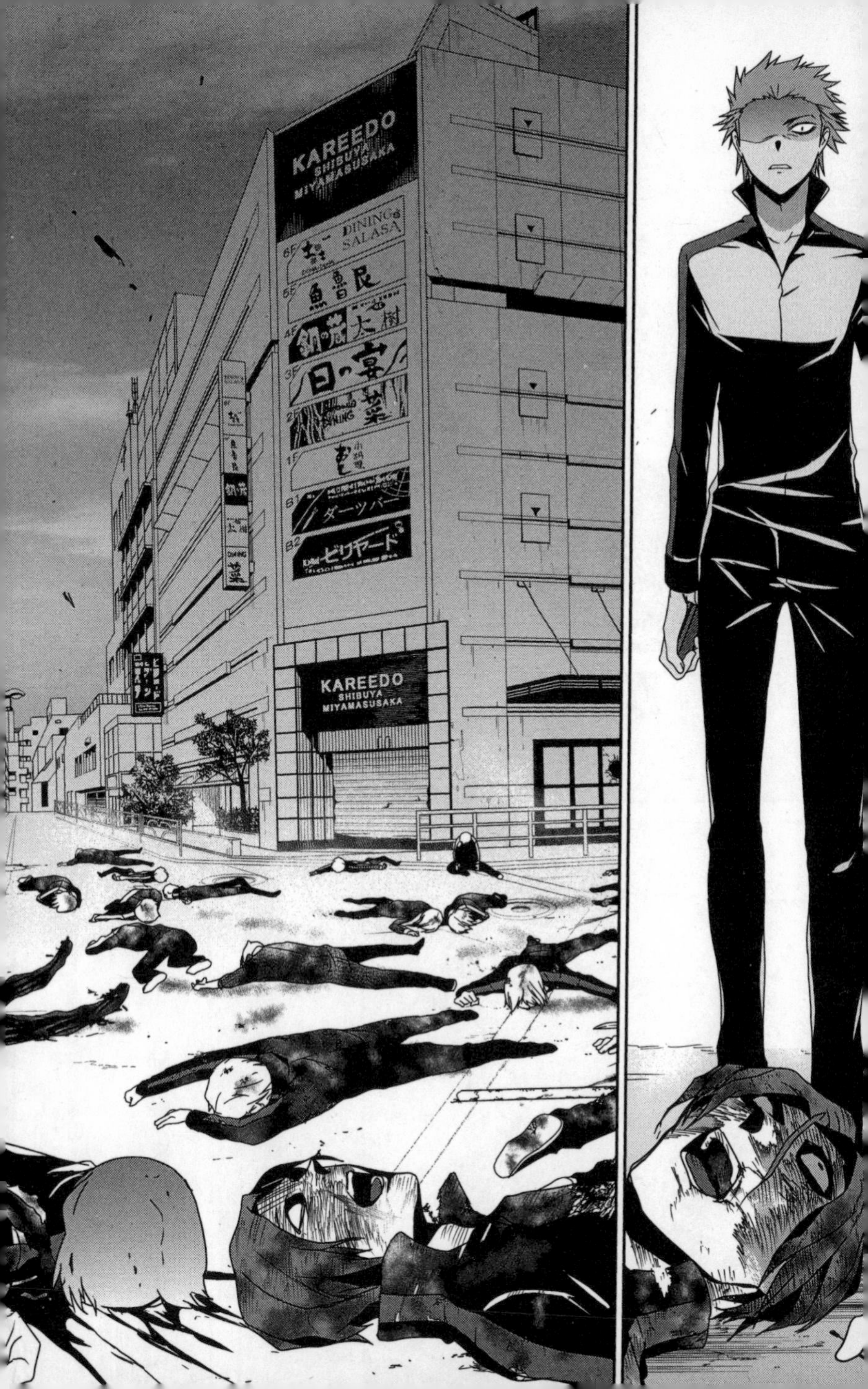
KAREEDO
SHIBUYA
MIYAMASUSAKA
DINING
SALASA
ダーツバー
ビリヤード
KAREEDO
SHIBUYA
MIYAMASUSAKA

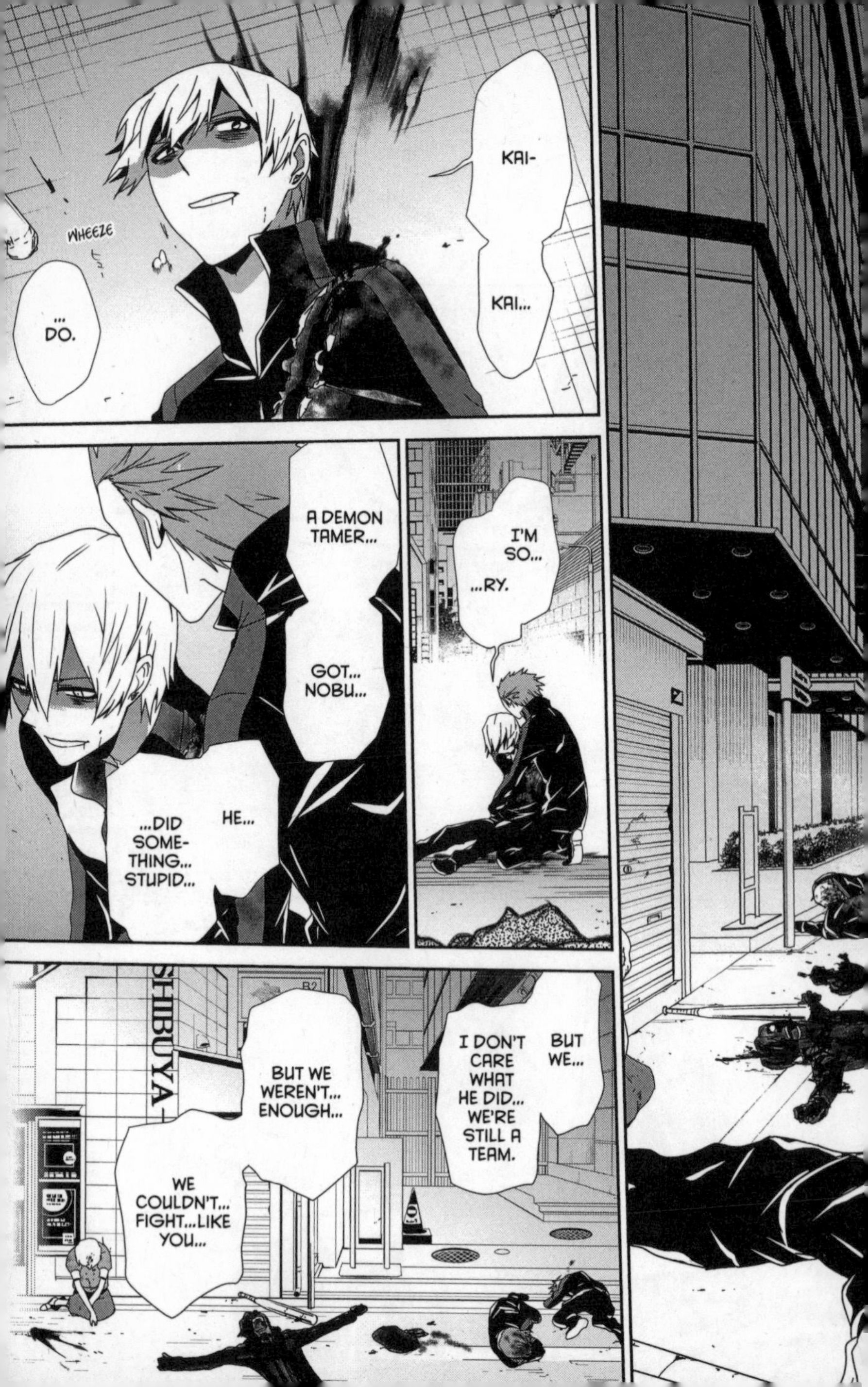
KAI-
KAI...
WHEEZE
...DO.
I'M SO... ...RY.
A DEMON TAMER...
GOT... NOBU...
HE...
...DID SOMETHING... STUPID...
SHIBUYA
BUT WE...
I DON'T CARE WHAT HE DID... WE'RE STILL A TEAM.
BUT WE WEREN'T... ENOUGH...
WE COULDN'T... FIGHT...LIKE YOU...

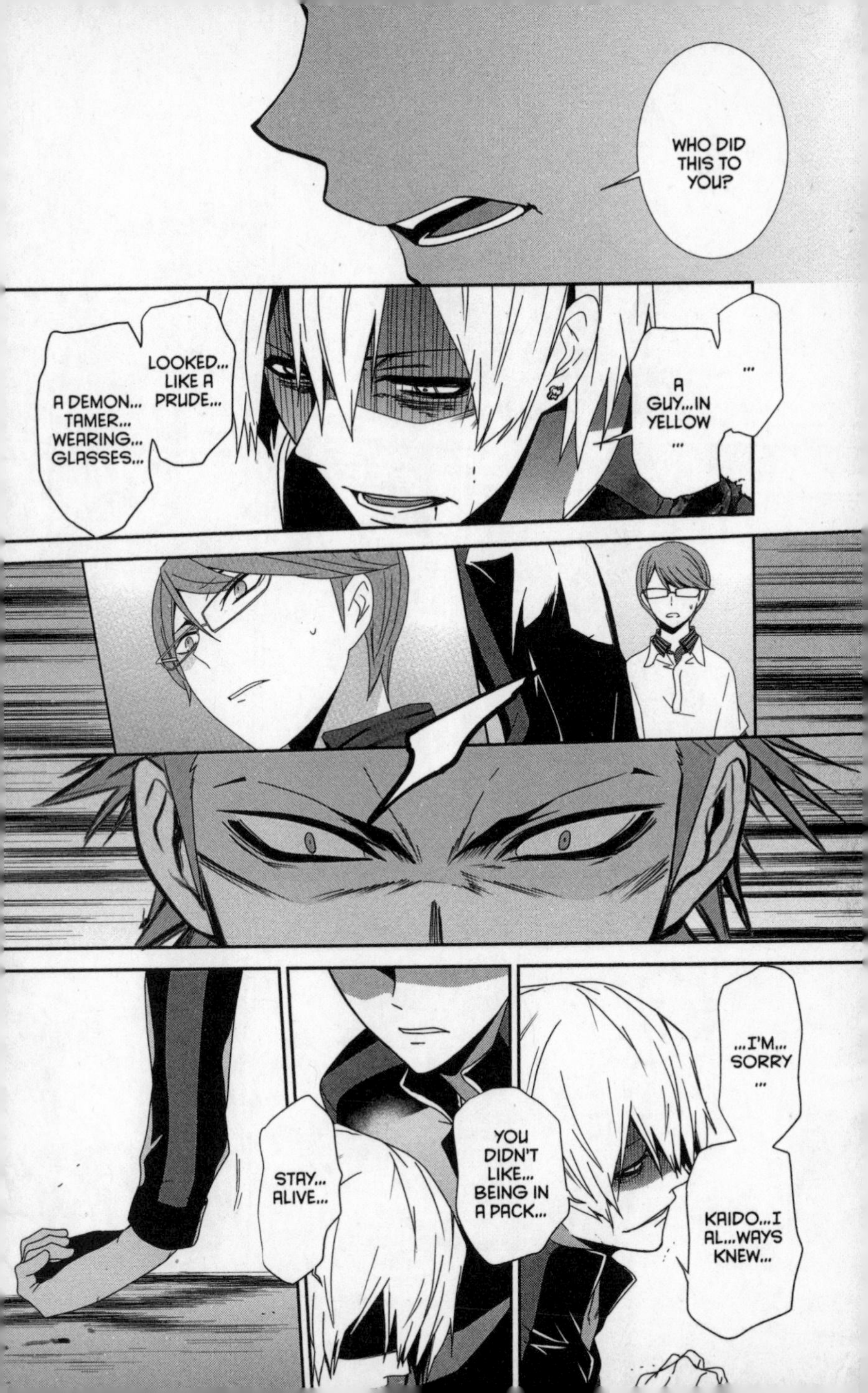
WHO DID THIS TO YOU?
... A GUY...IN YELLOW ...
LOOKED... LIKE A PRUDE...
A DEMON... TAMER... WEARING... GLASSES...
...I'M... SORRY ...
KAIDO...I AL...WAYS KNEW...
YOU DIDN'T LIKE... BEING IN A PACK...
STAY... ALIVE...

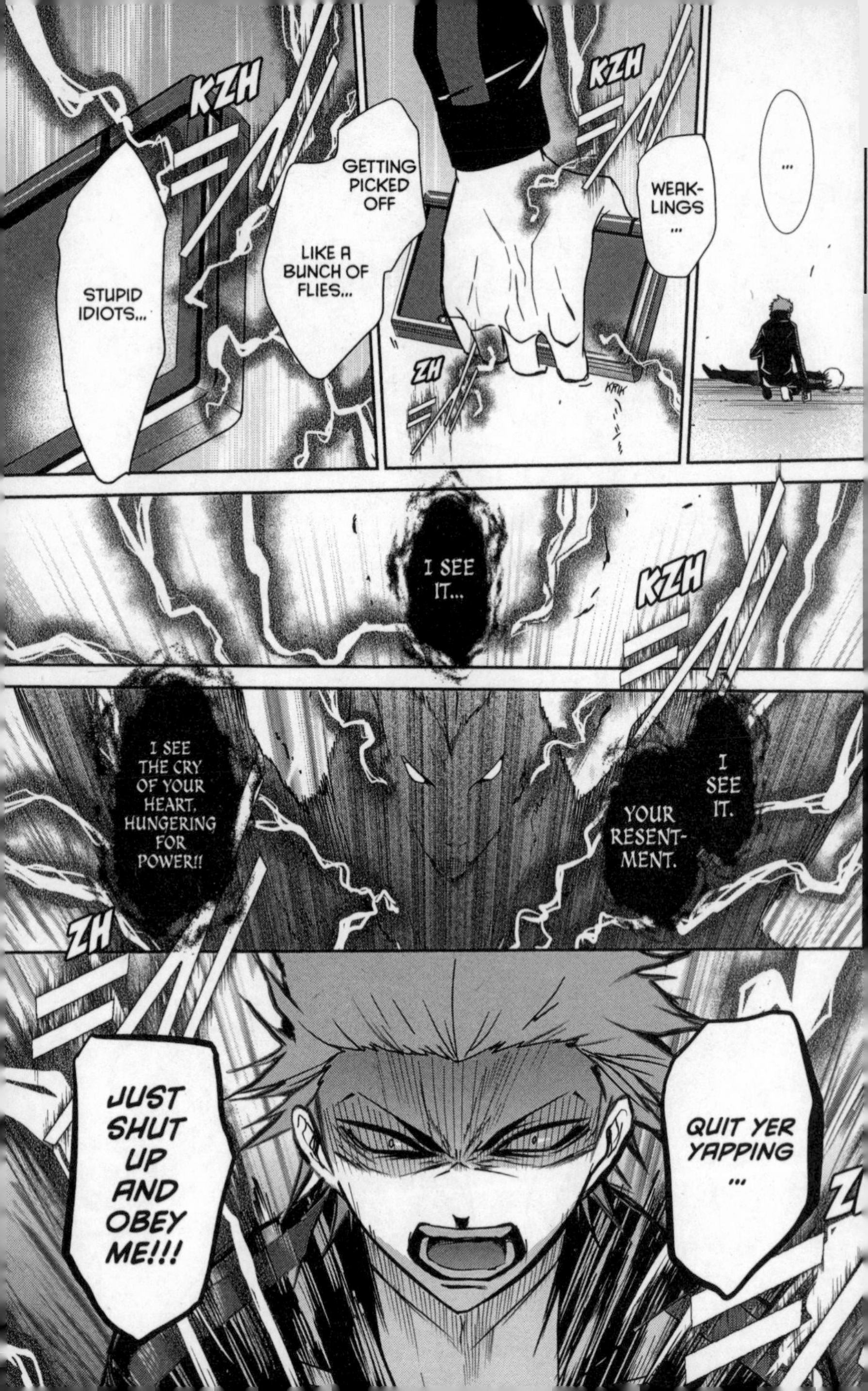
...
KZH
WEAK-LINGS ...
ZH
KRIK
GETTING PICKED OFF
LIKE A BUNCH OF FLIES...
KZH
STUPID IDIOTS...
KZH
I SEE IT...
I SEE IT.
YOUR RESENT-MENT.
I SEE THE CRY OF YOUR HEART, HUNGERING FOR POWER!!
ZH
QUIT YER YAPPING ...
JUST SHUT UP AND OBEY ME!!!

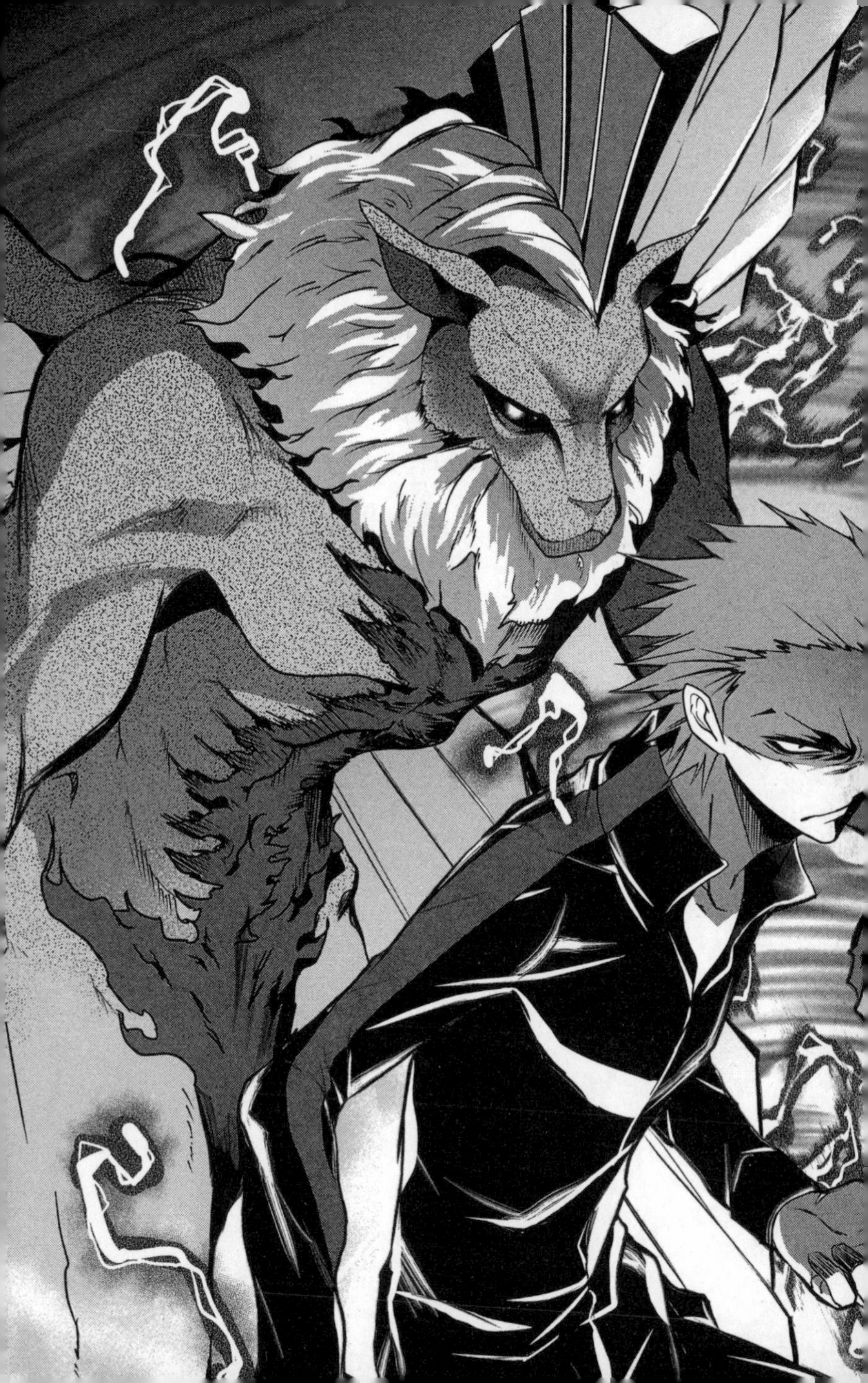

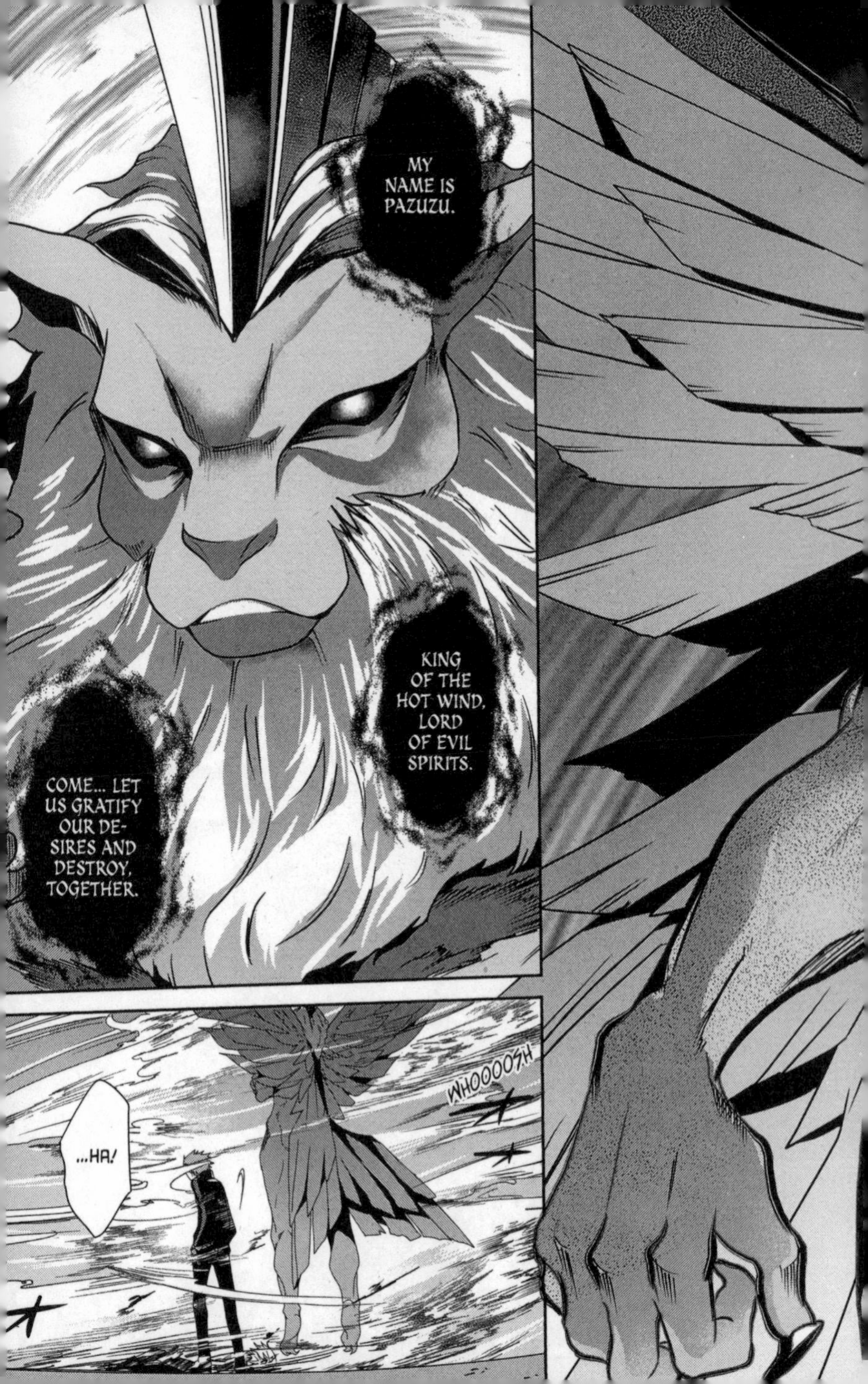
MY NAME IS PAZUZU.
KING OF THE HOT WIND, LORD OF EVIL SPIRITS.
COME... LET US GRATIFY OUR DESIRES AND DESTROY, TOGETHER.
WHOOOOSH
...HA!

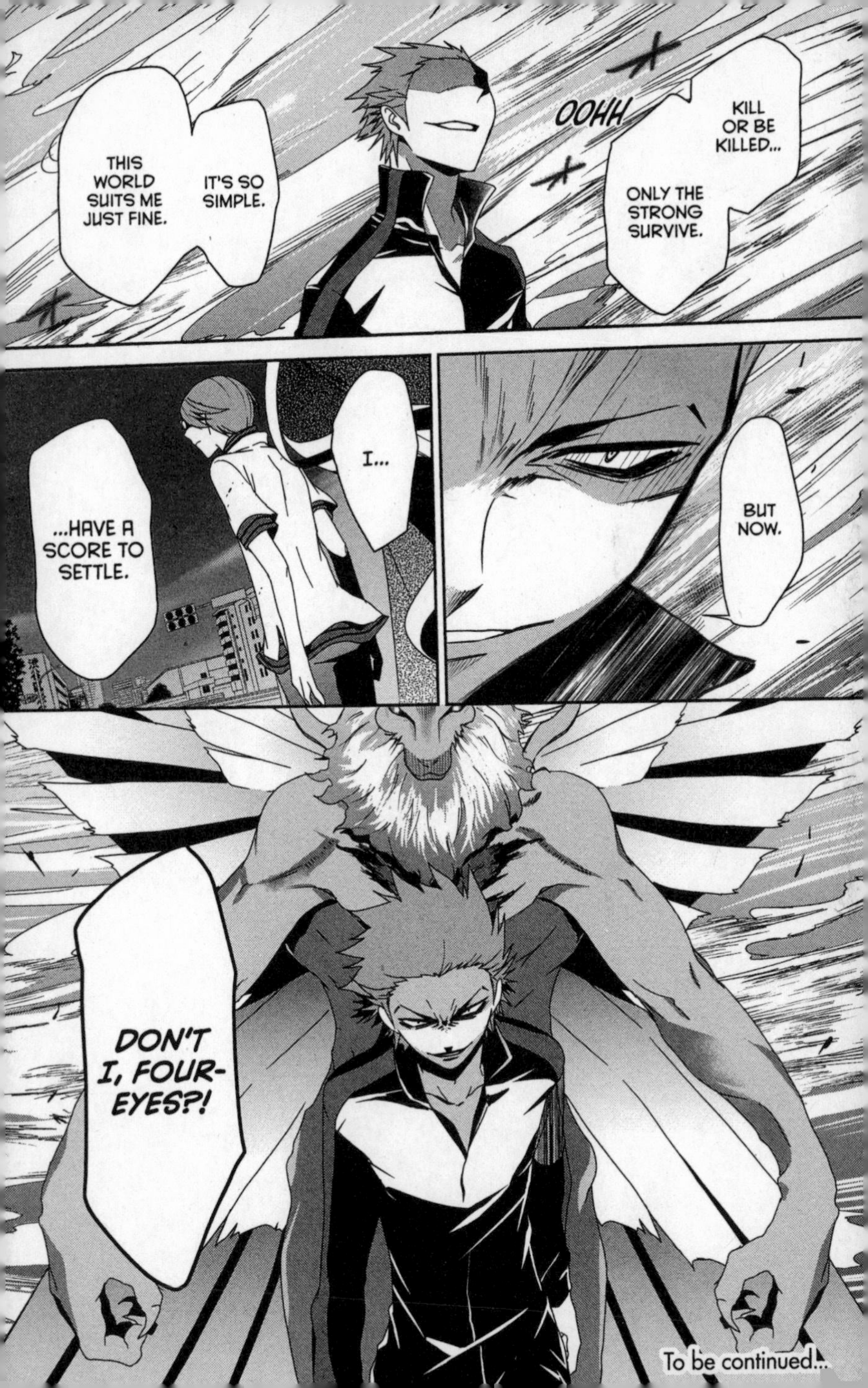
KILL OR BE KILLED...
ONLY THE STRONG SURVIVE.
OOHH
IT'S SO SIMPLE.
THIS WORLD SUITS ME JUST FINE.
BUT NOW.
I...
...HAVE A SCORE TO SETTLE.
DON'T I, FOUR-EYES?!
To be continued...

PROFILE

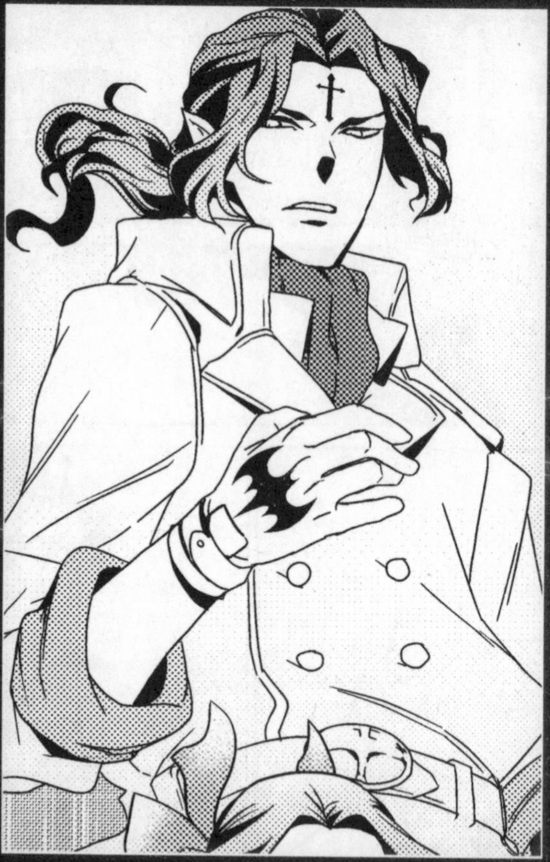

KRESNIK

A HOLY VAMPIRE HUNTER WHO IS BLESSED BY THE LIGHT. HIS NAME COMES FROM THE WORD FOR "CROSS." HIS ARCHNEMESIS IS THE SLOVENIAN VAMPIRE KUDLAK, AND THEIR BATTLES ARE UNPARALLELED. THEY BOTH ASSUME VARIOUS ANIMAL FORMS, SUCH AS PIGS, BULLS, AND HORSES, BUT KRESNIK'S FORMS CAN BE RECOGNIZED BY THEIR WHITE COLOR.

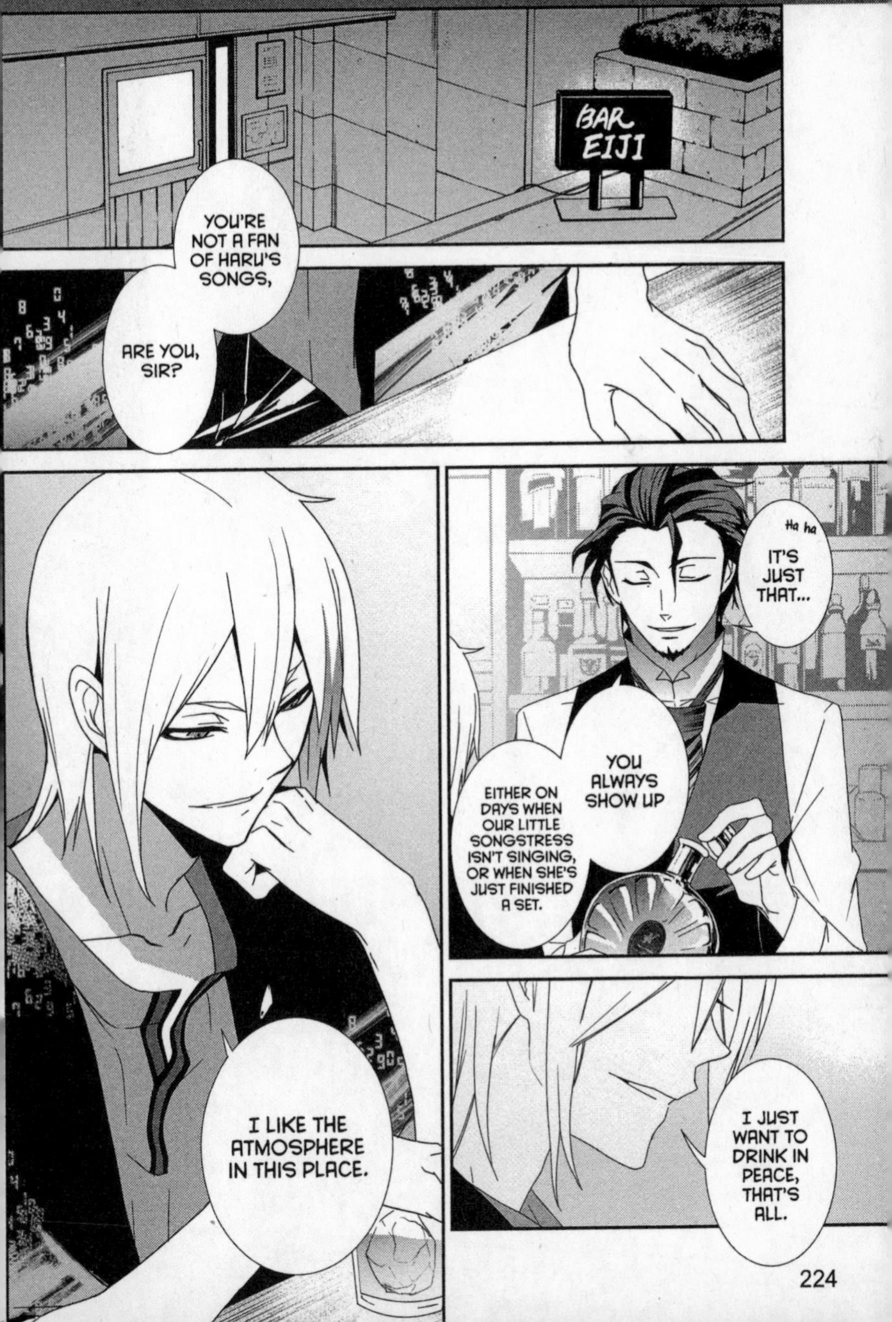
BAR EIJI
YOU'RE NOT A FAN OF HARU'S SONGS,
ARE YOU, SIR?
Ha ha
IT'S JUST THAT...
YOU ALWAYS SHOW UP
EITHER ON DAYS WHEN OUR LITTLE SONGSTRESS ISN'T SINGING, OR WHEN SHE'S JUST FINISHED A SET.
I JUST WANT TO DRINK IN PEACE, THAT'S ALL.
I LIKE THE ATMOSPHERE IN THIS PLACE.

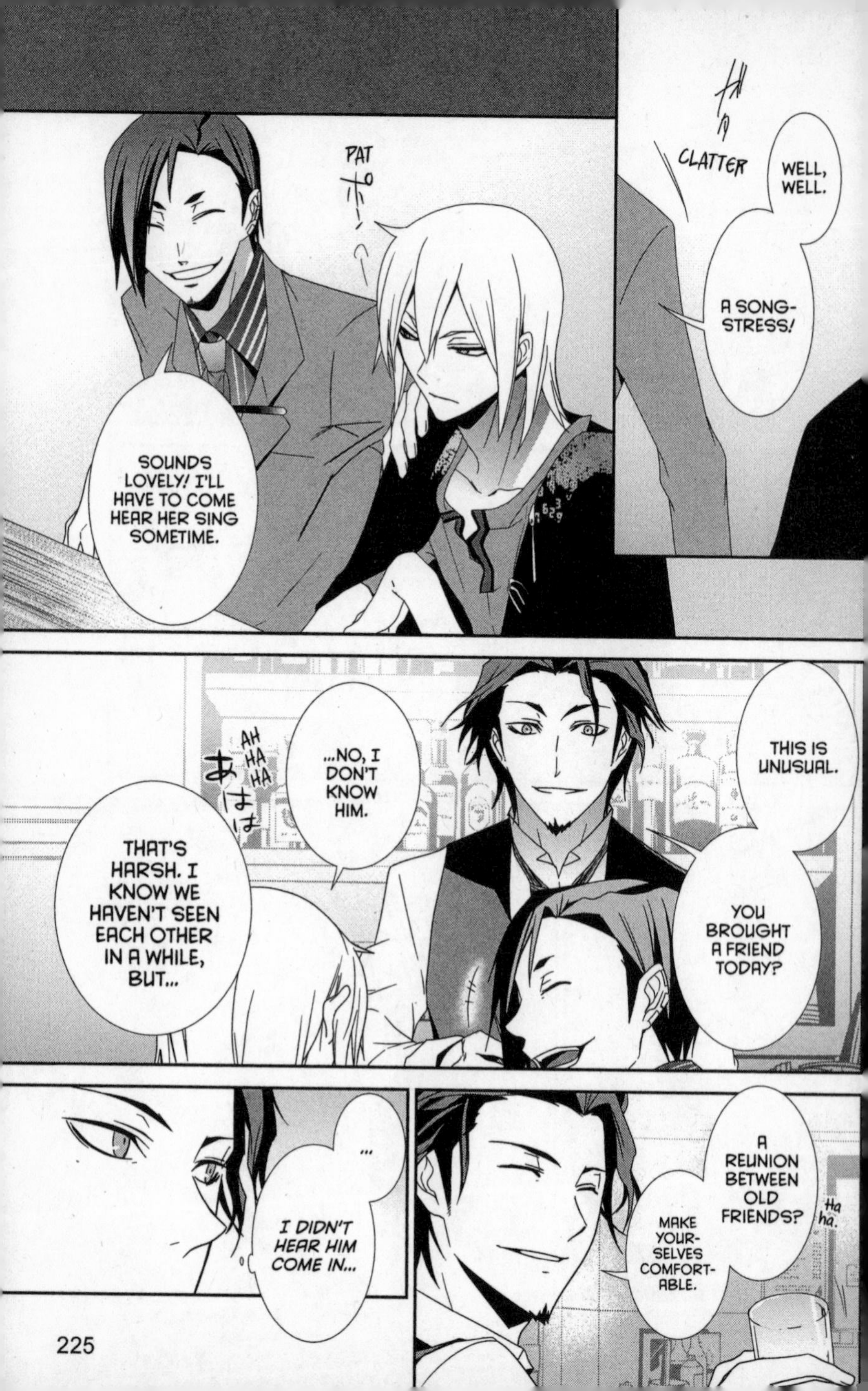
CLATTER
WELL, WELL.
A SONG-STRESS!
PAT
SOUNDS LOVELY! I'LL HAVE TO COME HEAR HER SING SOMETIME.
THIS IS UNUSUAL.
YOU BROUGHT A FRIEND TODAY?
...NO, I DON'T KNOW HIM.
AH HA HA
あはは
THAT'S HARSH. I KNOW WE HAVEN'T SEEN EACH OTHER IN A WHILE, BUT...
A REUNION BETWEEN OLD FRIENDS?
Ha ha.
MAKE YOUR-SELVES COMFORT-ABLE.
...
I DIDN'T HEAR HIM COME IN...

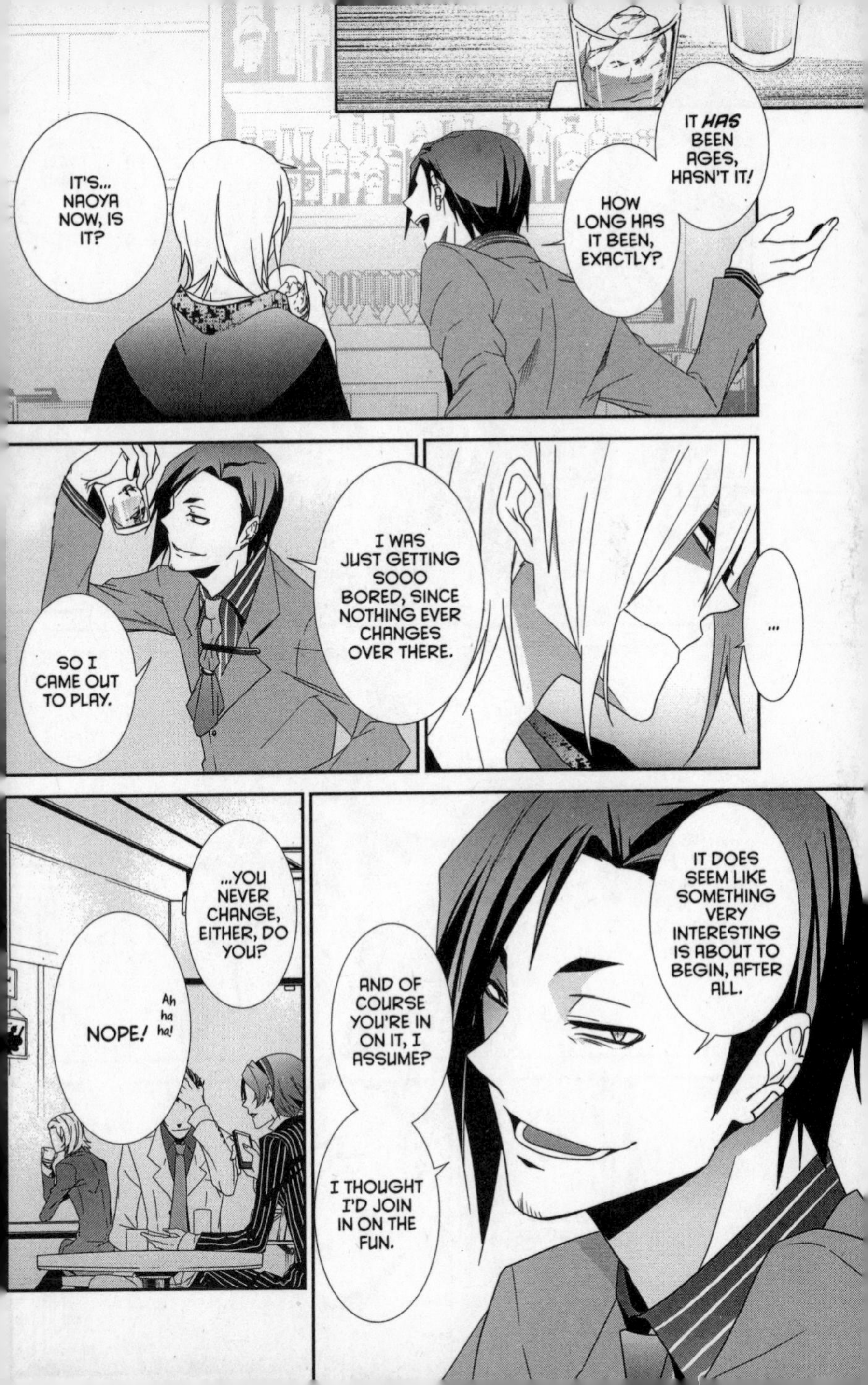
IT HAS BEEN AGES, HASN'T IT!
HOW LONG HAS IT BEEN, EXACTLY?
IT'S... NAOYA NOW, IS IT?
...
I WAS JUST GETTING SOOO BORED, SINCE NOTHING EVER CHANGES OVER THERE.
SO I CAME OUT TO PLAY.
IT DOES SEEM LIKE SOMETHING VERY INTERESTING IS ABOUT TO BEGIN, AFTER ALL.
AND OF COURSE YOU'RE IN ON IT, I ASSUME?
I THOUGHT I'D JOIN IN ON THE FUN.
...YOU NEVER CHANGE, EITHER, DO YOU?
NOPE!
Ah ha ha!

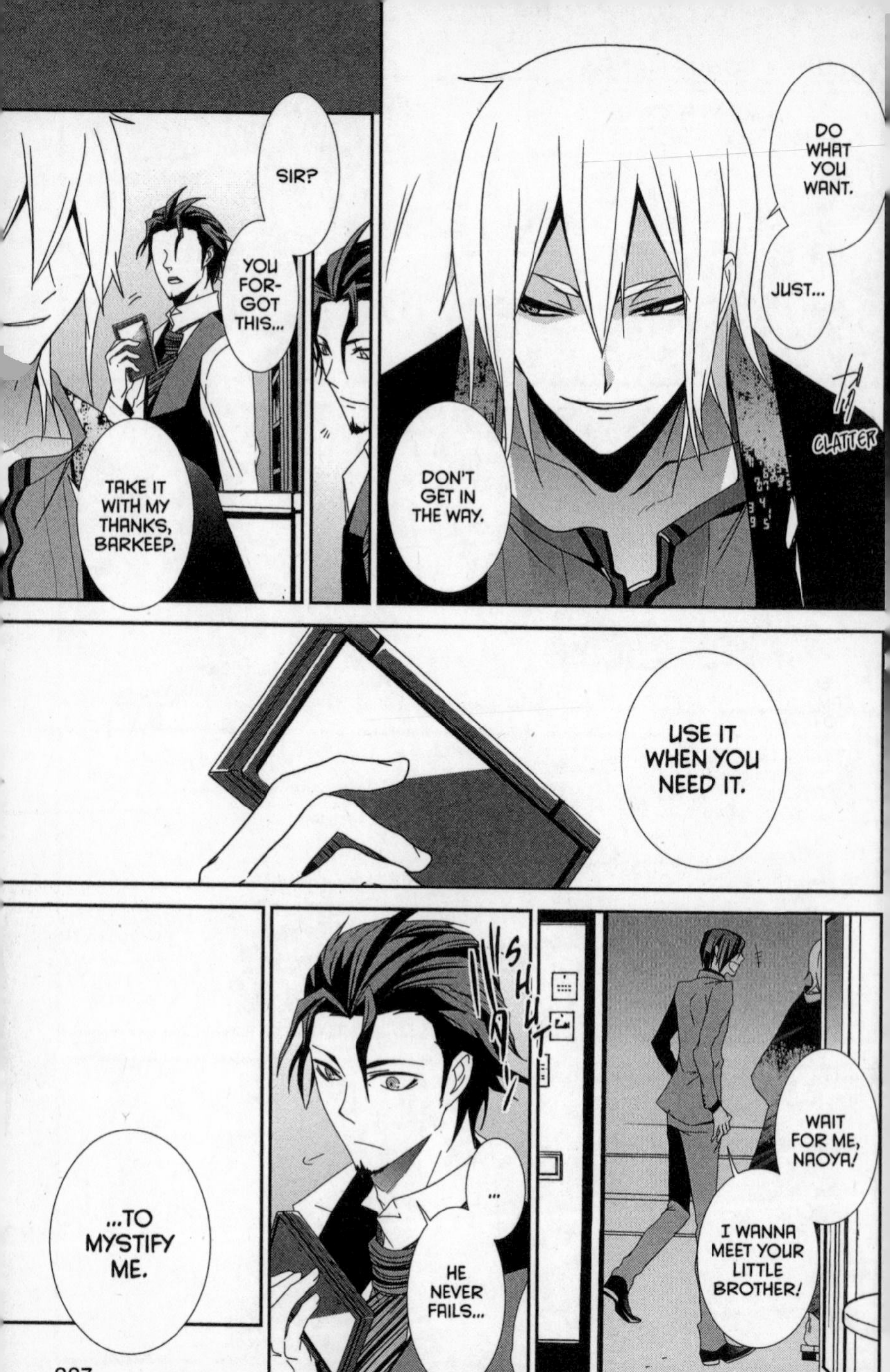
DO WHAT YOU WANT.
JUST...
DON'T GET IN THE WAY.
CLATTER
SIR?
YOU FOR-GOT THIS...
TAKE IT WITH MY THANKS, BARKEEP.
USE IT WHEN YOU NEED IT.
WAIT FOR ME, NAOYA!
I WANNA MEET YOUR LITTLE BROTHER!
SHUT
...
HE NEVER FAILS...
...TO MYSTIFY ME.

VOLUME 1 BONUS MANGA

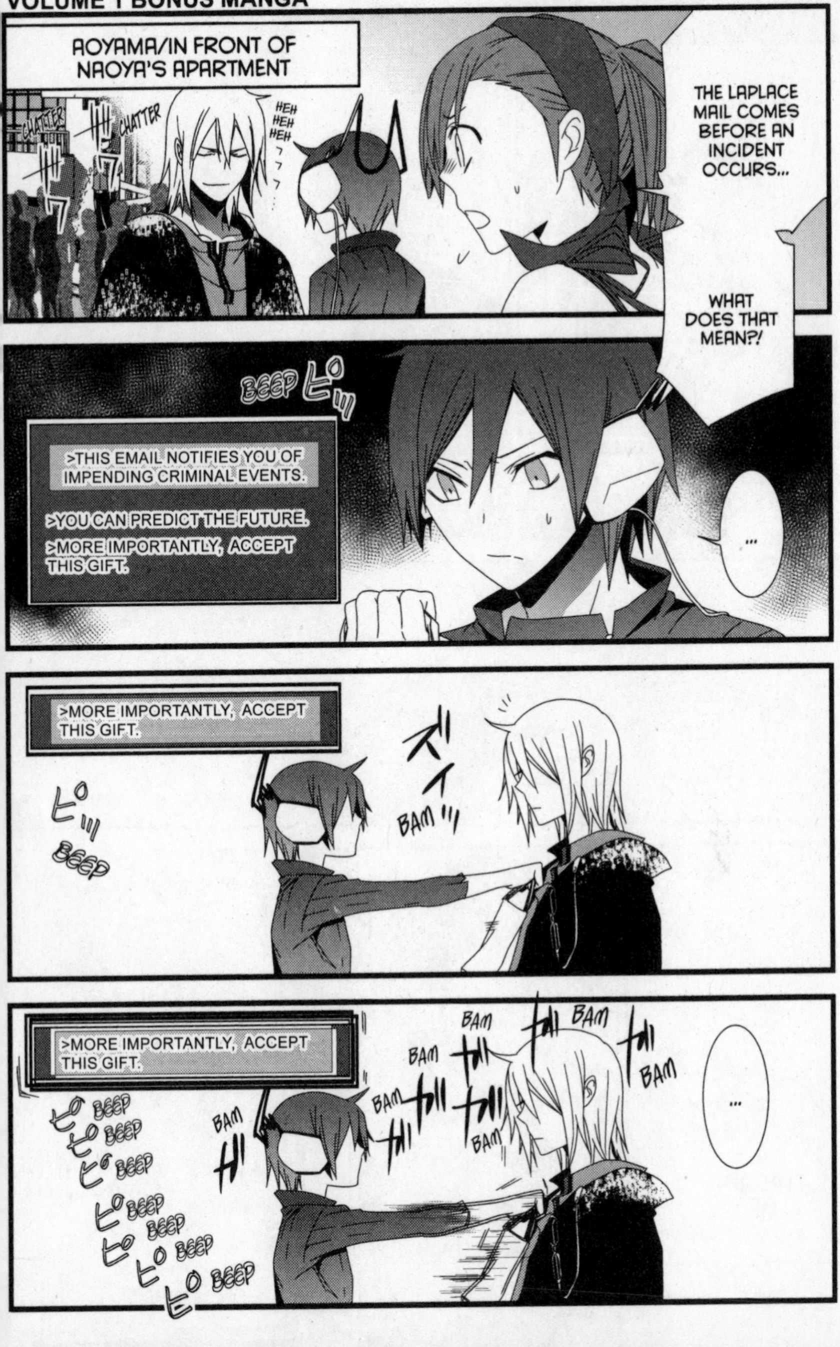
AOYAMA/IN FRONT OF NAOYA'S APARTMENT
THE LAPLACE MAIL COMES BEFORE AN INCIDENT OCCURS...
WHAT DOES THAT MEAN?!
HEH HEH HEH
CHATTER
...
BEEP
>THIS EMAIL NOTIFIES YOU OF IMPENDING CRIMINAL EVENTS.
>YOU CAN PREDICT THE FUTURE.
>MORE IMPORTANTLY, ACCEPT THIS GIFT.
BAM
>MORE IMPORTANTLY, ACCEPT THIS GIFT.
BEEP
...
BAM BAM BAM BAM BAM BAM BAM
>MORE IMPORTANTLY, ACCEPT THIS GIFT.
BEEP BEEP BEEP BEEP BEEP BEEP BEEP

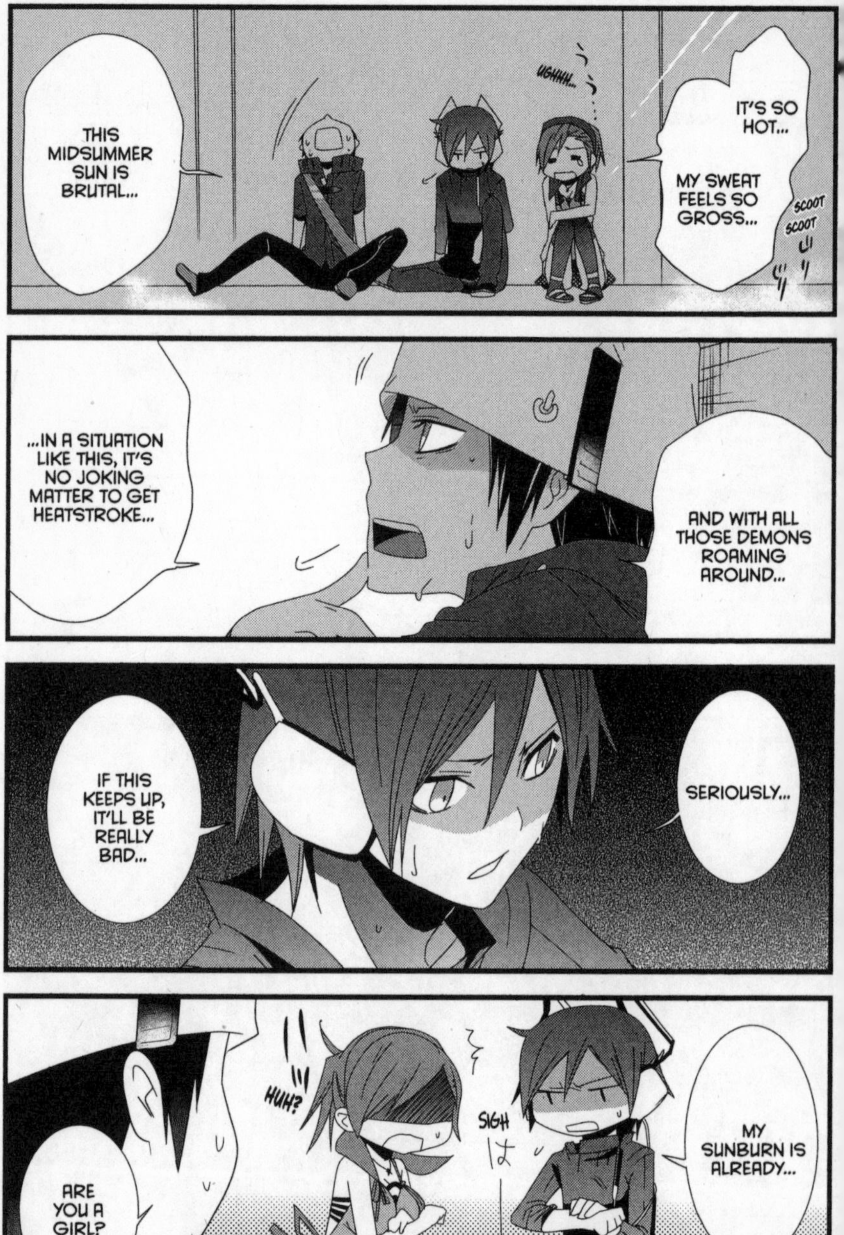
IT'S SO HOT... MY SWEAT FEELS SO GROSS...
SCOOT SCOOT
UGHHH...
THIS MIDSUMMER SUN IS BRUTAL...
AND WITH ALL THOSE DEMONS ROAMING AROUND...
...IN A SITUATION LIKE THIS, IT'S NO JOKING MATTER TO GET HEATSTROKE...
SERIOUSLY...
IF THIS KEEPS UP, IT'LL BE REALLY BAD...
MY SUNBURN IS ALREADY...
SIGH
HUH?
ARE YOU A GIRL?

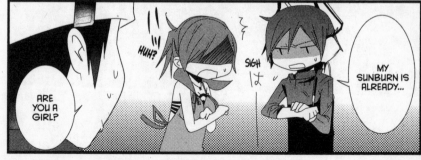

VOLUME 2 BONUS MANGA

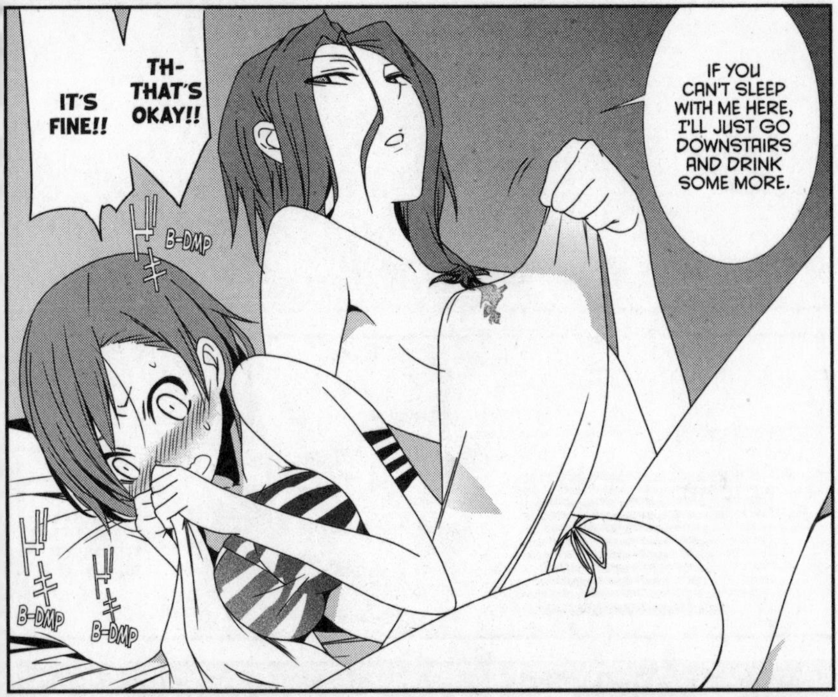
IF YOU CAN'T SLEEP WITH ME HERE, I'LL JUST GO DOWNSTAIRS AND DRINK SOME MORE.
TH- THAT'S OKAY!!
IT'S FINE!!
B-DMP
B-DMP
B-DMP

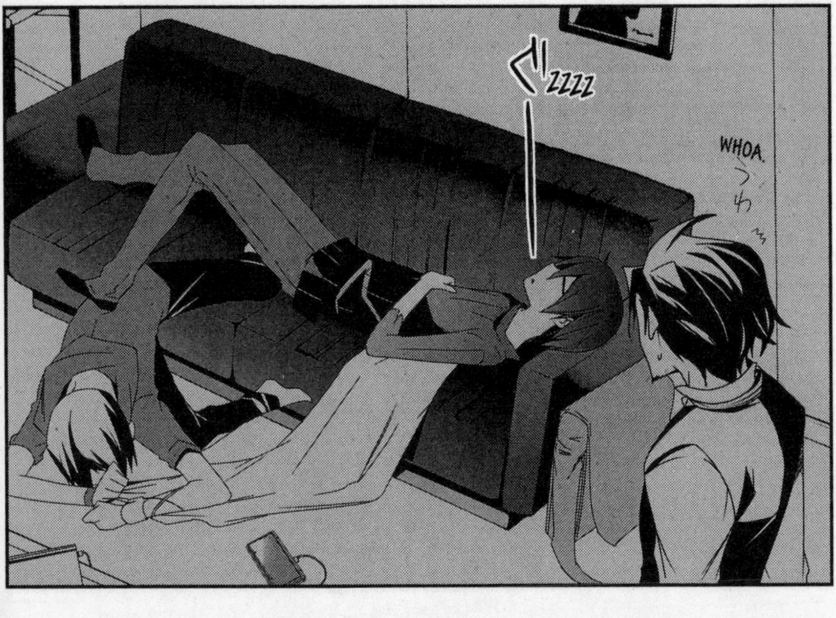
ZZZZ
WHOA.

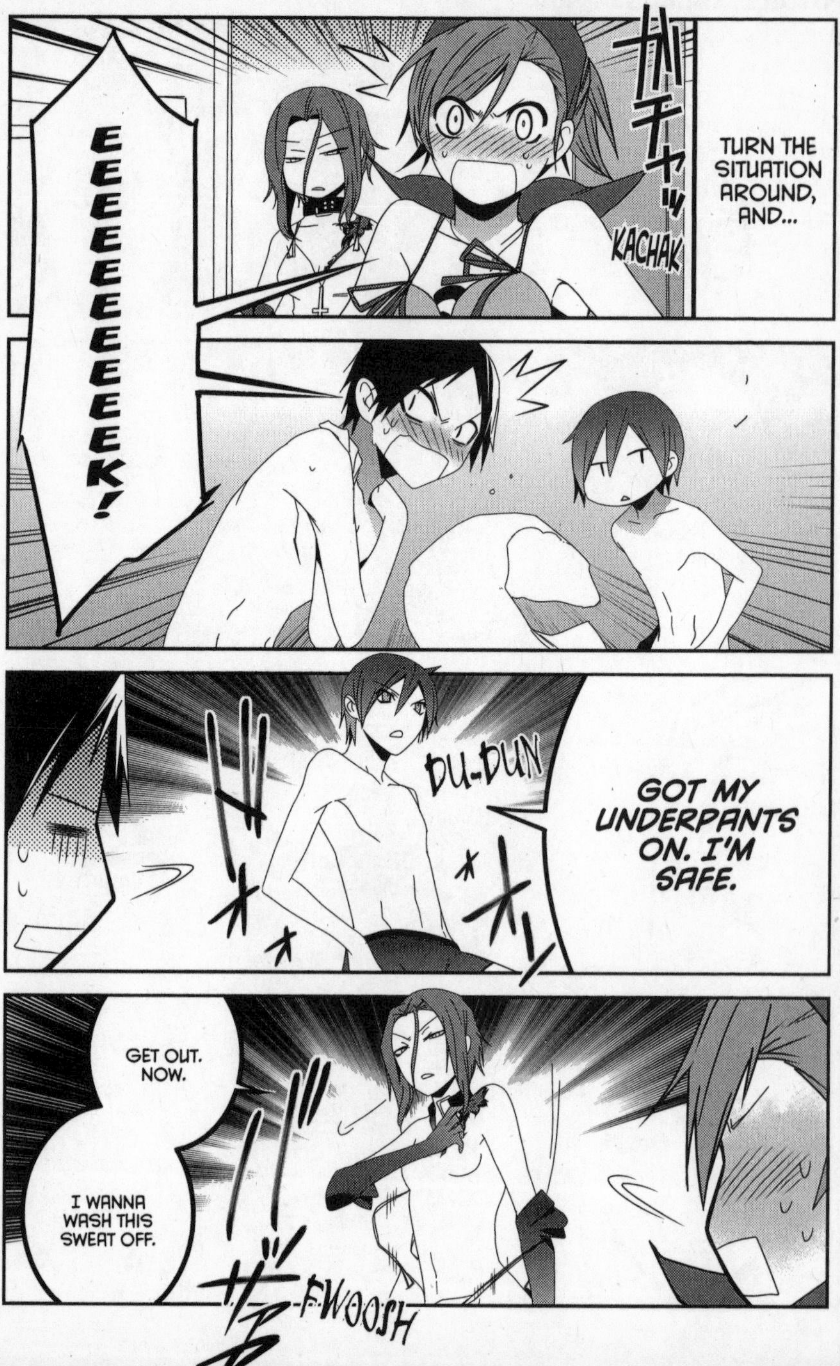
TURN THE SITUATION AROUND, AND...
KACHAK
EEEEEEEEEEEEK!
GOT MY UNDERPANTS ON. I'M SAFE.
DU-DUN
GET OUT. NOW.
I WANNA WASH THIS SWEAT OFF.
FWOOSH

VOLUME 3 BONUS MANGA

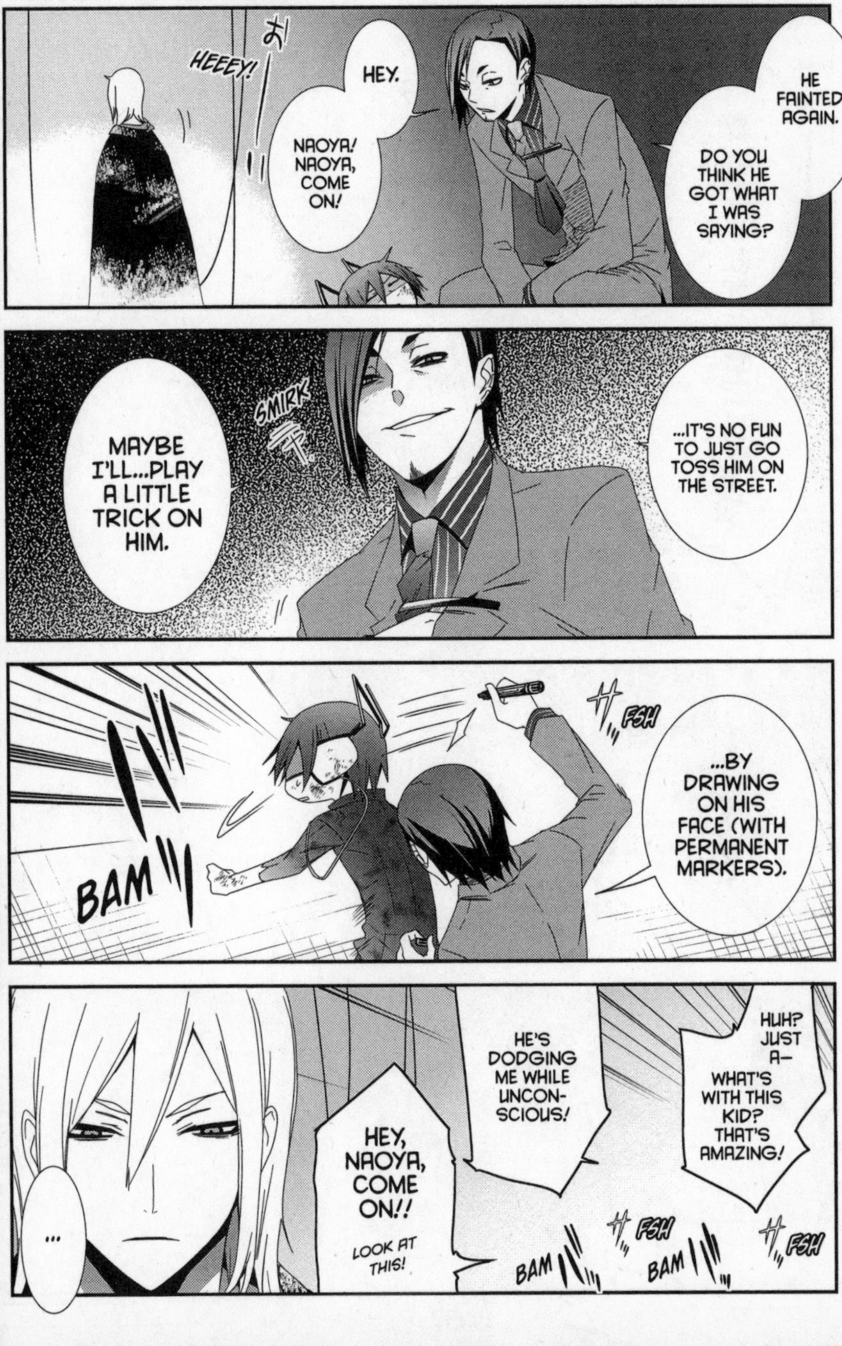

HE FAINTED AGAIN.
DO YOU THINK HE GOT WHAT I WAS SAYING?
HEY.
NAOYA! NAOYA, COME ON!
お
HEEEY!
...IT'S NO FUN TO JUST GO TOSS HIM ON THE STREET.
SMIRK
MAYBE I'LL...PLAY A LITTLE TRICK ON HIM.
...BY DRAWING ON HIS FACE (WITH PERMANENT MARKERS).
FSH
BAM
HUH? JUST A—
WHAT'S WITH THIS KID? THAT'S AMAZING!
HE'S DODGING ME WHILE UNCONSCIOUS!
FSH
BAM
FSH
BAM
HEY, NAOYA, COME ON!!
LOOK AT THIS!
...

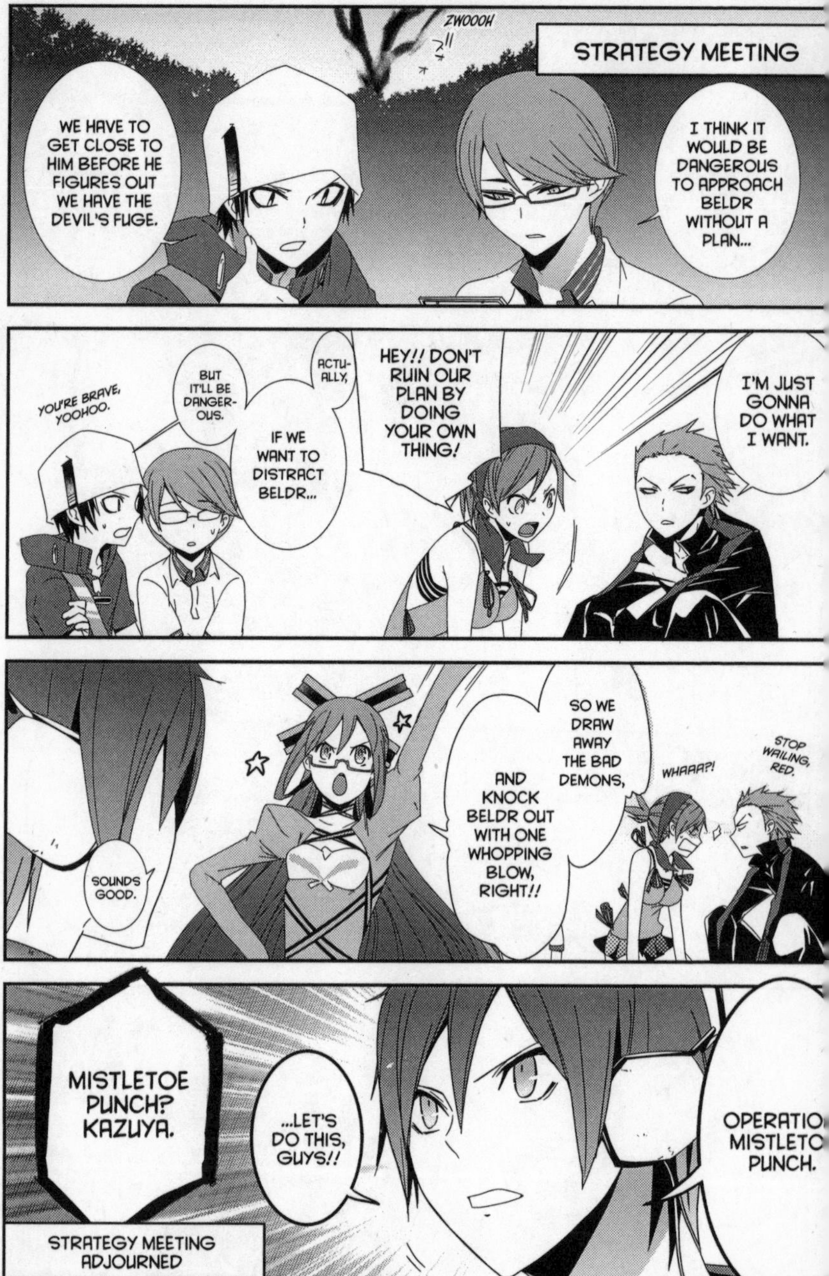
STRATEGY MEETING
ZWOOOH
I THINK IT WOULD BE DANGEROUS TO APPROACH BELDR WITHOUT A PLAN...
WE HAVE TO GET CLOSE TO HIM BEFORE HE FIGURES OUT WE HAVE THE DEVIL'S FUGE.
I'M JUST GONNA DO WHAT I WANT.
HEY!! DON'T RUIN OUR PLAN BY DOING YOUR OWN THING!
ACTU-ALLY,
IF WE WANT TO DISTRACT BELDR...
BUT IT'LL BE DANGER-OUS.
YOU'RE BRAVE, YOOHOO.
STOP WAILING, RED.
WHAAA?!
SO WE DRAW AWAY THE BAD DEMONS,
AND KNOCK BELDR OUT WITH ONE WHOPPING BLOW, RIGHT!!
SOUNDS GOOD.
OPERATIO MISTLETO PUNCH.
...LET'S DO THIS, GUYS!!
MISTLETOE PUNCH? KAZUYA.
STRATEGY MEETING ADJOURNED

VOLUME 4 BONUS MANGA

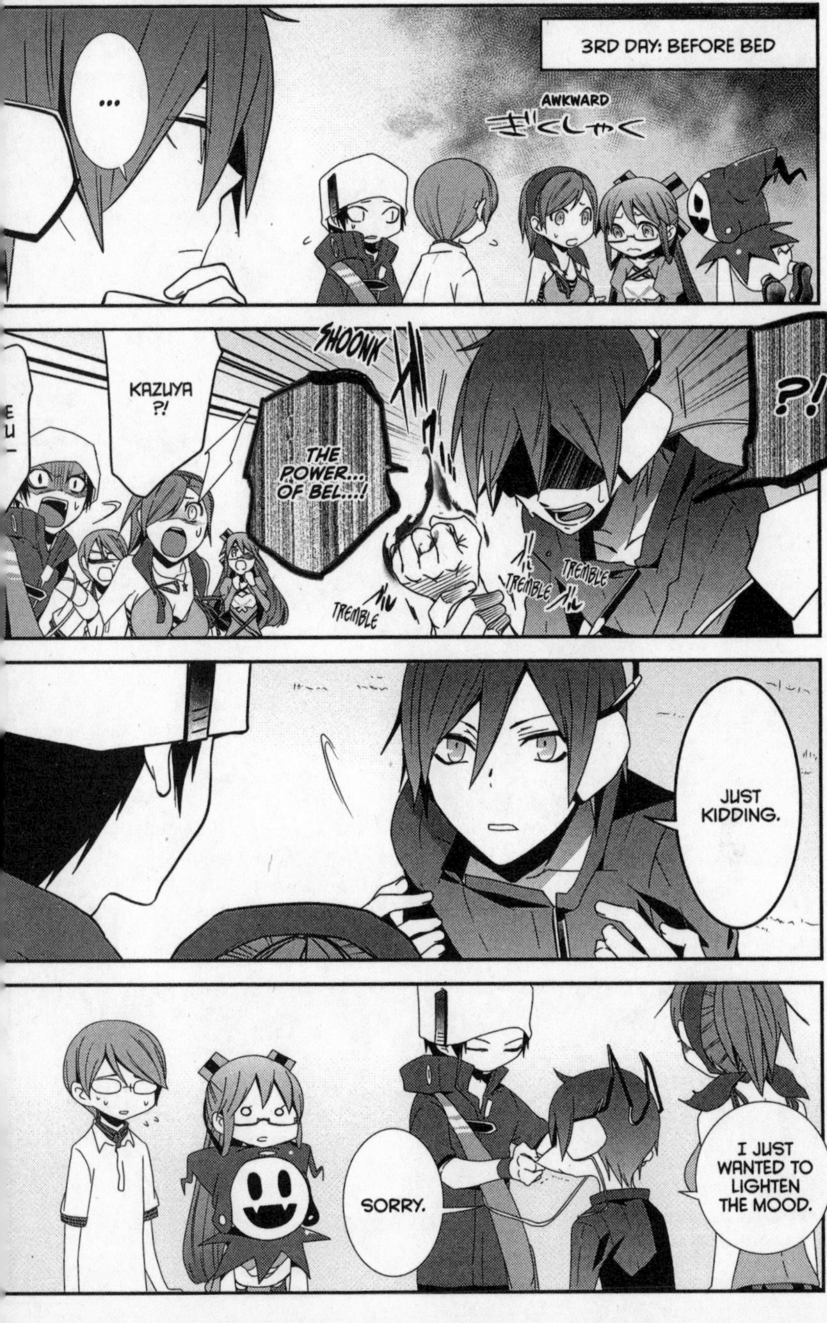
3RD DAY: BEFORE BED
AWKWARD
ぎくしゃく
...
?!
SHOONK
THE POWER... OF BEL...!
TREMBLE
TREMBLE
TREMBLE
KAZUYA ?!
JUST KIDDING.
I JUST WANTED TO LIGHTEN THE MOOD.
SORRY.

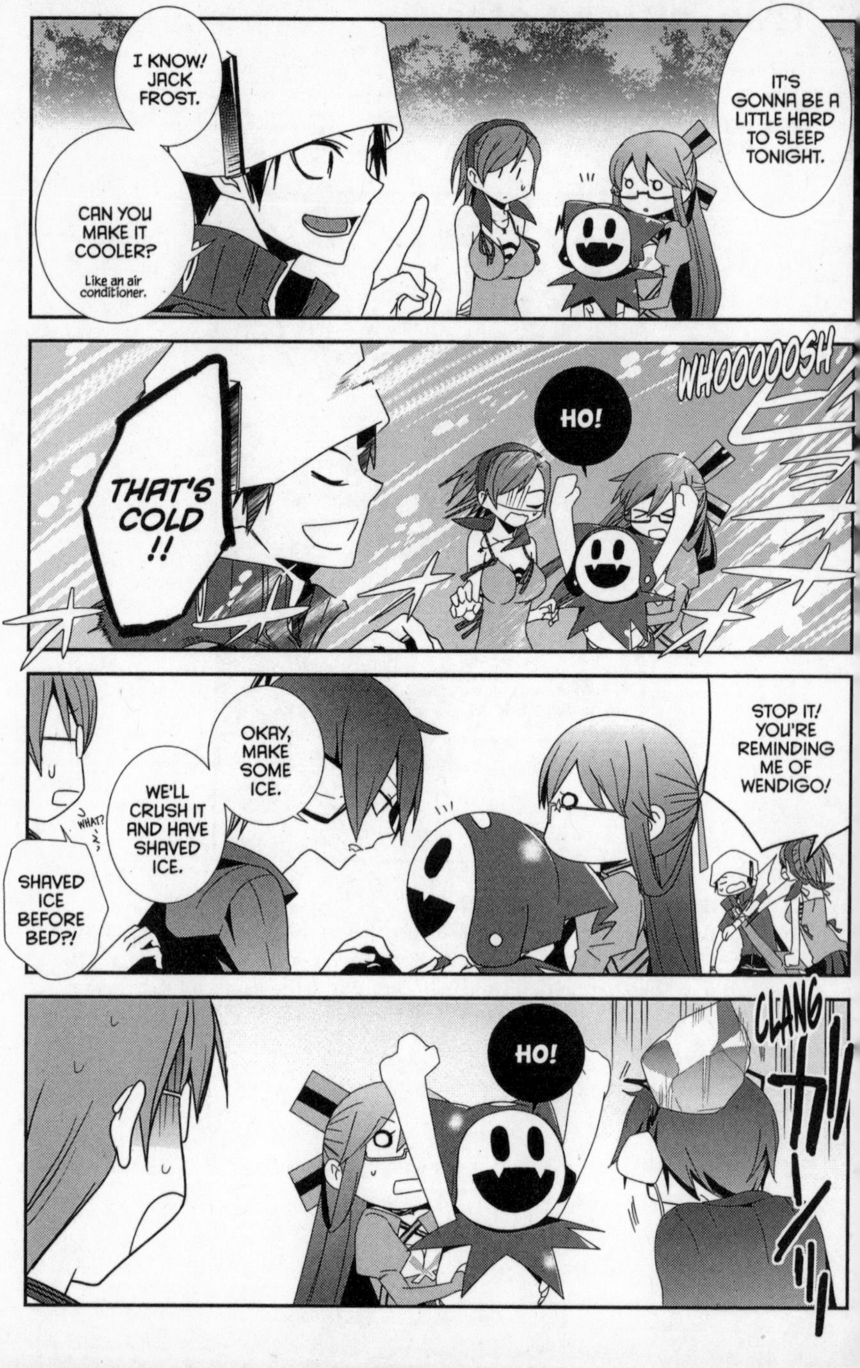
IT'S GONNA BE A LITTLE HARD TO SLEEP TONIGHT.
I KNOW! JACK FROST.
CAN YOU MAKE IT COOLER?
Like an air conditioner.
WHOOOOOOSH
HO!
THAT'S COLD!!
STOP IT! YOU'RE REMINDING ME OF WENDIGO!
OKAY, MAKE SOME ICE.
WE'LL CRUSH IT AND HAVE SHAVED ICE.
WHAT?
SHAVED ICE BEFORE BED?!
CLANG
HO!

Translation Notes:

Japanese is a tricky language for most Westerners, and translation is often more art than science. For your edification and reading pleasure, here are notes on some of the places where we could have gone in a different direction with our translation of the work, or where a Japanese cultural reference is used.

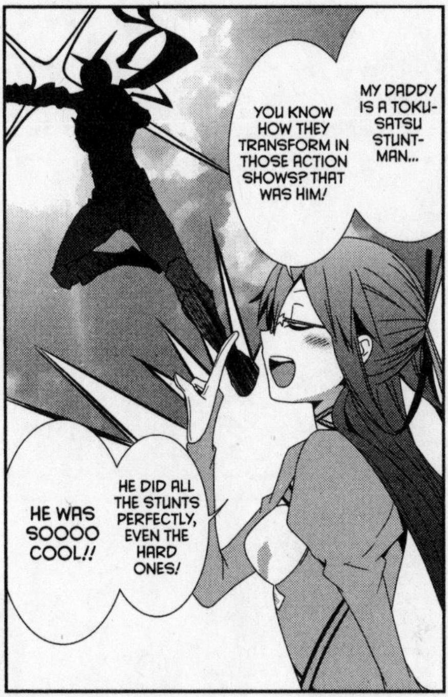
MY DADDY IS A TOKU-SATSU STUNT-MAN...
YOU KNOW HOW THEY TRANSFORM IN THOSE ACTION SHOWS? THAT WAS HIM!
HE DID ALL THE STUNTS PERFECTLY, EVEN THE HARD ONES!
HE WAS SOOOO COOL!!

Tokusatsu stuntman, page 89

Tokusatsu means "special effects," and usually refers to children's action shows like *Power Rangers*. Midori's father was specifically a "suit actor," which means he was the man to put on the superhero suit and mask, and did all the stunts, while the actor who played the character's alter-ego did voice-over.

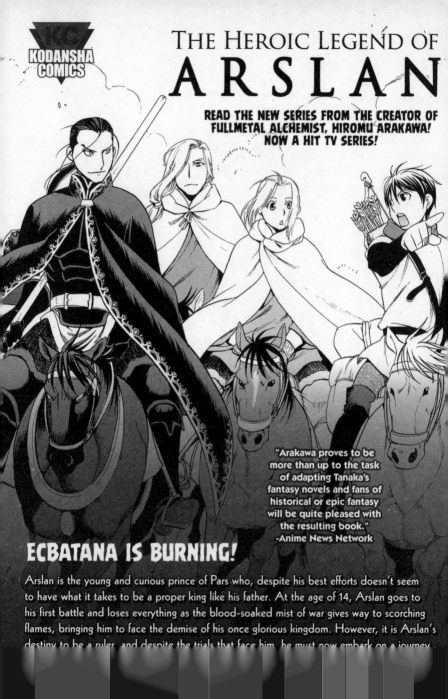

THE HEROIC LEGEND OF
ARSLAN

**READ THE NEW SERIES FROM THE CREATOR OF
FULLMETAL ALCHEMIST, HIROMU ARAKAWA!
NOW A HIT TV SERIES!**

"Arakawa proves to be
more than up to the task
of adapting Tanaka's
fantasy novels and fans of
historical or epic fantasy
will be quite pleased with
the resulting book."
-Anime News Network

ECBATANA IS BURNING!

Arslan is the young and curious prince of Pars who, despite his best efforts doesn't seem
to have what it takes to be a proper king like his father. At the age of 14, Arslan goes to
his first battle and loses everything as the blood-soaked mist of war gives way to scorching
flames, bringing him to face the demise of his once glorious kingdom. However, it is Arslan's
destiny to be a ruler, and despite the trials that face him, he must now embark on a journey

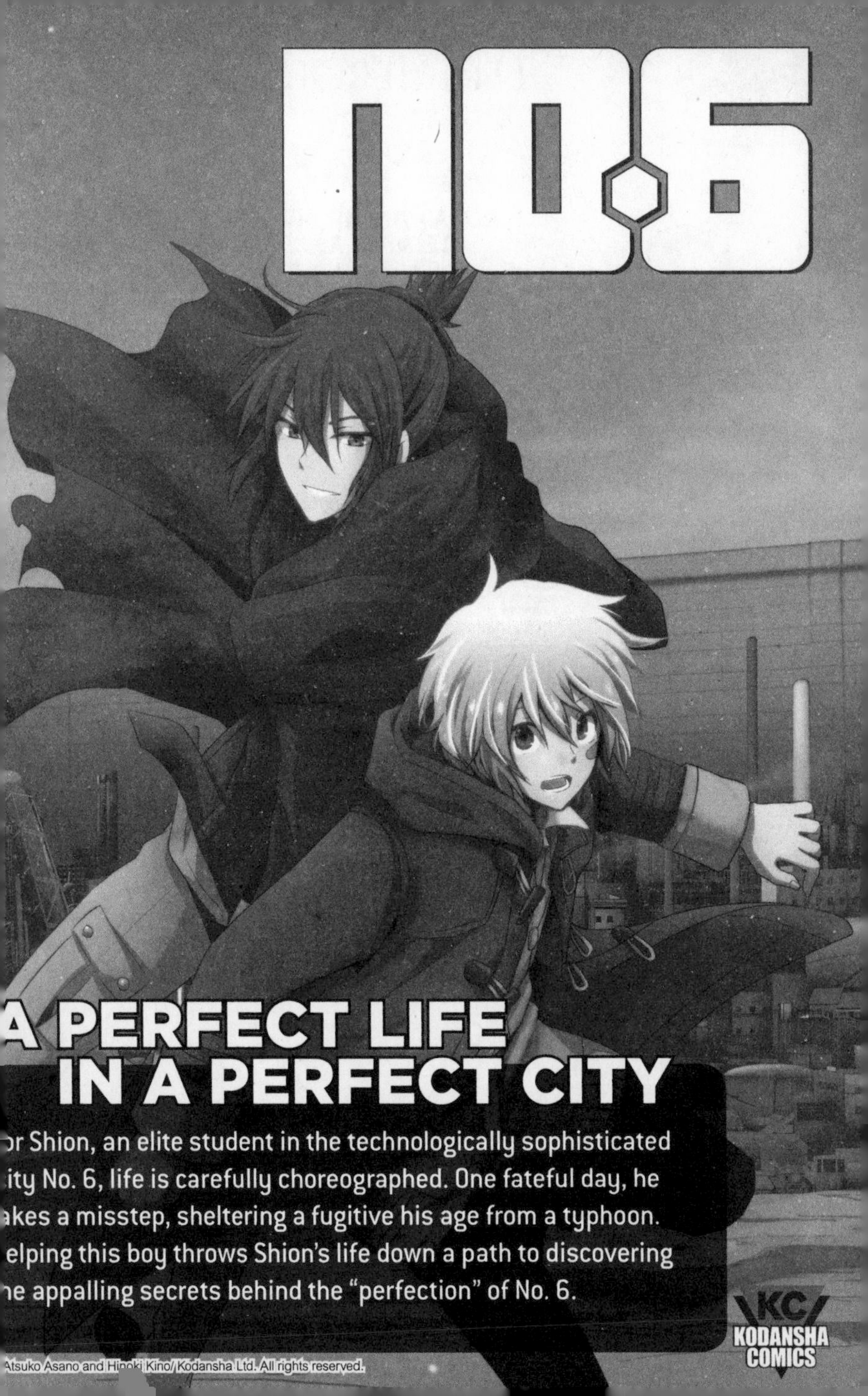
NO.6
A PERFECT LIFE
IN A PERFECT CITY
or Shion, an elite student in the technologically sophisticated ity No. 6, life is carefully choreographed. One fateful day, he akes a misstep, sheltering a fugitive his age from a typhoon. elping this boy throws Shion's life down a path to discovering ne appalling secrets behind the "perfection" of No. 6.
KC
KODANSHA COMICS
Atsuko Asano and Hinoki Kino/ Kodansha Ltd. All rights reserved.

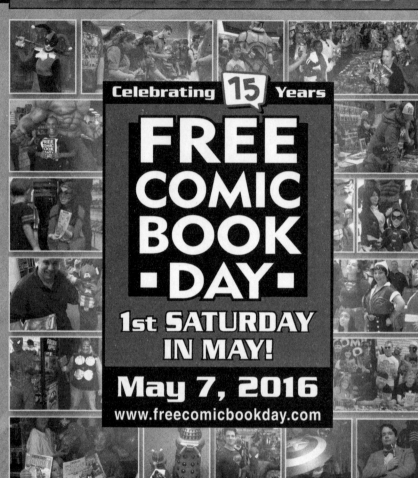
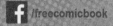

A Kodansha Comics Trade Paperback Original.

Devil Survivor volume 4 copyright © 2014 Index Corporation/SEGA/ Satoru Matsuba
English translation copyright © 2016 Index Corporation/SEGA/ Satoru Matsuba

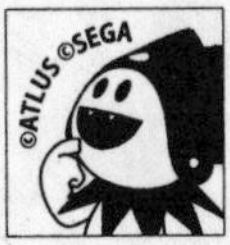

All rights reserved.

Published in the United States by Kodansha Comics, an imprint of Kodansha USA Publishing, LLC, New York.

Publication rights for this English edition arranged through Kodansha Ltd., Tokyo.

First published in Japan in 2014 by Kodansha Ltd., Tokyo.

ISBN 978-1-63236-272-8

Printed in the United States of America.

www.kodanshacomics.com

9 8 7 6 5 4 3 2 1

Translation: Alethea Nibley & Athena Nibley
Lettering: Paige Pumphrey
Editing: Lauren Scanlan

S0-BBT-040